DISCIPLESHIP

What you need to know and how you
can grow as a follower of Jesus Christ

Acknowledgements

Alyson Browning – *Project Manager & Content Editor*

Franklin Lugenbeel – *Graphic Designer & Photographer, LifeCoach Branding*

Elise Cox – *Graphic Designer, Workbook*

Nolan King – *Videographer & Video Editor*

James Harding – *Videographer & Video Editor*

Julie Herron – *Research & Administrative Assistant*

PocketCake – Jill Rogge, Jonathan Hockman, Hugh Welsh – *App Developers*

Jaci Herron – *Videographer & Video Editor Assistant*

Mark Browning – *Proofreader*

Ron Haley – *Discipleship Pastor, First Baptist Raytown*

Bobby Scott – *Videographer*

Andy Frojd – *Videographer*

Alex & Kelly Duckworth

Rich & Judy Hastings

Benetti's Coffee Experience

Blue Springs 8 Theatre

Premier Bowling Alley

St. Luke's East Hospital

Westside Family Church

Lee's Summit Airport

Cracker Barrel

Raytown South High School

iStockphoto.com by Getty Images

Shutterstock.com

Our *LifeCoach: Discipleship* Journey

Helpful tips before you begin ...

Connect with a *LifeCoach*

While you can complete *LifeCoach: Discipleship* on your own, it's much more impactful when you have someone to walk with you through this journey. If you already have someone in mind to be your coach, connect with them and discuss how you will go through this together. If you would like to be connected to a LifeCoach now, visit iLifeCoach. org to request one.

Daily Lesson Videos

LifeCoach: Discipleship is a 10-week program with five lessons per week, totaling 50 lessons for the entire journey. To accompany each of the 50 lessons, we have filmed short on-location videos to help bring the lesson to life and give you even more content. On the first page of each daily lesson, you will find a QR code that you can scan with your smart phone and immediately begin watching the video. You can also type URL into your web browser, and it will also take you to that day's video. We suggest watching the video before beginning that day's lesson to help get you started. To get the most out of the video teaching, we would encourage you to take notes and write down your insights in the margin of your notebook.

The *LifeCoach: Discipleship* App

Take *LifeCoach: Discipleship* with you wherever you go by downloading the mobile app in the App Store and Google Play. Search "LifeCoach with Brandon Park" to download the free app today.

Find out more about *LifeCoach: Discipleship*

Visit our webpage at www.iLifeCoach.org or email us at admin@iLifeCoach.org.

Download the App

This book was created to work in conjunction with the LifeCoach App which is available on Google Play and the App Store for iPhone, iPad and Android devices. Just search for "LifeCoach with Brandon Park."

SALVATION

week 1

Day 1

What Is the Gospel?

vimeo.com/138117628

On the first day of this discipleship journey, I want to make sure you fully understand the message of the gospel, which is why I am going to tell you five things that God does not know. That statement might surprise you. Maybe you're thinking, "I thought God knew everything?" That's true. God is *omniscient,* meaning He is all-knowing. In fact, God already knows everything about *you.* He knows when you went to bed last night, how many hairs are on your head, and even the number of heartbeats you have left. But it may surprise you to learn that there are five things God does *not* know:

God does not know how to love you more than He already does.

True love is always sacrificial. If you want to know whether somebody really loves you, find out what he or she is willing to sacrifice for you.

A father and son were traveling down a country road one afternoon in the spring when suddenly a bee flew in the window. Being deathly allergic to bee stings, the boy began to panic as the bee buzzed all around inside the car. Seeing the look of horror on his child's face, the father reached out and caught the bee in his hand. Soon, he opened his hand, and the bee began to buzz around once again. The boy began to panic. The father reached over to his son and opened his hand showing him the stinger, which was now lodged in his palm. He said, "Relax son, I took the sting for you. The bee can't hurt you anymore."

Because of Jesus' death and resurrection, He took the penalty of sin, death, and hell away from those who believe in Him. That's why Paul said, *"Where, O death, is your victory? Where, O death, is your sting?"* (1 Corinthians 15:55).

One man said, "I asked Jesus how much He loved me. He answered 'this much.' Then He stretched out His arms and died for me." Jesus stretched out His arms so that wicked people could nail Him to the cross – that's how much He loves us. He stretched out His arms to take the sins of the entire world – that's how much He loves us. He stretched out His arms to take away our penalty of death – that's how much He loves us. The cross of Jesus Christ is the clearest, loudest, most powerful "I love you!" ever proclaimed. It doesn't matter what you may have done in this life or where you are today. It doesn't even matter if you believe in God or not! The God you say you don't believe in died on the cross for *your* sins. Romans 5:8 says, *"God demonstrates His own love for us in this: While we were still sinners, Christ died for us."* You are loved more than you will ever know by Someone who died to know you.

God does not know how to ignore sin.

A story goes that everyone sitting in the courtroom had their eyes on the judge. After hearing the case, he looked up and slowly pronounced his judgment upon a young woman who was found guilty. He said, "I find you guilty and hereby fine you the maximum fine possible: $10,000." The courtroom gasped in astonishment. The judge then got up, took off his robe and walked to the front of the bench. Taking out his checkbook, he wrote a check for the full amount. Turning to the courtroom, the judge said, "This is my daughter, and even though I love her, I cannot overlook what she has done. Her actions still have repercussions, but I'm going to pay the penalty for those consequences."

I want you to think of the most horrendous sin you have ever committed. Do you have it? Do you remember it? Now, I want you to understand that it was *that* sin that God the Father saw when He looked down from Heaven and saw Jesus take your sin upon Himself. It was all of the sins – both large and small – that you and I have committed that Jesus took into His perfect body when He was dying on the cross.

Maybe you don't know what sin is. Sin is any thought, action, or attitude that goes against God and His standard of morality. Not only were we born with a sin nature (e.g. you never have to teach a toddler how to throw a temper tantrum), but also throughout our lives, we have all deliberately committed sinful acts. Scripture says, *"All have sinned and fallen short of the glory of God"* (Romans 3:23). All sins are serious and have serious consequences. It doesn't matter if you've committed one sin or committed a million. God's judgment of us will not be based on how we compare to other people; rather, it will be based on how we compare to His standard.

Even though God loves us, He cannot overlook the fact that we have sinned. The penalty for our sin must be paid in full. This is what happened when Jesus was on the cross. He took the full punishment for our sins. Someone has to pay for your sin – either Jesus pays or you do. If we personally accept His offer of complete payment for our sins, we will not be required to pay the penalty ourselves.

God does not know how to turn away anyone who comes to Him with repentance and faith.

"God couldn't love me. I'm not good enough." Have you ever thought that? Well, God isn't in the business of saving *good* people – just people who are truly repentant. God promised that *"if you confess with your mouth, 'Jesus is Lord,' and believe in your heart that God raised him from the dead, you will be saved"* (Romans 10:9-10).

It's important for us to understand that when Jesus died on the cross, He didn't die alone. He died in between two thieves who were being crucified because of crimes they had committed. One of the criminals railed at Jesus, saying, *"Are you not the Christ? Save yourself and us!"* The other thief watched how Jesus responded and put his faith and belief in Him, and to that man, Jesus said, *"Today you will be with me in Paradise"* (Luke 23:43). On that day, one man died on the *wrong* side of Jesus and another man died on the *right* side of Jesus. The way he got right is the way that we must get right. That second thief saw something about himself in those last minutes of his life. He saw his own sinfulness, and he placed his faith in the One who was dying next to him. Those two men are a representation of the decision that every person in this world has to make: Will I choose to receive Jesus or will I choose to reject Him? To not make any decision is a decision to reject

> " Someone has to pay for your sin – either Jesus pays or you do. "

NOTES _____

NOTES

Him. We will be judged not for the sins that we have committed but for the Light we have rejected.

Notice that the thief who believed had nothing to offer. There was nothing he could do to earn God's favor. This man didn't receive salvation because of his good works – he didn't have any. He wasn't saved because of church membership – he never joined one. He wasn't saved because he was baptized – he didn't have time. All he had was his faith and God's grace.

Ephesians 2:8-9 says, *"For by grace you have been saved through faith, and that not of yourselves, it is the gift of God, not of works, lest anyone should boast."* There is nothing you can do to earn your salvation. Salvation is not in the merit of man; it's in the mercy of God. It's not in the *goodness* of man; it's in the *grace* of God. Salvation is not a *reward for the righteous*; it's a *gift for the guilty*.

God has given His word that if you will come to Him in faith with a repentant heart, He will save you so you can spend eternity with Him in Heaven. There is no person so good that they need not be saved, but there is no person so bad that he cannot be saved.

God does not know another way to be saved but through Jesus.

Jesus is our way to God and God's way to us. Christianity is not a code, a cause, or a creed, but Christ. Jesus put it this way: *"I am the way, the truth, and the life. No one comes to the Father except through me"* (John 14:6). God has chosen to redeem mankind and save you through Jesus Christ. In 1 Timothy 2:5 we read, *"There is one God, and there is one mediator between God and men, the man Christ Jesus."* How many mediators? Just one, and His name is Jesus.

If you could get to Heaven by being a good person, why would Jesus have to die? You may be a moral person with wholesome values. You may be a good citizen who abides by the golden rule. But those things, while they are good, will not save you from your sins. Only Jesus can do that. *"Salvation is found in no one else, for there is no other name under heaven given to men by which we must be saved"* (Acts 4:12).

God does not know a better time to make this decision than right now.

In 2 Corinthians 6:2, Paul says, *"Behold, now is the favorable time; behold, now is the day of salvation."* If you sense God working in your heart today and drawing you to Him, you need to make this decision today. There is a danger that you may harden your heart to the point that you don't sense God drawing you to Him again. There is a danger that you may die before you get another opportunity to respond to Christ. You are living on borrowed time. Everyone faces death. Only a fool would go through life unprepared for something he knows is inevitable.

In 1829, a man named George Wilson attacked and robbed a mail carrier. He was sentenced to die, but received a pardon from the President of the United States. But to the shock of the Oval Office, Wilson rejected the pardon. The President of the United States had set him free, but George Wilson said, "No." The case went to the Supreme Court, and the issue was simply this: If the President gives you a pardon, aren't you pardoned? Can you reject a pardon given by a Sovereign? Chief Justice Marshall rendered the decision: "A pardon rejected is no pardon at all. Unless the recipient of the pardon accepts the pardon, then the pardon cannot be applied."

Because of Jesus' death, burial, and resurrection, you have been offered a pardon. But in order for the pardon to be effective, you must choose to *believe* and *receive*.

Are you certain of your salvation?

John 3:16 says, *"For God so loved the world, that He gave His only begotten Son, that whosoever should believe in Him, shall not perish but have eternal life."*

If you are not certain of your salvation and you would like to respond to the gospel in believing and receiving Jesus as your personal Lord and Savior, I want to encourage you to pray and make that decision. Praying a prayer doesn't save you. Salvation is an act of your will to respond to what God is doing in your heart.

"Dear Lord Jesus,
I know I am a sinner. I know I cannot save myself. I believe in who You are and what You came to this earth to do. I do not want to die in my sins. I want You to save me. Come into my life and make me a new person. I turn away from how I've been living, and for the rest of my days, I want to live for You. Thank you for giving me salvation and eternal life.
In Jesus' name, AMEN!"

If you prayed that prayer, you just made the greatest decision you'll ever make in your life! This is the first step on an exciting new journey!

Did you pray that prayer today and invite Jesus into your heart?

If you have already prayed that prayer, share briefly your experience of how you came to faith in Jesus Christ:

Based on your understanding of the Gospel, if you were to stand before God

NOTES

NOTES _____

_____

_____

_____

_____

_____

_____

_____

_____

_____

_____

_____

_____

_____

_____

_____

_____

_____

_____

_____

_____

_____

_____

_____

_____

_____

_____

_____

_____

_____

and He were to ask you, "Why should I let you into Heaven?" What do you think you would say?

_____

_____

_____

_____

_____

_____

_____

_____

_____

_____

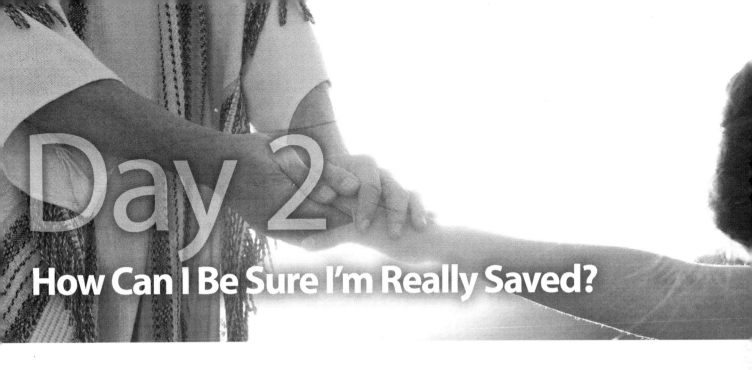

Day 2
How Can I Be Sure I'm Really Saved?

One basic thing that every Christian ought to know beyond any shadow of doubt is that he or she is saved, but how can you be sure?

Understanding salvation

Being born-again is a definite experience.

How dumb would it be if someone asked you, "Have you ever been born?" It would be even dumber if you responded, "Well, I hope so ... I'm doing the best I can!" Many times when you ask someone if they have been "born-again" their response is "Well, I've always been a Christian." That would be like saying, "I've always been born!" Just like birth is a definite experience, so is being born again.

Salvation has nothing to do with your self-effort.

Suppose a friend decides he wants to give you a Lamborghini Veneno, which is currently the most expensive car in the world, priced at $3.9 million dollars. You tell him that you can't accept such an extravagant gift and that you felt obligated to give him something to help cover the cost of the car. So you offer him a quarter and say "Thanks!" Then when you come pulling up in your neighborhood sporting such a nice ride and someone compliments you on your would be car, you say, "Thanks, my friend and I bought this car." Not only would that be ridiculous, but also gravely insulting to your friend. We try to do that same thing with God by adding our two bits of self-effort to His amazing grace. When we do that, we take the glory from Almighty God. There's nothing *you* can do to earn your salvation (Ephesians 2:9). When you get to heaven, all you're going to be able to say is, "Jesus paid it all!"

You can be 100% assured of your salvation.

Scripture makes that clear in 1 John 5:13: *"I write these things to you who believe in the name of the Son of God that you may know that you have eternal life."* We don't have a "hope-so" salvation; we have a "know-so" salvation.

The Apostle John wrote the Gospel of John as well as the epistles of First, Second, and Third John. Evidently, in the early church, some were having some serious questions and doubts about their salvation. In this small epistle of just five chapters, John uses the words "know" or "known" 38 times! It's been called "The Book of Assurance" because it was written to give us the assurance that we might *know* where we stand with God.

If you have doubts about your faith, that doesn't mean that you've never been saved. As a matter of fact, we only tend to doubt that which we believe. However, doubt is to your spirit what pain is to your body. Pain doesn't mean that you're dead. Pain means that there's something wrong

vimeo.com/138120209

NOTES _____

_____
_____
_____
_____
_____
_____
_____
_____
_____
_____
_____
_____
_____
_____
_____
_____
_____
_____
_____

> **"Christianity is not a religion; it's a relationship, and this relationship with God is basic to salvation."**

– something in your body isn't functioning as it ought to. So just as pain is a signal that there's something wrong in your body, doubt is a signal that there's something wrong with your spirit.

Why do you think some Christians have doubts about their salvation?

_____

_____

_____

_____

_____

_____

_____

Birthmarks of a believer

The first mark of a man made new is that he is under new management, and John writes that if someone is a genuine disciple of Jesus Christ, there will be clear evidences of that salvation. Throughout his book, he gives us many "birthmarks of a believer." Here are seven of the most dominant ones:

1. Are you enjoying a relationship with Jesus?

Christianity is not a religion; it's a relationship, and this relationship with God is basic to salvation. John gives us the first test in 1 John 1:2-3, *"This one who is life itself was revealed to us, and we have seen him. And now we testify and proclaim to you that he is the one who is eternal life. He was with the Father, and then he was revealed to us. We proclaim to you what we ourselves have actually seen and heard so that you may have fellowship with us. And our fellowship is with the Father and with his Son, Jesus Christ."*

It's a characteristic of any believer who loves God and Jesus Christ to have fellowship with Him. Salvation isn't just a cold hard fact – it's something we experience. We can enjoy knowing God intimately! Jesus said, *"I came that they may have life and have it more abundantly"* (John 10:10). We come to know and experience His comfort in hard times, His grace in our failures, His provision in our need, His strength in our weakness, and His joy when we feel like giving up.

Our fellowship with Him is the abundant life we experience! A six-year-old girl asked her father about "accepting Jesus." Her father led her in a prayer in which she asked Jesus into her heart. About a week later, she came to him and said, "Dad, how big was Jesus?" He said, "I don't know. He was a grown man, but people were shorter back then. I would guess about 5'10"?" She said, "Daddy, how tall am I?" "About 3'6"." "Daddy, I'm confused. If Jesus was 5'10" and I am 3'6", and Jesus came into my heart, wouldn't He just kind of poke out everywhere?"

There is a profound truth in what that little girl said. If the Jesus of eternal life has come to dwell in you, the evidence of that eternal life will overshadow you. So let me ask, are you enjoying a relationship with God and Jesus Christ? Do you sense His presence? Do you have a love for Him that draws you into His presence? Do you experience the refreshing, almost overwhelming sense of grace that comes upon you when you discover a new truth in His Word? If so, you're experiencing the fellowship of salvation.

2. Do you see a decreasing pattern of sin in your life?
A person who is truly saved has a growing sensitivity to sin in their life. In 1 John 1:5-6 we read, *"... God is Light, and in Him there is no darkness at all. Therefore if we say that we have fellowship with Him and yet walk in the darkness, we lie and do not practice the truth."* Adrian Rogers used to say, "A non-Christian leaps into sin and loves it; a Christian lapses into sin and loathes it." So test yourself: Do you now desire deliverance from the sin that used to entangle you? You were once self-confident and trusting in your own goodness. Do you now judge yourself as a sinner before a holy God? Do you yield yourself to Him? John goes on to say, *"If we say that we have no sin, we are deceiving ourselves and the truth is not in us."* One thing is sure: the person who is truly saved is sensitive to the sinful realities in their own life. It seems like the closer we get to the light of Jesus Christ, the more we begin to see our own imperfections.

John's letter goes on to say, *"Everyone who sins is breaking God's law, for all sin is contrary to the law of God. And you know that Jesus came to take away our sins, and there is no sin in him. Anyone who continues to live in him will not sin. But anyone who keeps on sinning does not know him or understand who he is ... Those who have been born into God's family do not make a practice of sinning, because God's life is in them"* (1 John 3:4-9).

I remember reading that Scripture shortly after I became a Christian, and I was very worried! I thought to myself, "I must not be saved because I know that I still have the ability to sin!" However, the verbs in this verse are in the present tense, which means the verse speaks of a continual, habitual course of action. This verse speaks of those who *"make a practice of sinning."* John is saying that a person who is born of God does not make sin his practice, his lifestyle, or his habit. Before I was saved, I was running towards sin; now I'm running from it! I may slip, I may fall, I may fail, but my heart's desire is to live for God!

Sometimes I get emails from Christians who doubt their salvation because they can't seem to break a sinful or unwise habit in their life. They fear that because they struggle with a particular sin, it must mean they're lost and don't know God. In I John 3:4 we read that a true believer cannot practice lawlessness. (In the original language of the Bible, that word means "living as if there were no law.") This is a person who doesn't care what God thinks about his habits. A true Christian can still sin, and they may struggle with the same temptation the rest of their lives; however, a Christian who sins but responds with confession and repentance is not the same as a non-Christian who shamelessly and unrepentantly practices sin. A true believer can't do that *"because God's life is in them."*

3. Do you strive to obey God's Word?
In 1 John 2:3 it couldn't be any clearer: *"By this we know that we have come to know Him, if we keep His commandments."* This is how Jesus described a true disciple when He gave the great commission: *"teaching them to obey all that I have commanded you"* (Matthew 28:19-20). The word translated "commandments" refers specifically to the orders of Christ rather than just laws in general. John doesn't beat around the bush here. He says, "Don't tell me you are really saved if you are not keeping God's commandments!"

Now let me be very clear: We are not saved because we keep His commands; we keep His commands because we are saved. If I'm being honest, I haven't always kept every single one of God's commandments, but that doesn't mean that I'm not saved.

The key to understanding the difficult passages in the Bible is to dig a little bit deeper into the original language to extract the full meaning. The word "keep" in the original Greek is *tereo,* and it simply means "to watch over." It was a word that sailors used back in the day. In the ancient world, they didn't have nifty GPS navigational systems to guide them. They navigated by the stars. They would keep their eye on the heavens, and they called that *tereo* – "keeping the stars."

> **"We are not saved because we keep His commands; we keep His commands because we are saved."**

NOTES

> **"If we love Him, and His love is in us, then we're going to love what He loves, which is His family, the Church."**

NOTES

"Keeping the stars" is much like keeping the commandments. Any sailor could occasionally get blown off course, get distracted, or waver around, but at the end of the day, they would look up to the stars and make sure their direction was in alignment with what they saw in the heavens. When we keep God's commandments, we steer by them. None of us is perfect, but from the moment that I gave my life to Jesus Christ, there has been a desire to keep God's Word. Martin Luther said, "My conscience is captive to the Word of God." Do you desire to obey God out of gratitude for all that Jesus has done for you? If so, you've passed an important test that indicates an evidence of salvation.

4. Do you see a decreasing love for the things in this world?

In 1 John 2:15 it says, *"Do not love the world, nor the things in the world. If anyone loves the world, the love of the Father is not in him."* When the Bible talks about the "world" in this sense, it's the Greek term *kosmos*, which refers to this world's system. It encompasses things like false religion, worldly theology, crime, immorality, and materialism. When you become a Christian, the same system of this world that used to attract you now begins to repel you. You may be lured into worldly things from time to time, but it isn't what you love; it's what you hate. Jesus said that those who follow Him are not of this world, just as He was not of this world.

5. Do you love the body of Christ?

We read in I John 2:9-10, *"Whoever says he is in the light and hates his brother is still in darkness. Whoever loves his brother abides in the light, and in him there is no cause for stumbling."* In other words, to say that you are *"in the light"* (to call yourself a Christian) should mean that your life shows the patterns of Christ. Loving fellow Christians comes naturally to the believer. Jesus said, *"By this all men will know that you are My disciples, if you have love for one another"* (John 13:35). Love is the nature of God and the characteristic of His children. If we love Him, and His love is in us, then we're going to love what He loves, which is His family, the Church. No single church or individual Christian is perfect, but we still love them regardless. One man said, "A church is comprised of people who have finally realized that they are sinners and banded themselves together to do something about it." Someone who is a genuine believer will *want* to be in church, loving the body of Christ and growing with other believers.

6. Do you experience answered prayer?

In 1 John 3:21-22 we read, *"Beloved, if our heart does not condemn us, we have confidence before God; and whatever we ask we receive from him, because we keep his commandments and do what pleases him."* One way you can know you are a believer is if God answers your prayers. God is more eager to answer the prayers of His children than we are to ask. God may not always answer our prayers the way we want Him to, but He does answer. There are a lot of people who may pray to God occasionally, but they don't even know the God to Whom they're praying. Because a true believer has entered into a relationship with God, they have a confidence that God can and will answer their prayers (1 John 5:14-15).

7. Are you experiencing criticism or rejection because of your faith?

John says, *"Do not be surprised, brethren, if the world hates you…"* (1 John 3:13). In the preceding verses, John uses a Bible illustration from the beginning of time to illustrate his point. Cain hated Abel and murdered him. Why did he do that? *"Because his deeds were evil, and his brother's were righteous"* (vs. 12). Because of the way you live your life before God and because of your stand for truth, you will face criticism for it. Have you ever experienced animosity, hostility, bitterness, alienation, or downright persecution for representing and advocating what is right? If so, that's a sign that you belong to the One who suffered the same way for the same reason (1 Peter 4:4; Philippians 1:28). When you are suffering because of Whom you belong to, don't ever think, "I wonder if God cares." Of course He does, so whenever this world persecutes you because of your faith, just remind yourself, "This is good because it's pretty clear Whom I am with!"

The evidence will be in the heartbeat

If you are saved, the evidence will be there. In Matthew 7:16, Jesus spoke of His true followers, *"You will know them by their fruits."*

There was a picture on the front page of a local newspaper, and if you had seen it, it would have certainly caught your eye. It was a photograph of a man in a hospital bed in what looked like the intensive care unit. Many tubes and health monitors surrounded his bed. And then the photo depicted a woman standing next to her husband's bed with her ear gently resting on her husband's chest – a very peculiar picture to say the least. Here's the back-story. This man was in dire need of a heart transplant. His heart was failing, and if he didn't receive a new heart soon, he would go into cardiac failure. Tragically, a young man was killed in a car accident, and it was his heart that was used in the transplant. But here is where the story gets interesting. The young man who was killed was this man's son, and it was their son's heart that was given to his father. And the picture was depicting this woman with her ear resting on her husband's chest, listening to the heartbeat of her son.

When I heard that story, I thought, "Lord, when people are around me, I want them to hear the heartbeat of your Son, Jesus Christ, living and abiding inside of me!" After all, Jesus gave Himself *for* me so that He might give Himself *to* me so that He could live His life *through* me. And if you are a genuine disciple of Jesus Christ, that will be your heart's desire as well.

Suppose someone were to ask you, "How do I know if I'm really saved?" How would you respond?

_____

_____

_____

_____

_____

_____

_____

Do you have any questions about what you're learning so far? If not, how can your coach pray for you today?

_____

_____

_____

_____

_____

_____

" **Jesus gave Himself *for* me so that He might give Himself *to* me so that He could live His life *through* me.** "

NOTES _____

_____

_____

_____

_____

_____

_____

_____

_____

_____

_____

_____

_____

_____

_____

_____

_____

_____

_____

_____

_____

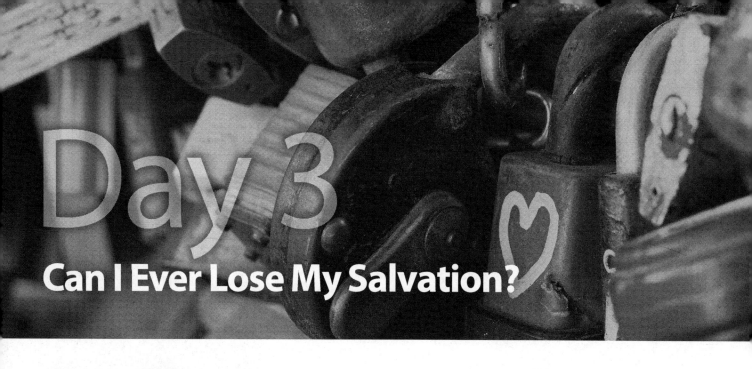

Day 3
Can I Ever Lose My Salvation?

vimeo.com/138120242

NOTES _____

_____
_____
_____
_____
_____
_____
_____
_____
_____
_____
_____
_____
_____
_____
_____
_____
_____
_____
_____
_____
_____

In 1937, the Golden Gate Bridge was built in San Francisco. The bridge was a dangerous and treacherous thing to work on as it began to rise hundreds of feet above the waters of the San Francisco Bay. The workers building it were afraid for their lives, and many of them fell to their deaths. In all, there were 23 people who died in accidental deaths building that bridge.

Finally, the management decided to do something about the problem, so they invested $100,000 in building a safety net under the bridge to prevent any more loss of life. It was actually a great savings because the work went 25% faster and no more lives were lost. As a matter of fact, only 10 (fewer than half as many before) fell into the net, and their lives were saved.

Why could those people work with more productivity? Because of their security. They knew the net was there, and that's the way it is with the Christian life. I don't know of any Christian who is spiritually productive who isn't first absolutely certain where they stand with God. When we know that our future is secure, we can concentrate on the present.

Permanent adoption

Ephesians 1:5 says, *"God decided in advance to adopt us into his own family by bringing us to himself through Jesus Christ. This is what he wanted to do, and it gave him great pleasure."*

God doesn't want you to feel insecure as a member of His family. Could you imagine what kind of state a child would be in if he wasn't sure if he was a part of his family? Perhaps one day he messed up and misbehaved and was kicked out of the house, left out in the cold, no longer a member of the family. Then after several weeks of being homeless, he was accepted back into his home once again and allowed to see his mom and dad, brothers and sisters. But sooner than later, he was kicked out again and left to be homeless. That poor kid would be an emotional wreck!

That's how it is with a lot of folks who believe they can lose their salvation. They think they are living in a foster home with God when in reality they are a part of His adopted family. We are sons and daughters of God!

John 10:27-29 says, *"My sheep hear my voice, and I know them, and they follow Me. And I give them eternal life, and they shall never perish; neither shall anyone snatch them out of My hand. My Father, who has given them to Me, is greater than all; and no one is able to snatch them out of My Father's hand."*

From John 10:27-29, you should understand that nothing can cause you to lose your salvation. Why is this?

_____

_____

_____

_____

_____

_____

_____

_____

_____

> **"** ... the God who saves you is the same God who secures you. **"**

NOTES

What that verse means is that the God who saves you is the same God who secures you. A person who has genuinely decided to place their faith in Jesus for their salvation is safe in the hands of God. This doesn't mean that just because a person joins a church or gets baptized he is automatically going to heaven. No, we're talking about genuine faith – those whose lives have been sincerely changed by the grace of God.

Jesus said in John 10:27, *"I give them eternal life ..."* How long is eternal? It never ends. If you could be saved for two years and then lose that salvation, what would that be called? Call it what you may, but it isn't "eternal life;" it is a "two-year life."

Sometimes people think it's possible to become a Christian but then to lose your salvation and fall away. Every once in a while, someone will ask, "What if a person says that they're saved, is baptized, and volunteers in the church, but after a few years, they walk away and turn their back on God completely? Didn't they lose their salvation?" The Bible answers that question in 1 John 2:19: *"They went out from us, but they were not of us; for if they had been of us, they would have continued with us; but they went out that they might be made manifest, that none of them were of us."*

In other words, it's possible to do all of the outward things that Christians do but not really be born-again.

Some might say they lost their salvation. John says, "No, they left because they were never a genuine part of the family of God to begin with." Adrian Rogers used to say a phrase that really sums this up: "The faith that fizzles before the finish had a flaw from the first."

God's promise

God made an amazing promise to you in Romans 8:38-39. I think this may be one of the most all-inclusive statements you will ever read in the Bible. Paul mentions ten strong opponents that can never separate us from God's love.

Read the verse below and highlight each of the 10 things that cannot separate us from God.

"For I am persuaded that neither death nor life, nor angels nor principalities nor powers, nor things present nor things to come, nor height nor depth, nor any other created thing, shall be able to separate us from the love of God which is in Christ Jesus our Lord." – Romans 8:38-39

NOTES

Wow! I'll give you a hundred bucks if you can think of anything that Paul left out! Let's look at each of these ten things individually:

- *Death* – You can't lose it when you die!
- *Life* – This covers anything that could potentially happen to you while you're living.
- *Angels* – Good angels or bad angels (Satan and his demons are fallen angels) – in other words, no unseen powers can separate a true believer from Jesus Christ.
- *Principalities* – That means the government can't come between you and God.
- *Powers* – That means any other authority.
- *Things present* – That's anything that is going on right now in your life.
- *Things to come* – That's anything that can possibly happen tomorrow.
- *Height* – That means anything in heaven.
- *Depth* – That means anything in hell.
- *Any other creature* – That was just in case we could think of anything that He left out.

God has made a solemn promise to you, and He covers all the bases! When you accept Him by faith, He fully and completely accepts you based on His grace. Hebrews 10:14 says, *"For by that one offering he forever made perfect those who are being made holy."* When you make the decision to accept God's free gift of salvation, God doesn't say to you, "I'm going to make the down payment, but now it's up to you to make the monthly installments." Notice the phrase, *"forever made perfect."* In the Old Testament, when people sinned, they had to come back and offer a sacrifice to atone for their sins again and again. Those sacrifices could never take away sin; they simply covered sin for the time being. But we are told in Hebrews 10 that when Jesus came to this earth, He offered Himself as the ultimate sacrifice – a sacrifice that is *"forever made perfect."* If a person thinks they can lose their salvation, they are reducing the sacrifice of Christ practically to the level of bulls and goats in the Old Testament.

Eternal security is not a license to do whatever you want, but the motivation to please God at all times. The mark of a genuine follower of Christ is that their life has been changed and they are now pursuing a closer, deeper walk with Jesus. If any man is in Christ, he is a new creation.

E.S.P.N.

One of the best ways to remember what Jesus did for you at the point of salvation is by using the acronym E.S.P.N. When you made that choice to believe and receive Jesus Christ, here's what happened:

E - Eternal Life. Your name was written in the Lamb's Book of Life. Those who are followers of Christ can rest in the confidence of knowing that when they close their eyes for the last time on this earth, they will open their eyes for the first time in Heaven.

S - Sins Are Forgiven. When we receive the salvation Jesus offers, our souls are power-washed! Salvation is an exchange of our sin for His righteousness. We can have a clear conscience knowing that we are at peace with God.

P - Personal Relationship. John 1:12 says, *"Yet to all who have received*

Him (Jesus) to those who have believed in His name, He gave the right to become children of God." God has given you a relationship with Himself through His Son, Jesus. God now offers to you and me the same power that brought Jesus back from the grave (Romans 8:11)! Our God specializes in taking dead things and bringing them back to life. Maybe you've felt like your dreams are dead. I've got great news. The same power that brought Jesus back from the grave is available in your life.

N - Never Leave You. In Hebrews 13:5, God makes this promise to His children: *"I will never leave you, I will never forsake you."* When you know that your future is secure, you can concentrate on your present. Though feelings come and go, God's love for us does not. Don't rest in your salvation experience. It is the Christ of your experience that keeps you.

Superman

In one of the Superman movies, Superman saves a man from a burning building. He rescues him from the top floor and is carrying him to safety by flying through the skies. The man looks at Superman and then looks down at the ground and says, "I'm scared, Superman. Look how far down that is."

Superman gives him a great answer. "Now if I delivered you from the burning fire, what makes you think I am going to drop you when I'm carrying you to safety?"

If God has delivered you from a burning hell, what makes you think He will drop you before He safely puts you down?

If someone were to ask you, "How can I know that I won't lose my salvation or that God won't give up on me?" How would you respond?

_____

_____

_____

_____

_____

_____

_____

_____

_____

How does knowing you can never lose your salvation affect your understanding of God and how you relate to Him?

_____

_____

_____

_____

_____

_____

_____

_____

_____

NOTES _____

_____

_____

_____

_____

_____

_____

_____

_____

_____

_____

_____

_____

_____

_____

_____

_____

_____

_____

_____

_____

_____

_____

_____

_____

_____

_____

_____

_____

_____

_____

Day 4

How Can I Grow in My Friendship with God?

vimeo.com/138120305

Helping us stay "connected" has become big business in our culture. Smart phones, Facebook, and Twitter give us instant access to the musings and activities of our friends and family members all over the world. But how much time do we actually spend building meaningful face-to-face relationships?

Let me ask you a question: How close are you to God? The answer is simple. You're as close to God as you want to be. How impersonal God seems is a measure of the distance you have put between yourself and God. Sure there are times when we really want to have a deeper friendship with God, but when it comes down to it, oftentimes we're not ready to pay the price. Don't just assume that because you go to a Bible-believing church that you're automatically close in your relationship with God. It requires investing in that relationship by consciously, constantly, and conscientiously drawing your heart towards Him on a daily basis. James 4:8 says, *"Draw near to God and He will draw near to you."* That verse contains both a precept and a promise. The precept is: you draw near to God. The promise is: God will draw near to you. He is always more eager to meet us than we are to meet Him, but we must initiate the first step.

Foundations of friendship

When you think about it, developing a friendship with God is no different than becoming friends with anyone else here on earth. Genuine friendship is built upon four foundations. If you want a real friend or if you want to be a real friend, it means that you must invest in these four things:

1. Time Spent Together

Two people will never grow in their friendship with one another if both parties never make any effort to hang out. We will never achieve that closeness we desire from God unless we make the effort in devoting time to be with him. We have to make the choice to "draw near to God" before He will draw near to us. Why? Because we are the ones who moved. We are the ones who get distracted from our walk with Him. Do you feel like you are "too busy" to spend time with the Lord each day? Then you are saying the immediate demands of your schedule are more important than enjoying that deep, satisfying communion with God.

2. Two-Way Communication

If you want to build a friendship with somebody, it involves actually communicating with them. Communication is not just a one-way monologue. How would you like it if you were trying to talk to someone but could never get a word in edge-wise? You know how it feels when you try to have a conversation with someone like that. Likewise, prayer is not a monologue; it is a dialogue. Prayer doesn't just mean you recite your wish list to God and go about your business. It means that you share your heart with Him but then be still long enough to hear His voice. God speaks primarily through His Word. So try interacting with the Spirit by praying as you read Scripture. As you meditate on His Word, ask Him questions: Lord, what are You trying to say to me? How does this apply to my life?

3. Vulnerability
It's very rare to find a friend you can truly and completely be yourself with. They say if you can find two to three friendships like this over a lifetime, you are a very blessed individual. An important factor in genuine friendship involves our willingness to be open, honest, and transparent about the deepest issues in our lives. The depth of any friendship is limited to the extent of our transparency with that other person. The same is true in our friendship with our Heavenly Father. God wants us to expose every area of our life to Him. Although the natural response is to shrink back from such vulnerability, we have to remind ourselves that God already knows us inside and out, yet He still loves us more than we can ever comprehend.

4. Shared Interests
Think about it. Your closest friends are people who you genuinely enjoy being around because you both like to do the same stuff. If we're going to grow in our oneness with God, it means we must learn to share His interests. We need to learn to love what He loves. We have to start caring about the things that He cares about. God is always attentive to our concerns, but do we care about His desires and purposes? Are you more interested in the Lord, or are you more interested in what He can give you? When our prayers are focused only on ourselves, when we neglect His Word, and when we are "too busy" for God, it communicates an unspoken message to Him: "I'm not interested in you."

On a scale of 1-10 (1 being as far away from God as you can get and 10 being as close to God as you can get on this earth), how would you rate your friendship with God today? What do you think your next step needs to be today to go to the next level?

_____

_____

_____

_____

_____

_____

_____

You are in control
You are in total control of the closeness you have in your friendship with God. But if you choose to be closer, then you must choose to do the things that foster a good friendship! We never grow closer to God when we just live life. It takes deliberate pursuit and attentiveness.

It's important for us to realize that in any relationship, intentionality is necessary to achieve intimacy. If you're married, chances are you and your mate didn't simply *drift* to the altar. You drew near to one another as you got

> **" You're as close to God as you choose to be. "**

NOTES *I have 2 true friend Danna & Karen*

> **"God is waiting on you to draw near to Him, and when you do, He will draw near to you."**

acquainted and spent time together. You went on dates. You talked on the phone. And when you weren't on the phone or on a date, you wished you were. Most marriages start off with a high level of passionate intimacy, but it's also common that as the years go by, you can find yourself starting to drift apart emotionally. When that happens, the main reason is because one or both parties are no longer *intentional* when it comes to investing in that relationship. God is waiting on you to draw near to Him, and when you do, He will draw near to you.

What does it mean to have God as a friend?

There's a principle of friendship that says over time you become like those you spend the most time with. That's our goal as disciples of Christ – to become like Him (Romans 8:29)!

There are some great Scriptures about what it means to have God as a friend:

- James 2:23 – *"'Abraham believed God, and God counted him as righteous because of his faith.' He was even called the friend of God."*
- In John 15:15, Jesus said to His disciples, *"No longer do I call you servants, for the servant does not know what his master is doing; but I have called you friends, for all that I have heard from my Father I have made known to you."*
- James 4:4 – *"Don't you know that friendship with the world is hatred toward God? Anyone who chooses to be a friend of the world becomes an enemy of God."*
- Exodus 33:11 – *"The LORD used to speak to Moses face to face, as a man speaks to his friend."*

Moses and God

Moses's friendship with God fascinates me. After Moses helped free God's people, the Israelites, out of Egypt, they were wandering in the desert for a period of forty years. Moses had some intense pressure on him as he led hundreds of thousands of nomads out in the desert, but he was also marked as a devoted friend of God.

What does it mean to you to have God as a "friend"?

_____

_____

_____

_____

_____

_____

_____

_____

_____

_____

Scripture says that the Lord spoke to Moses like a man speaks to his friend. There are really only two ways you can know God: casually or intimately. You can either know *about* God or you can really *know* God. The Bible says that the Israelites knew the *works* of God, but Moses knew the *ways* of God. Psalm 103:7 says, *"He made known his ways to Moses, his acts to the people of Israel."*

Moses knew God in a way the rest of the people didn't know. He understood God's ways. The rest of the people only saw the acts or the works of God. That describes many Christians today. There are Christians who know what God does, but they don't know who God is. They don't know God as an intimate friend.

When you read the Bible, you see that the Israelites were a very unstable people. They were constantly pushing the panic button, always in a frenzy, always worried, constantly complaining. Why? The writer of Hebrews put it this way: *"They always go astray in their heart; they have not known my ways"* (Hebrews 3:10). You see, the Israelites were fine as long as the works of God kept coming their way in their favor! But when God was no longer doing what they wanted Him to do, they panicked! The point is, if all you ever do is see the works of God, as long as the sun is shining, you'll be marching in the parade. But when difficulties come, you'll start questioning your faith. You've known God's works, but you've never come to understand God's ways.

There's one more thing I want you to see about Moses. Exodus 34 says, because Moses was spending so much time with God and basking in His glory, he did not know that the skin of his face shone with the radiance of God's glory. The people of Israel would see Moses coming down from the mountain and his face would shine so brightly that the Bible says Moses had to put a veil over his face. Your intimacy with God will increase your influence for God. When you spend time seeking God's face, the radiance of His glory will begin to show up on your face. People will know that there is something different about you.

After a while, Moses drifted away and wasn't spending much time in building his friendship with the Lord. As a result, he lost his glow, but he continued to wear the veil. He didn't want anyone else to know that the glow was gone.

As a kid, I used to have a lot of glow-in-the-dark toys. They're fun to play with because you can expose them to a light source, and then go in a dark room and watch them glow. But we all know what happens if you leave those toys in the dark too long. They lose their glow. If we don't spend time "re-charging" ourselves spiritually in the light of the presence of God, we too will lose our glow.

That's why the New Testament says, *"And we all, with unveiled face, beholding the glory of the Lord, are being transformed into the same image from one degree of glory to another"* (2 Corinthians 3:18).

How can we grow in our friendship with God?

There are many ways to grow that friendship, but here are some foundational practices that we'll dive into deeper later on in *LifeCoach: Discipleship*:

1. Communicate with God daily.

Prayer is simply communicating with God. Don't worry about the words that you use, because God knows your heart. Don't worry about whether you're sitting, standing, or kneeling. The main thing you need to know is that God wants to hear from you. I have three kids, and I love them with all my heart. When they want to speak to me, I couldn't care less about the position of their hands or the formality of their words. What I am drawn to is the genuineness of their hearts, and the same is true of our relationship with God.

2. Learn about God daily.

When I was a kid growing up, I hated reading. It's ironic that God called me to be a writer as an adult. Maybe you're not a person who reads much – that's ok. I'd encourage you just to read a chapter a day in the Bible, which doesn't take much time at all. Through the Bible, we begin to learn things about God we never knew. Someone once said that the Bible is like a vast ocean – shallow enough that a little child can play with no fear of drowning, yet so deep that scholars can swim in it and never touch bottom. The more you learn about God through His Word, the more you crave to know more

NOTES

> **"**As iron sharpens iron, so one man sharpens another.**"**
> – Proverbs 27:17

NOTES

about Him. Think of it this way – if prayer is speaking to God, then spending time reading the Bible is God's opportunity to speak to you. Many times, I've learned that if there's something I'm praying about, often the answer can be found in the section of the Bible I'm reading that day.

3. Become part of a local church.
God has intended the church to be a microcosm of what the Christian life is all about. Being a part of the "Body of Christ" means that you have a place to worship corporately with other believers, be equipped in the Word, and be empowered to serve in ministry. Getting involved in a church is vitally important. Since we live in an ever-increasingly busy world, we have to be intentional when it comes to protecting and prioritizing our time in being a part of a local church.

4. Find some Christian friends on the journey.
I discovered my most significant "spiritual growth spurt" when I found some friends who would help me along in my spiritual journey. There's nothing greater than knowing that you have the support system of a small group standing with you, praying for you, encouraging you, and sharing their insights from God's Word with you. Proverbs 27:17 says, *"As iron sharpens iron, so one man sharpens another."*

5. Go public with your faith through baptism.
We'll dig deeper into this with tomorrow's study. Baptism is a public symbol of the inward commitment you've made to follow Jesus. But baptism is also a command that Jesus gave to us. It's our way of publicly identifying with Him. What's interesting is that in a lot of foreign countries where it is illegal to convert to Christianity, nobody cares if you "prayed a prayer" or made a "decision" to follow Jesus. But when you are baptized, it shows them how serious you are about this decision, and in some instances, your very life could be in danger. Baptism is a clear symbol that we are now identifying ourselves as being in a relationship with Christ, and we are not ashamed of it. We want the whole world to know!

Life's most exciting adventure is intimacy with God. God wants to be your best friend, and He wants you to continually grow in your relationship with Him. The Christian life is like riding a bicycle; you're either moving ahead or falling off. I hope you will take the principles from today's lesson and begin your own exciting adventure.

Based on what you read in today's study, what should be your next step? What do you need to focus on today?

Day 5
Why Is Baptism Such a Big Deal?

Baptism. Is it really that important? Does it really matter to my faith and my walk in Christ? Is a person saved through baptism? You may have plenty of questions surrounding this topic, so we'll look to the Bible to get some answers.

Asked to explain baptism, a little boy answered, "It's when the preacher holds you under water, and you think about Jesus!" We can take heart in knowing that there is much more to the ordinance of baptism than that!

Baptism really is a big deal. In fact, the Bible talks about the subject of baptism 74 times! Jesus had an earthly ministry of three and a half years, and He commenced His ministry by being baptized, and He concluded his ministry by commanding his followers to *"Go and make disciples of all nations, baptizing them in the name of the Father, the Son, and the Holy Spirit ..."* (Matthew 28:19-20). Since baptism composed the bookends of the ministry of God's Son, that should tell us that it's a very big deal! What Jesus emphasizes, we should never de-emphasize, and we should never minimize what God has maximized!

Sometimes people have a tendency to think of baptism as something they *have* to do. Yet this is not something we *have* to do but rather something that we *get* to do. Once you truly understand its significance, you'll realize that it is a tremendous privilege!

Here's the key takeaway I want you to download into your heart: Baptism by immersion is the Biblical way a believer professes his faith in the crucified, risen Christ.

Why is the method of baptism so important?

There is only *one* kind of baptism taught in the Bible, and that is baptism by immersion. Since Jesus Christ is the example we pattern all of our life after, we should examine how Jesus was baptized.

Mark 1:9-10 says, *"At that time Jesus came from Nazareth in Galilee and was baptized by John in the Jordan. As Jesus was coming up out of the water, he saw heaven being torn open and the Spirit descending on him like a dove."* So if Jesus came up "out of the water," where was He? He was *in* the water. Jesus traveled over 60 miles in order to be baptized by John the Baptist at the Jordan River. John 3:23 tells us John the Baptist was baptizing at the Jordan because there was "much water there." Baptism by immersion is not always the easiest and most convenient thing to do. But if sprinkling and pouring were sufficient methods for Jesus to have been baptized, he could have saved Himself the hassle of making the 60-mile trip.

The word "baptize" comes from the spoken language back in Jesus' day known as Koine Greek. If you had lived back then, you would have heard

vimeo.com/138120369

NOTES _____

_____

_____

_____

_____

_____

_____

_____

_____

_____

_____

_____

_____

_____

_____

_____

_____

_____

_____

_____

_____

_____

_____

> **"Baptism is both a picture and a symbol of what Jesus has done for you and your new identity in Him."**

NOTES _____

_____
_____
_____
_____
_____
_____
_____
_____
_____
_____
_____
_____
_____
_____
_____
_____
_____
_____
_____
_____
_____
_____
_____

the everyday Greek word *baptizo*, which is where we get our word "baptize." *Baptizo* simply means "to immerse, to dunk, or to dip under." It was a word used to describe ships that had sunk into the sea. When a woman wanted to take a cloth and change the color of that cloth, she would immerse the cloth in dye, or *baptizo* the cloth. One ancient Jewish historian even described a man who was murdered by baptism! That's easy to understand. You would just put him under the water and not allow him to come back up!

As you can see, up until the time of Christ, this was a common word that had no religious meaning whatsoever until John the Baptist came along. So it's very clear from the Bible that immersion is the idea surrounding this topic of baptism.

What does baptism symbolize?

The reason Jesus was baptized has a lot to do with why we ought to be baptized – identification. In the early church, baptism was the way to "ID" those who were truly believers. When Jesus was baptized, He was identifying Himself with us being our model. When we are baptized, we are identifying ourselves with Him.

Both the method and the meaning of baptism are interwoven. If you change the method, you distort the meaning. The meaning of baptism is that it is an outward sign of an inward reality. It pictures what Jesus Christ has done for you. Just as Jesus died and was buried for the payment of your sins, when a believer goes under the water, it is a picture that he or she is "dying to self" and their former way of living. Just as Jesus was resurrected from the grave, when a baptized believer comes up out of the water, it is a picture of our new life with Christ and the fact that we will enjoy an eternal life with Him. Romans 6:4 says, *"We were therefore buried with him through baptism into death in order that, just as Christ was raised from the dead through the glory of the Father, we too may live a new life."*

So baptism is both a picture and a symbol of what Jesus has done for you and your new identity in Him. Suppose you had never met me, and you came up to my wife and said, "Carrie, do you have a picture of your husband?" And suppose she were to hold up a photograph of Brad Pitt. I can understand how she might get us confused because we look so strikingly similar. But you would see that photograph and you would say, "Carrie, that's not your husband - that's Brad Pitt!" And suppose her response was, "Well, any picture will do."

A true picture of anything always represents the reality of whatever you are trying to portray. You can't picture a burial by sprinkling a few drops of water on a person's head. Baptism is a picture of Jesus' death, burial, and resurrection and our identity with Him. The baptistery is in reality a "liquid tomb." Romans 6:5 says, *"We are buried in the likeness of his death."*

I like to look at a baptism as a funeral service of a person's former life of sin and a celebration service of their new life in Christ. On April 10, 1994, Brandon Park had his "funeral service." The only mourner there was the devil - he hated to see me go. I had been his good buddy. But the old Brandon Park was gone, and that was pictured by my going down into the water.

It is important to have your baptism after your salvation. To be baptized before you were saved would be like having your funeral service before you die. *"Anyone who is in Christ is a new creation ... old things have passed away ..."* (2 Corinthians 5:17).

In your own words, describe what your baptism is a picture or symbol of.

_____
_____
_____
_____

_____

_____

_____

_____

_____

Who should be baptized?

There are two things that always go together in the Bible: belief and then baptism. You never find one without the other, and you never find them in any other order. Every time you find an instance where someone decides to become a lifelong follower of Christ, you see them baptized.

For example, in Acts 18:8, we see, _"Crispus, the leader of the synagogue, believed in the Lord with all his household, and many of the Corinthians when they heard were believing and being baptized."_

If you have become a true follower of Christ and you want everyone to know that you are identifying yourself with Him, the way you do that is to be baptized by immersion.

As mentioned yesterday, in some countries it is a crime to be baptized into the Christian faith. They are not concerned with a person merely attending a church or claiming to be a follower of Christ, but once they are baptized, it is a sign to them that you are serious about your belief, which results in that individual's life being in jeopardy.

If you are a follower of Christ, and you're not ashamed of the God who has saved you, and you want everybody to know that you're a believer in Jesus, the way that you show that is through baptism by immersion. The way that you profess your faith in Christ is not just praying a prayer or walking down an aisle of a church. In the New Testament, the way a person professed their faith in Christ was by being baptized, and it is no different today.

We have many in our church who have come from a religious background where they have been baptized as infants. They later come to the realization that they need to be baptized by immersion now that they have made a decision to become a lifelong follower of Christ, but they don't want to offend their families. One woman expressed to her parents that when she was baptized as an infant, she acknowledged that her parents wanted her to be raised in the teachings of Christ and His Church. But now, as an adult, she is acting on that teaching for herself and making the personal decision to accept and follow Christ as her Lord and Savior.

When should a person be baptized?

In the Bible, baptism was always done immediately after one believes the gospel and receives Jesus Christ.

For example, there was a Philippian jailer who was saved under amazing circumstances. In Acts 16, after Paul and Silas were freed from their prison bonds, the Philippian jailer took Paul into his home and asked, _"What must I do to be saved?"_ And then the Bible says that _" ... immediately he was baptized."_

You find that pattern throughout the Bible. They were saved and then _immediately_ baptized. Why was it so quick? Because baptism is the way a believer identifies himself as a follower of Jesus Christ, and they were eager for others to know their decision.

This is so critical for us to understand: There is no record of an unbaptized believer in the New Testament. There is nothing in Scripture comparable to the excuses that people give today for not being baptized. "Well, I gave my heart and life to Christ as a child, but I've never been baptized." Or "I

> **"** Baptism is the way a believer identifies himself as a follower of Jesus Christ. **"**

NOTES _____

_____

_____

_____

_____

_____

_____

_____

_____

_____

_____

_____

_____

_____

_____

_____

_____

_____

_____

_____

_____

> **"Baptism is not necessary for salvation, but it is necessary for obedience."**

NOTES

32

accepted Christ 10 years ago, but I have never followed through on believer's baptism." There is no record of anything remotely similar to that in the Bible. Without exception, every believer in the Bible was immediately baptized.

When a police officer is sworn in, he immediately puts on the badge. When a man joins the army, he immediately puts on the uniform. When a couple gets married, they immediately put on their wedding bands.

Could you imagine how my wife would have felt on the day of our wedding if I had said to her, "Honey, I love you ... I just said 'I do' ... but let's talk maybe in another 20 years about putting on that wedding ring." I don't think that would have gone over very well. I wear that ring with pride because I want the world to know that she belongs to me and I belong to her! So the Bible says that once a man receives Jesus, understands the message of the gospel, and becomes a follower of Christ, they should immediately be baptized.

Are we fully saved after being baptized?

I cannot be more emphatic when I state the plain fact that baptism does not save you. You can be baptized so many times that you know every crack in the bottom of the baptistery and still not be saved.

Technically speaking, you become a Christian "by grace through faith." Ephesians 2:8-9 says, *"For it is by grace you have been saved, through faith - and this not from yourselves, it is the gift of God - not by works, so that no one can boast."*

There are two extreme viewpoints that people have when it comes to this issue, and both are incorrect. There is one group that says baptism is necessary for a person to go to heaven; therefore, it is a big deal. Yet there is another group that says baptism is not necessary to go to heaven; therefore, it is not a big deal. In this case, the truth lies in the middle because both groups are half right. Baptism is not necessary to go to heaven, but it is a very big deal.

As I share the gospel with people, I always ask them about their relationship with Jesus Christ, and many of them tell me, "Oh I was baptized as a kid." They somehow get the idea that all you have to do is be baptized, and then you're right with God. Getting baptized does not make you a follower of Jesus Christ.

I'm wearing a wedding ring right now. If I were to take my wedding band off of my finger and give it to a single man, would that make him married to my wife? Of course not. In a similar way, my taking the wedding band off does not make me unmarried. I am still married to my spouse regardless. So I can't make another man married by putting my wedding band on him, and I cannot make myself unmarried by taking the wedding band off. The wedding ring simply shows that I am married. And that's precisely what baptism portrays. Never mistake the symbol for the meaning just as you never mistake the ring for marriage.

Baptism is not necessary for salvation, but it is necessary for obedience. It is obedience that brings the blessing of God into your life. The Christian who is obedient to the Lord will be a Christian full of joy and full of fruitfulness in his life.

I've heard some individuals ask, "How come I can't understand the Bible? Why don't I sense the Lord at work in my life? Why don't I sense God's direction in important decisions I am facing?" Yet when I counsel and do a little prodding, we discover that there is some area of disobedience in that person's life. God says, "Why should I give you more light when I have already given you clear light in this matter that you have ignored?" The way to understand the part of Scripture that you don't understand is to obey the part of Scripture that you do understand. And when you begin to obey what you do understand, you will be amazed at how much more light will break into your life.

The waters of baptism, whether a spoonful or a tank full, cannot take away sin. But whenever possible, and as soon as possible, you should be baptized. There was a little kid who heard the gospel in children's church one Sunday and afterwards, told his mother, "Mom, I asked Jesus to come into my heart ... what do I do next?" She said, "After the worship service, just go up to the pastor and tell him that you have made the decision to follow Christ and you would like to be baptized." Well, he misunderstood what his mother said, so after the service, he walked up to his pastor and said, "I've decided to follow Jesus, and I want to be advertised!"

Although that may be incorrect terminology, it's great theology! Because that's exactly what baptism truly is – a symbol that you are "advertising" your faith in Jesus and your commitment to be a lifelong follower of the One who gave His life for you.

How would you describe baptism to an unchurched friend who has never witnessed a baptism before?

It shows the world you have taken Jesus as your Saviour and you want to live for Him. You are burying your past and Now a New Creation in Christ

Based on what you've studied today, have you been baptized the way Jesus was since your conversion as a follower of Christ?

I was baptized when I was 12 in a pond in the middle of a timber. It was pouring down rain & thunder + lightening.

NOTES

THE GOD QUESTIONS

week 2

Day 1

How Can I Know God Is Real?

vimeo.com/138213703

Many skeptics have asked, "If you can't see God, how can you believe in Him?" There are a lot of things that we believe in that we cannot see. Reality doesn't only encompass what we can see and touch in the physical world. Most everyone accepts the reality of things like emotions, beauty, and thoughts even though they don't physically exist. You can't see gravity, but if you jump off the Empire State Building, you will experience something very powerful that you cannot see. Some people assume that in order to believe in God, we have to check our brains at the door and just take a blind leap of faith. But God has never asked us to have a blind faith. He says, *"Come let us reason together"* (Isaiah 1:18). He invites us to come and consider Him and His truth. God not only exists, but the fingerprints of God have become exceedingly evident for anyone who is willing to search for them.

Read Romans 1:18-20: *"For the wrath of God is revealed from heaven against all ungodliness and unrighteousness of men, who by their unrighteousness suppress the truth. For what can be known about God is plain to them, because God has shown it to them. For his invisible attributes, namely, his eternal power and divine nature, have been clearly perceived, ever since the creation of the world, in the things that have been made. So they are without excuse."*

What does it mean when the Bible says, "What can be known about God is plain to them"?

_____

_____

_____

It's important for us to understand that atheists cannot prove that God does not exist and Christians can't prove that He does because proof requires scientific observation. I cannot prove that George Washington was our first president, but I can look at the evidence from history, which substantiates the fact that he did indeed exist. In this lesson, we'll look at a few incontrovertible evidences for the existence of God.

The Cosmology Argument:
Why does the Universe exist?

Every effect must have a cause. The Universe and everything in it is an effect.

There must be something that caused everything to come into existence. The often-asked question is, "If there is a God, why doesn't He reveal Himself so that everyone can believe in Him?" The very existence of anything and everything in the cosmos offers powerful evidence for the existence of God. Psalm 19:1 says, *"The heavens declare the glory of God; and the sky above proclaims his handiwork."* The word translated "handiwork" is scientifically specific. Hebrew lexicographers describe the word as meaning "motion of different parts of the same thing, at the same time, in opposite directions and with force." Robert Young defines the word as "to spread out or over." James Strong defines it as "to pound" or "to expand." When you think about it, that's a perfect scientific description of the Big Bang written in 1000 B.C.! Science has now demonstrated that the Universe had a beginning, necessitating a cause. Someone had to push the first domino and get the creation process started.

The Teleological Argument: *How do you explain the Universe's complex design?*

This argument states that since the Universe displays such an infinitely complex and sophisticated design, there must have been a divine Designer. For example, Charles Darwin asserted that all living creatures arose from a single-cell organism that sprouted from the primordial soup eons ago. However, back in the 1800's when Darwin wrote the *Origin of Species*, he did not fully understand how intricately complex a single cell is. A single cell is composed of millions of moving parts. Take a cell's protein molecule for example. The odds of a single protein molecule forming by chance is 1 in 10^{243} (that's a 1 with 243 zeroes behind it). A single cell is comprised of *millions* of these intricate protein molecules.

Many in the scientific community are talking about the "fine tuning" of the cosmos, which is really rattling the cages of the atheist community. One expert said that there are more than 75 physical or cosmological parameters that require precise calibration in order to produce a world that can sustain life. If any of them were "out of tune," we would die. Here are a few more examples of how complex our world is:

- If the elements of our atmosphere were just a few percentage points different, every living thing on Earth would die.
- If the Earth were 1 degree closer to the sun, we'd fry! If we were 1 degree further, we'd freeze!
- If the moon were any closer or larger, the tides would destroy the coastlines; if any smaller or further away, oceans would die from a lack of nutrient movement.
- If our distance from Jupiter were any greater, asteroids and comets would pepper the Earth; if we were any closer, Jupiter's gravity would make our orbit unstable.
- If Earth's gravity were any stronger, it would retain too much ammonia and methane and we couldn't breathe. If it were any weaker, Earth's atmosphere would lose too much water and we'd not have the liquid necessary to survive.
- If Earth's crust were any thicker, it would absorb too much of our oxygen. We wouldn't be able to breathe. If it were any thinner, the Earth would move and shake beneath our feet and would make life impossible.

The probability of these factors occurring anywhere in the Universe by chance are less than 12 in a hundred thousand trillion trillion trillion trillion trillion! If that's not wild enough, 100 billion other things had to

> ❝ The fact that our heart yearns for something earth can't supply is proof that Heaven must be our home. ❞
> – C.S. Lewis

NOTES

> "Deep within us is the recognition that there is something beyond this life and Someone beyond this world."

NOTES

happen for these 75 to exist! The probability of these factors converging is so infinitesimally small that cosmologists and astrophysicists now admit that it's more reasonable to believe that a divine Designer was involved than to assume it all happened by chance. Quite frankly, I don't have enough faith to be an atheist!

In 1959, scientists discovered the fact that the Earth is perfectly balanced. Wherever there is a mountain mass on one side of Earth, something of equal weight is on the opposite side of the Earth! That's why our planet doesn't wobble out of orbit. There is global weight distribution of land mass, mountains, valleys, and water! (Note that this weight balance of the Earth is described in Isaiah 40:12.)

If you are looking to see the evidence of God, look at these four points that can be easily remembered as CODA:

C - Creation – Every time you see a piece of machinery, an airplane, a ship, a car, or even a bicycle, you know it has a creator.

O - Order – Every time you see order, you know it has an "order-er." If you see a message spelled out using alphabet cereal, you know that someone arranged those letters to be in that specific order.

D - Design – Every time you see a wrist watch, you know it has a designer. How do you explain six feet of DNA coiled inside every one of our body's 100 trillion cells, which contain a four-letter chemical alphabet that spells out precise assembly instructions for all the proteins from which our bodies are made.

A - Art – Every time you see a thing of beauty, a piece of art like the Mona Lisa, you know it has an artist. When it comes to the beauty and intricacy of this world, the closer you look, the more you see God.

When we look at the Universe, what do we see that is so evident? We see creation, order, design, and art. If everything else in our society has a creator, order-er, designer, and artist behind it, isn't it reasonable to expect that behind this incredibly intricate, complicated, and awe-inspiring Universe, there is a Creator, Order-er, Designer, and Artist behind it?

Cambridge-educated Stephen Meyer demonstrated that no hypothesis could come close to explaining how information got into biological matter by naturalistic means. "Information is the hallmark of a mind," Meyer said. "And purely from the evidence of genetics and biology, we can infer the existence of a mind that's far greater than our own – a conscious, purposeful, intelligent designer who's amazingly creative."

The Ontological Argument: *Why does every culture throughout history have a concept of God?*

The ontological argument uses the concept of God to prove God's existence. From prehistoric times, the idea of God has existed in the mind of humanity, and evidence of such thought exists in the records of all world civilizations. Why does nearly every society, every culture, and every people group have a desire to worship a Being that is far greater and is outside of themselves? Scripture answers that: *"He has also set eternity in the hearts of men"* (Ecclesiastes 3:11). Deep within us is the recognition that there is something beyond this life and Someone beyond this world. We might try to fill this God-shaped hole in our lives in another way or we might deny this knowledge intellectually, but God's presence in us and all around is still obvious. Since the vast majority of people throughout history, in all cultures, in all civilizations, in all continents believe in the existence of some kind of

God, there must be something (or Someone) causing this belief.

In other words, the concept of God fits – almost as if our minds have a feel for God. So much so, in fact, that when people reject God, they invariably substitute something else in its place. Blaise Pascal said, "There is a God shaped vacuum in the heart of every man which cannot be filled by any created thing, but only by God, the Creator, made known through Jesus."

The Consciousness Argument:
How do you explain you?

Our existence has significance (or insignificance) depending on the existence (or nonexistence) of God. Many scientists are concluding that the laws of chemistry and physics cannot explain our experience of consciousness. According to a researcher who showed that consciousness can continue after a person's brain has stopped functioning, current scientific findings "would support the view that 'mind,' 'consciousness,' or the 'soul' is a separate entity from the brain."

Professor J.P. Moreland said, "You can't get something from nothing." If the Universe began with dead matter having no conscious, "how then do you get something totally different – consciousness, living, thinking, feeling, believing creatures – from materials that don't have that?" But if everything started with the mind of God, "we don't have a problem with explaining the origin of our mind."

The Moral Argument:
On what basis do we understand good and evil?

There are countless examples of goodness and virtue in our world. But a question arises: On what basis is something considered good or evil, right or wrong? Universally, we know that murder and rape and bigotry and racism are wrong, regardless of traditions, customs, or preferences. But where did we get this knowledge? Every culture throughout history has had some form of law. Everyone has a sense of what is right and what is wrong.

Love and compassion are either a part of God's nature (and therefore to be reflected in us), or they are products of a random biological accident (and therefore unnecessary). Where did this sense of right and wrong come from if not from a holy God? Mark Mittleberg remarks, "If we didn't invent it, if it transcends the realms of culture and politics, if it's something we can't get away from, then what is its source? Could it be that a Moral Lawgiver actually knit those moral standards, along with the ability to understand and operate by them, into the very fabric of what it means to be human?" Scripture actually answers that question for us. Romans 2:15 states, *"They demonstrate that God's law is written in their hearts, for their own conscience and thoughts either accuse them or tell them they are doing right."*

The Experiential Argument:
Why do people find God if He doesn't exist?

As Christians, we know God exists because we speak to Him every day. We sense His presence; we feel His leading; we know His love; we desire His grace. Things have occurred in our lives that have no possible explanation other than God.

One cloudy, windy day, a little boy was flying his kite. The kite had soared so high that it was now above the clouds and was no longer even visible to those who were still on the ground. An older gentleman happened to walk by the boy and said, "What are you doing there, young man?"

> " Things have occurred in our lives that have no possible explanation other than God. "

NOTES

39

> **"To look for scientific proof of God would be like taking a piano apart to look for a song."**

"Flying a kite, sir."

"Really, I don't see any kite. Are you sure it's still up there?"

The boy replied, "Oh yes, sir. I know the kite is still there because I can feel the pull."

Can we see God with our physical eyes? No. But for those who know Him, we have come to experience what it means to "feel His pull" on our hearts and in our lives. God has so miraculously saved us and changed our lives that we cannot help but acknowledge and praise His existence.

The evidence for faith

I want you to imagine a family of mice who lived all their lives inside a large piano. In their piano world, the music of the instrument filled all the dark spaces with sound and harmony. At first, the mice were impressed by it. They drew comfort and wonder from the thought that there was Someone – though invisible to them –above, yet close, who made them. They loved the thought of the Great Player who they could not see. Then one day, a daring mouse climbed up part of the piano and returned enlightened. He had found out how the music was made. The secret? Tightly stretched wires of graduated lengths that trembled and vibrated. They then had to revise their old beliefs. Now no enlightened mouse could still believe in the Unseen Player. Later, another explorer carried the explanation further. Hammers were now the secret. Scores of hammers were dancing and leaping upon the wires! This was a more complicated theory, but it all went to show that they lived in a purely mechanical and mathematical world. The Unseen Player soon came to be thought of as a myth, but regardless, the Pianist continued to play.

To look for scientific proof of God would be like taking a piano apart to look for a song. Ultimately, you can't prove God exists by using the scientific method, but the evidence for His existence is overwhelming. We cannot reason ourselves into the kingdom of heaven; it requires faith: *"And without faith it is impossible to please God, because anyone who comes to Him must believe that He exists and that He rewards those who earnestly seek Him"* (Hebrews 11:6). If God wanted to, He could have simply appeared and proved to the world once and for all that He does exist! But if He did that, there would be no need for faith. Jesus said, *"Because you have seen me, you have believed; blessed are those who have not seen and yet have believed"* (John 20:29).

Despite all of the evidence, the Bible warns us that some will reject the clear and undeniable knowledge of God and believe a lie instead. Romans 1:25 says, *"They exchanged the truth of God for a lie, and worshiped and served created things rather than the Creator."*

The reality is, none of these arguments can persuade anyone who refuses to acknowledge what is already obvious. Atheists tend to reject God for spiritual rather than intellectual reasons. An atheist has no more interest in finding God than a thief has in finding a policeman.

The true reason many refuse to admit that there is a God is because that admission comes with the realization that they are responsible to that God and in need of forgiveness from Him (Romans 3:23; 6:23). If God exists, then we are accountable to Him for our actions.

Struggling with doubts?

It's ok to struggle with doubt. I have found that in the times when I have really questioned my faith, I have been driven to find the answers. The end result is that my faith grows stronger than ever. When you find yourself questioning or doubting God, just remember, He made the brain cells you're thinking with. Mark Buchanan says: "The depth of our doubt is roughly proportional to the depth of our faith. Those with strong faith have equally strong doubts.

That principle bears out in the other direction as well: People with a trivial and shallow faith usually have trivial and shallow doubts."

If you or someone you know is struggling with doubts about the existence of God, understand that people who doubt usually have a story to tell about how they got to that point. James 1:19 says we need to *"be quick to listen, slow to speak, and slow to get angry."* Take time to respectfully listen to them and their point of view. If they do seem angry with God, ask them why. Listen with empathy and patience. Also understand that helping people think in new ways is usually a slow process. Transforming a hardened heart is actually the work of God Himself. Proving His existence isn't as important as telling the world what you know of His awesome nature.

Do you ever struggle with any doubts about God or His existence? If so, would you mind sharing what those doubts are?

How has the evidence for God presented in this chapter affected your faith? Can evidence strengthen one's faith?

NOTES

Day 2

Is the Bible Really the Word of God?

vimeo.com/138213874

The Bible spans centuries of history, contains a variety of literary styles, and culminates in the person of Jesus Christ. But how do we know the Bible is true?

When we say that the Bible is true, we're saying that we believe the Bible is inspired (literally "God-breathed"). How could imperfect men be expected to produce a perfect Bible? Peter answers that question: *"For no prophecy of Scripture was ever made by an act of the human will, but men moved by the Holy Spirit spoke from God"* (2 Peter 1:21). It's called God's Word even though God did not physically write it. Instead, God worked through ordinary people, inspired by Him, to record what we accept as the Bible. If the Bible is *inspired* that also means that it is *inerrant* because our God does not make mistakes. Simply put – the inerrancy of the Bible means that there is no untruth in the Bible.

How do we know that it's inspired? What if it's just a collection of stories and myths? How can we trust it completely? There are many astounding evidences that point to the inspiration of Scripture:

The Bible is scientifically correct.

This is where the Bible is so often attacked. Many skeptics say, "Of course, we know there are scientific errors in the Bible." Before you say that, make sure you know science, and make sure you know the Bible. In 1861, the Academy of Science in France wrote a book that listed 51 facts that proved the Bible is not true. Today, not a scientist on earth believes one of those facts. Our understanding of science is changing, but God's Word does not change.

A lot of skeptics today point to the miracles of the Bible as evidence that it should be relegated to the same shelf as myths and fairy tales. Are we really expected to believe the supernatural events it records? The reality is that if God exists and He is still at work in this world, miracles are not just possible; they are probable. If I believe in Genesis 1:1 that God created the world out of nothing (as science confirms through the Big Bang Theory), then I have no problem believing that God could part the Red Sea. If God is bigger and more powerful than all creation, and He steps into the world, wouldn't people be dazzled by what He does? Fantastic events are possible. Miracles can happen. You can't just disqualify them.

What we do find in Scripture are descriptions of science that were not proven scientific fact until hundreds, if not thousands, of years later. Let me give you some examples:

The earth is suspended in space (Job 26:7). This seems like common knowledge to us now, but the ancients didn't believe this. The ancient Egyptians believed the earth was supported by pillars, and the Greeks believed the world was carried on the back of Atlas. You don't find that mythology in the Bible. How did Job (the oldest book of the Bible) know that? Divine inspiration.

The earth is a sphere, not flat. When Christopher Columbus sailed the ocean blue in 1492, people warned him, saying, "Columbus, you'd better be careful you don't sail right off the edge of the earth!" Yet Christopher Columbus was convinced the earth was a sphere, not flat – because of reading the Bible. Isaiah 40:22 says, *"It is He who sits above the circle of the earth."* The Hebrew word for "circle" literally means "globe" or "sphere."

The stars cannot be counted. Hipparchus counted 1,022 stars. Later, Ptolemy came along and said, "Hipparchus is wrong. There aren't 1,022 stars, there are 1,056!" It wasn't until Galileo invented the telescope that he realized that when you look beyond the stars our eyes can see, there are billions of other stars behind them! Jeremiah 33:22 says, *"The stars are without number. The host of heaven cannot be numbered."*

There are many others, including an almost infinite extent of the sidereal universe (Isaiah 55:9), the law of conservation of mass and energy (2 Peter 3:7), hydrologic cycle (Ecclesiastes 1:7), the law of increasing entropy (Psalm 102:25-27), the paramount importance of blood in life processes (Leviticus 17:11), atmospheric circulation (Ecclesiastes 1:6), the gravitational field (Job 26:7), and many others.

The Bible is not a science book; it is not written to tell us how the heavens go, but how to go to heaven. Yet when the Bible does speak scientifically, it speaks with amazing accuracy that was hundreds of years before its time.

The Bible is historically reliable.

Despite common skeptical claims that the Bible has often been changed through the centuries, the physical evidence tells another story. There are a few minor differences in manuscripts called variants, but none of those variants impact or change Biblical beliefs or claims.

Apologist E.M. Blaiklock said, "Again and again archaeological discoveries have verified the accuracy of the historical and cultural references in the Bible. The more they did, the more it confirms the Bible." Dr. Nelson Glueck, probably the greatest modern authority on Israeli archaeology, said, "No archaeological discovery has ever controverted a Biblical reference. Scores of archaeological findings have been made which confirm in clear outline or in exact detail, historical statements in the Bible."

The Bible wasn't put together in secret; it was a very public process. People have been able to closely examine its claims all along, even to this day. And Christians welcome that kind of scrutiny, because we know our Bible can stand up to it. That's not true of the Book of Mormon. Mormons don't want that kind of scrutiny and historical research. The same thing applies with the Koran. A historical, critical study of the Koran is something Muslims do not want to do. But the Bible is very much an "open book."

The Bible contains many points of view. Four people tell me the story of Jesus, stories that were open to the public even in that day. People could read the stories and react to them. The life of Christ was evaluated, studied, and examined by the people who had lived with Jesus and could verify the accuracy of those stories – that's a valuable difference.

Compared to other ancient documents, the integrity of the text of the

> **"** Our understanding of science is changing, but God's Word does not change. **"**

NOTES

> **"The Bible is not a science book; it is not written to tell us how the heavens go, but how to go to heaven."**

Bible is also impressive. There are over 10,000 Old Testament manuscripts and over 5,700 Greek New Testament manuscripts that have been found, and when all of them are compared, they are in 99.99% agreement! This tells us that the earliest manuscripts have been copied precisely throughout the ages. No other ancient document comes anywhere close to that level of precision and accuracy. The next closest is Homer's *Iliad* which has about 670 manuscripts with less than 95% agreement. So by sheer number, date, and accuracy of these manuscripts, we can say with certainty that they are genuine and have not been altered over all the time they have existed.

The Bible is consistently unifying.

The Bible was written over a period of approximately 1,600 years by 40 different authors. Although it's viewed as one book, it's actually a collection of many books. The Old Testament is primarily a record of God's dealings with His chosen people – the Jews. The New Testament continues the record with first century accounts of the life and ministry of Jesus and the struggles faced by new Christians in a hostile culture. The Bible presents a coherent theology and worldview consistently throughout Scripture. It tells one big story of God's plan of salvation that culminated in Jesus Christ.

Considering how many authors wrote it over so many years, and that they all come to agreement and never contradict each other, that's pretty good evidence itself! Lee Strobel said that the chances of that happening are about the same as if a tornado ripped through a junkyard and came out with a functioning 747 airliner!

Erwin Lutzer put it this way: "Imagine various pieces of a cathedral arriving from different countries and cities, converging on a central location. In fact, imagine that investigation proves that forty different sculptors made contributions over a period of many centuries. Yet the pieces fit together to form a single magnificent structure. Would this not be proof that behind the project was a single mind, one designer who used His workmen to sculpt a well-conceived plan? The Bible is that cathedral, assembled by one super-intelligent architect."

When you take a book that was written over 1,600 years in three different languages by 40 different authors from all walks of life and bring it together, it makes one beautiful cathedral of truth! We can't say that just happened.

The Bible is prophetically accurate.

This is one of the most amazing and convincing proofs that give credibility to the Bible's inspiration. Fulfilled prophecy may be the primary authenticator of the Bible. Not only does the Bible have predictions of things that have yet to happen, but it also has predicted things in the past that *did* happen – nearly 2,000 prophecies to be exact! Prophecy is history that is pre-written. It's astonishing to see how history has fit into the sockets of Bible prophecy. No other book claiming to be "the word of God" can match the Bible's staggering accuracy in predicting events, yet hundreds of such prophecies can be found in the Bible. Detailed predictions about specific individuals, nations, and events were foretold hundreds of years before they occurred, and their fulfillments have been historically verified.

Isaiah prophesied that Judah would be taken captive by Babylon and that Babylon itself would be conquered by another nation, and he even gave the name of the king who would conquer them – Cyrus. King Cyrus would then allow the Jews to return to rebuild Jerusalem. And all of this was written 150 years before it happened! There is nothing vague about that prophecy at all – it's very specific.

Imagine if someone in the year 1850 predicted that one day America would be attacked by terrorists on its own soil. Furthermore, after that attack, the

President of the United States would order an invasion of Iraq. And the name of the United States President would be George W. Bush. What are the chances of someone predicting in 1850 the actions of a President who would not even be born for another 100 years? And yet that's essentially what Isaiah did.

Another astounding prophecy is found in Ezekiel. At one time, Egypt was the greatest nation in the entire world and the richest country on earth. In one prophecy about Egypt, the prophet Ezekiel said, "There shall no longer be a prince from the land of Egypt." Up until a few decades ago (before Egypt adopted a more democratic form of government) a prince had always ruled. But during the 2,500 years between this prophecy and Egypt's change of government, *none of its princes were Egyptian!*

That would be like prophesying that an American will never again be President of the United States and then having 2,500 years go by with no American president!

What's even more incredible are the detailed prophecies in the Old Testament concerning the Messiah that were fulfilled by Jesus Christ. Some critics say that Jesus arranged Himself so that he could fulfill all of these prophecies, but Jesus had to arrange being born in Bethlehem (Micah 5:2). He would then have to arrange Isaiah to write about the history of his life 700 years before he was born. He would have to arrange being executed by crucifixion on the cross (Psalm 22). When you read that Psalm, you read a description of the crucifixion as if a man was standing at the foot of the cross, looking upon pierced hands and feet and people gambling for the crucified's garments. Jesus was not looking back and quoting David; David was looking forward and seeing Jesus. When David wrote this, crucifixion was not even invented. Jesus also could not have arranged to rise from the dead and be seen by over 500 eyewitnesses. Matthew 26:56 says, *"But all of this was done so that the Scriptures of the prophets might be fulfilled."*

The prophet Daniel predicted in about 538 B.C. that Christ would come as Israel's promised Savior and Prince 483 years after the Persian emperor would give the Jews authority to rebuild Jerusalem, which was then in ruins. This was clearly, definitely, and miraculously fulfilled hundreds of years later when Jesus was born.

There are over 300 prophecies in the Old Testament concerning the Messiah that were all fulfilled in the life, death, and resurrection of Jesus Christ. According to one mathematician, the chances of Jesus fulfilling just eight of those 300 prophecies is 1 in 10 to the 17th power. To illustrate the high degree of improbability that figure represents, imagine taking 100,000,000,000,000,000 silver coins and laying them all over the state of Texas. Those coins would cover the entire state two feet deep! Then take one of those coins and mark it with a black "X" and throw it back into the pile. After you have thoroughly mixed up those coins, blindfold a man and allow him to walk all over the state and randomly pick up one of those silver coins. What are the chances that he would select the one marked with the black "X"? The same odds that Jesus could have randomly fulfilled eight out of the hundreds of prophecies about his life!

The Bible is personally transforming.

The one consistent theme of the Bible, developing in grandeur from Genesis to Revelation, is God's great work in the creation and redemption of all things, through His only Son, the Lord Jesus Christ. No other book has ever held such universal appeal nor produced such lasting effects. Multitudes of people, past and present, have found from personal experience that its promises are true, its counsel is sound, its commands are wise, and its wonderful message of salvation meets every need for both time and eternity. It's been said that the Word of God is so deep that scholars can swim in its

> **" It tells one big story of God's plan of salvation that culminated in Jesus Christ. "**

NOTES

> **"It's not the book of the month; it is the Book of the ages."**

NOTES _____

waters and never touch bottom, and yet so precious that a little child can come and get a drink without a fear of drowning.

I believe the Bible is inspired. When I read the Bible, I often sense something resonating in my own spirit. That's compelling and that gives me even more confidence. Many will choose not to believe this, and Scripture explains why in 1 Corinthians 1:18-2:14: *"For the word of the cross is folly to those who are perishing, but to us who are being saved it is the power of God...the natural person does not accept the things of the Spirit of God, for they are folly to him, and he is not able to understand them because they are spiritually discerned."*

I think God can give some understanding before a person is saved, but for me I had to believe before God really opened my eyes to the truth, and since then there has never been a doubt in my spirit that the Bible is the true, inspired word of God.

Maybe you have your doubts. That's okay. Test the Bible for yourself. Ask God to speak to you through His Word. Encounter the Bible on your own – don't just inherit somebody else's experience. I believe as you dive deeper into this Book, God will personally reveal Himself to you! And once He does, you'll have confidence in His Word.

You can trust the Bible. You will never become a great disciple until you first come to the point where you *know* the Bible is the inspired and inerrant Word of God. It's not the book of the month; it is the Book of the ages. It has outlived, outreached, and outranked all other books. And the more you become convinced that the Bible truly is the Word of God, the more time you will want to devote to reading it, knowing it, and meditating upon it.

Imagine this scenario: Someone you work with tells you that the Bible is a collection of myths and cannot be the Word of God. How would you respond to him? List two or three reasons why you believe the Bible is God's inspired Word:

_____

_____

_____

_____

_____

_____

_____

How does what you read today give you confidence that the Bible really is the word of God?

_____

_____

_____

_____

_____

_____

_____

How can we know Christianity is the right religion? Why is Jesus the only way to Heaven? If you are being active in talking about your faith, these are the types of questions you'll be asked at some point, or maybe you've asked those questions yourself.

In His earthly ministry, Jesus made a lot of bold statements. He told us to "love your enemies," to "pray for those who persecute you," and to "turn the other cheek." But by far, the most politically incorrect statement Jesus ever made is in John 14:6, *"I am the Way, the Truth, and the Life. No one comes to the Father but by Me."*

vimeo.com/138213996

Christianity is drastically different from every other religion.

Some people say that essentially, when you get right down to the bare facts, all religions teach roughly the same thing. Yet Jesus Christ boldly takes Christianity and puts it in a separate class all by itself saying He is the only way.

Acts 4:12 says, *"Salvation is found in no one else for there is no other name under heaven given to men by which we must be saved."* The reality is that Christianity cannot be reconciled with any other religion. The uniqueness of Christianity is based on the uniqueness of Jesus Christ Himself.

According to social anthropologists, the top five religions (from smallest to largest) are: Buddhism, Hinduism, Non-Religious, Islam, and Christianity. Each of these views has a different kind of god and vastly different means of reaching him. Because they are all different, they could all be wrong, but they cannot all be right. Outside of Christianity, every other faith is a "do-it-yourself" type religion. They think they can build their own highway to their god by being good enough to earn his favor.

Other religious leaders say, "Follow me and I will show you how to find the truth." Jesus said, "I am the truth."

Other religious leaders say, "Follow me and I will show you the way to salvation." Jesus said, "I am the source of eternal life."

Other religious leaders say, "Follow me and I will show you how to become enlightened." Jesus said, "I am the light of the world."

Other religious leaders say, "Follow me and I will show you many paths, many doors that lead to God." Jesus said, "I am the door."

All religions outside of Christianity are based on the idea of people struggling or striving to somehow earn the favor of God. Whether it be through Tibetan prayer wheels, pilgrimages, giving alms to the poor, praying a certain number of times a day, or going through a series of reincarnations,

NOTES _____

_____

_____

_____

_____

_____

_____

_____

_____

_____

_____

_____

_____

_____

_____

_____

_____

_____

_____

_____

_____

> **"**All other religions are spelled 'Do.' Christianity is spelled 'Done.'**"**

NOTES

they're all attempts of people to reach up to God. But Jesus Christ and Christianity is God's attempt to reach down to man. Jesus taught the exact opposite of what every other religious leader taught in that nobody can earn their way to heaven, so you might as well stop trying. All other religions are spelled "Do." Christianity is spelled "Done."

In 1 Corinthians 15:3-8, Paul wrote, *"For I delivered to you as of first importance what I also received: that Christ died for our sins in accordance with the Scriptures, that he was buried, that he was raised on the third day in accordance with the Scriptures, and that he appeared to Cephas, then to the twelve. Then he appeared to more than five hundred brothers at one time, most of whom are still alive, though some have fallen asleep. Then he appeared to James, then to all the apostles. Last of all, as to one untimely born, he appeared also to me."*

At one time, Paul hated Christians and began killing many of them. What caused Paul to switch teams? Based on that passage, what made him go from being a killer of Christ-followers to a follower of Christ?

_____

_____

_____

_____

_____

_____

_____

_____

Throughout history, there have been many who have claimed to be the "only way to God," but only Jesus Christ backed up His claim with unique credentials that gave him undeniable credibility. You can basically summarize these into four categories:

Jesus' fulfillment of prophecy

Jesus is the only person in all of human history to have been able to fulfill hundreds of ancient prophecies that were written about him hundreds of years before He was born. No one else can make this claim. Some skeptics have asserted that Jesus maneuvered his life around in order to fulfill these prophecies so that He would be perceived as the Savior of the world. For example, one of the prophecies states that Jesus would come riding into Jerusalem on a donkey before His crucifixion. So these skeptics would say that Jesus asked his disciples to go and get him a donkey because he was really anxious to get to Jerusalem and be crucified. However, when you look at each of these prophecies in detail regarding the coming Messiah, there is no way that he could have intentionally tried to fulfill these on His own. For instance, Jesus couldn't have arranged the place of His birth; He couldn't have arranged his ancestry. One ancient prophecy predicted the exact moment in history when the Messiah would be born – Jesus fulfilled that. He could not have arranged how he would be put to death – that prophecy was written hundreds of years before crucifixion was ever used. Jesus fulfilled ancient Biblical prophecies beyond any mathematical odds.

Jesus' unmatched character

Isn't it true that the more you get to know a person, the more obvious their weaknesses and shortcomings are? The exact opposite was true of Jesus. The more that people knew Jesus, the more they realized how perfect He really was. In fact, His closest followers who traveled with Him and spent every waking moment with Him marveled at His integrity, purity, and holiness. Nobody was closer to Jesus than His own disciples. In 1 John 3:5, John says, *"In Him is no sin."* Can you imagine living with someone every day for three years and never once seeing anything they did wrong? Even Peter, who was closest to Him, said that Jesus *"committed no sin, and no deceit was found in his mouth"* (1 Peter 2:22). Even Jesus Himself asked those around him, *"Can any of you prove me guilty of sin?"* (John 8:46). So His unique character validates His claim that He really was who He said He was.

Jesus' amazing miracles

Jesus said in John 10:37, *"If I do not do the works of My Father, do not believe Me."* In other words, Jesus was saying that anybody can claim to be the Son of God, but unless you visibly see me do the miracles of God, then you have no right to believe that I'm really the Messiah. Jesus did the miraculous in order to validate that He was the Son of God. He didn't just do them in a dark room somewhere but in broad daylight in front of hundreds of eyewitnesses. He performed miracles in front of His own skeptics. As a matter of fact, you can look through the ancient historical documents during Jesus' era and see that even those who were opponents of Christianity, as well as writers of ancient Jewish documents, admitted to the fact that Jesus did some incredible miracles that defied anything humanly possible. Even the Koran (the holy book of Muslims) admits that Jesus did amazing miracles.

Jesus' resurrection from the dead

This is the most important evidence that Jesus is who He said He was. Jesus Himself said time after time that He would die, but He would be resurrected from the dead (Matt. 16:21; 17:22-23; 20:18-19). Acts 1:3 says, *"He also presented Himself alive to them by many convincing proofs."* Let me give you three main reasons why I believe in the legitimacy of the resurrection of Jesus, and I encourage you to explore the evidence for yourself!

1. Jesus was definitely dead, and His body was buried in a guarded tomb.
Believe it or not, there are some skeptics who believe that Jesus never died on the cross. They think that He basically "passed out" and was unconscious and somehow revived Himself in the tomb and walked out. There are some doubters who don't believe that Jesus was *resurrected*; they believe He was *resuscitated*. There are many problems with that line of thinking. First, we're told in John 19:34 that just to make sure that Jesus was dead, a Roman soldier thrust a spear into his side, between his ribs, and punctured the lining of the heart and the heart itself, causing a water-like fluid and blood to come out. Medical experts say that is enough proof Jesus was already dead because the blood had begun to clot and separate from the watery serum.

As a matter of fact, the *Journal of American Medical Association* (the number one medical journal in the world) concluded: "Clearly the way that historical and medical evidence indicate that Jesus was dead before the wound to His side was inflicted supports the traditional view that the spear not only perforated the right lung but also the pericardium and the heart – thereby ensuring his death. Accordingly, interpretations based on the assumption that Jesus did not die on the cross appear to be at odds with modern medical knowledge."

In other words, the greatest medical experts in the world attest to the fact that Jesus was indeed actually dead. In addition, for someone to believe that

> **"** His unique character validates His claim that He really was who He said He was. **"**

NOTES

> **"... the greatest medical experts in the world attest to the fact that Jesus was indeed actually dead."**

NOTES _____

_____

_____

_____

_____

_____

_____

_____

_____

_____

_____

_____

_____

_____

_____

_____

_____

_____

_____

_____

_____

_____

Jesus never really died shows their ignorance in the Jewish burial customs. They would take the deceased body and wrap it in grave clothes and put up to a hundred pounds of spices in between the folds of the wrappings. Before they would wrap the head, they would put spices in the nostrils and in the mouth and then lock him away in an airtight tomb. For someone to believe that Jesus just resuscitated would mean that He would have to be a Houdini to take off those grave clothes and snort out those spices that would have blocked his airway preventing Him from getting any oxygen. Then, with those hands that had been nailed with spikes just days before, he would somehow roll away a stone that weighed several tons. Then when He came out He would face 16 Roman soldiers and kick it into Chuck Norris mode! The evidence just doesn't add up. Jesus was really dead and definitely buried.

2. The tomb of Jesus was empty.
Understand that for 2,000 years, no one has ever denied that the tomb was empty. It's never been disputed or debated. When the Romans soldiers reported to Caiaphas what had happened, the high priest paid a large sum of money to the soldiers and told them to say that the disciples came by night and stole his body while the solders were asleep. Of course, that doesn't make much sense because if they were asleep, how would they know what happened? So let's just suppose that a person or persons took Jesus out of the grave. It would leave only two possibilities: either His friends did it or His enemies did it.

What's the possibility that His friends took Him out of that tomb? Well, first of all, there were soldiers guarding it – 16 of them in all. They were the elite of the Roman guard. They knew of the rumors that Jesus was expected to resurrect from the dead, and they were stationed there to make sure that no one would steal the body to claim that He did. If you are a skeptic, you would have to believe that the same disciples who ran like scalded dogs at the crucifixion are the ones who had a sudden burst of courage to come back, take out those highly skilled Roman soldiers, and remove the body out of the tomb.

Second, there was the stone that was rolled in front of the tomb, which would have weighed many tons. It sat in a groove and rolled downwards to the front of the door. Modern scientists say that it would have taken 20 men to move such a stone just a few feet.

Third, the Bible says that when the stone was rolled in front of the tomb, it was given a Roman wax seal. Those Roman soldiers knew that if they went to sleep on their watch or if that seal had been broken, they would be burned alive because the penalty for allowing a Roman seal to be broken was death.

So if it is illogical and impossible for Jesus' friends to remove Him from the tomb, then what if His enemies did it? How absurd would that be? His enemies were doing everything possible to keep him in the tomb, not get him out of it. Even if they did, all they would have had to do to shut down Christianity 2,000 years ago was *just produce the body.*

So Jesus' friends didn't take His body – they *couldn't.* Jesus' enemies didn't take the body – they *wouldn't.* But there's one more fact to consider.

3. The disciples' lives were absolutely changed after the resurrection.
When you put all the accounts together, we are told that Jesus appeared on 10 different occasions over a period of six weeks to at least 516 people. These appearances were indoors and outdoors, mornings, afternoons, and evenings. Can you imagine the verdict a jury would give if you had something attested to by 516 witnesses corroborating one another 516 times? Yet even

more than that, many of those witnesses sealed their testimony with their own blood.

Think about what happened to the disciples. During the crucifixion, they ran from Jesus and went into hiding. They were afraid that the authorities would do to them what they did to Jesus. But something amazing happened to these same disciples after they saw the resurrected Christ. They went out boldly proclaiming that Jesus was alive! All but one of the eleven disciples suffered a violent death as a martyr. Peter was crucified upside down in Rome in 66 A.D. Andrew was martyred in Greece after he led the wife of a Roman governor to Christ. As a result, he was bound to death and killed in 74 A.D. James, son of Zebedee, was martyred by Herod Agrippa when they cut off his head with a sword (Acts 12:1-9). When they tried to martyr John, he actually lived through it, so they eventually banished him to a life of solitary confinement on the Island of Patmos where he died in 96 A.D. Phillip was stoned to death for preaching the Gospel in Heliopolis in 52 A.D. Bartholomew preached Jesus in Persia and India. He was beaten, crucified, and then beheaded in 52 A.D. Thomas made it all the way to India to share the Gospel, but he was stabbed by a spear in East India in 52 A.D. Matthew was slain by a sword in Ethiopia in 60 A.D. James, son of Alphaeus, was thrown from a building and then beaten to death in 60 A.D. Thaddeus was shot by arrows in 72 A.D. Simon, the Zealot, took the gospel north and preached in the British Isles. He was crucified in Persia in 74 A.D.

Here's the point: all of the disciples of Jesus suffered horrible, violent deaths because they would not disavow that Jesus Christ was indeed the Son of God, who bodily appeared to them after He had died. It's a psychological fact that someone might live for a lie, but no one will willingly give their own life for what he knows to be a lie.

The empty tomb is God's receipt that the payment for your sins was made in full. Romans 1:4 says, *"And Jesus Christ our Lord was shown to be the Son of God when God powerfully raised Him from the dead by means of the Holy Spirit."* You don't have to believe in the resurrection of Jesus Christ, but you do have to deny overwhelming evidence to the contrary if you reject it. It doesn't matter what you're right about if you're wrong about Jesus.

What is the most convincing proof to you that Jesus really is who He said He was? Why?

_____

_____

_____

_____

_____

_____

_____

" The empty tomb is God's receipt that the payment for your sins was made in full. "

NOTES _____

_____

_____

_____

_____

_____

_____

_____

_____

_____

_____

_____

_____

_____

_____

_____

_____

_____

_____

_____

_____

_____

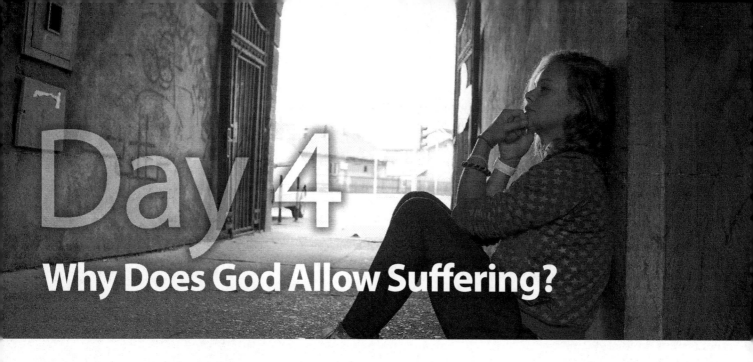

Day 4
Why Does God Allow Suffering?

vimeo.com/138214069

George Barna did a nation-wide scientific poll in which he asked people, "If you could ask God any one question and you knew He would give you an answer, what would you ask?" The result? The number one issue on people's minds was, "Why is there so much suffering in this world?"

Maybe you've wondered that too. If God is all-powerful and all good, why would He allow this to take place? Couldn't He stop it? Why is it that bad things happen to good people?

The Bible says that while we are in this world, we don't have perfect knowledge because we are finite human beings (1 Corinthians 13:12). It's almost as if a fog shrouds our understanding of some of these deeper issues like why there is pain and suffering. But there are some key Biblical truths that shine through the fog.

Our choice
God gave man the choice to choose to love and follow God or not. We need to understand, first of all, that God is not the creator of evil and suffering. So how do we reconcile an evil and troubled world with a good Creator God? The Bible's opening chapter says that every piece of God's creation was good when He created it. Genesis 1:31 says, *"God saw all that He had made, and it was very good."*

God made humans with the highest reasoning capacity and the ability to make choices for themselves. Another term for the ability to make choices is *free will.* So why did God give us free will? He gave it because the greatest value in the universe is love – to love God and to love other people. And the only way that the highest value of love can really be attained or expressed is if we have free will. We must be able to make the choice to love or not to love if love can be real at all.

My daughter has a Hello Kitty doll, and if you push her paw, you will hear a little voice say, "I love you. I love you." Now, does Hello Kitty really love you? Of course not. She's programmed to say that. She has no choice. As long as her batteries are working, every time you push her paw, she's going to say it. That's not real love. When God created man, God didn't create human robots. God knew that you must be able to make the choice *not* to love in order for your expression of love to be true.

Man made the wrong choice, and as a result, sin and suffering entered the world. Evil and suffering are the result of the choice made by our first parents, Adam and Eve: *"When Adam sinned, sin entered the human race. Adam's sin brought death, so death spread to everyone, for everyone sinned"* (Romans 5:12).

All suffering can be traced back to people disobeying God. As a result of Adam and Eve's decision, three kinds of evil were introduced into the world:

1. Moral evil – This is the immorality and pain and suffering that result when we make the choice to be selfish and arrogant, uncaring, or abusive. Someone has estimated that 95% of the suffering in this world is the result of sin done by ourselves or by other people. People today ignore God and then blame Him for the chaos that results.

2. Natural evil – This is earthquakes, tsunamis, tornadoes, hurricanes, etc. These too are the result of sin having been allowed into the world. Genesis 3:18 says that because of sin, nature was corrupted and thorns and thistles entered into the world. Romans 8:20 says, *"Against its will, everything on earth was subjected to God's curse."* One author put it this way: "When we human beings told God to shove off, he partially honored our request. Nature began to revolt. The earth was cursed. Genetic breakdown and disease began. Pain became part of the human experience."

3. Social evil – This includes such things as poverty, hunger, and homelessness. People look at starving children in Africa and say, "Where is God in all of this?" The truth of the matter is, we produce enough food on this planet to give every man, woman, and child 3,000 calories a day. It's because of our own selfishness, irresponsibility, and misplaced nationalism that people around the world are starving.

So God is not responsible for the evil in the world. We, as human beings, are responsible. God created the fact of freedom; we perform the acts of that freedom. He made evil possible; we make evil actual.

All evil and suffering is the result of sin.

A lot of people think, "Well, God created everything that exists and evil exists ... so God created evil." Let's follow that logic of thought for a moment.

Does cold exist? If you live up north, you'd probably give an emphatic yes! Cold does exist, especially in the middle of January. But technically speaking, cold does not exist. According to the laws of physics, cold is in reality just the absence of heat. Absolute zero (-460 F) is the total absence of any heat. We can't measure coldness; really all we can do is measure heat. So technically cold doesn't exist. We've just created this word to describe how we feel if we have no heat.

Does darkness exist? You'd say, "Well, yeah. You can turn out all the lights in a room and it will be completely dark." But in reality darkness doesn't exist either – it's just the absence of light. You can't measure darkness; you can only measure the amount of light present. Darkness is a term used by man to describe what happens when there is no light present.

So now let me ask you another question: Does evil exist? I'd submit to you that evil doesn't exist unto itself. Evil is simply the absence of God. It is just like darkness and cold, a word that man has created to describe the absence of God. God did not create evil. Evil is the result of what happens when man does not have God's love present in his heart. It's like the cold that comes when there is no heat or the darkness that comes when there is no light. Ultimately, the heart of the human problem is the problem of the human heart.

It's not because of evil that God doesn't make any sense; it is because of God that we can make sense of evil. How do we do that? By remembering this truth: God is so good and God is so great that He can take the negative of evil and turn it into the positive of good.

> **" All suffering can be traced back to people disobeying God. "**

NOTES _____

_____
_____
_____
_____
_____
_____
_____
_____
_____
_____
_____
_____
_____
_____
_____
_____
_____
_____
_____
_____
_____
_____
_____
_____
_____

> **"It's not because of evil that God doesn't make any sense; it is because of God that we can make sense of evil."**

NOTES _____

_____

_____

_____

_____

_____

_____

_____

_____

_____

_____

_____

_____

_____

_____

_____

_____

_____

_____

A strengthened faith

God can accomplish something positive out of the negatives of life. God can use pain to draw us closer to Him. Peter Craaf said, "Only after suffering, only after disaster did Israel, do nations, do individuals turn back to God." Suffering brings repentance. Sometimes we have to learn the hard way. It's certainly true in my own experience. If you're going through good times in your life when everything's going great, the marriage is wonderful, the money is rolling in, and the job is great, it's in those seasons that we easily neglect to turn to God. But when pain and suffering come, when heartbreak takes place, what's the first thing we do? We get on our knees and say, "God I need you! Lead my life! Help me in this situation!"

One of my favorite verses when it comes to suffering is 1 Peter 5:10. It says, *"And after you have suffered for a little while, the God of all comfort, who called you to His eternal glory in Christ, will Himself perfect, confirm, strengthen, and establish you."* Faith is strengthened when we go through the valleys of life.

Some of the times when I have felt closest to God were in those times when I was going through a very difficult time. Has that also been your experience as well? Why or why not?

_____

_____

_____

_____

_____

_____

_____

_____

_____

_____

_____

I heard about a woman once who had lived a very wild life. She had been far from God when she contracted cancer and found out it was terminal. She had a very short time to live. In her desperation and in her pain and suffering, she reached out to God, and God embraced her. She had the most beautiful relationship with Him and made this statement before she died: "If it took cancer for me to meet Jesus Christ, I say thank God for cancer." That is a very radical statement.

If that doesn't compute with you, if that doesn't make sense to you, one reason might be that you don't know Jesus yet in that way. I pray the day will come when you will know Him in that way and be able to say, "Regardless of what it took for me to come to this point, it was worth it for this." You don't have to know the why when you know the Who.

In Genesis, we read about how Joseph was sold into slavery by his own brothers. He would later suffer a hard life, spending twelve years in prison after being falsely accused. But later, he was elevated to a great role of authority, where he was now in a position to save the lives of the same brothers who had sold him into slavery years before. He said to his brothers about the sufferings he went through: *"You intended to harm me, but God intended it for good to accomplish what is now being done, the saving of many lives"* (Genesis 50:20).

The end of evil and suffering

Have you ever wondered why God doesn't just step in right now and cause suffering to cease and judge evil? The answer is: Just because He hasn't done it yet doesn't mean He's not going to do it. That would be like picking up a John Grisham novel and closing it up halfway through, saying, "I can't believe this book! He doesn't tie up all the loose ends of the plot!" We need to remember that the book of God's unfolding history is not done. God is doing something, but we may not be seeing the whole story. One of the reasons God doesn't end it all right now is because of His love for humanity. It says in 2 Peter 3:9, *"The Lord is not slow in keeping His promise as some understand slowness. He is patient with you not wanting anyone to perish, but everyone to come to repentance."*

Paradise is coming.

Our worst suffering here on earth will pale in comparison to the glory God has in store for us in eternity. I think sometimes, as believers, we forget that this isn't heaven. We were made to long for the world to come (2 Corinthians 5:2). There is coming a day when God will judge the world, separating sin, evil, and death from all that is good and from all who have been forgiven by trusting in Christ. Paradise will be restored in what the Bible calls, *"The new heaven and the new earth,"* in *"... a world where everyone is right with God"* (2 Peter 3:13).

The Apostle Paul had his fair share of suffering while he was on this earth. He said in 2 Corinthians 11:23-27, *"I have worked harder, been put in jail more often, been whipped times without number, and faced death again and again. Five different times the Jews gave me thirty-nine lashes. Three times I was beaten with rods. Once I was stoned ..."* Yet in the same letter, when Paul talks about what he will experience in the life to come, he says, *"Our present troubles are quite small and won't last very long. Yet they produce for us an immeasurably great glory that will last forever."*

Lee Strobel once described a scenario in this way: Imagine that on the first day of the year, you had the absolute worst day of your life. You woke up with a migraine headache. The pain was so great you thought you were going to die. On the way to the doctor's office, you were hit head-on by an uninsured motorist and your car was totaled. It was the car that you had always dreamed of owning. Then on the same day, you found out that your company was downsizing and your name was at the top of the list. The whole day was just like that – every hour on the hour it was just one terrible consequence after the other. Your first day of the new year was like a reprint of the children's book *Alexander and the Terrible, Horrible, No Good, Very Bad Day.*

Then suppose that the next day on January 2, you wake up to a phone call from another company offering you a better job with twice the pay. Suppose every day the entire rest of the year turns out to be just like that. One day you inherit a million dollars from an unknown relative. You buy a lottery ticket and you win $10 million dollars. Your children are excelling in school and getting straight A's! They are so good, the teachers ask you out to dinner because they want to meet the parents of such outstanding children. Your marriage is perfect. You get voted "Person of the Year" by the local newspaper. You play against Tiger Woods in golf and *you win*! You're in the best health and have never felt better in your life!

At the end of the year, on December 31, suppose someone asks you, "So how was your year?" You'd probably say, "Oh, it was unbelievable!"

"Really? But didn't you say that January 1 was the worst day of your life?"

You'd reply, "Oh yeah, it was really bad, but everything else has gone so

> **"** You don't have to know the *why* when you know the Who. **"**

NOTES

NOTES

_____
_____
_____
_____
_____
_____
_____
_____
_____
_____
_____
_____
_____
_____
_____
_____
_____
_____
_____
_____
_____
_____
_____
_____
_____
_____
_____
_____
_____
_____
_____
_____
_____
_____

well, I had almost forgotten about it."

What happened? When you looked at the totality of the year – when you put everything into perspective – it was a tremendous year.

You may go through 90 years of chronic pain and turmoil in this life. But after a hundred million days of perfect bliss in the presence of God and the eternity that awaits you, suppose someone comes up to you and says, "How has your existence been?" You'd say, "It's been unbelievable! Heaven is so great! I just could have never imagined it would be this good!"

"But wait a second...didn't you have such a tough life before you got here?" And you look back over your earthly life and say, "You're right. I don't want to minimize that. I did suffer a lot. But when I put that in context, in light of God's incredible outpouring of goodness and joy that He has infused into my life, those bad days of my existence are not even worth comparing with the eternity of joy that I have experienced with God here."

When I was a kid, I remember reading a novel for the first time. I was so captivated by the story and wondering how things would pan out for the main character, that I remember turning to the back of the book and sneaking a peek of the last chapter. Having the knowledge that the good guy wins in the end gave me the confidence to continue reading the book.

I've got great news for you! If you're a follower of Jesus, I've read the last chapter in the novel of our existence and I can tell you with joyful confidence how your story ends. That is the hope that God gives. *"No eye has seen, no ear has heard, and no mind has imagined what God has prepared for those who love him"* (1 Corinthians 2:9). If your life is a living hell right now, you can praise God that this life is the only hell you will ever know. We have the assurance of how our story ultimately ends – and the good guy wins.

Are you going through a difficult time right now? How can your LifeCoach pray for you today?

_____
_____
_____
_____
_____
_____
_____
_____

Day 5

How Can I Understand the Trinity?

The doctrine of the Trinity may be the greatest distinctive of Christianity. No other religion in the world has ever been Trinitarian. Even though the word "trinity" is not found in the Bible, the truth of the Trinity is found throughout the Bible. The very word "trinity" comes from the Latin word *trinitas*, which literally means "a group of three." The prefix *tri-* means "three" and *unity* means "one." You put it together and you have *tri-unity* – three in one. While there is only one God, the Godhead consists of three distinct persons – the Father, the Son, and the Holy Spirit. All of them are equally omniscient (all-knowing), omnipotent (all-powerful), and omnipresent (presence is everywhere), but each person of the Trinity has unique functions.

Trying to explain how God is one God who has revealed Himself in three different ways is pretty inexplicable and incomprehensible. But the purpose of theology and being a disciple involves trying to understand all of God we can; however, we can never understand all that God is.

That's why God told Isaiah, *"For my thoughts are not your thoughts, nor are your ways My ways,' says the Lord. 'For as the Heavens are higher than the earth, so are My ways higher than your ways, and my thoughts than your thoughts.'"* (Isaiah 55:8-9).

The doctrine of the Trinity is not beyond logic and reason, but just above it. It's not a contradiction because we're not saying that God is both one person and also three persons. We are saying that God is one in essence and three in person. When you stop and think about it, our Creator has left His triune imprint on His own creation. Everything that God has made in this world is a reflection of His triune nature; it reflects His tri-unity. The world has a lot of things that are illustrations and shadows of the Trinity. God left His fingerprints on the work of His creation, and we see in it a reflection of the trinity. For example, the *universe* is made up of time, space, and matter. *Space* consists of length, width, and depth. *Matter* is energy, motion, and phenomena. *Time* is past, present, and future. The Bible says that *mankind* is triune in nature through body, soul, and spirit. Even *light* itself is actually constituted of three rays or groups of wavelengths distinct from each other, not one of which without the other would be light! The first ray originates, the second ray illuminates, and the third ray consummates. The first ray, called invisible light, is neither seen nor felt. The second is both seen and felt, and the third is not seen but is felt as heat. Light has three strands but only one ray. That's a pretty accurate picture of who God is and what each person in the Trinity does for us! God the Father originates, Jesus the Son illuminates, and God the Holy Spirit consummates.

Any way we try to illustrate the Trinity to help our feeble human minds comprehend it will always fall short. But one way to think about the Trinity

vimeo.com/138214127

NOTES

57

> **"God the Father originates, Jesus the Son illuminates, and God the Holy Spirit consummates."**

is by comparing it to the Sun. We understand the Sun as one entity, but we experience it in three distinct ways. The Sun is a mass, a giant star that holds our solar system together. Without the mass of the sun and its gravitational pull, our planet would soar into outer space. The Sun is also our primary source of light. Without its light, no life could exist and nothing could grow. Yet the Sun also has a third component. We feel it as heat, especially in the summer months! Without the Sun's heat, everything on our planet would freeze causing all life forms to become extinct.

How does that compare to our understanding of God? God the Father is like the mass of the Sun that holds everything together. The Father designed and organized how mankind would be redeemed (Galatians 4:4-5). He also set into motion a complex set of events, actions, and prophecies, which culminated in the life and death of our Savior. God the Son carried out the Father's plan. He became the "light of the world" (John 8:12) so that we could understand what God is really like. He became God in human flesh, which we call the "incarnation." The Holy Spirit, like the heat of the Sun, is that part of the Godhead that we can feel each day. He sees to it that every person feels a call toward God's saving grace (John 14:26; John 16:8; Romans 1:19-20) and then begins to work in and through the lives of those who receive salvation. Adrian Rogers said, "God the Father is all there is. The Holy Spirit is all we will feel. And Jesus is all we will ever see."

It's important to understand that we do not serve three gods; we have one God in three persons functioning uniquely and perfectly. The Father, Son, and Spirit are equal in their divine attributes while at the same time relating to mankind in a different way because of each of their unique roles.

The Trinity throughout the Bible

- From the very first verse in the Bible, we can see the Trinity. Genesis 1:1 says, *"In the beginning God created the heavens and the earth."* The Hebrew word for God is *Elohim*, and the suffix -*im* in Hebrew gives the singular noun a plural form. For example, a cherub is one angel but cherubim are several angels.
- In Genesis 1:26 we read: *"Let Us make man in Our image according to our likeness."* But then in the very next verse, we read, *"So God* [Elohim] *created man in His own image."* The word "Our" refers to God's plurality, and "His" refers to God's singularity. He is one in essence, but three in personality.
- In Deuteronomy 6:4, we have a verse that's known as the bedrock of the Jewish faith known as the Shema. It says, *"The Lord our God – the Lord is One!"* The word "one" is a fascinating word in the Hebrew language because it means "one in multiple" or "one as in a group."
- You also see instances of an unnamed individual all throughout the Old Testament. He appeared to Abraham at Mamre, Jacob in the wilderness, and was the fourth man in the fiery furnace with Shadrach, Meshach, and Abednego. Generally, you see him referred to as the Angel (with a capital A) or (Messenger) of the Lord in the Old Testament. Most Bible scholars believe that this is the second person of the Godhead – Jesus Christ.
- There are about 100 references to the Spirit of God in the Old Testament. Even as far back as Genesis 1, we find the *"Spirit of God hovering over the waters"* when creation began.
- In the New Testament, there are 12 places where the three names "Father, Son, and Holy Spirit" are grouped together, and they are all arranged in different ways. That's important to understand that none of the persons in the Godhead are either inferior or superior to the other one. The Godhead is co-equal and co-eternal.

Now what does all of this have to do with you and me? Well, if you want to know God you can only know God in the Trinity. You cannot get to God the Father unless you go through God the Son. Jesus said, *"No one comes to the Father except through me"* (John 14:6). But you cannot get to the Son unless you are brought by the Holy Spirit (John 16:13). Let's take a look at each of those roles more in depth.

Read Galatians 4:4-7. Notice how each person of the Trinity is mentioned in this passage. In your own words, write down what role God the Father, God the Son, and God the Holy Spirit play in your salvation:

_____

_____

_____

_____

_____

_____

_____

_____

_____

God the Father thought of our salvation.

Galatians 4:4 says, *"But when the fullness of the time had come, God sent forth His Son."* The word "fullness" refers to an appointed time. Why was Jesus born at the exact moment He was born? Why not a hundred years earlier or later? Because God had planned the birth of Jesus down to the exact day of the calendar. The setting was perfect 2,000 years ago to receive the Messiah. The time was right *spiritually*. Israel had come out of Babylonian captivity as a broken nation. They would never again return to idolatry. The time was right *socially*. Alexander the Great had built a world empire and made Greek a near universal language. Christians would be able to preach the gospel all over the world in a language that all could understand. The time was right *politically*. Because of the control of the Romans, it was a time of economic and political stability. How do you explain that? It wasn't a coincidence. It was providence – God the Father was in control.

Has it ever occurred to you that nothing ever occurs to God? If you're ever tempted to think that your world is spinning out of control, just remember: God the Father is still on His throne. This is difficult for us because we want God to act on our clock and our calendar, but God acts according to His plan and principles. Everything is moving and flowing through the providential hands of a sovereign God. We need to understand that with God, time means nothing, but timing is everything. God is never early. God is never late. God is always right on time – His time. History is really His Story.

God the Son bought our salvation.

According to Galatians 4:4, who did God send in the fullness of time? He sent "His Son." That refers to His deity; Jesus came as God. But it also says that He was *"born of a woman."* That refers to His humanity; He came as a man. Jesus was just as much man as if He weren't God and as much God as if He weren't man. He was *"born under the law,"* which refers to His impeccable character. Jesus came to reveal the character of God, not to display the

> 66 *But when the fullness of time had come, God sent forth his Son, born of woman, born under the law, 5 to redeem those who were under the law, so that we might receive adoption as sons. 6 And because you are sons, God has sent the Spirit of his Son into our hearts, crying, "Abba! Father!" 7 So you are no longer a slave, but a son, and if a son, then an heir through God.* 99
> - Galatians 4:4-7

NOTES _____

_____

_____

_____

_____

_____

_____

> "Because of Jesus, law has been replaced with grace, sin has been replaced with righteousness, and death has been replaced with eternal life."

NOTES _____

grandeur of God. He was the only person who ever lived who never sinned against God's law. Jesus had to be sinless and blameless because He came to be our perfect sacrifice and die for the sins of the world. If Jesus was not God, He could not have been a pure substitute because only God can forgive sins. If Jesus were not a man, He would not have been the proper substitute because only a man can die for men. Jesus could not have done what He did if He had not been who He was.

So what was the purpose of God the Son? Galatians 4:5 tells us that it was *"to redeem those who were under the law, so that we might receive adoption as sons."* The first part of His purpose was to *"redeem us"* from our sins. He was born for the express purpose of dying for you and me. The word "redeem" there literally means, "to buy out of the slave market." Jesus came to redeem us out of spiritual slavery because every person is in bondage to LSD: the law, sin, and death. Because of Jesus, law has been replaced with grace, sin has been replaced with righteousness, and death has been replaced with eternal life.

The result of that redemption is so *"that we might receive adoption as sons."* In the Roman world, the custom of adoption was mainly a privilege of the wealthy as the poor could not afford to adopt anyone. A wealthy person could adopt one of his slaves or an orphan child and make him his very own son or daughter. It was a transaction binding on all parties. At the exact moment that this legal transaction was completed, all prior obligations of the person adopted were canceled, and that individual was made an official part of the new family, with the same name, same standing, same position, and same privileges he would have had if he were a son by birth. This is such a cool truth! Spiritually, we are born into the family of God, but legally we are adopted as sons of God. Redemption changes my condition; adoption changes my position. I am no longer just free; I am now a full-fledged child of God with all the rights, standing, and privileges. Galatians 4:7 says that you are also *"an heir of God through Christ."* Paul repeats this truth in Romans 8:17, where he says that we are *"heirs of God and joint heirs with Christ."* Legally, we're familiar with what a joint heir is; it means you share and share alike. What that means is everything that Jesus has now belongs to you! Jesus became as I am so that I might become as He is. We are sons of God and joint heirs with Christ.

God the Holy Spirit brought our salvation.

Galatians 4:6 says, *"And because you are sons, God has sent forth the Spirit of His Son into your hearts, crying out, 'Abba, Father!'"* If you are a child of God, you have the Holy Spirit. It's the first gift the Father gives to His children. He is living in you, working through you, praying with you, and He wants to reveal to you the tremendous privileges that are yours as a son of God! The word "Abba" is the Aramaic word for "Daddy." Only a child of God, through the Spirit of God, can truly call on God as his Father.

When it comes to salvation, God the Father thought it, God the Son bought it, and the Holy Spirit brought it and wrought it into our lives! I have been selected by the Father, saved by the Son, and sealed by the Spirit. Ephesians 2:18 is a great verse that describes the Trinity in one single statement: *"Now all of us can come to the Father through the same Holy Spirit because of what Christ has done for us."* You go to the Father, through the Son, by the Holy Spirit.

You might be thinking, "I'm still a little bit confused about this whole subject." Well, join the club. We may not fully understand the Trinity this side of heaven, but we certainly should believe it. Someone once said concerning the Trinity, "Define it and you'll lose your mind; deny it and you'll lose your soul." Studying the Trinity and coming to a renewed understanding of who God really is refines our relationship with Him. Charles Spurgeon used to say, "Nothing will so enlarge the intellect and magnify the whole soul of man as a devout, earnest, continued investigation of the whole subject of the Trinity."

One of my favorite stories is one I read a long time ago about a wealthy Roman who had a faithful and capable slave named Marcellus. But he also had a son who was a real disappointment to him. When this Roman died and his will was opened, it was found that he had left all of his estate to Marcellus, the slave. However, his will decreed that his son could choose one item, and only one item, from the estate, before the will was settled. When the administrator asked the son what one thing he would take out of his father's estate, he said, "I'll take Marcellus!"

When he took Marcellus, he got it all! God the Father, God the Son, and God the Holy Spirit – they're all for one and they're one for all. And they will be all for you when you take Jesus!

What does it mean that there are three distinct persons in the Trinity? How do you find yourself relating to each person of the Trinity? Are you drawn more toward one over another? Why do you suppose that is?

_____
_____
_____
_____
_____
_____
_____

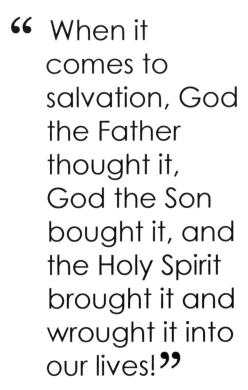

> 66 When it comes to salvation, God the Father thought it, God the Son bought it, and the Holy Spirit brought it and wrought it into our lives! 99

NOTES _____

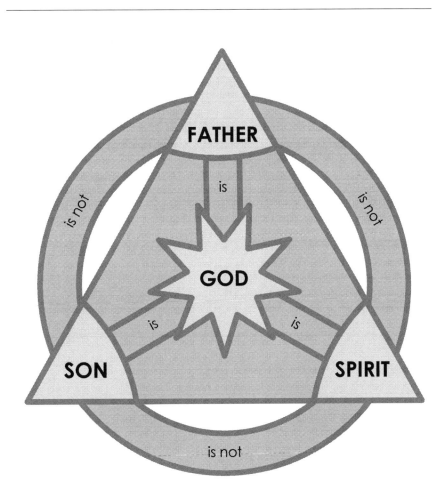

BIBLE STUDY

week 3

Day 1
Why Should I Read the Bible?

vimeo.com/138214253

NOTES _____
_____
_____
_____
_____
_____
_____
_____
_____
_____
_____
_____
_____
_____
_____
_____
_____
_____
_____
_____
_____
_____
_____

The quality of our Christian walk will never rise higher than the quality of our time spent in God's Word. Our spiritual growth is intricately tied to our commitment to Scripture. How can we know the God of the Bible if we don't know the Bible of God?

Sometimes Christians blame others for the fact that they aren't growing spiritually, but that's not a good explanation. If you want to grow spiritually, you must take responsibility for your growth. In 1 Timothy 4:7, Paul says, *"Train yourself to be godly."*

Successful people do daily what unsuccessful people do occasionally. We know that the secret of your success is discovered in your daily routine, so this week we're going to look at how to have a devotional time in God's Word. We'll also look at some practical tips and techniques that help create an environment for you to have accelerated growth in your relationship with God. But today, we are going to look at what the Bible is and why we should read it.

What is the Bible?
Willie White provides this description of the Bible:

This book contains the mind of God, the state of man, the way of salvation, the doom of sinners, and the happiness of believers. Its doctrines are holy, its precepts are binding, its histories are true, and its decisions are immutable. Read it to be wise, believe it to be safe, and practice it to be holy. It contains light to direct you, food to support you, and comfort to cheer you. It is the traveler's map, the pilgrim's staff, the pilot's compass, the soldier's sword, and the Christian's charter. Here paradise is restored, heaven opened, and the gates of hell disclosed. Christ is its grand object, our good its design, and the glory of God its end. It should fill the memory, rule the heart, and guide the feet. Read it slowly, frequently, and prayerfully. It is a mine of wealth, a paradise of glory, and a river of pleasure. It is given you in life, will be opened in judgment, and be remembered forever. It involves the highest responsibility, will reward the greatest labor, and will condemn all who trifle with its sacred contents.

There are tons of metaphors that have been used in the Bible to describe the Bible. Jesus said that the Bible is like a seed that grows. Isaiah said that the Bible is like a hammer that breaks and a fire that burns. But in the passage of Scripture we're going to study in depth today, we're told that the Bible is like a sword that cuts.

Hebrews 4:12 says, *"For the word of God is living and active, sharper than any two-edged sword, piercing to the division of soul and of spirit, of joints and of marrow, and discerning the thoughts and intentions of the heart."*

The Bible is the "Word of God," which means that it is divine in its origin. Even though it was penned by 40 different writers, who wrote 66 different books over a period of 1,600 years, it only has one author – God. Nowhere does the Bible claim to be the words of man; it claims to be the word of God. Someone once made this observation about the Bible, "I know man did not write this Book. A good man would not have written it because it claims to be from God, and a good man would not make a false claim. A bad man would not have written this Book because it condemns his own evil, so it must be written by God!" Over three hundred times, you find in the Bible the phrase "the word of God" or "the word of the Lord." Phrases such as "God said" or "God spoke" occur nearly 4,000 times. **When the Bible speaks, God speaks.**

Since it is the Word of God, the Bible is inspired. As we saw in one of our lessons last week, 2 Timothy 3:16 says that *"All Scripture is given by inspiration of God ..."* That means that if it is *inspired*, it must be *inerrant* in its original document because God would never inspire error.

Characteristics of the Bible
Because the Bible is the Word of God, the writer of Hebrews tells us that it possesses two characteristics that you would expect:

1. God's Word is Alive.
Hebrews 4:12 says, *"The word of God is living ..."* The Greek word for "living" is the word that gives us our word "zoology." This is a book that pulsates with life. No other book ever written has life, and no other book ever written *gives* life. Jesus said in John 6:63, *"It is the Spirit who gives life; the flesh profits nothing. The words that I speak to you are spirit, and they are life."* When you open this Book, it is almost as if Jesus Himself steps right off the pages and into your heart. God used His words to speak the universe into existence. God breathed into man and man became a living soul. God breathed into this book and it became a living book. The Greek word for "inspired" literally means "breathed out." The same breath that gave life to man is the same breath that gives life to this Book.

2. God's Word is Active.
"The word of God is living and active ..." Some Bible versions translate this word as "powerful." In the Greek, it's the word *energeo*, which is where we get our English word "energy." It's a word that literally means "activity that produces results." Think for a moment just how powerful, energizing, and activating God's word really is. Hebrews 11:3 says, *"By faith we understand that the universe was created by the word of God, so that what is seen was not made out of things that are visible."* There was once a time when there was no universe, and at the word of God, planets began to rotate on their axes. Or consider the miracles of Jesus Christ. All He had to do was speak the word and diseases were cured, storms quieted down, and dead men came back to life.

Based on Hebrews 4:12-13, why is it important that God's Word is alive and active? Have you experienced the Bible in this way for yourself?

_____

_____

_____

_____

_____

> " ... if you want to grow spiritually, you must take responsibility for your growth. "

NOTES _____

> **"**No other book
> ever written
> has life, and
> no other book
> ever written
> gives life.**"**

The power of God's Word

Scripture has the *power to convict*. When Stephen was preaching the Word of God, Acts 7:54 says that *"When they heard these things they were cut to the heart."*

It has the *power to convert*. We are saved by grace through faith in Jesus Christ. But we come to that understanding through the Word of God. Romans 10:17 says, *"So then faith comes by hearing, and hearing by the word of God."*

The Bible has the *power to cleanse* our heart. Jesus said in John 15:3, *"You are already clean because of the word which I have spoken to you."*

The Word of God also has the *power to conquer*. The Bible says that in the last days, when Jesus comes back and defeats the devil for the last time, He is going to have only one weapon. Revelation 19:15 says that the weapon is the sword of the Lord, the Word of God. When you internalize, meditate, and memorize the Word of God, you have the power to conquer your greatest struggles as well!

A two-edged sword

In Hebrews 4:12, the Bible is compared to a sword: The Word is *"sharper than any two-edged sword, piercing even to the division of soul and spirit, and of joints and marrow, and discerning the thoughts and intentions of the heart."*

In other words, this Book can not only tell you what you do, it can tell you why you do it. The Bible not only gets under your skin, it can get into your heart. A physical sword cuts living people to make them dead, but this spiritual sword cuts dead people to make them live. Friend, God's Word is not only able to divide and discern; it is able to deliver. There is no heart so hard that the sword of the Spirit cannot pierce and penetrate it, bringing that person to a saving knowledge of Jesus Christ.

Why does it say that this sword is "two-edged"? It's taken from the Greek word *distomos* and it's unquestionably one of the strangest words in the New Testament. The prefix *di*, means "two" and the word *stomos* means "mouth." When you combine them together, you get *distomos*, which literally means a "two-mouthed" sword.

The Word of God is like a sword with two edges cutting both ways. Ephesians 6:17 calls it *"the sword of the Spirit, which is the word of God."* The term "word" is taken from the Greek word *rhema*, which describes "something that is spoken clearly, vividly, in unmistakable terms and undeniable language." Here's an example of a *rhema*: Maybe you're praying about some situation, and suddenly, a Bible verse you read or studied rises up from inside your heart. At that moment, you're consciously aware that God has given you a verse to stand on and claim for that situation. You've received a word that came right out of the mouth of God and dropped into your spirit! That word from God is so sharp that it cuts through all of your questions, your intellect, and your natural logic, and it lodged its way deep into your heart.

When you spend time meditating on that *rhema*, or quickened word from God, it begins to release its power inside of you. You'll start to declare what it is that God has said to you and when it comes out of your mouth, it will be like a mighty blade that drives back the forces of evil that have been marshaled against you, your family, your business, and your relationships.

First, the Word of God comes out of the mouth of God. Next, it comes out of *your* mouth! When it came out of your mouth, it became a "two-edged," or more literally a "two-mouthed," sword. One edge of this sword came into existence when the Word initially proceeded out of God's mouth. The second edge of this sword was added when the Word of God proceeded out of your mouth! When you and God come into agreement with His Word, it releases His power into the situation at hand!

The power contained in this Book is absolutely mesmerizing! **We may read other books, but the Bible reads us.**

God's Word within us

A couple decided that they should do something to strengthen their marriage. They decided to go duck hunting together. They'd heard of other people going duck hunting with dogs, so they figured they needed to buy a good hunting dog. They got all of their equipment and their dog and took off for a day of duck hunting. They tried getting some ducks, but they came back at the end of the day and hadn't gotten a single one. The husband looked at the wife and said, "Honey, we've got to be doing something wrong here. We haven't caught a duck yet!" The wife said, "Well, maybe if we throw the dog up a little higher, he can catch a duck this time!"

That's what a lot of us are doing. We're trying to get a dog to do what a gun was meant to do. We're trying to accomplish things in our lives with tools that don't work or don't make sense. A dog is not the right weapon to get ducks. You need firepower to bring a duck down.

A lot of us have "hound dogs" trying to fix the problems of our lives. We're on the phone with "hound dog" friends. All they're doing is barking us up into more of a mess. We're doing everything except using the firepower from heaven. It's not enough that we're trying to fix our problems. But the real focus needs to be on *what* we are trying. The Word of Christ must dwell in us richly. It has to be the basis of our decisions.

1 Thessalonians 2:13 says, *"And we also thank God for this, that when you received the word of God, which you heard from us, you accepted it not as the word of men but as what it really is, the word of God, which is at work in you believers."*

When you read the Bible, don't just read it as you'd read the newspaper. Read the Scriptures with a prayerful heart. Take a moment before you begin reading to ask God to open your eyes to the wonders it contains. Never underestimate the power of asking God to open your eyes to His Word. God wants to reveal His truth to you.

What are the benefits of studying God's Word? Can you be equipped to change your world without being rooted in God's Word? Why or why not?

_____

_____

_____

_____

_____

_____

_____

_____

> **"When you and God come into agreement with His Word, it releases His power into the situation at hand!"**

NOTES _____

_____

_____

_____

_____

_____

_____

_____

_____

_____

_____

_____

_____

_____

_____

_____

_____

_____

_____

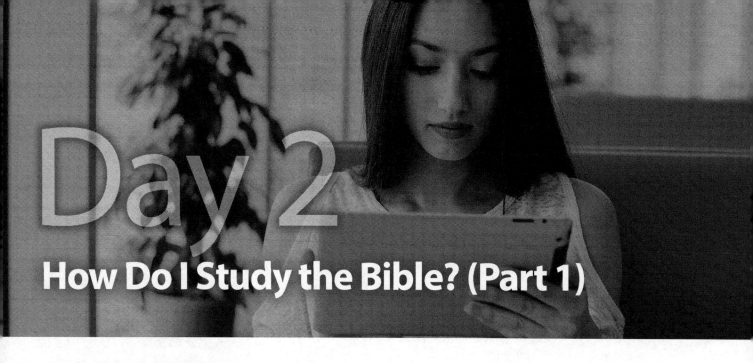

Day 2

How Do I Study the Bible? (Part 1)

vimeo.com/138214308

NOTES _____

_____

_____

_____

_____

_____

_____

_____

_____

_____

_____

_____

_____

_____

_____

_____

_____

_____

_____

_____

The Bible was given to us not simply to inform but to transform, not just to give us bigger heads but also to give us bigger hearts, so that we can live life to the fullest the way that God intended. The ultimate purpose of the Bible is to change our lives. In 2 Timothy 3:16-17 we read, *"All Scripture is given by inspiration of God ... so that the man of God may be complete, thoroughly equipped for every good work."* When we study the Bible, it changes our convictions, our character, and our conduct.

There are many ways you can study the Bible. One of the best books ever written on this subject is *Rick Warren's Bible Study Methods*. In each of these methods, you use different kinds of tools and ask different kinds of questions to extract the full meaning of Scripture. Over the next two days, we will learn from Rick Warren one of the best methods to study the Bible – the devotional method of Bible study. The greatest aspect of this method is that you can use it any time, anywhere, and you don't need any special tools other than your Bible!

There are six simple steps to the devotional method of Bible study. Today, we'll look at and practice the first three.

Pronounce It!

This is really quite simple. You read a verse (out loud if possible), and each time, stress a different word in the verse, emphasizing one word at a time. It's really the simplest way to start unlocking the full meaning of Scripture, but it's amazingly powerful. Each time you emphasize a different word, you see a different perspective and a different meaning begin to develop. Let's try this method with the most well-known Psalm in the Bible, Psalm 23:

Psalm 23:1 says, *"The Lord is my shepherd, I shall not want."*

Now, let's emphasize each word in that verse:

THE Lord is my shepherd, I shall not want.
The **LORD** is my shepherd, I shall not want.
The Lord **IS** my shepherd, I shall not want.
The Lord is **MY** shepherd, I shall not want.
The Lord is my **SHEPHERD**, I shall not want.
The Lord is my shepherd, **I** shall not want.
The Lord is my shepherd I **SHALL NOT** want.
The Lord is my shepherd, I shall not **WANT**.

Do you see what just happened here? You got eight different facets on that one verse just by repeating it over and over again with a different emphasis on a different word each time. It's called the pronouncing method of Bible meditation.

With each emphasis, stop and make a note about what insight that word gives to you. Here's what each word spoke to me:

"**THE**" tells me there is only one God, He's not just "a god" – He is the one and only true God. "**LORD**" reminds me that I have submitted myself to His Lordship. He is the boss and the owner of my life, and I can trust Him with everything. "**IS**" is a present tense verb. The God I serve is not the God of the past, He is the God of my present, and I know He will take care of my future. What He is offering in this verse is available to me today. "**MY**" tells me He's not just offering this promise to the spiritually elite; He is my very own personal shepherd. A "**SHEPHERD**" cares for the needs of his sheep, just like I need God's protection from danger, His provision for my needs, and His Spirit to convict me when I wander astray. "**I**" shows that with the knowledge that the Lord is my shepherd, that benefits me directly. "**SHALL NOT**" is a pretty emphatic statement. There isn't any room for question or doubt. This is based on a certainty. With God, I will not have a single "**WANT**." In other words, when God is my shepherd, I can rest in His presence. I can be content. Everything that I need for life, God promises to supply.

Do you see how easy that was? You don't need a seminary degree or any special tools to do that. Now let's have you try:

Use the *Pronounce It!* method of Bible meditation using the first phrase of Colossians 3:15. Make a note of what each word means to you:

"Let the peace of Christ rule in your hearts." – Colossians 3:15

_____

_____

_____

_____

_____

Which word has the most meaning to you? How does that verse apply to your life right now?

_____

_____

_____

_____

Picture It!

This method works best when you're reading a story or a parable in the Bible. Try to picture the Biblical scene in your mind. What would you think, feel, or do if you were in this situation? Then see yourself as a different character in the story, and ask yourself the same questions again.

Next, ask yourself these questions: With whom do I identify most in this

> **" The ultimate purpose of the Bible is to change our lives. "**

NOTES _____

_____

_____

_____

_____

_____

_____

_____

_____

_____

_____

_____

_____

_____

_____

_____

_____

_____

_____

_____

_____

_____

_____

_____

> 66 *And when he returned to Capernaum after some days, it was reported that he was at home. ² And many were gathered together, so that there was no more room, not even at the door. And he was preaching the word to them. ³ And they came, bringing to him a paralytic carried by four men. ⁴ And when they could not get near him because of the crowd, they removed the roof above him, and when they had made an opening, they let down the bed on which the paralytic lay. ⁵ And when Jesus saw their faith, he said to the paralytic, 'Son, your sins are forgiven.' ⁶ Now some of the scribes were sitting there, questioning in their hearts, ⁷ 'Why does this man speak like that? He is blaspheming! Who can forgive sins but God alone?' ⁸ And immediately Jesus, perceiving in his spirit that they thus questioned within themselves, said to them, 'Why do you question these things in your hearts? ⁹ Which is easier, to say to the paralytic, "Your sins are forgiven," or to say, "Rise, take up your bed and walk"? ¹⁰ But that you may know that the Son of Man has authority on earth to forgive sins'—he said to the paralytic— ¹¹ 'I say to you, rise, pick up your bed, and go home.' ¹² And he rose and immediately picked up his bed and went out before them all, so that they were all amazed and glorified God, saying, 'We never saw anything like this!' 99*

- Mark 2:2-12

story? How does their situation apply to my life right now? What is God trying to say to me? Then take a few minutes to write down your thoughts, observations, questions, or any action items you need to take.

When I read Exodus, I like to picture in my mind what it must have been like to cross the Red Sea. When I read Joshua, I try to picture in my mind how amazing it must have been to watch the walls of Jericho fall. When you start picturing a scene on the movie screen of your mind, Scripture comes alive to you and you begin to see it in a whole new light.

Read Mark 2:1-12 in the margin. Using the *Picture It!* method and visualize yourself from the perspective of the people in this story.

Picture yourself as the man on the mat ... What must it have been like to be so helpless? Is there any area of your life where you feel paralyzed right now – with fear, indecision, self-doubt, guilt, or sorrow? Is there anything your LifeCoach can pray for today?

_____

_____

_____

_____

Picture yourself as one of the men on the roof ... What kind of faith and determination did it take for them to do what they did? Do you know of anyone who needs your help right now? Does someone need help finding their way to Jesus? What is blocking the way?

_____

_____

_____

_____

Picture yourself as the homeowner ... Have you ever been inconvenienced because of someone in need? In light of this man's healing, was it worth the trouble you were put through?

_____

_____

_____

_____

Picture yourself as one of the people in the crowd ... Why did you come to the house? How do you feel about the guy who just cut in line? What have you seen Jesus do in other people's lives and how has it strengthened your faith?

_____

_____

_____

_____

Probe It!

If you remember, in the video I said that one of the secrets to good Bible study is asking the right kind of questions. Many times I'll get stuck in a passage. I'll ask a question that I have a difficult time answering. Most of the time, when that happens, I just take out my smartphone and Google the question. Of course, you need to be careful with this, as you can't trust everything you read on the Internet. But over time, you'll discover some websites and online commentaries that you can trust. For any question you have about the Bible, someone has asked that question before, and there are many articles you can read that will help you dig deeper.

Rick Warren developed a list of good questions you can ask about a text using the acrostic: **S.P.A.C.E.P.E.T.S.**

> **S** – Is there a **SIN** to confess?
> **P** – Is there a **PROMISE** to claim?
> **A** – Is there an **ATTITUDE** to change?
> **C** – Is there a **COMMAND** to obey?
> **E** – Is there an **EXAMPLE** to follow?
> **P** – Is there a **PRAYER** to pray?
> **E** – Is there an **ERROR** to avoid?
> **T** – Is there a **TRUTH** to believe?
> **S** – Is there **SOMETHING** to praise God for?

Notice that every phrase in those questions contains an action verb. They are all action-oriented, and they are designed to drive us towards applying what we are reading, which is the goal of all Bible study! I would encourage you to take a moment and write down these questions in your Bible so you'll always have them with you to remember and reflect on as you study.

Read Joshua 1:8 and work through each of the S.P.A.C.E.P.E.T.S questions and write down your observations:

"Do not let this Book of the Law depart from your mouth; meditate on it day and night, so that you may be careful to do everything written in it. Then you will be prosperous and successful."

_____

_____

_____

_____

_____

_____

_____

_____

There you have it! Those are the first three methods of devotional Bible study. Tomorrow, we will look at three more methods you can use to study God's Word.

> 66 When you start picturing a scene on the movie screen of your mind, Scripture comes alive to you and you begin to see it in a whole new light. 99

NOTES _____

_____

_____

_____

_____

_____

_____

_____

_____

_____

_____

_____

_____

_____

_____

_____

_____

_____

Day 3

How Do I Study the Bible? (Part 2)

vimeo.com/138214375

NOTES _____

olossians 3:16 says, *"Let the word of Christ dwell in your richly."*
The Bible says that the Holy Spirit will bring a verse to your mind when you need it. But He can't bring something to your mind if there's nothing in your mind. You have to dwell on it richly. You have to let it into your heart.

Then you should ask, "How do I need to apply this to my life?" or "Who do I need to share this truth with?" The quickest way to let it dwell in your mind is to tell it to someone else. The people who learn the most are the people who are passing it on to others.

Just to review, yesterday we covered the first three methods of devotional Bible study.

Pronounce It! When you're reading your Bible and you come to an important verse, stop and read it slowly. Emphasize each word in the verse, extracting the meaning of each word.

Picture It! When you're reading a story or a narrative, put yourself in the shoes of those in the story. A picture is worth a thousand words.

Probe It! The key to good Bible study is asking great questions. Look for ways you can apply the Bible to your life by using the S.P.A.C.E.P.E.T.S. list of questions.

Now, let's take a look at the last three methods:

Paraphrase It!

The goal of this method is to be able to explain the entire verse or passage in your own words. It's not enough just to know what the Bible says; you also need to understand what it means. If you can't put something in your own words, then you don't really understand the meaning.

Think of this as a two-way communication. God speaks to you through His Word, and you are speaking back to Him what it is you heard Him say to you using your own words.

Let me give you an example. In John 8:31-32, Jesus says, *"If you hold to my teaching, you are really my disciples. Then you will know the truth, and the truth will set you free."* In my own words, that verse means: "One of the ways that I know I'm a disciple of Jesus is if I hold fast to His teaching. That means that I cherish it and obey it. When I do that, I'll come to a knowledge of what truth really is, and that knowledge will give me victory in this life!"

So the *Paraphrase It!* method is easy. You simply:
- Read through the verse thoroughly to get an understanding of it.
- Think about what God is saying to you.

- Put it into your own words.
- Search your heart to see how this verse applies to you.
- Talk to God about it.

Put Proverbs 3:5-6 into your own words and share what God is saying to you in this passage: *"Trust in the LORD with all your heart and do not lean on your own understanding. In all your ways acknowledge Him, and He will make your paths straight."*

_____

_____

_____

_____

_____

_____

_____

Six Easy Steps to Bible Study:
1. Pronounce It!
2. Picture It!
3. Probe It!
4. Paraphrase It!
5. Personalize It!
6. Pray It!

Personalize It!

You personalize the Scripture when, as you're reading it, you put your name in place of the pronouns or nouns that are used in the text. For example, insert your name in the blanks below:

"For God so loved _____ that He gave His one and only Son, that if _____ believes in Him, _____ shall not perish but have eternal life." – John 3:16

Author Diane Stark writes:

When my daughter had a crush on a boy, I asked her to place his name in 1 Corinthians 13:4-6.
Put your name in here
She did. "Sean is patient and kind; Sean does not envy or boast; Sean is not arrogant or rude. Sean does not insist on his own way; Sean is not irritable or resentful; Sean does not rejoice at wrongdoing, but rejoices with the truth."

She frowned. "I saw him pick on another boy in the hallway. I guess he wasn't very kind." She began to rethink her interest in him.

This verse has not only given my daughter greater discernment about others, but it also helped her reflect on her own behavior. I asked my daughter to substitute her own name into that passage. Then I explained that when we become more like Jesus, we become the right type of person for someone else to like.

Pray It!

As you're reading Scripture, turn it into a prayer and pray it back to God. A prayer based on Psalm 23 might go something like this: "Thank you Lord for being my Shepherd, and that I lack nothing. *Thank you for making me lie down in green pastures and for leading me beside the quiet waters. I know that you are the only One who can truly bring peace into my life. Thank you for restoring my soul."*

It never hurts to write down your thoughts and your prayers back to

NOTES _____

_____

_____

_____

_____

_____

_____

_____

_____

_____

_____

_____

_____

_____

_____

_____

_____

_____

_____

_____

NOTES _____

God. Ask yourself, "Based on what I just read, what does God want me to know, what does He want me to do, and what does He want me to feel?" When you pray Scripture back to God, you are using Scripture to be that mirror to your own soul and you're communicating back to God what you see based on the light of that truth.

You now have all six methods of devotional Bible study. I really hope you will use them to enhance your study of God's Word. Now, let's take a look at some principles of Bible study and interpretation that will help you as you study:

Principles of Bible study and interpretation

Devotional books should supplement your Bible reading, not replace it. Our Christian stores have shelves filled with books to guide our spiritual life and walk us through reading the Scriptures. Devotional books are a great supplement to your spiritual walk. But would you rather hear someone talk about what your significant other said about you or would you rather read directly from them yourself? Don't depend on other spiritual leaders to be the sole source of spiritual growth for you.

Know the context of the Scripture you're reading. Before you read a passage, make sure you know where it's coming from. Was it written before or after Jesus came to earth? Who was it written by? Who was it written for? Why was it written? Many study Bibles provide this context in the introduction of each book or in the footnotes of the study Bible. Other times, you can just do a little simple research with a search engine on the Internet.

Let Scripture define Scripture; let the Bible be your dictionary. The Bible is its own best commentary. Scripture best explains and interprets Scripture. By looking up other verses on the same topic, you will get a much bigger, clearer picture of what God has to say about it. A good way to practice this principle is to get a Bible with cross-references in the margins. You'll be provided with a list of other verses that also relate to the verse that you're reading. For example, one verse on the subject of prayer will also be cross-referenced with another similar verse on prayer.

Always interpret unclear passages in light of clear passages. God tells us to correctly handle the word of truth (2 Timothy 2:15). We need to look at the *"whole counsel of God"* (Acts 20:27) when it comes to those verses that seem unclear. For example, Acts 2:38 says, *"Repent and be baptized for the remission of your sins."* So does that mean that you have to be baptized in order to be saved? No. Because the Bible makes it clear in the rest of the New Testament that salvation is by grace through faith, not by works of any kind. In this particular verse, the confusion is the word translated "for" in our Bibles. In other Scriptures, this same Greek word is translated "because of" or "as the result of." That makes more sense in light of everything else we know about how to be saved. That verse can literally be read *"Repent and be baptized [because of or as a result of] the remission of your sins."*

Read the Old Testament with the New Testament in mind, and read the New Testament with the Old Testament in mind. The Bible is a collection of 66 books, with Jesus and His story of redemption as the scarlet thread weaving through it, bringing it all together. The New Testament is hidden in the Old and the Old Testament is revealed in the New. The Old Testament is the New Testament concealed; the New Testament is the Old Testament revealed. A lot of Christians seem to dismiss the Old Testament and read it as if it's not as important as the New. That's a big mistake. Paul said, *"For everything that was written in the past was written to teach us, so that through the endurance taught in the Scriptures and the encouragement they provide we might have hope"* (Romans 15:4).

Read the Bible literally. Scripture should be read literally unless it's obvious that a particular passage was written allegorically, symbolically, or figuratively. For instance, Revelation is full of symbols and allegory that paint a prophetic picture of what the end times will be like. Although we take the Bible literally, there are figures of speech contained within its pages. When someone says, "It's raining cats and dogs outside," you know that cats and dogs are not literally falling from the sky. It means it's raining very hard. There are figures of speech that are symbolic of the greater spiritual reality, and it is the spiritual reality that we need to take literally.

If the plain sense makes sense, you have the right sense, so seek no other sense! What I mean by that is as I look back on my years of wrestling with the Word of God, I have come to realize that the only interpretation that makes the Bible alive and meaningful is the interpretation that takes Scripture exactly for what it says. Too often, the average Christian believes simply and uncritically what others write or preach, trusting in the interpretations of man rather than what is simply written in the Word of God. Yet Paul instructed the church at Corinth that *"we write nothing else to you than what you read and understand, and I hope you will understand until the end"* (2 Corinthians 1:13). Paul was writing this to ordinary people, many of whom were uneducated. Yet he said that if they had eyes to read God's Word or ears to hear it, they could understand it. God's Word was written plainly and simply in order that plain and simple people like you and me could understand it.

The Bible has only one meaning, but many applications. Sometimes you hear Christians in a Bible study ask one another, "What does that verse mean to you?" Finding the meaning of Scripture is an objective, not a subjective experience. It has only one meaning, which is what the original author intended for it to say. Bible scholars use what is called the "historical-grammatical" method of interpretation. This means that in the unclear passages of Scripture, we can still interpret it properly.

Don't interpret the Bible based on your own personal experiences; interpret your personal experiences based on Scripture. The point of Bible Study is not to try to shape Scripture to agree with your opinion. We call that *eisegesis*, which means that you read into the text some idea or theory that you want to see there. Instead, *exegesis* is drawing out of the text the truth that God put there and allowing that truth to shape your life.

True or false: The Bible has only one interpretation or meaning. What is the basis of your answer?

_____

_____

_____

_____

_____

> **" God's Word was written plainly and simply in order that plain and simple people like you and me could understand it. "**

NOTES _____

Week 3

Day 3: **How Do I Study the Bible? (Part 2)**

> **"**That's what devotional reading is all about – not just knowing the Word, but getting to know the Author personally.**"**

NOTES _____

Love letter

I want you to think of your Bible study or devotional time as your personal meeting with God. Many times people say, "Well, I just don't have the time to do this." Here's one thing about human psychology that no one can deny: You always have time to do those things that are important to you. You've got to spend some time with God in His Word and in personal devotions each day because it's like filling up your gas tank. It keeps you going.

When my wife, Carrie, and I were dating, I loved to get love letters from her. Regardless of whether it came as a card or a written note, I remember opening them with butterflies in my stomach. I couldn't wait to see what her message to me was. I would ponder over the exact shade of meaning of every word, every comma. Reading it would cause a hundred questions to formulate in my mind. "Would she have said that to anybody?" or "I wonder what she meant when she used that word?" were questions rapidly firing through my mind. After I read it once, I set the note down for a few minutes to think about it. Then I picked it back up and re-read it. By the end of that day, I had that love letter practically memorized word-for-word.

That's the kind of attitude God wants us to have when it comes to His Word. The Word of God is His love letter to you. And He wants you to open it and experience the joy of getting to know Him through His Word. That's what devotional reading is all about – not just knowing the Word, but getting to know the Author personally. Read God's story, His love letter to you, for yourself.

There are two things you can count on in your life that are absolutely immutable, meaning that they don't change. Those are God's Word and God's promises. When everything else in your life seems unstable and fluid, you can count on those two things being stable and constant.

Day 4
How Do I Apply the Bible?

The Bible wasn't written to increase our knowledge, but to change our lives. Applying what the Bible says to your life is where the rubber meets the road. There's a saying that we only believe the parts of the Bible that we actually *do*. As Christians, our job is to listen to God and obey His voice, and the primary way that God will speak to you is through His word. **We study the Bible to know *about* God; we obey the Bible to really *know* God.** Knowledge on its own doesn't equate to spiritual growth. Knowledge without application is like having keys to a treasure chest you never open.

Jesus taught us to hear the words of God and act on them in John 13:17: *"If you know these things, blessed are you if you do them."* Storing information in your brain doesn't change your life. Having knowledge that you put into practice, on the other hand, makes all the difference.

Just because you have a Bible doesn't mean that you're going to get the benefit from it. James, one of the most practical books in the Bible, gives us some steps for how we can respond to God's Word and apply it to our lives.

James 1:21-25 says, *"Therefore, putting aside all filthiness and all that remains of wickedness, in humility receive the word implanted, which is able to save your souls. But prove yourselves doers of the word, and not merely hearers who delude themselves. For if anyone is a hearer of the word and not a doer, he is like a man who looks at his natural face in a mirror; for once he has looked at himself and gone away, he has immediately forgotten what kind of person he was. But one who looks intently at the perfect law, the law of liberty, and abides by it, not having become a forgetful hearer but an effectual doer, this man will be blessed in what he does."*

Why do we often *hear* and not *do* when it comes to Scripture? What does this say about our faith?

_____

_____

_____

_____

_____

_____

_____

vimeo.com/138214434

NOTES _____

> **"We study the Bible to know about God; we obey the Bible to really know God."**

I think what James is trying to say here is that most of us are educated far beyond the level of our own obedience. We know what the Bible says we are to do; we just don't put it into practice. We have more revelation than our current level of application. Our problem isn't access to the Word; we have a problem with the application of the knowledge we already have access to.

I heard about a missionary serving in another country where the Bible is illegal. In order to get people access to Scripture, they have to sneak the Bibles in along with the parts of cars to get them across the border. When they get the Bibles, their method is to cut the pages of the Bible into squares of four verses on each side of the paper. Then they distribute them through the community – eight verses at a time, four verses on each side. At the end of each week when the children are playing outside, they slip out of their shoes the old verses and trade it in for a new square of verses so that each family can have a new passage to study that week.

That's hard for us to imagine here in our country. We're spoiled. We buy half a million Bibles *per week*! We have tremendous access, but it results in so little application. You can call it "spiritual obesity," which is the result when your Biblical knowledge exceeds your obedience. The point that James makes in this passage is that we have a knowledge surplus, but an obedience deficit. So how do we apply the Bible to our daily lives? James offers us three steps:

1. Receive the Word with a ready heart.

James tells us in verse 21 to *"put aside all filthiness and all that remains of wickedness, and in humility receive the word implanted ..."* In order to receive the word, you must get rid of one thing and welcome another. It says, *"put aside all filthiness."* The Greek word used for "filthiness" was also used to refer to getting the wax out of your ear. If you have excess wax in your ears, it has to be removed because it will limit your ability to hear. We can have trouble hearing spiritually too. Paul had trouble getting through to the Hebrews because they had become *"dull of hearing"* (Hebrews 5:11). The word "dull" suggests an interesting image – it literally means "mule-headed." A mule can be pretty stubborn when it comes to doing what his master tells him to do. James is telling us that before we go before the Word, we need to ask God to reveal any sinful thing in our lives that would limit us from being able to hear what His Spirit desires to speak into our hearts through our reading that day.

Once we've put aside and confessed anything that might limit our hearing, James says we are to *"receive the word implanted."* The word "receive" is a hospitality term, which means "to welcome with gladness" or "to receive gladly." If we're going to apply the Bible to our lives, we've got to welcome it into our hearts. James compares the Word of God to a seed that is planted within our hearts. How is it possible to take two seeds that are exactly the same and plant them in two different locations and get two different crops in terms of fruitfulness? The difference is the soil. One soil is prepared and the other is not. How can you take two people and put them in front of a Bible and one person will be blown away and blessed by its message and the other doesn't get anything out of it? One was prepared, and the other wasn't. If we allow the weeds of sin and spiritual dullness to grow up around our hearts, the seed of the Word of God may not grow and produce to its maximum ability. The old timers used to say that we need a 12-inch revival. There are approximately 12 inches between your head and your heart. We need to get the information that is up in our head down into our heart.

When you sit down to unfold what God's Word has to say to you each day, make sure that you have a ready heart. Ask the Holy Spirit to reveal anything in your life that isn't glorifying to Him. Take a moment to confess it and forsake it and ask for His cleansing and forgiveness. Many times I pray just a simple prayer before opening God's Word: "Lord, show me what it is you have to say to me today." And then go into that study looking for His response. That's a prayer God loves to answer.

2. Reflect on the Word with an open mind.

After we've received the Word, we must properly reflect on it so its truth can shape and guide our lives. James 1:22 says, *"But prove yourselves doers of the word, and not merely hearers who deceive themselves."* When you are exposed to the teaching of Scripture, you have only two responses: progress or regress. You can do what it says and respond by making positive progress, or you can choose not to do anything about it and regress spiritually. The Christian life is like riding a bicycle; either you're moving forward or you're falling off! You're either going forward or backward. There's no such thing as neutrality for a disciple of Jesus. It would be better to do more with less knowledge than to do less with more knowledge.

James says, *"Do not merely listen to the word and so deceive yourselves."* Have you ever watched someone deceive themselves? I think of the contestants on *American Idol* or *America's Got Talent*. Some of these people thought they had great talent, but they needed someone like Simon Cowell to give them a reality check. It's possible that we can deceive ourselves into thinking that we're good with God and growing in the Christian walk because we're surrounded by Biblical teaching. But the Bible says that we are blessed according to what we *do*, not according to what we *know*. You can go to church week after week, but if you're doing nothing to serve God, and you're not living with integrity, you're deceiving yourself. The dangerous thing is, you think you're good because you heard it. You've gotten inoculated.

When you hear the Word and do it, that's application. When you hear the Word and you *don't* do it, that's inoculation. When you get inoculated with a vaccine, you get a form of that disease that prevents you from getting the real thing. My fear is that many Christians have become inoculated with the Word of God. They've gotten just enough of it to keep them from getting the real thing.

James uses another great illustration here. He compares God's Word to a mirror: *"For if anyone is a hearer of the word and not a doer, he is like a man who looks at his natural face in a mirror; for once he has looked at himself and gone away, he has immediately forgotten what kind of person he was."*

Do you remember back in the 90's when those *Magic Eye* optical illusions were all the craze? They were posters of 2D abstract images that if you looked at them long enough, you were supposed to be able to see 3D objects. I remember looking at those things, putting my nose right up to it, and then moving farther away without losing my focus in order to see the 3D figures. I think a lot of people look at the Bible as more of an optical illusion than they do a mirror. We think that if we stare at it long enough and in just the right way, then all of a sudden a hidden meaning is going to jump out at us from the text. Don't get me wrong, God's Word is deep. We should meditate on it and take it apart piece by piece. But God never intended His Word to be an optical illusion. God's Word is simple, but not simplistic. It is mysterious, but not mystical. James says that the Bible is a mirror that shows you the real you and enables you to see the real Jesus.

The purpose of a mirror is to evaluate ourselves. We get up in the morning and one of the first things we do is to look in the mirror to assess the damage that has been done the night before, and then before we head off to work, we (hopefully) do something about what we see.

Have you ever seen yourself in the Bible? Hebrews says that God's Word detects the thoughts, intents, motives, and desires of the heart (Hebrews

> " If we allow the weeds of sin and spiritual dullness to grow up around our hearts, the seed of the Word of God may not grow and produce to its maximum ability. "

NOTES

> **"... the primary purpose of the Bible is to be a mirror – to reveal who you really are in light of who God really is."**

4:12). Many years ago, Queen Elizabeth I ordered that all of the mirrors be removed from the palace because she couldn't stand to face the fact that she was growing old. A lot of people don't read the Bible because they're afraid. They're unwilling to face themselves and see themselves as they really are. The purpose of a mirror is to be an accurate reflection of what you look like so you can discern your imperfections and do something about them. The Word of God plainly shows you what is actually there. According to James, the primary purpose of the Bible is to be a mirror – to reveal who you really are in light of who God really is. The world is kind of like a funhouse mirror: it throws back distorted images of who you really are based on culture and the opinions of others. But God, through His Word, can show you who you really are in light of who He really is. When you see yourself in light of the Word of God and you allow it to reflect back to you who you really are, it clears up your perception thereby enabling your obedience. When you see yourself as you really are in light of who God really is, it's life transforming. When you see God as holy, it causes you to become more holy because **we become what we behold.** On the other hand, if you fill your mind with a steady diet of junk, or you fill your heart with images that are contrary to God's Word, you will likewise become what you behold.

This is important to remember: Looking in a mirror doesn't make you any prettier! Looking in the mirror doesn't make you any more toned. You may have heard it said that the Bible changes our lives. To be technical, that isn't true. It is the *application* of the Bible through the power of the Holy Spirit that changes our lives. Our churches today are packed with people who know definite facts about Jesus, but have no dynamic faith in Jesus.

Just glancing in the mirror doesn't improve your appearance. It's what you do with what you see that makes you who you ought to be. Here's the equation I regularly teach my church about the importance of applying the Bible to our lives: **Information + Application = Transformation.** The mirror shows you what God sees in your heart, and it reflects back to you who you really are in light of who God really is.

3. Respond to the Word with intentional obedience.

James says in verse 25, *"But one who looks intently at the perfect law, the law of liberty, and abides by it, not having become a forgetful hearer but an effectual doer, this man will be blessed in what he does."*

So how do we respond to the Word of God?

Read it carefully. Verse 25 says, *"but one who looks intently ..."* He's talking more about careful research than casual reading. The word "look" in the Greek means "to stoop down and gaze in." It's the same word used when Peter went to the tomb on that first Easter Sunday when he stooped down and examined the empty grave of Jesus. He investigated it. So how do we do that with the Word of God? Go back and look at the previous two lessons on how to study the Bible. Use the S.P.A.C.E.P.E.T.S. acrostic to help you mine out and extract those little gold nuggets. After all these years of preaching, every time I read the same passage I've read dozens of times before, I still find myself learning something new about God, about the Bible, and about myself.

Review it intentionally. James says that it is he that *"abides by it"* that will be blessed by the Bible. The word "abides" means "to continue to do so." The Bible also calls this meditation. Remember, meditation does not mean putting your mind in neutral and contemplating the lint in your navel. It means to think about something seriously over and over again. Let me make this easy for you. If you know how to worry, you know how to meditate.

When you take a negative idea and you think about it over and over again, that's called worry. When you take a concept in God's Word and you think about it over and over again, that's called meditation. This is so important because Jesus said, *"If you continue in my Word, then you are truly my disciples"* (John 8:31-33).

Remember it habitually. Tomorrow we're going to look at another tool for spiritual growth, Scripture memorization. Nothing will do more for your spiritual life than developing the habit of memorizing Scripture. We remember what's important to us. Take notes. Write things down. If you value God's Word, you're going to want to take notes on it. Hebrews 2:1 says, *"Write things down so we don't let slip what we've heard."* Psychologists did a study and found that we forget 95% of what we hear within 72 hours, but we remember 90% of what we *do*! James says that when it comes to applying the Bible to daily life, we should read it, review it, and respond to it.

When I was in seminary, I began to realize that my heart was growing cold and that I was becoming very calloused to God's Word. I was reading it, studying it, and hearing it taught so much that I was radically decreasing in my desire to apply what I had learned. I made it the desire of my heart that every time I come before God's Word, whether it be in a sermon or in my daily Bible study, I am going to find the *one thing* that I can apply directly from that message. Call it the "One Thing Principle." I would encourage you to come before God's Word with that same perspective. Be a doer of the Word. Don't merely listen. Put it into practice.

In what area of your life could you do a better job applying God's Word rather than just listening to it?

NOTES

81

Day 5
How Do I Memorize Scripture?

vimeo.com/138214496

The Bible compares itself to a sword. Ephesians 6:17 says, *"Take up the ... sword of the Spirit, which is the word of God."* We need to understand that we are in a spiritual battle (Eph. 6:12), and the grip we have on God's Word, the sword of the Spirit, is the only offensive weapon we have. But here's the thing: most of us have a very weak grasp of the Word of God.

The Bible talks about five ways we can expose ourselves to the teachings of God's Word:

1. **Hearing** – We remember 15% of what we hear within 24 hours of hearing it.
2. **Reading** – We remember 30% of what we read.
3. **Study** – We remember 60% of what we study.
4. **Memorize** – We remember 100% of what we commit to memory.
5. **Meditate** - We also remember 100% of what we continually review.

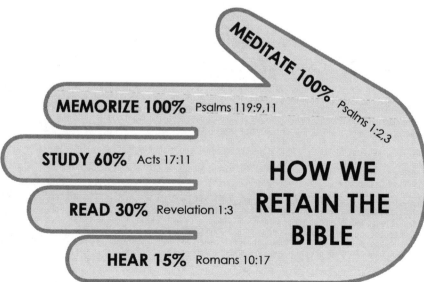

MEDITATE 100% Psalms 1:2,3

MEMORIZE 100% Psalms 119:9,11

STUDY 60% Acts 17:11

HOW WE RETAIN THE BIBLE

READ 30% Revelation 1:3

HEAR 15% Romans 10:17

For most Christians, the only exposure they get to God's Word is on Sundays when they hear a pastor's message. That means they might internalize 15% of the teaching that day at best (that is *if* they were paying attention and taking good notes). I want you to imagine that you were a soldier in the ancient world and you tried to go into battle by only holding your sword with your pinky finger. You probably wouldn't look like much of a threat to the enemy, and you would easily get that sword knocked out of your hand. We wonder why we never feel like we have any power in our life and why we always feel beaten down. It's because we're not firmly grasping the greatest tool God has given to us – the Word of God.

Now, I know what you're probably thinking. "I don't even remember what I ate for breakfast this morning. How am I supposed to memorize verses in the Bible?" You can memorize anything if you put your heart into it. You've memorized your phone number and social security number. If you're a husband, hopefully you've memorized your wife's birthday and anniversary. You can memorize verses of Scripture that mean a lot to you. As a matter of fact, in their book *How God Changes Your Brain*, Drs. Newberg and Waldman demonstrate that Scripture meditation and memorization actually enlarges your capacity to remember things. Did you ever think that your brain would grow in proportion to the Scriptures you memorized and meditated on?

Why memorize?

The goal of Scripture memory is not for you to have bragging rights and be able to spout off long monologues of the Bible in an effort to impress people. The goal is really three fold:

1. To meditate on the Word. Today, when most people think of meditation, they think of some sort of New Age practices. Biblical meditation has nothing to do with "looking within ourselves," but has everything to do with looking into God's holy Word. The end result of meditation is that you're not just getting into the Word, but the Word is getting into you.

2. To allow the Holy Spirit to bring God's Word back to your memory when you need it.

3. To carry the Bible with you wherever you go. Paul's exhortation to believers was to *"let the word of Christ dwell in you richly"* (Colossians 3:16). In order for God's Word to dwell in you, you must memorize it.

Church Swindoll, in his book *Growing Strong in the Seasons of Life*, said, "I know of no other single practice in the Christian life more rewarding, practically speaking, than memorizing Scripture. No other single exercise pays greater spiritual dividends! Your prayer life will be strengthened. Your witnessing will be sharper and more effective. Your attitudes and outlook will begin to change. Your mind will become alert and observant. Your faith will be solidified."

There are actually a ton of Bible verses that deal with this topic of memorizing and meditating on Scripture.

Read Joshua 1:8 and write that verse in your own words:

_____

_____

_____

_____

_____

_____

_____

_____

> **❝** We need to understand that we are in a spiritual battle, and the grip we have on God's Word, is the only offensive weapon we have. **❞**

NOTES _____

_____

_____

_____

_____

_____

_____

_____

_____

_____

_____

_____

_____

_____

_____

> ❝In order for God's Word to dwell in you, you must memorize it.❞

Benefits of memorizing Scripture

1. Memorizing Scripture leads to loving obedience to God.
Deuteronomy 6:5 says, *"You shall love the Lord your God with all your heart, with all your soul, and with all your strength."* Then in the next few verses, he tells them to memorize the Word and keep it before themselves and their families continually. For many people, the Bible is like the Queen of England. She holds the top position, but she has no real power. Many people say they love the Word of God, but because they're not hiding its words in their heart, it has no real power in their life.

2. Memorizing Scripture causes us to prosper and be successful for God.
Joshua 1:8 tells us that when we meditate on God's Word day and night, *"you will make your way prosperous, and then you will have success."* Success simply defined is "progressing in the will of God for your life." That one verse teaches us that if we want that kind of success we must 1.) memorize it by repeating it constantly, 2.) meditate on it day and night, and 3.) obey all that is written in it.

3. Memorizing Scripture causes you to live a life of joy and comforts you in times of difficulty.
Psalm 19:8 says, *"The precepts of the LORD are right, giving joy to the heart. The commands of the LORD are radiant, giving light to the eyes."* Scripture also says in Isaiah 26:3, *"My son, do not forget my law, but let your heart keep my commands; for length of days and long life and peace they will add to you."*

4. Memorizing Scripture produces a vibrant, stable, and consistent life.
Psalm 1 talks about how the person who memorizes and meditates on the Word as being one *"planted by the rivers of water, that brings forth fruit in its season, whose leaf also shall not wither."* What is this referring to? You know when you're around someone like this. You usually leave their presence feeling blessed or inspired because he or she overflows with the Word of life. When you invest yourself in meditating and memorizing Scripture, you too can produce the spiritual fruit God intends for you to produce.

5. Memorizing Scripture gives you great wisdom and guidance.
Wisdom is simply the ability to apply knowledge to everyday situations. Psalm 119:99 says, *"I have more understanding than all my teachers, for Your testimonies are my meditation."* In other words, spending time in the Word will give you more wisdom and guidance than any other source of formal education. I know of a psychologist who started memorizing Scripture soon after he was saved, and over time, he had committed 60 verses to memory. He said that he learned more about how to relate, counsel, and get along with people from memorizing Scripture than he did in his entire 40 years of studying psychology. If you feel like you are lacking in wisdom, memorize Scripture! If you feel like you need guidance in making a decision, memorize the Word! The will of God is revealed in the Word of God. The better I know the Word of God, the better I know His will for my life. Psalm 37:31 says, *"The Law of his God is in his heart; none of his steps shall slide."*

6. Memorizing Scripture gives you victory in your thought life.
Every time Jesus was tempted in the wilderness, He quoted Scripture to combat Satan's temptation. He did that in order to give us a model to follow. I believe that the greatest battle faced by most Christians is the struggle we have with our thought life. It could be worry, anxiety, discouragement, or

lustful thoughts. In 2 Corinthians 10:5 it says that we are to be *"casting down arguments and every high thing that exalts itself against the knowledge of God, bringing every thought into captivity to the obedience of Christ."* Whenever we are facing some struggles in our thought life, we need to follow the pattern of Jesus. Memorize specific verses that deal with those areas, and review and recite them when you're facing a struggle in your mind.

Recently, I went through a season of discouragement and depression, but what I found that helped me the most was memorizing some specific verses that dealt with the self-defeating thoughts that kept ruminating around in my head. Our sinful minds are cleansed as the water of God's Word flows through them, flushing out the corrupt thoughts of our old nature, and replacing them with the pure ways of God's thinking.

7. Memorizing Scripture helps us teach and counsel others.
Deuteronomy 6:6-7 talks about how parents can use the Scriptures they've internalized in their own heart to enable them to take advantage of those teachable moments. The reason most Christian parents aren't able to transfer Biblical principles to their kids is because they don't know the Word for themselves.

Look back over those reasons why it's beneficial to memorize and meditate on God's Word. Which one of those reasons resonates as being most important to you at this time in your life? What do you need God's Word to do for you most?

_____

_____

_____

_____

_____

_____

_____

_____

_____

How can I memorize Scripture?
Anyone who wants to memorize verses in the Bible can! The main reason most people never think they can memorize is because they haven't been shown a practical method to do so. I'm going to share with you some practical steps, but first, you must make up your mind to do it. No method is going to help you unless you first purpose in your heart that it's something that you need to do. At the age of 24, Augustus Van Reign learned that he was going blind. It was at that point that he decided to use all of his free time to memorize God's Word. By the time he reached 35 years of age, he had memorized word-for-word the entire New Testament as well as the books of Psalms and Proverbs.

Someone has said, "The greatest waste of time is the time wasted getting started." So let this spiritual discipline piggyback on some other activity or some other habit you already have. If you go to the gym each day, then memorize Scripture while you're on the elliptical machine. Or try doing it at the breakfast table or while you're sitting at red lights in traffic.

Here are some practical steps you can take to get started:

> **"** ... spending time in the Word will give you more wisdom and guidance than any other source of formal education. **"**

NOTES _____

_____

_____

_____

_____

_____

_____

_____

_____

_____

_____

_____

_____

_____

_____

_____

_____

_____

> 66God will be overjoyed with our efforts to commit His life-changing Word to memory. When we hide His Word in our hearts, we are saying to God, 'Your Word is important to me.'99

NOTES _____

_____

_____

_____

_____

_____

_____

_____

_____

_____

_____

_____

86

1. Select verses to memorize that are meaningful to you.
The more meaningful the verse is to you and the more purpose you attach to it, the easier it is to memorize. Every once in a while when we're reading our Bible or listening to a sermon, we stumble across a verse that seems to jump off the page and into our heart. We have those moments where we feel like that verse was meant specifically for us for that specific moment in time. When that happens, keep a running list of those verses in the back of your Bible, and that will eliminate having to decide what verse to memorize next.

2. Spend some time meditating on that verse.
How do we do that? It's really simple:
- **Picture It** – What does this spiritual truth look like? Try to visualize what this text is saying in your own mind. Picture it as a reality in your life.
- **Ponder It** – Mull over it in your mind as you think about it over and over again. Repeat it over and over to yourself. What do these individual words mean? What is God trying to express?
- **Personalize It** – What does this mean specifically in your own life? What actions need to happen for that truth to become a reality in you?
- **Pray Over It** – Ask God to bring this truth to life in your everyday experience. Ask Him to make this truth real to you and to show you how you need to respond.

3. Write verses on cards you can carry with you.
I keep a stack of index cards with me when I'm reading my Bible so that when a verse or two really speak to my heart, I simply jot them down on the card and put it in my pocket so that I can periodically reflect on it throughout the day.

In 1898, Dr. Oscar Lowry wrote a book on how to memorize Scripture by using a card system. He was able to personally memorize almost 20,000 verses, which is almost two-thirds of the entire Bible! There are some advantages to the card system in that cards can be kept in your pocket or purse and reviewed any time in any place. Having cards also makes it easier to put those verses on your wall or bathroom mirror. You can even keep all of your verses in one place, and it makes them easier to file or rearrange.

There are even some great apps out there that allow you to memorize Scripture from your smartphone. Check out these apps in your device's app store: Verses – Bible Memory, Bible Memory: Scripture Typer (my personal favorite), or Fighter Verses. These are all excellent resources that make this spiritual discipline more practical and convenient for you.

So whether you put them on your phone or write them on a card, the key is to meditate on them often enough that they are logged into your memory bank.

I'll be honest. Scripture memorization can be difficult at times. Many times people start off on this journey strong, but then after two or three weeks, the gusto is lost in our busy lives. That's why I want to also point you to a great resource called The Verses Project. A group of worship leaders and musicians have put together a complete online music library of Scripture memory songs put to music. When you hear and sing God's Word, it sticks with you all day, just like a song that you *don't* want to get out of your head! Check it out online at theversesproject.com.

When we get to heaven, God isn't going to be impressed with how many sports statistics we can recall or how many one-liners from movies we know by heart or how many words of popular songs we can recite. But God will be overjoyed with our efforts to commit His life-changing Word to memory. When we hide His Word in our hearts, we are saying to God, "Your Word is important to me."

PRAYER

week 4

Day 1

Why Is Prayer So Powerful?

vimeo.com/138214583

NOTES _____

_____

_____

_____

_____

_____

_____

_____

_____

_____

_____

_____

_____

_____

_____

_____

_____

_____

_____

There is nothing in life that is outside the reach of prayer. Christianity is not some dry, dusty, ancient religion. It's living daily in a warm, personal, intimate friendship with the living God. We need to learn to bring all of our concerns before God because if it's big enough to concern you, it's big enough to concern Him.

Do you sometimes feel as if your prayers just aren't getting above the light bulbs? I think if you were to ask the average Christian what their biggest challenges are when it comes to prayer, there are two common answers: "I just don't know if God is really hearing me," and "I have trouble staying faithful and consistent in my prayer life."

This week we're going to tackle both of those big struggles and more! Today, we'll look at how we can know that God really is hearing and answering our prayers.

I'm sure you've had the experience where there are certain things you pray for time and time again, but you never get an answer to those prayers. You're seeing nothing happen, and as a result, you're getting discouraged. It appears as though God isn't moving because our circumstances don't seem to be changing. I believe one of the major reasons that happens is because our prayers have the wrong focus. Every prayer that you and I pray ought to be focused on one thing and one thing only – the will of God. Praying in the will of God is the key to getting your prayers heard and answered.

The assurance is found in 1 John 5:14-15: *"This is the confidence we have in approaching God: that if we ask anything according to his will, he hears us. And if we know that he hears us – whatever we ask – we know that we have what we asked of him."*

1 John 5:14-15 is perhaps the greatest promise in the Bible on the subject of prayer. Read this passage and jot down in your own words what God is saying to you:

_____

_____

_____

_____

_____

_____

Praying God's will

The power of prayer is not the result of the person praying. Rather, the power resides in the God who is being prayed to. John says, *"This is the confidence that we have in approaching God ..."* The word "confidence" means "boldness" or "assurance." It pictures a person so confident that when he speaks, he has no doubt about what he is saying. In the context of prayer, this word presents the picture of a believer who is so confident he is right in asking that he asks unashamedly and confidently.

What can give us that kind of confidence? The verse goes on to tell us *"... if we ask anything according to His will, he hears us."*

A prayer prayed in the will of God is guaranteed to accomplish the work of God. Henry Blackaby illustrated this concept in a really insightful way. His son's birthday was coming up, and he and his wife decided to buy their son a blue bicycle for his birthday. They bought the bike and then hid it in the garage. Now they only had to get their son to begin to *want* the bike for his birthday. So they began talking to him about bicycles, talking about how fun it would be to go out on family rides. They took him to bike stores and showed him bicycle magazines, and before long, his son was asking for a bike for his birthday! What he asked for he received because his father had it in storage for him long before he even wanted it!

That's exactly how God acts toward us. When we pray, if we are listening for His Holy Spirit, He will place upon our hearts desires that are really His desires. Adrian Rogers said, "The prayer that gets to Heaven is the prayer that starts in Heaven. We just close the circuit." Prayer is the Holy Spirit finding a desire in the heart of the Father and putting that desire in our hearts to return it in the form of a request to Him. God promises to answer the prayer prayed in accordance to His will. The will of God is what you would want if you knew everything from God's viewpoint. The key to finding it is to abide in Christ. If you abide in Him (John 15:7), you will find that God will guide and direct your prayers, and you will be praying in the will of God.

We need to remember that prayer does not change the mind of God. Prayer is not overcoming God's reluctance; it is laying hold of God's will. God doesn't change. Yet He will do things when we pray that He will not do if we don't pray (James 4:2). Prayer affects what God does, but it doesn't change Him.

Take a look at some of these power-packed promises about prayer prayed in the will of God:

- **Matthew 7:7** – *"Ask, and it will be given to you; seek, and you will find; knock, and it will be opened to you."* In the original language, there's some ascending intensity in these verbs of *ask, seek,* and *knock*. It's like starting off with some politeness by asking. Then you get a little more aggressive by seeking. And then you're knocking on the door and not letting go, like Jacob, who wrestled with the Lord and refused to let go until He blessed him (Genesis 32:22-32).
- **Matthew 21:22** – *"And whatever you ask in prayer, you will receive, if you have faith."* God usually meets us at our level of expectancy. That's what faith is all about!
- **Mark 11:24** – *"Therefore I tell you, whatever you ask in prayer, believe that you have received it, and it will be yours."* Sometimes when we pray, we ought to thank God in advance for the answers to our prayers.
- **John 14:13-14** – *"Whatever you ask in my name, this I will do, that the Father may be glorified in the Son. If you ask me anything in my name, I will do it."*

> **"** Every prayer that you and I pray ought to be focused on one thing and one thing only – the will of God. **"**

NOTES

> **"The will of God is what you would want if you knew everything from God's viewpoint."**

Remember, the power of prayer doesn't flow from us. The power of prayer comes not from saying special words, praying in a certain position, or holding certain artifacts. The power of prayer comes from the omnipotent One who hears our prayers and answers them. Prayer is the hyperlink that connects us to His Almighty power.

God does answer prayer in response to faith, but sometimes God will still answer our prayers in spite of our own lack of faith. In Acts 12, the church was praying for Peter's release from prison (vs. 5), and God directly answered their prayer (vs. 7-11). Peter then went to the door of where the prayer meeting for him was taking place and knocked, but those who were praying refused, at first, to believe that it was really Peter! They prayed for him to be released, but deep down they didn't really expect God to answer their prayers.

God always answers

We need to keep in mind that God *always* answers prayer! But sometimes it's not answered exactly as we planned. Here are four ways God answers prayer:

1. Sometimes the answer is *direct*. That is, you pray and ask God for something and He gives it to you almost immediately. Has that ever happened to you? Recently, I prayed on a Saturday that God would send me a leader to start a specific ministry in our church. The next day, a couple came up to me after the service and said that they felt God drawing them to our church and if we ever need a volunteer to serve in this specific ministry, they would be happy to! I took that as a direct answer! And God has blessed us tremendously through them! Sometimes our prayers are answered so directly, it is the unmistakable hand of God.

2. Sometimes the answer is *different*. God doesn't give us what we ask for; He gives us something better than we ask! I'm so grateful God doesn't always answer our prayers the way we want Him to! If that were the case, I would have married the wrong woman three times! If God doesn't give you what you ask, He will give you something that is better for you.

3. Sometimes the answer is *denied*. God simply says "no" because what you're asking for is wrong. Perhaps to answer it may not help you, or it may create problems for someone else. He will not give you something that could harm or hurt you. God always has your best interests in mind (Romans 8:28).

4. Sometimes the answer is *delayed*. Quite simply, God wants for you what you want for yourself, but on a different timetable. That's why God's Word says that we are to keep on asking, keep on seeking, and keep on knocking. We must always remember that God's delays are not necessarily His denials. There are several examples in Scripture of how we are to persist in prayer. In Luke 18, Jesus told a parable about the persistent widow. She had a dispute with another person and could not get justice. So she kept coming to the judge repeatedly, over and over again, saying, *"Give me justice against my adversary!"* At first, the judge was unwilling, but later he said to himself, *"I will give her justice, so she doesn't wear me out by her persistent coming."* Then Jesus made this application: *"Will not God grant justice to His elect who cry out to Him day and night? Will He delay to help them?"* (Luke 18:7). Jesus isn't saying that God is like the unjust judge. The point is that this woman wouldn't stop asking! You find this pattern over and over again in the Bible (see also Luke 11:5-10).

Did you know that one of the largest veins of gold ever discovered in California was found only three feet from where the previous miners had stopped digging? Christians often experience the same problem. Many times we quit just before we receive God's greatest blessing. Charles Spurgeon said, "Prayer pulls the rope below, and the great bell rings above in the ears of God. Some scarcely stir the bell, for they pray so languidly; others give but an occasional pluck at the rope; but he who wins with heaven is the man who grasps the rope boldly and pulls continuously, with all his might."

Can you think of an example of how God has answered a prayer in one of these four ways for you? What did God teach you about Himself in how He answered?

_____

_____

_____

_____

_____

_____

_____

_____

_____

When it comes to prayer, when the idea is not right, God says, "No!" When you are not right, God says, "Grow." When the timing is not right, God says, "Slow." When everything is right, God says, "Go!"

When should you stop praying?

We've established the fact that God wants us to persist in prayer. It's the _"fervent prayer of the righteous man that accomplishes much"_ (James 5:16). But is there ever a time when you should stop praying about something? Let me give you two thoughts on this.

First, you can stop asking when although you don't have the answer in your hand, you do have the answer in your heart. There have been times when I've prayed about things before, and I have sensed God say, "Brandon, you are asking me to do something that I'm not going to do. But what you really need is _this_ and I have heard your prayer." I may not have had it in my hand, but I did have it in my heart.

Secondly, you stop asking when God says, "No." I think of the Apostle Paul for example. He had a health issue that he called "the thorn in his flesh." We don't know exactly what it was, but we don't need to know. Paul asked God three different times to take it away from him, but God answered, "No." Instead, God revealed this truth to Paul: _"My grace is sufficient for you, for my power is made perfect in weakness."_ What was Paul's response back to God? _"Therefore I will boast all the more gladly of my weaknesses, so that the power of Christ may rest upon me"_ (2 Corinthians 12:9). So why is prayer so powerful? According to the Bible, the power of prayer is, quite simply, the power of God who hears and answers prayer.

Prayer changes you and your perspective

Dr. Andrew Newberg of Thomas Jefferson Hospital has been studying the effect prayer has on the human brain for more than 20 years. He wanted to get a better understanding of why prayer showed a propensity to heal the human body when a person prayed. So he injected radioactive dye into his

NOTES _____

_____

_____

_____

_____

_____

_____

_____

_____

_____

_____

_____

_____

_____

_____

_____

_____

_____

_____

_____

_____

_____

_____

_____

_____

_____

_____

_____

_____

_____

_____

_____

_____

_____

_____

_____

> ❝What God does in us while we wait for Him to answer our prayers is just as important as what it is we're praying for.❞

subjects and watched what changed inside their heads when they pray. His results were pretty insightful. The area of the brain associated with the sense of self began to "shut down," according to Newburg. "You become connected to God. You become connected to the world," he said. "Your self sort of goes away." That's exactly what the Bible says prayer does for us.

Prayer has a way of not just changing your circumstances; it also changes us. What God does in us while we wait for Him to answer our prayers is just as important as what it is we're praying for. Waiting upon the Lord is not just something that we have to do until we get what we want. Waiting is part of the process of becoming what God wants us to be. He is teaching us to be dependent upon Him

When I was a teenager, I had a hammock on our back porch. I spent time every single evening on that hammock praying and dreaming about what God could do with a life fully devoted to Him. In *The Adventure of Prayer*, Catherine Marshall wrote, "Dreaming is praying." I think she's right. In my own experience, the more I pray, the more I dream. Dreaming is a form of praying, and praying is a form of dreaming. Catherine Marshall says, "There is no limit to what this combination of dreams and prayer can achieve."

It's been said that a change of *pace* plus a change of *place* can equal a change in *perspective*. Allow yourself time to *"be still and know that He is God,"* and He will begin to renew your perspective from His heavenly viewpoint. Luke 5:16 says that *"Jesus often withdrew to lonely places and prayed."* The word "often" means it was His habit. We need to spend time alone with God every day and cultivate this habit as well.

Confidence in the Father

It's been said that during the U.S. Civil War, Abraham Lincoln issued an order that for a certain time, no man was to go home on furlough. During that time, a young soldier made his way to the nation's capital to see the President, but no one would allow him access. The soldier said that his wife was dying and he wanted to go home to see her, but they still refused to allow his admission. As he turned away from the White House, he made his way down the street to a park bench, sat down, and began to sob uncontrollably. When a little boy who was walking by saw the soldier, he stopped and asked him what was wrong. He turned to the boy and said, "My wife is dying and I need a furlough to go and see her, but they won't allow me in to see the President." "Very well," said the boy, "You take my hand and I'll take you in. I'll get you to the President." The boy led him past the guards into the White House, past the secretaries, past all the other government officials. They walked hand in hand up the stairs all the way to door of the President's office. The guard at the door told the young boy, "The President is busy." But the little fellow was not to be put off. He yelled through the door, "Daddy, tell this man to let me come in!" Abraham Lincoln immediately dropped his pen and said to the officer, "Let him in." The boy, little Tad Lincoln, came in with his newfound friend and told the man's story. Immediately President Lincoln dipped his pen in the ink, signed an official order of furlough, and sent the man home.

I love that story because it illustrates the confidence that we have to get to God the Father through His Son Jesus Christ (Hebrews 10:19-22). Not only that, but because of Jesus, we are now adopted into God's family as sons and daughters of the King of Kings and the Lord of Lords. We have instant access into His presence at any time. What makes prayer so powerful is not the one offering the prayer but the One who has the power to answer.

When you pray, how confident are you that God is hearing your prayers? What Scriptural prayer promise did you read today that you need to cling to?

_____

_____

_____

_____

_____

_____

_____

_____

_____

NOTES _____

_____

_____

_____

_____

_____

_____

_____

_____

_____

_____

_____

_____

_____

_____

_____

_____

_____

_____

_____

_____

_____

_____

_____

_____

_____

Day 2
How Should I Pray?

vimeo.com/138214638

NOTES _____
_____
_____
_____
_____
_____
_____
_____
_____
_____
_____
_____
_____
_____
_____
_____
_____
_____
_____
_____
_____

In some ways, prayer is one of the most mysterious aspects of our walk with God. We wonder if God really hears our prayers, if our prayers have any bearing in our lives, what we should pray about, and how we should pray. Studying the Lord's Prayer helps us answer those questions.

Jesus was a continual source of amazement for His disciples. They watched and listened to everything He did. They witnessed Jesus take a boy's school lunch, and, after praying and blessing it, use it to feed five thousand people. They observed in awe how Jesus raised the dead to life, made the blind see, and the deaf hear. But one of the things that impressed the disciples the most was His ability to pray and be connected to His Heavenly Father. They noticed that Jesus' prayer life was intimate, relational, and supernatural! That's why they asked Jesus, *"Lord, teach us to pray."* If you feel like you're not where you want to be in your prayer life, you're in good company. The first followers of Jesus needed prayer guidance as well. In fact, the only tutorial they ever requested was on prayer. The disciples could have asked Jesus for instruction in a variety of topics such as preaching, teaching, or performing miracles, but they wanted to have the power in prayer they saw in Jesus.

Many people misunderstand the Lord's Prayer to be a prayer we are supposed to recite word for word, but this isn't a canned prayer. The disciples said, "Teach us to pray," not, "Teach us a prayer." It's only an example of how to pray and the things that should go into prayer – worship, trust in God, requests, confession of sin, prayers for protection, etc. We are to pray for these kinds of things while speaking to God in our own words. It's not a rote prayer; it's an outline of how we can communicate with God.

In Matthew 6:9-13, Jesus teaches us to include these things in our prayers: *"Our Father in heaven, hallowed be your name. Your kingdom come, your will be done, on earth as it is in heaven. Give us this day our daily bread, and forgive us our debts, as we also have forgiven our debtors. And lead us not into temptation, but deliver us from evil."*

The Lord's Prayer could really be called the "Disciple's Prayer." Notice that it can be divided into two categories. The first half deals with God's glory; the second half deals with our needs. Let's take this model prayer apart and look at it more in depth:

"Our Father in heaven ..."

We approach God on the basis of an intimate relationship. Only children can call their parent "Father." This word for Father is actually the word *Abba* in the original language, and it was a word of affection that a small child would use toward his father. It literally means "Daddy." This is the first time in the Bible you ever find this word used to describe God. Jesus invites us to approach God the way that a child approaches his or her daddy. You don't have to approach God with big churchy words or formalities. Let your prayer be natural. Don't put a steeple in your throat and act like you're speaking through stained glass. You come before Him as a child comes before a loving father. It's pretty awe-inspiring to think that the God who created the sun, moon, and stars is the same God we have the privilege of calling Daddy. Prayer is simply a heartfelt conversation between a loving Father and His child. I was talking to a new believer who felt intimidated when it came to her prayer life. "What if I say the wrong things? What if I pray in the wrong way?" The reality is, just as happy children cannot "mis-hug" their daddy, a believer cannot "mis-pray."

"Hallowed be your name ..."

Our prayers should include a time of worship, giving all that we know of ourselves to all that we know of Him. To "hallow" God's name means that we declare it is holy. You recognize that He is set apart. This opening line in the model prayer recognizes the fact that God is both our Father and our King. He loves us, and He is far greater than us. Prayer can be as ordinary as picking up the phone, but as awesome and incredible as discovering that Almighty God is on the other end of the call! It acknowledges our inability and God's ability. We come with empty hands but high hopes.

"Your kingdom come ..."

Before Jesus ascended back to Heaven, he said to His disciples, *"the Kingdom is within you"* (Luke 17:21). He was referring to the work of the Holy Spirit in the life of those who believe. To pray for His kingdom to come, you are asking His Spirit to dominate every part of you and for His purposes to come to fruition through your life. No matter what heartache or frustration you may have in your life today, when you pray "Your kingdom come," you are reorienting your attention to the fact that this world is not your home (John 18:36). Someday, in eternity, God will restore a new heaven and a new earth without all the effects of sin and suffering (Revelation 21). It's for *that* kingdom that we should live primarily. When we come to God in prayer, it's all about Him – not about us. What are His priorities for us? How does he want us to spend our money today? So many times we come to Him and think God is like a Divine vending machine – just say a prayer, and He will deliver it to you. God does want to answer your prayers, but first He wants you to come to Him with the realization that life is not about us, it's about Him. When we pray, we acknowledge that we are there to fulfill His priorities and seek His plans over ours.

"Your will be done on earth as it is in heaven ..."

You're saying, "God what you want is what I want, and I want you to use me so that the plans you have in Heaven will result here on earth." Nothing lies outside the reach of prayer except that which lies outside the will of God. John 15:7 says, *"If you remain in Me and My words remain in you, ask whatever you want and it will be done for you."* To "remain" or "abide" means to lean upon Jesus moment by moment. That verse can literally be translated, "If you are in living communion with Me, and my words are at home in your heart, I command you at once to ask for whatever you desire and it will be done for you." This is what the Bible calls "praying in the Spirit." We pray *to* the Father, *through* the Son, and *in* the Holy Spirit. So what is the purpose of prayer? It's for His kingdom to come and for His will to be done on this earth and in our lives. Prayer is not saying, "Dear God, please do for me what I want," but, "Please do in me, with me, and through me what you want."

NOTES

95

> **"If we do not allow prayer to drive sin out of our life, sin will drive prayer out of our life."**

"Give us this day our daily bread ..."

This is praying for your daily needs. In the first century, bread had to be made on a daily basis. They had to rely on God to provide for their needs one day at a time. When we pray, "Give us each day our daily bread," we are saying that we trust God as the source to supply all the physical needs of our lives, and we affirm that He will take care of everything we need. Philippians 4:19 says, *"My God shall supply all your needs according to His riches in glory in Christ Jesus."* What does it mean to supply it "according to His riches?" A millionaire may give you ten bucks *out* of his riches, but that's not *according* to His riches. As children of God, we can boldly and confidently come before God and say, "Lord, please meet the needs that I have in my life." Once you've acknowledged who God is, and you have aligned yourself with His agenda, you can now share with Him the desires of your heart. What do you want God to do for you? God is committed to providing for our needs, but we need to put His will and His desires first. When we make God's desires our desires, He will give us the desires of our heart (Psalm 37:4).

"And forgive us our debts ..."

Sin is like a debt that must be paid. Either Jesus pays for it or you do. Our greatest need is to be forgiven. Without God's forgiveness, we are dead in sin (Ephesians 2:1). With His forgiveness, we are made alive in Christ (Colossians 2:13). Every time you sin, you go into debt with God. You've taken on an obligation that you cannot possibly meet. It's like charging $100,000 to a credit card with a $1,000 limit when you only have a $1 bank balance. Sooner or later, the collection agency is going to come looking for you. Sin makes us overdrawn debtors to God (even after we become Christians). It breaks our fellowship with Him. Only confession and forgiveness can balance the books. Saying, "God I want to ask Your forgiveness for the sin in my life," ought to be a regular part of our prayer life. It's been said that the secret of all failure is our failure in secret prayer. If we do not allow prayer to drive sin out of our life, sin will drive prayer out of our life. The sinning man will stop praying, but the praying man will stop sinning. Disciples who aren't praying are straying.

"As we also have forgiven our debtors ..."

There's a condition that we have to meet in the Lord's Prayer. God forgives our debts to the extent that we also have forgiven our debtors. God expects that there be no grudges or unforgiveness in your heart towards others as you approach Him in prayer. Because we are forgiven, we are also called to forgive. This verse reminds us that it is wrong to ask from God what we are not willing to give to other people. Is there anyone who comes to mind right now who is in need of your forgiveness? Have you been holding someone captive by the grudge you've harbored in your own heart? Forgiveness is more for the person who has been offended than it is for the one who carried out the offense. It's not healthy spiritually or emotionally to hold a grudge. Bitterness is like drinking poison and waiting for the other person to die. When we fail to forgive someone, we set ourselves up as a higher judge than God Himself. Our relationship with God cannot be right if our relationship with others is not where it should be. You can confess your own sins until you're blue in the face, but if you're still holding a grudge or refusing forgiveness towards someone else, you're robbing yourself of the joy of fellowship with God.

"And do not lead us into temptation, but deliver us from evil."

There are temptations we face on a daily basis, but it's our submission to

NOTES

God that gives us the power and ability to avoid that temptation. You might be facing a temptation to do something or to put yourself in a situation that you know would not bring God glory. It's in those moments that we need to stop and pray, "God, give me Your power, Your supernatural ability to walk away from this temptation." In 1 Corinthians 10:13 God promises us that He will answer that prayer: *"...with the temptation, he will also provide a way of escape, that you may be able to endure it."*

As you look back over the model prayer Jesus gave to His disciples, what phrase or aspect of the Lord's Prayer is the most meaningful to you? Why?

_____

_____

_____

_____

_____

_____

_____

Follow the model

An unknown author put together this great summary of the Lord's Prayer:
I cannot say "our" if I live only for myself.
I cannot say, "Father" if I do not endeavor each day to act like His child.
I cannot say, "hallowed be your name" if I am playing around with sin.
I cannot say "your kingdom come" if I am not allowing God to reign in my life.
I cannot say "give us this day our daily bread" if I am trusting in myself
instead of in God's provision.
I cannot say, "Forgive us our sins" if I am nursing a grudge or withholding
forgiveness from someone else.
I cannot say, "lead us not into temptation" if I deliberately place myself in
its path.

In his book *Before Amen*, Max Lucado summarizes the main aspects of the Lord's Prayer in a simple, easy-to-remember pocket-sized outline:
Father, you are good.
I need help – heal me and forgive me.
They need help.
Thank you. In Jesus name, Amen.

Max Lucado says, "Let this prayer punctuate your day. As you begin your morning, 'Father, you are good.' As you commute to work or walk the hallways at school, 'I need help.' As you wait in the grocery line, 'They need help.' Keep this prayer in your pocket as you pass through the day."

Through the Lord's Prayer, Jesus taught us everything we need to know to develop a vital, intimate, and powerful prayer life. When we follow His model, we can be assured that nothing is coming in between us and God or keeping Him from hearing our prayers.

There's a big difference between air and breath. Air is all around us. It's presently bringing 14.7 pounds of pressure per square inch on our bodies. Though, only when you relax and let air in does it become breath. As with air, God surrounds us all the time. When you relax spiritually and let Christ into your thoughts, that's when they become prayer. I honestly believe that a lot

> ❝ The number one thing God wants to give you in response to your prayer is Himself! ❞

NOTES _____

_____

_____

_____

_____

_____

_____

_____

_____

_____

_____

_____

_____

_____

_____

_____

_____

> **"The number one thing God wants to give you in response to your prayer is Himself!"**

NOTES

of Christians miss incredible opportunities and blessings because they have taken a completely passive role in their prayer lives.

When it comes to prayer, more people are concerned with what they are praying for than with the One to Whom they are praying. We pray to God. Think not about your weakness but about His strength. It may be acceptable for a kid to give his dad a Christmas list of all that he wants, but if that's the only relationship they have, it's not a good one. Don't treat God like a Santa where the only time He hears from you is when you want something. Prayer is not a supernatural credit card, an opiate to tranquilize nervous Christians, or a magic wand to persuade God to do something. The number one thing God wants to give you in response to your prayer is Himself!

In *Living Faith*, Helen Roseveare wrote about a time when she was a missionary doctor in the Congo at a medical clinic and orphanage. One day, a mother died in labor, leaving behind a premature baby and a two-year-old girl. The facility at the clinic had no incubator or electricity. Dr. Roseveare's first task was to keep the baby warm. She sent a midwife to find a hot water bottle, but the nurse soon returned with bad news. The only bottle they possessed had burst when she filled it. It was their last one. A solution was not easily found. The clinic was in the heart of the jungle. Help was many miles away, and the life of a newborn child was in jeopardy. The following day, Helen mentioned the concern to the children of the orphanage. She told them of the frail baby and the sad sister, and the children prayed.

A ten-year-old girl named Ruth decided on her own to take her problem to Jesus. "Please, God, send us a hot water bottle. It'll be no good tomorrow, as the baby won't live another day, so please send it this afternoon. And, while You are about it, would You please send a dolly for the little girl who lost her mother so she'll know You really love her?"

The doctor was stunned. That prayer was so bold and so filled with faith, it could only be answered by a miracle.

Later that afternoon a twenty-two-pound package from back home was delivered to Helen's door. After nearly four years at the clinic, she had *never* received a single package. When she called the children to come and help her open it, she could feel the tears begin to well up in her eyes. Could it be? They pulled off the string and unwrapped the paper. In the box, they found bandages, jerseys, raisins ... and a brand new hot water bottle. And at the bottom of the box was a doll for the little girl. The box had been shipped five months earlier. God had heard and responded to that prayer months before it was even offered.

God wants your time of prayer to be your time of power. Before you face the world today, face your Father. He's looking forward to having a conversation with you.

What have you learned or been reminded of about prayer today?

_____

_____

_____

_____

Do you have any unanswered questions about prayer?

_____

_____

_____

_____

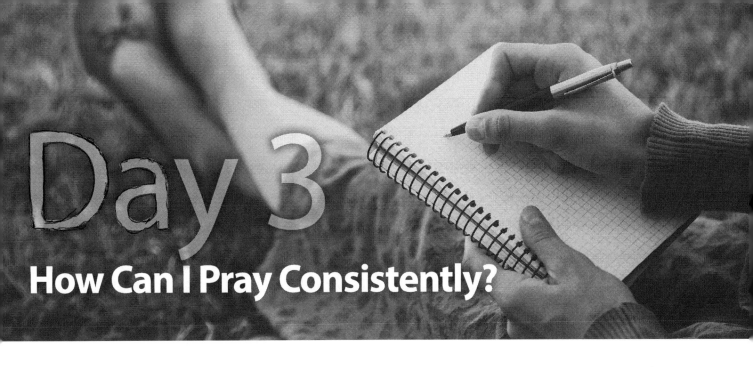

Day 3
How Can I Pray Consistently?

A little girl was watching her mother one night as she was rubbing cream onto her face. She said, "Mom, why do you do that?" She replied, "To make myself beautiful." This little girl kept watching as her mother began to remove the cream she had just put on and the girl said, "What's the matter, Mom, are you giving up already?"

I sometimes wonder if God looks at our puny, inconsistent, non-persistent prayer lives and asks, "Are you giving up already?"

Read what Jesus said about prayer in Matthew 7:7-11 (see pg. 100) and circle the three key words that spell the acrostic A.S.K.: Ask, Seek, Knock.

Based on this passage, what words would you use to describe the parent-heart of God?

_____

_____

_____

_____

_____

_____

There are basically four reasons why people don't pray:
1. A lot of people are not sure how to pray.
2. Many get bored or distracted when trying to pray.
3. Many think their requests are too small for God.
4. Many people are not sure their prayers will make a difference.

In my opinion, the best way to overcome these obstacles to prayer is through the practice of keeping a prayer journal. Journaling has been defined as "the recording of your thoughts today for the recollection of your past tomorrow." The great thing about keeping a prayer journal is that it helps you to overcome all of these obstacles, and I have found it to be the greatest tool that has helped me to keep a consistent and persistent prayer life. Keeping a prayer journal is a lot like writing letters to God. It gets rid of all the flowery phrases we think we have to say to "impress God," and it digs right down into the nitty gritty of bringing your needs, hopes, worries, and fears into the presence of God.

vimeo.com/138214730

NOTES _____

_____

_____

_____

_____

_____

_____

_____

_____

_____

_____

_____

_____

_____

_____

_____

_____

_____

_____

> **"** *⁷ Ask, and it will be given to you; seek, and you will find; knock, and it will be opened to you. ⁸ For everyone who asks receives, and the one who seeks finds, and to the one who knocks it will be opened. ⁹ Or which one of you, if his son asks him for bread, will give him a stone? ¹⁰ Or if he asks for a fish, will give him a serpent? ¹¹ If you then, who are evil, know how to give good gifts to your children, how much more will your Father who is in heaven give good things to those who ask him!* **"**
>
> *- Matthew 7:7-11*

Benefits of keeping a prayer journal

1. Having a prayer journal helps you stay balanced in your prayer life.
Some people use a simple notebook or journal to keep track of their prayer requests. For me, I use a three-ring binder with loose-leaf notebook paper. Then I have five dividers in my notebook to help me remember my five topics of prayer:

- Praise – written prayers for things I'm grateful for, answered prayers, etc.
- Family – what I'm asking God for concerning my wife and children
- Others – how I'm interceding for specific needs of church members, friends, missionaries, etc.
- Myself – my personal needs or concerns
- Goals – I keep my list of yearly goals in my prayer journal so I can ask for God's help to reach them.

One of the life principles I learned in Sunday school as a kid is that if you want to have J.O.Y. in your life, you need to put Jesus first, Others second, and Yourself last. By dividing my journal up in this way, it reminds me of what those priorities need to be. I also keep another section where I can just jot down a prayer to God, without having to think about what category I'm going to put it in.

2. Having a prayer journal gives you a record of God's faithfulness in answering your prayers.
I would suggest you use a blue or black pen to write down your prayers to God, and be as specific as possible. Then use a red pen to write down answers to prayer or whatever you sense God wants you to do as you pray about that need. (Sometimes God is waiting on us to be the answer to our own prayer.)

It's such an awesome blessing to have a written record of "proof" that God really does hear you when you pray. Having a hard copy of your prayers before God is evidence of that.

3. Having a prayer journal keeps you consistent in having a prayer time.
Every day, make a decision to write something down in your journal and pray about that. Just by opening it up, you'll also be reminded to pray about other things that are in there as well.

4. Having a prayer journal keeps you from being distracted in your prayer time.
This has been my biggest struggle with my prayer life. I have a mild case of Attention Deficit Disorder, so my mind tends to wander when I pray. The benefit of prayer journaling is that it keeps the task at hand literally *at your hand*. Writing out your prayers takes a little longer than just "thinking" them, but as you're writing, at least that time is actually spent in prayer.

5. Having a prayer journal can help you lay your burdens down before the Lord.
Every once in a while, there's something that bothers me and occupies my thinking so much that I need to do something to get it off my chest. There's something about writing it down that enables me to lay that burden down at the feet of Jesus.

I keep a small decorative box on my desk that I call my Trusting God Box. Whenever I have something that is occupying my mind and my thinking, and I just can't stop worrying about it, I write it down on a piece of paper and place it inside this box. It's a simple act where I'm acknowledging that I am trusting God with this detail of my life, and I cannot allow it to consume my thoughts or worries any longer. When I place it in the box, I am laying it down before God. But here's the catch: if I find myself continuing to dwell on and struggle with worry with that same issue, I must remove that piece of paper out of the Trusting God Box because that shows exactly what I've done. I've stopped trusting God to handle that issue in my life.

Jesus gave us an awesome promise in His Word. In Matthew 11:28, He said, *"Come to Me, all who are weary and heavy burdened, and I will give you rest."* Journaling your prayers to God is just one way to physically and symbolically transfer that burden.

6. Having a prayer journal will serve as a diary of your spiritual growth.

If you're like me, you probably have a hard time remembering what you had for breakfast this morning, let alone trying to remember what God was doing in your life six months ago. The weakest ink is still better than the best memory. Dozens of times throughout the Bible, we find Scripture replete with this simple command: "Remember!" "Do not forget what the Lord has done for you!" Journaling helps chronicle the work of God in your life, and your faith grows when you see just how faithful He has been to you!

7. Having a prayer journal will cause you to spend more time in prayer and see God at work in your life.

Praying almost becomes an addiction! Especially when you see God working in and through you. Sometimes I'll be sharing with someone how God answered a prayer in such a specific way, and it's hard to believe that it really happened, but when I can point back to that request in my prayer journal, it not only builds my faith but theirs as well.

Have you ever thought about keeping track of your prayer requests and answers to prayer? How might this habit benefit your prayer life?

_____

_____

_____

_____

Never give up

I think if there was one person who could talk about the power of prayer, it would be George Mueller. In the 1800's, Mueller testified that in his lifetime, 50,000 specific prayers were answered. Years before he died, about the middle of his career, he affirmed that up to that time 5,000 of his definite prayers had been answered on the day of asking. He made it a habit to keep a notebook with two-page entries. On one page he gave the request and the date, and on the opposite page he entered the date of the answer. By keeping a prayer journal, he was able to keep a record of definite petitions and their specific answers, and he recommended this as a tool to other believers who desired specific results to their prayers.

God called Mueller to establish many Christian orphanages, but he never asked for money or for donors to finance his work. He believed in praying for his needs and asking God to provide. One day, the housemother of the orphanage informed him that the children were dressed and ready for school but there was no food for them to eat. George asked her to take the 300 kids into the dining room and have them sit at tables. He then said a prayer to give God thanks for the food. Then they waited. George knew that God would provide for the children as he always did. Within minutes, a baker knocked on the door. "Mr. Mueller," he said, "last night I could not sleep. Somehow

> **"** *Come to me, all who labor and are heavy laden, and I will give you rest.* **"**
> - Matthew 11:28

NOTES _____

> **"When you pray, you have a Father who will hear you and a King who will answer you."**

NOTES _____

I knew that you would need bread this morning. I got up and baked three batches for you. I will bring it in."

Soon there was another knock at the door. It was the milkman. His cart had broken down in front of the orphanage. The milk would spoil by the time he would be able to get the cart repaired, so he asked George if he could use some free milk. George was smiling from ear to ear as the milkman brought in 10 large canisters of milk. It was just enough for the 300 thirsty children.

George said, "I live in the spirit of prayer. I pray as I walk about, when I lie down and when I rise up. And the answers are always coming. Thousands and tens of thousands of times have my prayers been answered. When once I am persuaded that a thing is right and for the glory of God, I go on praying for it until the answer comes. George Mueller never gives up!"

Assurance of answered prayer

So what is the assurance that God is going to hear and answer us? God answers that for us in Matthew 7:9-11: *"What man among you, if his son asks him for bread, will give him a stone? Or if he asks for a fish, will give him a snake? If you then, who are evil, know how to give good gifts to your children, how much more will your Father in heaven give good things to those who ask Him!"*

Based on those verses, there are at least three reasons we know we can have the assurance of answered prayer:

1. Because God is good. I'm a parent, and I know how much I love my own children and how I enjoy blessing them and providing for their needs. Yet I have a sinful human nature. I'm far from perfect. Jesus said if we who are evil know how to give good gifts to our own kids, how much more does our Heavenly Father, who is perfect, desire to bless us and hear us when we pray.

2. Because God knows what we need. He is wise enough to know what's best for us. If we ask for a fish, Jesus says He's not going to give us a snake. No loving parent would do that. One of my favorite verses is Psalm 84:11, which says, *"The Lord thy God is a sun and a shield. The Lord will give grace and glory. No good thing will He withhold from them who walk uprightly."* He is too wise to make a mistake, and He withholds no good thing for those who walk with Him.

3. Because God is able. Notice how verse 11 says that He is our Father *"in heaven."* Think about it. Your *Father* is the Creator and the *King* of all Kings! When you pray, you have a Father who will hear you and a King who will answer you. When you pray, you have the *sympathy* of a Father and the *sovereignty* of a King.

Begin today *asking, seeking,* and *knocking* on the door of Heaven! Remember you are on Jesus' prayer list (John 17). He knows you by name, and He calls you by name. The Lord God is waiting to hear from you!

What do you need to pray about today? What's the biggest burden on your heart?

_____

_____

_____

_____

_____

Day 4

How Does God Talk to Us?

vimeo.com/138214785

Prayer is not a monologue; it's a dialogue. It can be frustrating because we sometimes feel like prayer is a one-sided conversation. Have you ever gotten yourself into a difficult situation where you just pleaded with God and said, "Lord, just tell me what I need to do!" When we think of people hearing from God, the image that pops into most people's minds is that of hearing a deep audible voice from the clouds, but that's not how God speaks.

One of the most basic claims of Christianity is that God speaks to people. You find these phrases all throughout the pages of the Bible: "And God said ..." and "The word of the Lord came ..." God does want to have a relationship with you, and there is no real relationship without communication.

Prayer is you talking to God. Listening is waiting for God to talk to you. Jesus said, *"He who has an ear, let him hear."* In order for you to hear from Him, you must be tuned in to His voice. There's a difference between hearing and listening. Listening is *wanting* to hear. You have to listen *for* God before you can listen *to* God. If you are going to hear God's voice and recognize it, you must be listening for Him.

The problem with hearing God's voice is not an external problem; it's an internal problem. Isaiah 6:9 says, *"They kept on hearing but did not understand. They kept on seeing but did not perceive."* Hearing from God is not something mystical. In fact, one of the proofs that you know Jesus Christ is that you hear His voice. John 10:27 says, *"My sheep hear My voice, and I know them, and they follow Me."* A lot of people know *about* God but they don't really *know* God. Since Christianity is a relationship, not a religion, we need to learn how to hear and recognize His voice.

Here are five of the most common ways God speaks to us:

God speaks through Scripture.

In 2 Timothy 3:16 we read, *"All Scripture is given by the inspiration of God and is useful for teaching, rebuking, correcting and training in righteousness, so that the servant of God may be thoroughly equipped for every good work."*
Notice that word "inspiration." It literally means, "God breathed." The Word of God is pulsating with power. It can be counted on. It will guide you, correct you, comfort you, and help you. So if we don't continue to expose ourselves to the Bible on a daily basis, we're missing out on the number one way God wants to talk to you.

If you're not reading the Bible, your phone is off the hook. God's getting the busy signal and He can't get through to you.

Scripture says the Bible is living and active and useful in all kinds of

NOTES

> **"Prayer is not a monologue; it's a dialogue."**

ways. Notice what sticks out to you when you read. What words resonate deep within your soul? This might be how God is speaking to you.

God speaks through impressions.

In other words, He puts ideas in our minds. Every once in a while, we feel inspired, and God gives us a creative idea. Where do you think that creative idea came from? It came from the Creator! Rick Warren says, "When God puts an idea in your mind we call it an inspiration. When the devil puts an idea in your mind we call that a temptation."

Scripture says that God has given us the Holy Spirit to be our counselor and guide. John 14:26 reads, *"The Holy Spirit will be your teacher and will bring to your mind all that I have said to you."* The Holy Spirit does for me internally all that Jesus did for me externally. Notice that phrase *"bring to your mind."* It's the Holy Spirit that gives us those impressions, ideas, hunches, or gut feelings. Some of your most brilliant ideas weren't yours. They were God's.

Now please understand that not every idea or impression you get comes from God. You need to test it first. 1 John 4:1 says, *"Do not believe every spirit but test the spirits to see whether they are from God."* The Bible says we need to learn to distinguish God's voice and figure out if it's really God or not. Here are six ways you can test an impression. To help you remember them, I've use the acrostic **S.P.E.A.K.S.**:

S - Scripture – *Does it agree with the Bible?*

Hebrews 4:12 says, *"For the word of God is living and active, sharper than any two-edged sword, piercing to the division of soul and of spirit, of joints and of marrow, and discerning the thoughts and intentions of the heart."* God will never tell you to violate anything in this Book. Never. God will never tell you to ignore or disobey anything in this Book. God's voice is absolutely always consistent with His Word. The Bible tells us very clearly, "Pay your taxes," so God is not going to give you the impression to lie or cheat on your taxes. Most of God's will for your life is already right here in the Bible. You don't even have to pray about it. Just do what it says.

P - Peace – *Do I sense God's peace about it?*

In 1 Corinthians 14:33 we read, *"God is not the author of confusion."* At the time of this writing, my wife and I had the opportunity to purchase our "dream home." On paper, it seemed like the perfect fit for us. It was right in our price range. But as we toured the home and prepared to make an offer, we both felt a very distinct lack of peace in making that decision.

So if you're feeling confused, that confusion is not coming from God. It may be coming from yourself or other people, but it's not coming from God. If you feel pressured and overwhelmed and driven to make a hasty decision, a major decision in life, and you're very pressured to make it, you need to question it. That's not the way God works. There's not one single example in the Bible where God says, "Rush!" to a major decision. Colossians 3:15 says, *"Let the peace of God rule in your hearts."* That word "rule" literally means, "umpire." In other words, we are to allow the peace of God to umpire, to call the shots in our life. If God is genuinely speaking to you, and you think this idea is from God, it's going to bring peace to your heart if you follow it. God's Spirit produces a calm spirit.

E - Encourage – *Do my Christian friends confirm it?*

God never meant for you to make a major decision in life on your own. He wants you to get help and advice from wise, mature Christians, other believers who are grounded in the faith and have a little more Bible under their belt than you might have. Ephesians 3:10 says, *"God's intent is that through the church the manifold wisdom of God should be made known."* If God has genuinely spoken to you, He's going to confirm it with other believers. Proverbs 11:14 says, *"Where no counsel is, the people fall: but in the multitude of counselors there is safety."* You need to get people who love you enough to level with you.

A - Area of Responsibility – *Does it concern my responsibility?*

If it's not your responsibility, why would God talk to you about it? God will reveal His will to you for your life, not necessarily for someone else's life. Romans 14:10-12 says, *"We will all be judged one day not by each other's standards or even by our own, but by the judgment of God. It is God alone that we shall have to answer for our actions."* A lot of well-meaning (albeit presumptuous) Christians have done a lot of damage because they thought that God was talking to them about what somebody else should do. Now God certainly does want to use others to communicate His will to us, but God will often use that word to confirm what He's already saying to us in our heart.

K - Kind – *Is it convicting rather than condemning?*

Conviction is the voice of God; condemnation is the voice of the devil. What's the difference? Conviction points the way to change; condemnation just makes you feel like a very bad person. When God convicts you of sin, it's always something very specific. God says, "Here's an attitude, behavior, or something else in your life that needs changing." When Satan condemns you, he makes you feel like a loser in general. Satan will try to tell you, "You're a worthless person. You stink. God could never use you. Forget ever trying to live the Christian life." Revelation 12:10 says that Satan is the *"accuser of the brethren."*

S - Sharpening – *Does it make me more like Christ?*

Jesus is the standard by which we measure everything we do. God says very clearly in the Bible that His goal for your life is to make you more like Jesus. James 3:14,17 says, *"If you harbor envy and selfish ambition, such wisdom does not come from heaven ... the wisdom that comes from God is pure, peace loving, considerate, submissive, full of mercy, impartial, and sincere."*

Let me just pause here and say that I've seen some people do some pretty stupid things because they thought God told them to do something. Then when God didn't bless what they did, they wondered what happened and became upset with God. The problem was not that God fooled them. The problem was that they really didn't hear His voice and charged off with their own agenda instead. God's communication to us is personal, understandable, specific, and reliable.

You need to remember that when God is speaking to you, He will almost always use more than one of these other channels to communicate with you, and the message will be consistent in all of them.

Review the S.P.E.A.K.S. acrostic and write down the six ways you can test an impression:

_____

_____

_____

_____

_____

_____

_____

> " If God is genuinely speaking to you, and you think this idea is from God, it's going to bring peace to your heart if you follow it. "

NOTES _____

_____

_____

_____

_____

_____

_____

_____

_____

_____

_____

_____

_____

_____

_____

_____

_____

NOTES

God speaks through other people.

There are two types of people you want to listen to, as they are the ones God often uses the most to speak to us. They are godly Christians and gifted teachers.

Godly Christians. Your LifeCoach is one of those people for you! Has there ever been a time in your life when another godly Christian gave you a word of counsel that resulted in a major turning point in your life? We can be the conduits that God uses to speak to other people. As you continue to grow in Christ, God will often speak through you to others without you ever even knowing it. He has the ability to get into your mind without you even thinking about it. God plants those ideas that are communicated.

Gifted Teachers. Have you ever sat in a church service and felt like God was speaking directly to your heart? He was. God often uses other people to share His word with us and to help us apply it to our lives. In 1 Thessalonians 2:13, Paul says, *"For this reason we also constantly thank God that when you received the word of God which you heard from us, you accepted it not as the word of men, but for what it really is, the word of God, which also performs its work in you who believe."* God speaks through teachers, communicators, and pastors, and it changes our lives when we listen to them. That's why I hate to miss church. I think to myself, "What if God had that pastor prepare that message directly for me, and what if I miss it?" I don't ever want to miss God talking to me. I want to show up whenever I can. The more teaching that you hear, the more God will have the opportunity to speak to you.

God speaks to us through special circumstances.

God can speak to you through *painful circumstances*. Are you familiar with this one? It's been said that we don't change when we see the light; we change when we feel the heat. We fear change, and we don't change until the pain of staying the same becomes greater than the fear of change. God sometimes uses painful experiences to get our attention redirected back to Him. Perhaps He has tried to communicate with you in other ways, but you were too distracted to listen. Pain can become our best hearing aid to listen to the voice of God. God whispers to us in our pleasures, but he shouts to us in our pain. It's God's megaphone. Proverbs 20:30 says, *"Blows and wounds scrub away evil, and beatings purge the inmost being."*

God can speak to you through *open and closed doors*. When talking about hearing from God in special circumstances, we often use the analogy of a door. Sometimes you hear people say things like, "God, open the door for us to move there," or, "God, please close the doors to all schools you don't want me to go to." This works especially well when God has something specific in mind for us to do. If there's a job he wants you to take, it may be the only option left. Or if he wants you to go to a certain school, he may provide a generous scholarship to aid in your decision. But God's voice through circumstances doesn't always come in the form of doors opening and closing. Sometimes it's more subtle than that.

God can speak to your through *confirmations*. Sometimes there are smaller, less definitive circumstances that point us in a direction. Pay attention to the things you're seeing and hearing. What are they discussing at church or in your small group? What events are unfolding around you? Those can often be a way of hearing God's voice even when it doesn't come in the form of a door slamming or swinging wide open.

God speaks through dreams and visions.

I share this last one reluctantly because we need to exercise great caution here. However, we can't ignore the fact that this does seem to be a way that God communicated to individuals in the Bible. Joel 2:28-31 says, *"And it shall come to pass afterward, that I will pour out my spirit upon all flesh; and your sons and your daughters shall prophesy, your old men shall dream dreams, your young men shall see visions."*

Job 33:14-16 says, *"For God speaks in one way, and in two, though man does not perceive it. In a dream, in a vision of the night, when deep sleep falls on men, while they slumber on their beds, then he opens the ears of men and terrifies them with warnings."*

Why would God speak to us when we're asleep? It could be because we're relaxed, not distracted, and our defenses are lowered at that moment. Many times as I'm falling asleep, I'll ask God a question. I'll say something like, "Lord, what do you want me to do about this specific situation?" Then I'll go to sleep. Most of the time, I don't get any answer at all this way. But sometimes I do. It's up to how God wants to reveal that to me. Sometimes I'll pray and ask God to show me His next step for my life. Then when I wake up, I've got the plan all there! It just comes together.

When it comes to listening to the Lord, pray and ask God a question, but then make yourself available to sit in silence and give Him the opportunity to speak. Open up the pages of Scripture. Sit in silence before God. And when you do, you'll find that the antenna of your heart is tuning into the station of God's Holy Spirit, and you will hear His voice.

Based on what you read today, what are some of the channels that God can use to speak to you?

_____

_____

_____

_____

_____

_____

_____

_____

Do you have any questions or additional insights about today's study?

_____

_____

_____

_____

_____

_____

_____

_____

NOTES

Day 5

How Can I Listen to God's Voice?

vimeo.com/138214869

NOTES _____
_____
_____
_____
_____
_____
_____
_____
_____
_____
_____
_____
_____
_____
_____
_____
_____
_____
_____
_____
_____

Psalm 46:10 says, *"Be still and know that I am God."* God speaks louder to us when we get quiet. It is that inner calm that opens up the intercom to God so that you can hear His voice. Mother Theresa said, "In the silence of the heart God speaks. If you face God in prayer and silence, God will speak to you. Then you will know that you are nothing. It is only when you realize your nothingness, your emptiness that God can fill you with Himself. Souls of prayer are souls of great silence."

Whenever I'm talking, I'm not listening. You may have heard the saying: God gave us two ears and one mouth for a reason. It's because we should listen twice as much as we speak. When you are dealing with a situation in which you need God's wisdom, you need to be silent in prayer and let your spirit pick up on what the Holy Spirit wants to say to you. Psalm 62:1 says, *"My soul waits in silence for God only; from Him is my salvation."* David wrote this when he was in a time of stress and major distress. He knew only God could meet and satisfy his deepest needs. I wonder if you feel that way today.

To hear from God is not that difficult. The problem is that our lives are so full of distractions that we never take the time to get quiet before Him. You need to ask yourself, "Is the ambient noise level of my life low enough for me to hear the whispers of the Lord?"

Why do you think it is so difficult for people to hear God's voice today?

_____
_____
_____
_____
_____
_____
_____
_____
_____

Listen expectantly

We know that God is listening to us, but are we listening to Him? If you're like 95% of all Christians, your prayer time is almost always you doing all the talking with God doing all the listening. But there is another way to pray altogether. It is prayer where we talk very little while God speaks volumes.

Maybe you're facing an issue in your life where you need guidance: "Lord, should I be dating this person?" "Should I change jobs?" "How do I deal with my children in these circumstances?" "Should I make this investment or not?"

God is interested in every detail of your life. In fact, He's more interested in the details of your life because He made you. So don't you ever insult God by thinking, "Oh I can't pray about that ... it's something so small, God wouldn't care about it." He's far more interested than you think He is. So when you're looking for guidance from God, ask a specific question. The more specific you ask, the more God is able to answer it. When I pray, I often say things like: "God, what do you think about ...?" "What should I do here?" "How do I do it?"

Over 20 times in the New Testament, God commands us to "Ask!" We need to believe He wants to answer. James 1:5-6 in the Living Bible, puts it this way: *"If you want to know what God wants you to do, ask him, and he will gladly tell you, for he is always ready to give a bountiful supply of wisdom to all who ask him; he will not resent it. But when you ask him, be sure that you really expect him to tell you ..."* Notice that word "expect." When you expect answers to your prayers, you *really* pray. And when you *really* pray, you *really* get answers!

In two places at once

Ephesians 2:6 totally transformed my prayer life. It says, *"And God raised us up with Christ and seated us with Him in the heavenly realms with Christ Jesus."*

Now, let's do some inductive Bible study and ask some questions.

Who is the "us" in this passage? That's you and me! It encompasses all believers.

What does this verse say we are doing? We are sitting.

What do you have to possess to be sitting? A chair.

Now let's get real practical. Where are all of these believers sitting? It says that we're seated with Christ in the Heavenly realms. So if I'm still here on this earth serving Jesus, how can I be seated with Him in heaven? This is where it gets really fun. The Bible tells us that our greatest source of strength and victory is recognizing how very close to Him we actually are!

I want you to picture heaven as having an enormous throne. Jesus is seated on that throne, and He is praying and interceding to the Father on behalf of all of us. Around that huge throne are all of these rows of chairs, but out of all of those chairs, there's one chair with your name on it. Now don't rush past the implications of what this verse is saying: *There's a chair in heaven in the front row at the throne room of God, and it's your chair!* Because your spirit is linked to God's spirit, you can go to that chair any time you want. You can sit at His feet, feel His embrace, and hear His voice any time you want. All you need to do is sit in that chair.

Think of it this way. If you have a smartphone, you probably have FaceTime or Skype. When I'm traveling, I love FaceTime because I can be in another country at night and yet be able to talk with my wife and kids face to face while they're eating breakfast that morning. It enables me to be two places at the same time. Well, God had this figured out long before Apple or Google ever discovered it. Prayer enables you to be in two places at the same time. When we pray, we are seated with Christ in the heavenly places.

When you go to pray, where do you see yourself? Do you pray upwards, hoping your prayers make it above the light bulbs? Or do you pray with an understanding that you are next to God, hearing His heartbeat and seeing things from His point of view?

> " Is the ambient noise level of my life low enough for me to hear the whispers of the Lord? "

NOTES

> **"There's a chair in heaven in the front row at the throne room of God, and it's your chair!"**

NOTES

How does picturing yourself seated with Christ in Heaven change your perspective about prayer?

Habakkuk's prayers

Habakkuk was struggling with a lot of things in his relationship with God. In Habakkuk chapter 1, he asks God six specific questions. Then in chapter 2, he waits and listens to God answer, and he writes down what he hears.

Habakkuk 2:1-2 says, *"I will climb up to my watchtower and stand at my guardpost. There I will wait to see what the LORD says and how he will answer my complaint. Then the LORD said to me, 'Write my answer plainly on tablets, so that a runner can carry the correct message to others.'"*

The first thing Habakkuk said was *"I will climb my watchtower."* That's a Hebrew expression that basically means, "I'm going to get alone with God. I'm going to find a place where I can eliminate distractions so that I can hear God speak." The reality is, we can't hear the still small voice of God as long as the radio is on, the TV is on, and your cell phone is always giving you notifications.

Next Habakkuk says, *"... I will stand at my guardpost. There I will wait to see what the LORD says ..."* Habakkuk was saying, "Lord, I'm not going to move until you move! I'm not leaving this guardpost until I know that You have revealed Yourself to me." God speaks to the person who takes time to listen. It's been said that hurry is the death of prayer.

Habakkuk then says, *"I will look out to see what He will say to me."* Why does the Bible say, "look"? It seems like it would make more sense to say, "I will listen to what God says." An important key to hearing God is to understand that God's voice is often visual. God often wants to speak to you through a mental picture. We see a lot of examples in Scripture where people were praying and God gave those people a mental picture, an image, or a vision inside of someone's head. I think that may be the reason why Jesus says several times, *"Watch and pray."* God created most of us to be visual thinkers. When we read a book, we don't just read the story, we see the story unfolding in our minds like a movie. God often speaks to us by giving us an image, a visual in our mind's eye.

The last thing that Habakkuk says in this passage is: *"The LORD gave me this answer, 'Write down clearly what I reveal to you.'"* Habakkuk writes down his prayers to God as well as God's answers back to him. One of the best personal practices I've ever developed is keeping a prayer journal. It's nothing elaborate, just a simple three-ring binder where I can write down my prayers, what God is saying to me as I pray, and how God is answering those prayers. The benefits of doing this is that it keeps my prayer life focused, and it allows me to remember what I've said to God and what God has said back to me.

Wow. Now. How.

My friend, Dan Southerland wrote a book entitled *Chair Time: A Simple Life Changing Way to Pray.* He provides a simple outline for how to pray and listen to God using three simple words: Wow – Now – How.

Wow. This is coming before God and celebrating what Jesus has done for you. Picture yourself coming into God's presence and taking your personalized chair in the front row of the throne room of God. I pray something like this: "Heavenly Father, I am totally wowed and awed by all that you have done for me. You saved me, and you're still working on me to make me more like you! Thank you for allowing me to partner with you in your Kingdom work. I am totally wowed by who You are!" Scripture tells us that the fastest way to enter into His presence is through praise and thanksgiving (Psalm 100:4). So if you're going to take your chair in the throne room of God, you can't help but use some "wow" words!

Now. This is when I shift from speaking words of "wow" to keeping a worshipping attitude going on in my heart. "Now I'm here in this moment, Jesus, to hear from You. I'm going to be silent. I'm going to listen. Now I ask you to speak. Help me to hear You if there's something You need to say to me."

How. How comes after I have heard God speak. The focus of my "how" time is, "Lord, what do You want me to do about this?" This could end in one of two ways. Some days I simply say, "Lord, I didn't hear anything from You today ... but I'm still so wowed by You, and I still enjoyed being with You in Your presence. Lord, help me be open to You today if there's something You want to speak to me about." God doesn't answer or speak every time. Some days I sense in my spirit that God does have the answer, but it's not the right time for Him to tell me in that moment.

Other days, I might pray, "Lord, thank you for speaking to me today and helping me to hear Your voice. I want to apply what you said, so please show me what to do about what I heard from You. You promised to give me wisdom when I ask for it (James 1:5). I will be listening. Give me a chance to apply this truth today, and I will obey you."

I've got a confession to make. I used to be bored to death with the idea of prayer. I used to picture my prayers as a one-sided conversation with God. I never really expected an answer. All of that changed when I learned this discipline of not just speaking to God, but waiting in His presence to hear His voice. Christianity is a relationship, and if you're in a relationship where you are the only one who is doing all the talking, it's not a relationship!

Describe a time when you felt like God was speaking to your heart. What was it like to hear His voice?

_____

_____

_____

_____

_____

_____

_____

NOTES _____

WORSHIP

week 5

Day 1 How Can I Live a Lifestyle of Worship?

Day 2 How Can I Be Filled with the Holy Spirit?

Day 3 What Is the Power of Praise and Worship?

Day 4 How Can I Increase My Faith?

Day 5 How Can I Grow in My Generosity?

Day 1

How Can I Live a Lifestyle of Worship?

vimeo.com/138214938

NOTES
_____
_____
_____
_____
_____
_____
_____
_____
_____
_____
_____
_____
_____
_____
_____
_____
_____
_____
_____
_____
_____
_____
_____
_____

Worship is giving all that I am to all that He is. It isn't something that just happens in a church service on Sunday; it's something that encompasses everything we do and everything we are throughout the week. Worship is not an event; it's a lifestyle. I believe that we have been wired from the start to live lives for worship – lives that are billboards for the greatness and glory of God. He doesn't want just a place in your life. He demands and deserves preeminence. God's throne is not a duplex.

I don't know whether or not you would consider yourself a worshipping kind of person, but you cannot help but worship *something*. It's what you were made to do. If for some reason you choose not to give God what He desires, you'll still worship something. You'll exchange worship of the Creator for something He has created. That "thing" might be a relationship. A dream. Friends. Status. Money. Success. Some kind of pleasure. It's worship because you are admitting that a person, a thing, or an experience is what matters most to you. It's the thing you put first in your life; it's whatever is worth most to you. As a result, worship determines our actions and becomes the driving force behind all we do.

In other words, whatever you worship you become. You can worship whatever you want, but there will always be a last twist to the story: Whatever you worship you become obsessed with, whatever you become obsessed with you imitate, and whatever you imitate you become. If you worship money, you will become greedy at the core of your heart. If you worship a sinful habit, that sin will grip your soul and poison your character. We become what we worship. So if you don't like the person you're becoming, take a quick inventory of the things that are on the throne of your heart.

Body, soul, and spirit

In week two, we looked at how God is a Trinity: Father, Son, and Holy Spirit. In a sense, God made us to be triune in our nature as well because the Bible says that God created man in his own image (Genesis 1:27), and you would expect to see the same nature of the Father in His children. So we too have a threefold nature: body, soul, and spirit.

The Bible talks about your triune nature of body, soul, and spirit in two places:
- 1 Thessalonians 5:23 – *"Now may the God of peace Himself sanctify you completely. And may your spirit, soul, and body be kept sound and blameless for the coming of our Lord Jesus Christ."*
- Hebrews 4:12 – *"For the word of God is living and active, sharper than any two-edged sword, piercing to the division of soul and of spirit, of joints and of marrow, and discerning the thoughts and*

intentions of the heart."

- Dr. Clarence Larkin developed a chart to help us visualize how your human nature consists of three parts:

THE THREEFOLD NATURE OF MAN

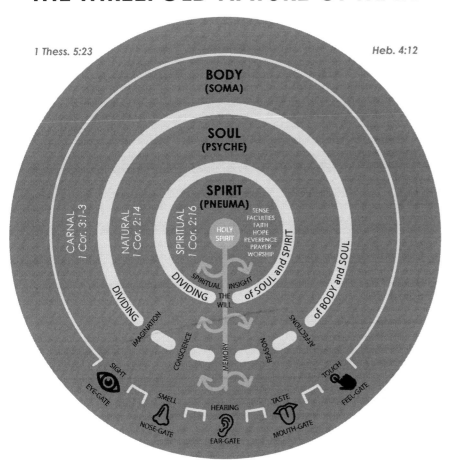

1 Thess. 5:23   *Heb. 4:12*

> **"** Worship is giving all that I am to all that He is. **"**

NOTES _____

1. You have a spirit. This is that part of your nature that was dead before you came to know Christ. When you made the decision to believe and receive Jesus as your personal Lord and Savior, your spirit came alive and you were "born again." Your spirit is that part of your nature that gives you the ability to connect with God. It's the Holy Spirit that has come to live and dwell within you! Sometimes we talk as if our soul is the part of us that is made new at salvation. We say things like, "Jesus saved my soul." Well, if you want to get real technical, the aspect of your nature that is made immediately new when you become a Christian is your spirit.

2. You have a soul. This is the part of your nature that gives you your personality or your personhood. It's comprised of your intellect, your emotions, and your will. It's what makes you the wonderful person that you are! However, your soul has been damaged and scarred with your own sin, as well as the sins of others, and by the environment of the sinful world in which you live.

3. You have a body. This is the most obvious, but it's the part of your nature that gives you the ability to communicate with your environment.

> ❝Worship is when your spirit connects with His spirit through the Holy Spirit.❞

NOTES

The gateways that you use to communicate with your world involve your five senses: touch, taste, see, smell, and hear.

That's the order through which God works in our lives – spirit to soul to body. The order of that is important. Your spirit is the only thing about your nature that's perfect because that's actually the person of the Holy Spirit residing in you beginning at the point of your salvation. Once grabbed hold of by the Holy Spirit, the human spirit changes the nature of your soul. The Bible calls this sanctification, the process of God making you more and more like Jesus. As the soul is improved on the inside, the soul dictates how the body should act and therefore changes how the body reacts on the outside. So if you want to change what happens in the body, you have to first change the nature of the soul. But in order to change the nature of the soul, you've got to be influenced by the dominance of the Spirit.

Worship by seeking the Spirit.

Jesus said, *"Yet a time is coming and has now come when the true worshipers will worship the Father in spirit and truth, for they are the kind of worshipers the Father seeks. God is spirit, and those who worship Him must worship in spirit and truth"* (John 4:23-24). Simply put, until the Holy Spirit of God comes into your human spirit, with the birth of new spiritual life, your spirit is so dead it cannot worship God. You cannot worship God unless your human spirit has been made alive by the Holy Spirit.

Jesus said true worship takes place in your spirit. So why is that important? To worship God, you have to worship Him with your body, but many people have the idea that if they just bodily come to church and bodily show up and bodily sit in a seat, they've worshipped God. They think if they come to the right place at the right time and go through the right motions, they've worshipped. Obviously, you do worship God with your body. You use your voice to sing, ears to hear, eyes to see, hands to clap. All of those things are expressions of worship, but they are not the essence of worship.

It's unfortunate that today so many believers are looking on the outside for a power that only resides on the inside. They are searching externally for that which God has planted internally. Ephesians 3:16 says, "that you might be strengthened with power through His spirit in the inner man." Remember that you are the visible part of the invisible Christ. He is the invisible part of the visible me.

Worship is when your spirit connects with His spirit through the Holy Spirit. That's what it means to worship Him "in spirit and in truth." Always remember this: God operates primarily, not in the realm of the physical, and not in the realm of the emotional, but in the realm of the spiritual. Where you truly meet God in worship is with a spirit that is focused on Him and wants to fervently give Him the worship He desires.

It is impossible to truly experience the presence of God and not be changed by it. When you experience God, you don't walk out the doors the same way you walked in. Some people wonder if you should get emotional when you worship. When worship is genuine, I don't see how you can't get emotional. I don't see how a believer can be in a church service and stand there like a statue with no emotion and no participation. If you ever grab hold of a live wire that is surging with electricity, something will happen inside of you. I believe when you truly connect to the God of this universe, something will happen inside of you that people will be able to see on the outside of you.

Worship by sanctifying your soul.

Jesus said in Matthew 22:37, *"Love the Lord your God with all your heart, and with all your soul, and with all your mind."* That really does cover all the bases: your intellect, your emotions, and your will.

God wants you to allow yourself to be *"transformed by the renewing of your mind"* (Romans 12:1-2). As I'm sure you've probably figured out by now, you don't instantaneously become perfect when you become a Christian. Your soul (mind, will, emotions) are in the process of being sanctified and made new over time. That's why you can become a Christian but still have an addiction, be angry all the time, or struggle with a certain sin. God loves you just the way you are, but He loves you too much to let you stay that way. The spirit of God goes to work to bring about the transformation in your heart. Just because you struggle with a sin doesn't mean that you're not a Christian. But being a Christian does mean that you've changed the direction of your life because the Holy Spirit is alive in you!

Back in World War II, when the allied forces were trying to take back some Pacific islands from Japanese control, the allies would bomb the island until they could establish a beachhead. A beachhead meant that they had finally achieved a physical presence on the island. And from the point of that beachhead, the allied forces could take over more and more territory until they had completely taken possession of the entire island. Some days they would get pushed back and be forced to retreat, but most of the time their advances worked. Once the allied forces were able to establish a beachhead, they never once failed to take total control over the island.

I like to look at salvation in a similar way. Perhaps God allowed a few bombs to go off in order to get your attention. You saw your need for Christ, believed and received Him into your life, and at that moment, the Holy Spirit established a beachhead. But from this point forward, God begins the work of taking over more and more territory from the enemy's control over your life. He'll give you greater victory, and the things that used to be an issue for you are no longer an issue. As you begin to follow Christ, that problem with anger will be replaced by His patience, but only if you allow the Holy Spirit to take control and have total possession over you.

The devil wants you to ignore the power of the Spirit to influence your soul. He wants to convince you that you can change your life on your own by focusing on managing your mind, will, and emotions by yourself. He wants you to think that way because Satan knows that you'll never be able to completely fix those things on your own. The work of God's Spirit is to pump new life into your soul so that eventually, your born-again spirit becomes the major influencer in what you think, feel, and do.

This is one of the major differences between having religion versus a relationship. Religion tries to change a person from the outside. Religion tells you that if you want to be more victorious, you just need to go to church more, be a better person, give more, serve more, sing louder, and try harder. But those things simply produce more and more weary and defeated Christians. The real victory happens on the inside when the new spirit pumps God's truth into the different areas of our life. Just as our hearts pump blood to the different parts of our bodies, the spirit pumps the truth of God into our souls – our mind, will, and emotions.

Worship by surrendering your body.

When God looks at our body, He sees two things. First, God sees something that is meant to be sacrificed on the altar. Romans 12:1 says, *"Therefore I urge you, brethren, by the mercies of God, to present your bodies a living and holy sacrifice, acceptable to God, which is your spiritual service of worship."* Just as the priests would make sacrifices on the altar in the Old Testament, the Bible says that God is looking for us to make our bodies "living and holy" sacrifices to Him. When you offer a sacrifice, it involves total and complete surrender. You are no longer your own. You have given up any right that you

> **" The work of God's spirit is to pump new life into your soul so that eventually, your born-again spirit becomes the major influencer in what you think, feel, and do. "**

NOTES _____

> **"Life begins once Jesus becomes the reason you live it."**

once thought you had in order to consecrate yourself to the will of God.

Secondly, not only does God see a sacrifice, but He also sees His temple. In 1 Corinthians 6:19, Paul says, *"Or do you not know that your body is a temple of the Holy Spirit who is in you, whom you have from God, and that you are not your own?"* When God sees our body, He doesn't primarily see flesh and blood, eyes and teeth, hands and feet. God sees a house, a temple where He lives.

If you go back to the Old Testament, the central institution of the Israelites was the Temple. It was the spiritual headquarters of the nation where the presence of God literally dwelt. It was the place of worship. In the Old Testament, God had a Temple for his people; but in the New Testament, God has a people for His temple. That means that my body is not just a temple on Sunday. The Holy Spirit lives in this temple 24 hours a day – through every waking moment.

The Apostle Paul reminds us: *"You are not your own; you were bought at a price. Therefore, honor God with your body"* (1 Corinthians 6:19-20). That is the bottom line. A big part of worship is surrendering your body, every day, for God's honor. Worship is doing everything in the name of Jesus and giving God thanks for it. You can stop trying to *do*, and just live out of what He has already *done*! His life is in you.

Sometimes we like to compartmentalize our life and think about it in segments. We think church is church, work is work, home is home, and everything fits nicely into its own little independent box. People who think that their relationship with God is both personal and private tend to look at life this way. It's one thing to talk about God at church, but some people don't want to bring Him up at work. That's just too weird. However, nowhere in the Bible do you find this compartmentalization of the sacred and the secular. Christianity isn't a religion; it's a relationship. When you have a relationship with someone, that doesn't change based on the day of the week or your geographical location. Can you imagine saying to your spouse, "Honey, when we're home, I'm married. I'll talk about you, and I'll acknowledge you. But when I go to work on Monday, I don't have to act married because home is home and work is work." That would definitely not go over too well, now would it? Here's what I want you to understand. You can't leave your worship of God at home or at the church. To be in a relationship with Christ means that we take Him with us wherever we go.

So as you can see, worship is really just walking in a state of complete surrender to the will of God with your whole being – body, soul, and spirit. When I get up in the morning, my attitude needs to be, "General Jesus, this is Private Brandon reporting for duty. What would you have me do for you today?" I want to encourage you today to walk in the same new awareness of the Holy Spirit, who is living and abiding in your heart, and continue to worship Him throughout your day.

Life begins once Jesus becomes the reason you live it.

People will always worship something. What are some things people waste their worship on?

What will be the consequences for failing to worship God?

_____

_____

_____

_____

_____

_____

_____

_____

_____

NOTES _____

_____

_____

_____

_____

_____

_____

_____

_____

_____

_____

_____

_____

_____

_____

_____

_____

_____

_____

_____

_____

_____

_____

_____

_____

_____

_____

_____

Day 2

How Can I Be Filled with the Holy Spirit?

vimeo.com/138214984

NOTES _____

I want you to use your imagination for a moment. Picture a man who for the first time in his life bought a brand new car and invited all of his friends over to admire it. But he had never driven it. He was very proud of it, and he was grateful for it, but everywhere he went he pushed it. Then someone finally showed him how to put the key into the ignition and start up the car! You might be thinking, "Ok, that's pretty dumb." You're right; nobody could be that dumb except the Christian who doesn't understand that when they got saved, God put an engine in their salvation. For many people, their Christianity is something they're proud of, but it is almost a burden to them. Rather than it carrying them, they're pushing it because they have not discovered the power of a Spirit-filled life.

Read Ephesians 5:18-21: *"And do not get drunk with wine, for that is debauchery, but be filled with the Spirit, addressing one another in psalms and hymns and spiritual songs, singing and making melody to the Lord with your heart, giving thanks always and for everything to God the Father in the name of our Lord Jesus Christ, submitting to one another out of reverence for Christ."*

The Holy Spirit does in me internally all that Jesus Christ did for me externally. The Holy Spirit is that person of the trinity that is most readily with us right now. But there is a difference between having the Holy Spirit in our heart because of our salvation and having the Holy Spirit fill us or control us. When we accept Jesus Christ as our Savior, the Holy Spirit enters our body, but when we are filled with the Spirit, He empowers our body. Think of it this way: When we are saved, the Holy Spirit becomes resident; when we are Spirit-filled, the Holy Spirit becomes president. He wants to empower us, take control of us, and use us for the glory of Jesus Christ!

The Bible says in Ephesians 5:18, *"And do not be drunk with wine, in which is dissipation; but be filled with the Spirit."* The verb "be filled" is in the imperative mood, which means this isn't a suggestion or a request; it's a command. It's the will of God for every Christian to be filled with the Holy Spirit. That's why Paul immediately preceded this verse by saying, *"Understand what the will of the Lord is"* (vs. 17). It's also worth noting that this verb is in the present tense, and in the original language of the Bible, that denotes continuous action. In other words, we are to be continuously filled with the Holy Spirit. The filling of the Holy Spirit is something that is to be renewed each day. Anyone knows that you can fill your gas tank, but that one filling will not last. When you leave the gas station and drive around, you will begin to run low on fuel. Likewise, no matter how full of the Spirit you are today, what you receive today will not last until tomorrow. And when you're running on empty, you have no power.

The word "filled" was a word used to describe the wind filling up a sail and carrying a ship along in the water. To be filled with the Holy Spirit is to allow the ship of your life to be guided by the wind of the Holy Spirit of God. Just as the wind guides the sail that guides the ship, so every thought we think, every word we say, every deed we do should be directed by the Holy Spirit of God.

I have always found it fascinating that Paul contrasts being drunk with being Spirit-filled. Why did he use that analogy? Because when you're under the influence of alcohol, you literally do whatever the alcohol wants you to do. It takes control of your intellect, your emotions, and your will. In the same way, the Holy Spirit dominates you and directs you to be able to do things that can only be explained by the power of God.

How would you describe what it means to be filled with the Holy Spirit?

> **"** The Holy Spirit does in me internally all that Jesus Christ did for me externally. **"**

NOTES

What does the Holy Spirit do?
I can see from Scripture at least four things that the Holy Spirit wants to do in your life.

1. The Holy Spirit will commission you. Acts 1:8 says, *"But you will receive power when the Holy Spirit comes on you; and you will be my witnesses in Jerusalem, and in all Judea and Samaria, and to the ends of the earth."* The word there for "power" is *dunamis*, which is where we get our English word "dynamite," and it literally means "a force; a miraculous power; the explosive power of God." When you are filled with the Spirit, you can't help but talk about Jesus. Without the filling of the Spirit, your witness will be ineffective, but with the filling of the Holy Spirit, your witness will be inevitable. In Luke 24:49, Jesus told the disciples to *"tarry in the city of Jerusalem until you are endued with power from on high."* Before Jesus sent His disciples into the world, He sent the Spirit into His disciples. And the same is true of us. Our lives are only spiritually productive and effective when we are filled with His Spirit. I have said before that God does not want us to do His work for Him; He wants to do His work through us.

2. The Holy Spirit will comfort you. The Holy Spirit is called a Comforter, and He will comfort you when you are hurting. Jesus said, *"And I will pray the Father, and he shall give you another Comforter, that he may abide with you forever"* (John 14:16). Even when you are hurting deeply, you can turn to the Holy Spirit and sense His comfort. He will then enable you to experience that peace that surpasses all understanding.

121

> **"**It is not your responsibility to persuade God to fill you with His Spirit; it is simply your responsibility to permit Him to do so.**"**

3. The Holy Spirit will counsel you. He is your Counselor or the Guide you need to navigate through life. The Holy Spirit is to a Christian what instinct is to an animal. When you don't know what to do, the Holy Spirit will direct you. Jesus said in John 16:13, *"But when He, the Spirit of truth comes, He will guide you into all truth."* There are times when I need to make a decision, but I just don't know what to do. So I start by praying and asking the Holy Spirit to give me direction, wisdom, and discernment. Isaiah 30:21 says, *"Whether you turn to the right or to the left, your ears will hear a voice behind you, saying, 'This is the way; walk in it.'"* Sometimes that voice will say, "Reach out to that person," or, "pray for them right now," or, "make this decision," or, "Don't say what you're thinking about saying. That won't please God." He will lead you, but never drive you. I love what Jesus said to His disciples in Luke 12:11-12: *"When you are brought before synagogues, rulers and authorities, do not worry about how you will defend yourselves or what you will say, for the Holy Spirit will teach you at that time what you should say."* Jesus is saying when you are required to speak out for your faith, don't worry about what you are going to say. The Holy Spirit will put the words in your mouth that you need to say. But *when* does this happen? When you are "brought before the authorities." If you're not experiencing the power of the Holy Spirit in your life, maybe you're not outspoken about what you believe. The Holy Spirit is called a Comforter, but why do you need a Comforter if you're already comfortable? We experience the Holy Spirit's power the most when we are out in the world making true disciples.

4. The Holy Spirit will convict you. Jesus said, *"When [the Spirit] comes, he will convict the world of guilt in regard to sin and righteousness and judgment"* (John 16:8). There may be something in your life that's not as it should be, and all of a sudden you are feeling this sense of, "I shouldn't have done that." What is that? It's the presence of the Holy Spirit convicting you.

I want to challenge your thinking about the Spirit-filled life for just a moment. When you talk about the Spirit-filled life, most Christians are looking to answer two questions: 1.) What? and 2.) How? But there's a much more important question to ask first: "*Why* do I want to be filled with the Holy Spirit?" Do you want to be filled with the Holy Spirit so you can use God or so that God can use you? The Holy Spirit was not given for your enjoyment, but for your employment. There are a lot of people who talk about the *filling* of the Spirit, but what they are really interested in is the *feeling* of the Spirit. They are after what I call the "thrill of the fill." Some people pray and say, "Oh, God, if I could just have more of you in my life … if I could just have more of your Holy Spirit living and working in me!" We need to understand this: It is not your responsibility to persuade God to fill you with His Spirit; it is simply your responsibility to permit Him to do so.

How do we become filled with the Holy Spirit?

1. Surrender yourself completely to the Holy Spirit. 1 Corinthians 6:19-20 says, *"Do you not know that your bodies are temples of the Holy Spirit, who is in you, whom you have received from God? You are not your own; you were bought at a price. Therefore honor God with your bodies."* You are a temple, and He wants to come and take complete control of His temple. Ask yourself if there is any area of your life that is out of bounds with God in your finances, thought life, ambitions, or other areas. To be filled with the Spirit means that Christ occupies every square inch of our being. God will not fill a dirty vessel. We must first be cleansed of everything that doesn't belong in a child of God. The Holy Spirit will never leave a surrendered vessel unfilled or unused.

2. Continue to give Him control over you. We must not forget the command to "be filled." We must continue to surrender to His control in our thoughts, speech, and actions. How does a person get drunk? By drinking. How does a person stay drunk? By continually drinking. We must continue to "be filled" with the Holy Spirit. Adrian Rogers said, "I know too many Christians once Spirit-filled but have now sobered up!" Living a Spirit-filled life involves a continual control of you renewing and rededicating your life to the Lord every day.

3. Ask the Holy Spirit to fill you. How did you get saved? You asked Christ to be your Savior. How do you get filled? You ask God to fill you with His Spirit. When a person prays and asks Jesus to save them, that is a prayer that God always answers because it is always the will of God for a person to be saved. When a person prays and asks the Holy Spirit to fill them with His presence and His power, that is a prayer that God always answers because it is always the will of God for His children to be filled with His Spirit.

Far too often we ask for what we already have. If you are saved, the Holy Spirit is already living and dwelling in our lives. Ephesians 1:3 says that we have already been blessed with every spiritual blessing! Everything we need to live the Christian life is supplied to us by the Holy Spirit.

So many times we pray, "God give me more love for that person who's hard to get along with." Scripture says, *The love of God is shed abroad in your hearts*" (Romans 5:5).

We pray, "God I need more grace!" but 2 Corinthians 12:9 says, *"My grace is sufficient for you."*

We pray, "O Lord, I need more strength." Philippians 4:13 says, *"You can do all things through Christ who strengthens you."*

We pray, "O God guide me!" while Romans 8:14 says, *"As many as are led by the Spirit of God, they are the sons of God."*

I want you to imagine that I have a glove sitting on a table. What would happen if I told that glove to pick up a book or play the piano? Absolutely nothing. The glove itself can't play the piano. But if I put my hand in the glove and play the piano, what happens? Music! When I put my hand in the glove, the glove moves! The glove doesn't get all pious and say, "O hand, please guide me! Show me the way to go!" It just goes! Judges 6:34 says that the *"Spirit of the Lord clothed Gideon."* Gideon was so full of and controlled by the Spirit of God, the Lord wore him like a suit of clothes! That's what I want God to do in my life as well!

Review what you just read. In your own words, how can a person be filled with the Holy Spirit?

> **"** I think it's interesting that the first mark of a Spirit-filled life is not mountain-moving faith, speaking in tongues, or even dynamic speaking ability, but rather it is a heart that sings. **"**

NOTES

123

NOTES

What does a Spirit-filled life look like?

Your life will be marked with joy.
Scripture goes on to say that as a result of the Spirit's filling, we will find ourselves *"speaking to one another in psalms and hymns and spiritual songs, singing and making melody in your heart to the Lord"* (v.19).

I think it's interesting that the first mark of a Spirit-filled life is not mountain-moving faith, speaking in tongues, or even dynamic speaking ability, but rather it is a heart that sings. In other words, when you are filled with the Spirit, there will be a song in your soul. Regardless of whether you can sing or not, when you're filled with the Holy Spirit, there's going to be a genuine joy in your heart. The phrase "singing and making melody in your heart" in the Greek language literally means "to strum your heart like a musical instrument." When we sing, we may listen to our voice, but God is listening to our heart.

Your life will be marked with thankfulness.
Verse 20 says, "*... giving thanks always for all things to God the Father in the name of our Lord Jesus Christ.*" A Spirit-filled life is a thankful life. When you are filled with the Holy Spirit, you will literally be able to give thanks in all things. The only way you can be thankful to God in difficult circumstances is to be filled with the Holy Spirit.

Your life will be marked with graciousness.
Verse 21 says, "*... submitting to one another in the fear of God.*" The word "submit" is a military term that refers to one equal submitting to another equal. When we are filled with the Holy Spirit, we will always treat others as being more important than ourselves, and we will do as much as we can to meet their needs rather than our own.

As parents we know we're not supposed to live vicariously through our kids, but there's one Parent who does want to live vicariously through His children. Our Heavenly Father wants to fill us with His power and presence so that we might live a life of purpose. The great preacher, Charles Haddon Spurgeon, once made this observation: "If there were only one prayer which I might pray before I died it would be this: 'Lord, send your church men and women filled with the Holy Spirit and with fire.'"

Describe what a Spirit-filled Christian looks like:

_____

_____

_____

_____

_____

_____

_____

_____

_____

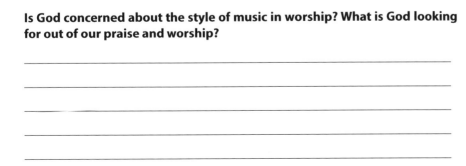

Day 3
What Is the Power of Praise and Worship?

A Sunday school teacher was teaching a class of four year olds about how, when the Temple was built, the presence of God filled the temple. Instantly, all the eyes in the room got wide, full of excitement, and the kids couldn't wait to learn more. Soon the teacher discovered that the source of their excitement was not because God had come to dwell in the Temple, but because they were imagining a building full of the presents of God! I think a lot of times we're not much unlike those kids. We are more easily excited about our *presents* and blessings from God than we are about being in the *presence* of God.

So what is praise and worship? Simply put: it is our response to God's presence. Eugene Peterson said, "Worship does not satisfy our hunger for God – it whets our appetite. Our need for God is not taken care of by engaging in worship – it deepens. It overflows the hour and permeates the week."

There is a slight difference between praise and worship. Praise is celebrating God for who He is and what He has done for us. Interestingly enough, the Bible actually has more to say about praise than it does about the subject of prayer. Psalm 18:3 says, *"I will call upon the Lord, who is worthy to be praised ..."* Praise is closely intertwined with thanksgiving. It doesn't really require much from us, and it can be applied to other relationships as well, like when we praise our spouse, our kids, or a fellow co-worker for something good they have done.

Praise can be a part of worship, but worship goes far beyond praise. Worship is the art of losing self in the adoration of another. It gets to the heart of who we are. In order to worship God, we have to let go of our worship of self. John the Baptist said, *"He must increase, but I must decrease"* (John 3:30). Although, we can worship many things in this life (a relationship, success, etc.), Scripture says that it's something that should be reserved for God alone (Luke 4:8). Just as praise is synonymous with thanksgiving; worship is synonymous with surrender.

Is God concerned about the style of music in worship? What is God looking for out of our praise and worship?

_____

_____

_____

_____

vimeo.com/138215029

NOTES _____

_____

_____

_____

_____

_____

_____

_____

_____

_____

_____

_____

_____

_____

_____

_____

_____

_____

_____

_____

> ❝You will praise the Lord in direct proportion to what you think of Him.❞

126

Why is praise and worship such a big deal to God?

Read Psalm 147. Here are at least five reasons we can find in these verses:

1. Praise and worship shows how much reverence you have for God. The word "worship" literally means "worth-ship." When you worship, you are saying, "This one is worth more; I am worth less." To the degree that you worship and how you worship is an outward expression of how much you think God is worth to you. You become like what you worship. If your life's pursuit is towards superficial things in life, you'll become worldly and materialistic. If you worship the true God, you'll become godly.

Psalm 147:1 says, *"Praise the LORD. How good it is to sing praises to our God, how pleasant and fitting to praise him!"* One of the reasons God created us is so that we would praise Him and that our lives would bring Him glory. Did you know that you will praise the Lord in direct proportion to what you think of Him? If your concept of God is low, your worship will be lethargic. But if your concept of God is Biblically accurate, your worship will be full of passion, energy, and enthusiasm. If you find that worship is boring, it's because your concept of God is boring. You will never worship God correctly until you come to really know God personally.

2. Praise and worship will refresh you spiritually. It isn't just for God; it's also for us. There's something energizing that happens in our spirits when we begin to genuinely praise Him. Like you, I have some days that are more difficult than others. I get exhausted, and there are some days that I just don't know if I can keep going at the same pace that I'm currently living. So on my way home from the office, I'll play some praise and worship music, and a change begins to happen on the inside of me. As I begin to praise, He begins to refresh. Psalm 147:2-3 says, *"The LORD builds up Jerusalem ... He heals the brokenhearted and binds up their wounds."* There is a refreshment and a healing of wounds that takes place in our heart when we praise Him. Here's another key truth: You cannot praise and pout at the same time. Isaiah 61:3 says, *"Put on the garment of praise in the spirit of heaviness."* The Lord is willing to make an exchange with you. If you have a heavy heart that is burdened by the cares of this world, He wants you to exchange that with the garment of praise. When we come to God just as we are, carrying our burdens and wearing our scars, God's Spirit steps in and begins to do His work in restoring us spiritually and refreshing us emotionally. The more you praise and worship God, the more you plug into His power. The less you praise and worship Him, the less power you will have.

Psalm 100:2 says, *"Serve the Lord with gladness, come before Him with joyful singing."* This is one of the most distinct things about Christianity. Do you know of any other religion in the world that speaks of a God that wants us to come before Him not just with songs, but with joyful singing? What are the great songs of Islam, Buddhism, or Hinduism? There are none. When you come face-to-face with God in worship, there ought to be a song in your heart.

3. Praise and worship will release your faith. In other words, praise gives your faith a vitamin shot. The Psalmist calls your attention to how great our God is. Psalm 147:4-6 says, *"He determines the number of the stars and calls them each by name. Great is our Lord and mighty in power; his understanding has no limit. The Lord sustains the humble."* When you concentrate on how awe-inspiring God is, it increases your faith! Not only does He call the stars by name, but He also knows the number of the hairs on your head (Luke 12:7). Scripture also says that we are to *"Magnify the name of the LORD; let us exalt His name together"* (Psalm 34:3). The idea of "magnifying" the Lord has two meanings. First, it means "to enlarge." When you look at something through a magnifying glass, you make it larger in *your* eyes. Your worship doesn't make God any larger than He already is – He's infinite. But when you worship, you make Him larger in your eyes. His power and might become larger than any obstacle or adversity that you're experiencing at that current moment. When you pray, you tell God how big your problems are, but when you praise and worship, you tell your problems how big your God is!

The second meaning of "magnify" is "to concentrate." If you were to take that same magnifying glass outdoors, you can harness the rays of the sunlight into a single beam strong enough to start a fire! True worship involves being still, removing the distractions, and concentrating all of your energies on being in His presence (Psalm 46:10).

4. Praise and worship reflects our gratitude.

The way that we worship shows how much we appreciate who God is and what He has done for us. Verse 7 says, *"Sing to the LORD with thanksgiving; make music to our God on the harp."* When you study the ancient documents describing the early church, their worship was similar and yet different than how we worship in the modern era. For them, worship was not a performance by a handful of people on stage; everyone in the church participated. It was prayerful. There would be hours of prayer before the worship service even started, and they would ask for God's presence to meet them where they were. During worship, the early believers would pray out loud all at the same time. Their worship involved dancing along with boisterous and joyful singing. When you think about it, these early believers didn't have much to be happy about. They were facing intense persecution; many of them were being killed for their faith. Many churches were forced to meet in catacombs so they wouldn't draw unnecessary attention. And yet their worship was joyful and it was powerful. It doesn't matter what style of music you prefer. If your worship is not joyful, engaging, and exciting, it's not true worship.

Listen carefully to the prophet Isaiah, *"The Lord says: 'These people come near to me with their mouth and honor me with their lips, but their hearts are far from me. Their worship of me is made up only of rules taught by men'"* (Isaiah 29:13). Isaiah is talking about people who come into worship as if it were another formality, a duty if you will, and although they sing the songs and say their prayers with their mouths, their hearts are far from God. One of the surest signs that you are losing your passion for the Lord is when your mouth goes into autopilot during worship. Your physical body may be singing, but your mind and your heart are somewhere else.

If worship is mindless, it is meaningless. We need to be specific when we praise and worship Him. If someone approached you and repeated the same phrase, "I praise you! I praise you!" twenty times, you would probably think, "For what?" You would rather receive two specific compliments than 20 vague generalities. So would God.

Is your worship an adequate reflection of how thankful you are for His hand upon your life? When the American hostages came home on January 20, 1981, after being held captive in Iran, the first thing they did when they got off the plane was to get down on their knees and kiss the ground. After being prisoners for so long and being given back their freedom, their hearts were so full of gratitude for their country that they bowed down and kissed the asphalt of that airport. Why? They knew where they had been and they knew where they were now.

Do you know why many of us stop bowing and stop worshiping? It's because we forget where we've come from. We forget that we were once held hostage in Satan's territory, but now we have been set free. Let your worship reflect the level of thankfulness you have in your heart.

5. Praise and worship resists our enemy.

> **"** It doesn't matter what style of music you prefer. If your worship is not joyful, engaging, and exciting, it's not true worship. **"**

NOTES

NOTES

Psalm 147:10-14 says, *"His pleasure is not in the strength of the horse, nor his delight in the legs of a man; the Lord delights in those who fear him, who put their hope in his unfailing love."*

When you feel like you are experiencing spiritual warfare, just begin to praise the Lord. When Paul and Silas were in prison, they didn't despair; they began to sing! And their worship became their weapon that ushered in God's presence and broke them out of prison. There's a fascinating story in 2 Chronicles 20: Jehoshaphat, King of Israel, was afraid because he was facing what seemed to be a hopeless situation. A coalition of three enemy nations was plotting to overtake Israel. Jehoshaphat prayed and sought the face of God, and he asked his entire nation to fast and pray. I love how God responded to them. He said, *"Do not be afraid or discouraged because of this vast army. For the battle is not yours, but God's."* On the day of the battle, the Israelites were ready to move forward in faith, believing that God would fight this battle for them. Jehoshaphat had so much faith that he actually appointed a choir to be on the frontlines of the battlefield singing and thanking God for His faithfulness. So what happened? The three enemy armies coming against the Israelites ended up getting confused and they thought they were killing the Israelites, but in reality they were killing each other! By the time God's people had arrived, the battle was already over, and all they had to do was pick up the plunder. Why did God do it this way? He did it as a visual lesson to teach us to praise Him in faith before the victory has even taken place.

Psalm 22:3 says that God inhabits the praises of His people. God is always present, but He really manifests His presence when His people begin to praise Him with a genuine spirit. In the movie *Field of Dreams*, we get one of the most famous lines in film: "If you build it, they will come." When it comes to worship, "If you worship Him, His presence will come!" When all hell breaks loose in your life, begin to praise and worship and allow the truth of God's Word to take root in your heart. You may not sing your blues away, but I'll bet you'll feel the presence of a powerful friend.

How is God's worth being displayed through your praise and worship of Him?

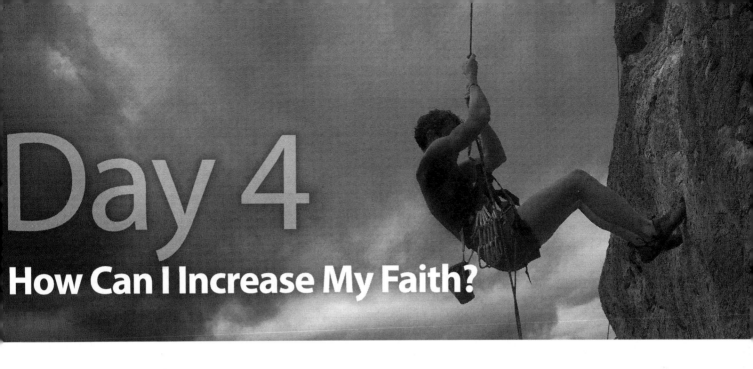

Day 4
How Can I Increase My Faith?

vimeo.com/138215088

Faith is so vital to the Christian life that Scripture tells us that without it, it is impossible to please God (Hebrews 11:6). Faith does not make things easy. It makes them possible (Luke 1:37). Faith is like Wi-Fi. It's invisible, but it has the power to connect you to what you need. Stress makes you believe that everything has to happen right now. Faith reassures you that everything will happen in God's timing. Faith is seeing light with your heart when all your eyes see is darkness.

In Luke 17:5, the disciples made a request of Jesus: "Increase our faith." They wanted Jesus to help them believe more because it was obvious to them that they weren't believing enough. The disciples felt that much of what the Lord was asking them to do just didn't seem normal or natural. In effect, they were saying, "Lord if you're asking us to do that, you're going to have to give us more faith than what we already have."

Isn't it true that much of what God asks us seems out of our reach? It seems beyond what we're able to do with the faith we have. We know what God wants us to do, but sometimes it just doesn't seem practical. We feel like we don't have the patience or the power to carry it out.

Our faith grows when we walk with God through difficulty.

Faith is like a roll of film: it develops best in the dark. When I was a little kid growing up in Port St. Lucie, Florida, we lived near a convenience store. Around the age of nine, I remember asking my dad for permission to ride my bike down to the other end of the neighborhood, where our convenience store was, to buy some candy. I was shocked when my dad said, "Yes." I felt so grown up and independent riding my bicycle that far away from home. Just recently, I brought that up with my dad and said that I couldn't believe he would let me ride my bicycle that far away from home all by myself at such a young age. My dad started laughing and said, "You really thought you were alone when you went to that convenience store?" He said, "I followed you the entire time. I walked along behind you and stayed behind the trees so you couldn't see me. The entire time you were in that convenience store, my eyes were upon you. You thought you were alone. But you were never alone."

Isn't that so much like our relationship with God? There are times when we feel so alone and so isolated. We feel like God may have even forgotten about us. If only we would remind ourselves that His presence has been with us the entire time and His watchful eye has never left us.

There are 10 Scriptural references to the promise that God will never

NOTES _____

_____
_____
_____
_____
_____
_____
_____
_____
_____
_____
_____
_____
_____
_____
_____
_____
_____
_____
_____
_____
_____

129

> **"Faith does not make things easy. It makes them possible."**

forsake or abandon you! For example, Hebrews 13:5 says, *"I will never leave you; nor forsake you."* Sometimes, we're tempted to think, "Lord, why have you left me alone? Why is your hand not on me? Are you really aware of what is going on in my life? Do you really care?"

And all along, God is saying, "When you thought I wasn't there, I was walking right behind you. When you thought I wasn't aware of what was going on, my eyes never left you. When you thought that I didn't care, I was behind the scenes working in your life." Faith is trusting God even when you don't understand His plan.

Our faith grows when we remember God's faithfulness in the past.

Faith believes in spite of the circumstances and acts in spite of the consequences. I saw a sign once that gave this acrostic of F.A.I.T.H.: Forwarding All Issues to Heaven. We learn in 1 John 5:4 tells us, *"This is the victory that has over come the world – our faith ..."* On the cross of Jesus Christ, all the sin (past, present, and future) of the entire world and its consequences were nailed to Jesus Christ. If Jesus was able to overcome those sins and resurrect in victory over them, and then be seated at the right hand of God, His indwelling presence can surely overcome any destructive force you're facing right now. If a weight lifter can bench 500 pounds, is he going to have any problem carrying 25 pounds of groceries for you? Your part is to believe that Jesus can enable you to overcome, and *then* you act on that belief. God has never asked you to do anything that He is not absolutely certain you can do through Him.

When you read Biblical examples of audacious faith in the Bible, it ought to cause your own spiritual circuit board to light up! And when you look back on your own life at how God has been faithful to you, it increases your faith.

We must never allow our feelings to get in the way of our faith. Faith is not equal to feelings. To allow your feelings to guide your faith is like a truck driver being controlled by the cargo in his truck rather than by the wheel he is steering. It is the wheel that controls the cargo, not the cargo that controls the wheel.

Our faith grows when we mature in our understanding of who God is.

The reason that God honors faith is that faith honors God. Hebrews 11:1 says, *"Now faith is the substance of things hoped for, the evidence of things not seen."* Faith has to have substance. If after a child has lost a tooth, their parent goes to bed saying, "I am trusting in the tooth fairy to put a dollar under my son's pillow," that's just wasted conversation. There's no substance. In order for faith to do something, it must be based on something. We are told to have faith in our God and His Word.

In a message one Sunday, I picked a couple out of the crowd and asked them how long they had been married. The husband said they had been married for 29 years. My next question was, "Would you say that you love your wife more now than you did when you first got married?" He said, "Yes!" (Good answer, by the way!) I then asked him if he loved his wife with 100% of his heart on their wedding day? He said, "Yes!" (Another good answer!) So what happened? You can't love someone more than 100%, right? I'll tell you what happened. Your capacity to love grew over time. You weathered some difficulties, you went through some storms together, and you had fights and had to forgive one another. Your love has grown more seasoned over the years, which has increased your ability to grow in your love for your spouse.

That's how our faith grows as well. The more faith you have, the more ability you have to grow in your faith.

After hearing the story of Jonah and the whale, a little boy asked, "Dad, how could a fish swallow Jonah?" His dad said, "Well, if God can make the world simply by speaking the word, then surely He could speak the word and make a fish large enough to swallow a man." The little boy said, "Well, I didn't know you were going to bring God into it." When you bring God into the equation of faith, you don't need a lot of faith. You just need a lot of Him! You don't need more faith. What you need is the right kind of faith.

When Jesus was in His hometown of Nazareth, the Bible says that Jesus could do no mighty works there because of their unbelief (Matthew 13:58). Even though Jesus was fully God, He was limited because of the people's unbelief. It was their lack of faith that kept Him from doing some mighty works in their lives. Remember, Jesus taught us, *"According to your faith, be it unto you"* (Matthew 9:29).

Some people say that "faith moves mountains." That is not true. It is God that moves mountains. Jesus told us in Mark 11:22 to *"have faith in God."* Your faith is no better than its object. Faith in faith is just positive thinking, and that's a recipe to get discouraged. You must place your faith in God. It's not the size of your faith, but the object of your faith that really counts.

When you look through the Bible, almost everyone who received a blessing from God was an individual with *weak* faith! There were a few who had very strong faith in Jesus, but most of them didn't. There was a man whose son was demon possessed, and he came to Jesus saying, *"If you can do anything for my son, please do it."* Jesus said, *"If you believe – all things are possible to him that believes."* The man said, *"Lord, I believe, but help my unbelief"* (Mark 9:24). Have you ever been there? "Lord, I believe. I have a modicum of faith. But Lord, help my unbelief." That's what God is looking for as a starting point. Remember this: God still demonstrates His power and supplies His provision in direct proportion to the faith of His children.

The size of our faith isn't determined by who God is, but by who you *believe* God is and whether you have the courage to respond accordingly.

Our faith grows when we believe in God's promises.

One of the simplest definitions I've heard on this subject is that "Faith is acting as if God is telling the truth." Another way of saying it is: "Faith is acting as if something is so even when it appears to not be so in order that it might be shown to be so simply because God said so." Faith simply means you believe God to do what He said He will do. God's promises are not mottos to hang on the wall; they are checks to take to the bank. Faith is taking God at His Word. Romans 10:17 says, *"So faith comes from hearing, and hearing through the Word of Christ."* That means that faith comes from *outside* of you; you don't generate faith. The way we grow in our faith is by growing in our understanding of God's Word and the promises He makes to us.

In Luke 17:6, Jesus said, *"If you have faith as small as a mustard seed, you can say to this mulberry tree, 'Be uprooted and planted in the sea,' and it will obey you."* Notice that Jesus says, *"If you have faith as small as a mustard seed."* A mustard seed is extraordinarily small. It's not gargantuan. It's tiny. Weak faith in the right object is better than misplaced faith in any object. Weak faith in God is better than strong faith in anything else. Jesus is saying that mustard seed faith is really all you need. While a mustard seed is really small, it packs a lot of life. Because you when you plant a mustard seed, it gives you a tree that grows up to 15 feet.

Jesus then tells his disciples what that mustard seed faith could do. He said you could speak to a mulberry tree to be uprooted and planted in the sea, and it will obey you. That may not sound like much to you, but to the disciples, this was a staggering statement due to the nature of the mulberry tree. A mulberry tree (or a sycamore tree) has an in-depth root system that

> **"** Faith is trusting God even when you don't understand His plan. **"**

NOTES

12 Faith Confessions

1. **I am fully forgiven and free from all shame and condemnation.**
(Romans 8:1-2;
Ephesians 1:7-8;
1 John 1:9)

2. **I act in audacious faith to change the world in my generation.**
(Joshua 10:12-14;
John 14:12)

3. **I have no fear or anxiety; I trust in the Lord with all my heart.** (Proverbs 3:5-6;
Philippians 4:6-7;
1 Peter 5:7)

4. **I am able to fulfill the calling God has placed on my life.**
(Exodus 3:9-12;
Psalm 57:2;
Colossians 1:24-29)

5. **I am fully resourced to do everything God has called me to do.**
(Deuteronomy 8:18;
Luke 6:38;
Philippians 4:13)

6. **I have no insecurity, because I see myself the way God sees me.**
(Genesis 1:26-27;
Psalm 139:13-16;
Ephesians 5:25-27)

7. **I am a faithful spouse (if you're single, you can insert the word future**

not only goes way down into the ground, but it intertwines itself with its roots and anything else in the neighborhood. It was said of a mulberry tree that once it's planted, you might as well leave it alone, because you'll never be able to uproot it. They could live for up to 600 years! That's how solid and deep their roots went. Yet Jesus said that if you have faith as small as a mustard seed, you could say to it, "Get up and get out," and it will go!

Some of the problems you have in your life are like mulberry trees. Those roots run deep. They've been hanging around a long time. And try as we may, we've been unable to untangle them. It just keeps on, year after year, producing new problems in our lives.

Let's look at another instance when Jesus talks about mustard seed faith. When the disciples came back discouraged because they were unable to drive out an evil spirit in a demon-possessed boy, they asked Jesus why they could not drive it out. Jesus responded: *"Because of your little faith. For truly, I say to you, if you have faith like a grain of mustard seed, you will say to this mountain, 'Move from here to there,' and it will move, and nothing will be impossible for you"* (Matthew 17:20).

A mountain was something too high to get over. It was an obstacle too great for you to climb. It represents something too big for you to handle. Jesus says, "Don't allow the magnitude of that obstacle to intimidate you. A mustard seed faith will do."

Notice that in both of those Scripture passages, Jesus tells us to demonstrate our faith by *speaking* to the mulberry tree or to the mountain. In the Bible, whenever God wanted something to take place, He would just speak it (see Psalm 33:9; Hebrews 11:3). When Jesus was on this earth and He wanted something to happen, He would simply speak and things changed. The Bible says that life and death are in the power of the tongue (Proverbs 18:21).

Faith is the medium of exchange in Heaven. If you need an answer to prayer, spend a little faith. That's why Jesus said, *"According to your faith, be it unto you"* (Matthew 9:29). One man put it this way: "Pray and doubt; you'll do without. Pray and believe; you will receive."

Our faith grows when we step outside our comfort zones.

Peter was the only disciple who walked on water, but he was also the only one willing to get out of the boat. You will never walk on water and reach your full potential unless you have the courage and the boldness to take a step of faith and do what God has put in your heart. God made you and He knows what you're capable of. Throughout your life, He's going to present you with opportunities that, in the natural sense, you may not think you can handle. You'll be tempted to shrink back with fear. But God will empower you to do His will. Anything God orders, He will pay the bill.

Too many people are living in the safe zone, but God wants you to step out into the faith zone. Have some courage and boldness to pursue what God has put in your heart.

Growing up, I was extremely shy. I had a speech impediment and a severe stuttering problem. Being a communicator and mega church pastor would have been the last thing my parents could see me doing when I grew up. However, when I stepped out and got beyond my own natural ability, that is when God stepped in and gave His supernatural ability. He brought gifts out of me that I never even knew I had. You too have incredible things on the inside of you that you probably never knew you had!

Many times we say, "God, if you'll just show me the blueprint ... if you'll just give me the details, then I'll be a whole lot more comfortable." No. If God did that, it wouldn't require any faith on your part. You sometimes have to take a step of faith and then God will lead you and show you the next step.

God told Abraham, *"Leave the place where you are and I will show you where I am sending you"* (Genesis 12:1). We think just the opposite: "God you show me and I'll go!" Instead God says, "You go and I'll show you." In other words, God wants us to take the first step of faith. It's interesting that when God parted the Jordan River for the children of Israel to cross, the Bible says that the waters did not open up until the priests first put their feet in the waters (Joshua 3:13). Don't you know that it took faith to go out there walking in the water expecting God to open it up? We think to ourselves, "God, if you part the seas in my life, I'll go running through them!" No, God says, "You get out there and get your feet wet and watch me do supernatural things in your life." Faith is directly tied to an action done in response to a revealed truth.

Our God is a progressive God. Once you reach a certain level, He might leave you there for a little while, but He's not going to let you stay that way too long. He's going to push you. He doesn't want you to stay stagnant, mediocre, or comfortable for too long because your spiritual growth will come to a screeching halt.

Maybe you have an opportunity right now in which God is calling you to take a step of faith. Or maybe God is preparing you today to have faith for whatever future opportunities may hold. When you step out in faith and take God up on His Word, you will live a life of worship and honor the God for whom you serve.

Has there ever been a time in your life when your faith hit a low point? What led to your loss of faith, and what helped you regain it again?

_____

_____

_____

_____

_____

_____

_____

_____

_____

Today you read five ways God grows our faith. Which one has made the biggest difference in your confidence in God? Why?

_____

_____

_____

_____

_____

_____

_____

_____

_____

_____

in there) and a godly parent – our family is blessed. (Deuteronomy 6:6-9; Ephesians 5:22-25; Colossians 3:18-19; 1 Peter 3:1-7)

8. **I am completely whole – physically, mentally, and emotionally.**
(Psalm 103:1-5; Matthew 8:16-17; 2 Corinthians 5:17; 1 Peter 2:24)

9. **I am increasing in influence and favor for the kingdom of God.**
(Genesis 45:4-8; 1 Samuel 2:26; Acts 2:37-47)

10. **I am enabled to walk in the sacrificial love of Christ.**
(2 Thessalonians 2:16-17; 1 John 3:16; 4:9-12)

11. **I have the wisdom of the Lord concerning every decision I make.**
(2 Chronicles 1:7-12; Proverbs 2:6; Ecclesiastes 2:26; James 1:5)

12. **I am protected from all harm and evil in Jesus' name.**
(Genesis 50:20; Psalm 3:1-3; 2 Thessalonians 3:2-3)

Source: *Sun Stand Still* by Steven Furtick

133

Day 5

How Can I Grow in My Generosity?

vimeo.com/138215142

NOTES _____

I'll never forget what it was like to get my first paycheck. I was 16 years old, working my first job, and I remember getting a check for almost $100 and thinking to myself, 'This is *my* money! Nobody gave it to me. I earned it! It belongs to *me*!" At the time, that logic seemed completely right and completely reasonable. But I was dead wrong. The first thing I had to learn early on was that it wasn't my money.

The work that you and I do is simply the way God puts money into our hands, but it's not our money. It belongs to *Him*. God is the One who gives us our life, health, and ability to work, as well as the job that you have to bring home that paycheck. So in reality, every dime you earn comes from Him and His blessing on your life.

When King David took up an offering to build the Temple, he offered this prayer up to God: *"But who am I, and who are my people, that we should be able to give as generously as this? Everything comes from you, and we have given you only what comes from your hand"* (1 Chronicles 29:14).

Where did David say the money they offered the Lord came from? How does that perspective change how you view your own personal finances?

_____

_____

_____

_____

_____

_____

_____

_____

Before I got my first job, if I wanted to buy some Christmas presents for my parents, I had to do so with *their* money. I'd say, "Dad, can you spot me some twenties so I can go shopping and buy you and Mom a present." So then I'd go to the store and pick out something nice for the both of them, wrap it up, and I would feel really good about just how generous I was! It never really occurred to me at that age that they were buying their own presents. I was just the one going to the store. Everything I had came from them, so what I *gave* to them *came* from them. What David was literally saying in that verse is, "God, what we have just put into your left hand we really just received from your right hand." There's an old saying that says some people live hand to mouth. Can I be honest with you? We all live "hand to mouth" – from God's hand to our mouth.

In 2 Corinthians 8:7 we learn, *"But just as you excel in anything, in faith, in speech, and knowledge and complete earnestness and in your love for us, see that you also excel in the grace of giving."*

It's called the "grace of giving" because you need God's grace to get to the next level. In today's video, we introduced the concept of the generosity ladder. I want you to imagine that you have a ladder with five different rungs that each represents the four different stages of giving. Let's climb each step and look at it individually so that we too can *"excel in the grace of giving."*

Step 1 – First-Time Giving Level
This is just basic level giving. It's where generosity starts. When you make your first offering to God, you get on the ladder. You've just taken the first step to honoring God with your finances. This is a great place to start, but not a great place to stop. One of the things that every disciple of Jesus needs to understand is that the offering in your church service is not separate from your worship, but it is an important part of your worship to God.

In 1 Corinthians 16:1-2, Paul says, *"Now about the collection for God's people: Do what I told the Galatian churches to do. On the first day of every week, each one of you should set aside a sum of money in keeping with his income."*

The Bible never talks about a specific dollar amount that you are to give. Instead, it speaks of a percentage or proportion of money in keeping with your income. Back in Bible times, everybody got paid on the last day of the week, so they would bring a percentage of that paycheck to worship on the first day of the week. The Bible says that we are to honor the Lord with the first fruits of all our increase (Proverbs 3:9-10). I chose to honor that verse personally by setting up online giving where the very first thing that gets taken out of my checking account when I get paid is my tithe (10% of my income).

Step 2 – Occasional Giving Level
This is the person who gives to the church, but they don't do so consistently. They give every once in a while, but there's nothing systematic or regular in their giving. If you've just given something for the first time, I encourage you to continue giving when you worship so that you can grow and develop the habit of generosity.

Step 3 – Intentional Giving Level
This is the person who has given more than occasionally. They are now intentional and consistent in their giving, but they still give less than 10% of their income. They've grown in their giving to the point that they give regularly, but they're still short of the obedience level that God has asked each of us to give.

Step 4 – Tithing Level
This could also be called the obedience level of giving. The Bible talks a lot about the concept of tithing. The word "tithe" simply means a "tenth." We are to return 10% of what we earn back to the Lord for His Kingdom work. So that means if my paycheck is $1,000, my tithe needs to be $100. John D. Rockefeller, one of the wealthiest millionaires in his day, was once asked

> "Honor the Lord with your wealth and with the firstfruits of all your produce; [10] then your barns will be filled with plenty, and your vats will be bursting with wine."
> - Proverbs 3:9-10

NOTES

135

> **"If God has blessed you financially, perhaps it's not for you to raise your standard of living but to raise your standard of giving."**

what the secret was to his money management. He said it was simple. You tithe 10%, save 10%, and live on the remaining 80%. That's a great rule of thumb to live by.

The first three levels are not a bad place to start, but they are a bad place to stay. As soon as possible, you need to get to the point where you are on the obedience level of offering your full tithe to the Lord. When you tithe, in essence you're saying, "Lord, all that I have came from You in the first place, and if it weren't for You, I wouldn't have it to begin with, so I'm going to give the first portion back to You." Maybe you're thinking, "Ok, why does God want the first 10% of everything I make? Is it because He needs it?" Absolutely not. Do you know what your money represents to God? It represents your heart. And God wants your heart. If you say that God is first in your life, but He's not first in your finances, then He's not really first in your life at all, and you need to quit kidding yourself.

In Malachi's day, the Israelites had allowed their money to master them instead of them mastering their money. Because of that, God told them, *"Will a man rob God? Yet you are robbing Me! But you say, 'How have we robbed You?' In tithes and offerings."* Israel had gotten away from God, and they didn't even know it. But when God talks about how they had gotten away from Him, He doesn't mention their morals; He mentions their money. Why? Because God continuously uses our attitude toward money to take our spiritual temperature, and it's a very accurate thermometer. For a new or growing Christian, giving is usually the last thing they will commit to. God cannot bless your finances unless you are giving Him the whole tithe. Malachi 3:10 says, *"Bring the whole tithe into the storehouse, so that there may be food in My house, and test Me now in this,' says the LORD of hosts, 'if I will not open for you the windows of heaven and pour out for you a blessing until it overflows."'*

Notice that God says, *"test me now in this."* Do you realize that there is only one instance in the Bible where we are told to "test" God, and this is it! When you do that, God says, "Ok … you're demonstrating that you've put me first in your life. Now let me tell you what I'm going to do. I'm going to bless your socks off! You will receive a blessing until it overflows."

Step 5 – Extravagant Giving Level

This is the peak level of giving. This is living a life of generosity. The New Testament pattern of giving goes far beyond tithing. When you look at the early church in the Book of Acts, many were selling land and giving away as much as they possibly could because they were so passionate about their mission as a church.

So "extravagant giving" means that you go beyond just giving 10%. You're now giving a tithe *and* an offering! Perhaps that extra offering above and beyond your tithe can go to missions or to feed the hungry. Maybe it's leaving a large and generous tip to a waitress who is struggling through a hard time. It means you're quick to sponsor someone going on a missions trip, or you're the first person to step up when you hear there is a need. Perhaps it means increasing your giving to the Lord by a percentage point, giving 11% or maybe even 15-20% to expand God's kingdom work. If God has blessed you financially, perhaps it's not for you to raise your standard of living but to raise your standard of giving.

For years, I was tithing 10%, and I felt pretty good about myself, but I wasn't really growing in my generosity. I felt like I had stagnated. I had been tithing for so long, it was second nature to me. A few years ago, I made a commitment to the Lord that every time I got a raise, I would increase my giving by one percentage point. So the first year, I gave 11%; the second year, I increased my giving to 12%; and so on. I am now giving more than

I've ever given before, and God continues to bless me financially like never before! His promise is true in my life, and I know that when you take Him at His Word, He too will *"put out for you a blessing until it overflows."* Stanley Tam says, "It's what you sow that multiplies, not what you keep in the barn."

We need to understand that the tithe was never meant to be the ending point of your generosity. It's the starting point. Tithing is like the training wheels of generosity. It's really cute when you see a four-year-old riding his bicycle with training wheels. It's not so cute when you see a 40-year-old doing the same thing! Tithing, like the training wheels, is meant to teach you to ride the bike of a generous life. It gives you an easy-to-understand system of stable giving in your life. But somewhere along the way, as you mature as a Christian, you are supposed to take those training wheels off and drive that bicycle to an ever-increasing level of generosity. God wants you to increase your giving over time.

Philemon 1:6 says, *"You are generous because of your faith. And I am praying that you will put into action the generosity that comes from your faith as you understand and experience all the good things we have in Christ."*

What are the reasons people give for not tithing? What do our reasons reflect about our belief in God and our hearts toward Him?

Look at the chart below. How much are you currently giving to your church? Based on your income, what is the amount that you should be giving?

Annual Income	Monthly Income	Semimonthly Income (2x)	Weekly Income	Weekly Giving									Tithe		
				1%	2%	3%	4%	5%	6%	7%	8%	9%	10%	12%	15%
$12,000	$1,000	$500	$231	$2	$5	$7	$10	$12	$14	$16	$18	$21	$23	$28	$35
$15,000	$1,250	$625	$288	$3	$6	$9	$12	$14	$17	$20	$23	$26	$29	$35	$43
$18,000	$1,500	$750	$346	$3	$7	$10	$14	$17	$21	$24	$28	$31	$35	$42	$52
$21,000	$1,750	$875	$404	$4	$8	$12	$16	$20	$24	$28	$32	$36	$40	$48	$61
$24,000	$2,000	$1,000	$462	$5	$9	$14	$18	$23	$28	$32	$37	$42	$46	$55	$69
$30,000	$2,500	$1,250	$577	$6	$12	$17	$23	$29	$35	$40	$46	$52	$58	$69	$87
$36,000	$3,000	$1,500	$692	$7	$14	$21	$28	$35	$42	$48	$55	$62	$69	$83	$104
$42,000	$3,500	$1,750	$808	$8	$16	$24	$32	$40	$48	$57	$65	$73	$81	$97	$121
$48,000	$4,000	$2,000	$923	$9	$18	$28	$37	$46	$55	$65	$74	$83	$92	$111	$138
$54,000	$4,500	$2,250	$1,038	$10	$21	$31	$42	$52	$62	$73	$83	$93	$104	$125	$156
$60,000	$5,000	$2,500	$1,154	$12	$23	$35	$46	$58	$69	$81	$92	$104	$115	$138	$173
$66,000	$5,500	$2,750	$1,269	$13	$25	$38	$51	$63	$76	$89	$102	$114	$127	$152	$190
$72,000	$6,000	$3,000	$1,385	$14	$28	$42	$55	$69	$83	$97	$111	$125	$139	$166	$208
$78,000	$6,500	$3,250	$1,500	$15	$30	$45	$60	$75	$90	$105	$120	$135	$150	$180	$225
$84,000	$7,000	$3,500	$1,615	$16	$32	$48	$65	$81	$97	$113	$129	$145	$162	$194	$242
$96,000	$8,000	$4,000	$1,846	$18	$37	$55	$74	$92	$111	$129	$147	$166	$185	$222	$277
$108,000	$9,000	$4,500	$2,077	$21	$42	$62	$83	$104	$125	$145	$166	$187	$208	$249	$312
$120,000	$10,000	$5,000	$2,308	$23	$46	$69	$92	$115	$138	$162	$185	$208	$231	$277	$346

> **"When you choose to obey God, He will show up in your life!"**

NOTES

Which "rung of the ladder" would you say you are on right now? What is your plan to get to where you need to be in your generosity?

Nelson Searcy once shared how he was challenging the people in his church to give a tithe, and he was challenging his people to test God in this. There was a man that came up to Nelson after the service and said, "I'm an atheist. I don't even believe in God, but I'm coming to this church because I like the band and the music, and there are some pretty girls here, but I'm going to take you up on this tithing challenge, and I'm going to prove to you once and for all that God doesn't exist." So he told Nelson how much he made and how much he was going to give over a period of time, and he wrote that on a piece of paper.

Nelson prayed and said, "Ok, God, You have got to come through on this one!" So this atheist put God to the test, and after just a few months of doing this, he prayed to receive Christ, he was baptized in the church, and he was even promoted as an air traffic controller. God showed up in a BIG way!

When you choose to obey God, He will show up in your life! If you want to know that God exists, start tithing. If you want God's blessing on your life, start giving.

I want to challenge you to set some goals in the area of giving to your church. Resolve right now that you are immediately going to go up another rung on the ladder. Allow generosity to motivate you to impact the lives of others for God's kingdom.

EXTRAVAGANT — I give beyond my tithe to my church.

TITHING — I faithfully give 10% of my income to my church.

INTENTIONAL — I give consistently to my church but less than 10% of my income.

OCCASIONAL — I give to my church but not consistently.

FIRST TIME — This will be my first gift to my church.

SIN & TEMPTATION

week 6

Day 1

What Happens When a Christian Sins?

vimeo.com/138215190

NOTES _____

_____
_____
_____
_____
_____
_____
_____
_____
_____
_____
_____
_____
_____
_____
_____
_____
_____
_____
_____
_____

A husband and wife, who had been married for over 25 years, were driving down the road in a single cab pickup truck. The wife looked over at her husband and said, "You know, we used to be so in love. We would sit so much closer to each other in this thing." The husband looked over at his wife and said, "That's true, but I'm not the one who moved."

If you ever feel far away from God, guess who moved? In Acts 17:27 we read, *"He did this so they might seek God, and perhaps they might reach out and find Him, though He is not far from each one of us."* When a Christian sins against God, we do not lose our relationship with Him, but we do lose our *fellowship*.

I have three kids. If one of them does something wrong and they "sin" against their mom and dad, they do not lose a relationship with us. They are still our kids, and we love them unconditionally! In fact, they could never lose a relationship with us because our nature is a part of who they are. They're our own flesh and blood. However, when our kids sin against us, even though they may not lose *relationship*, they do lose *fellowship*. We may not feel as close to them as before. We may not feel, at that moment, like giving them a big hug or taking them out for ice cream. Why? It's because the kids' unrepentant sin has driven a wedge in their relationship with their parents.

I tend to look at our relationship with God the same way. We will always be His kids, but when we sin knowingly and unrepentantly against our Heavenly Father, we're not able to enjoy close intimacy and fellowship with Him. That is why we confess our sins to God – not to maintain our salvation, but to bring ourselves back into close fellowship with the God who loves us and has already forgiven us.

How do you feel when there is unconfessed sin in your life? How does God convict you of your sin?

_____
_____
_____
_____
_____
_____
_____
_____

Three aspects of salvation

It's important for us to understand that salvation really has three aspects that are mentioned in the Bible: justification, sanctification, and glorification. Those are all big words, but they're easy to understand.

"Justification" means we are saved from the *penalty* of sin. When we choose to believe and receive Jesus, God transfers our sin account onto His Son. To be "justified" means "just-as-if-I've-never-sinned." We have gained access to God and become one of His children (Romans 5:1).

"Sanctification" means we're being saved from the *power* of sin. This is the process that the Holy Spirit is working on in our lives here on earth after we make the choice to follow Christ. We still mess up, but through confession and repentance, we're growing in our faith and becoming more like Jesus (1 Thessalonians 5:23).

"Glorification" means we will be saved from the *presence* of sin. Someday when we leave this life and enter into eternity, the full benefit of our salvation will be realized as God once and for all eradicates sin (Romans 8:30).

Sometimes, when the Bible uses the word "salvation," it's talking about all three of those aspects, or it's talking about a specific one of those three, and based on the context of Scripture, we can understand which one it is talking about.

What happens when we sin?

Read Psalm 51.

If there's anything that David teaches us, he demonstrates that if you're bound to sin, you're bound to suffer. In Psalm 51, we find David in the aftermath of the effects of sin in his life. He had committed adultery with a woman named Bathsheba, tried to cover up the unwanted pregnancy, and ultimately put Bathsheba's husband in a position where he would be killed in war. David had committed something both horrible and hurtful, but David was a child of God. In this Psalm, he is looking back on the consequences of his sin, and he leaves this record for us to learn from his experiences as to the consequences when we sin against God. What are those consequences?

Sin will make our souls dirty.

In verse 2, David praye*d*, *"Wash me thoroughly from my iniquity, and cleanse me from my sin."* Now think about that for a moment. David was a king. He lived in a palace. He probably took baths in a marble tub and slept on the cleanest sheets! No one in Israel lived in a more clean and pristine environment than David did, and yet he felt grimy and dirty. If you are a child of God and you sin, you're going to feel dirty. If you can sin and get away with it without feeling unclean or without remorse and shame, that's a sign that you don't really know God.

Sin will dominate our minds.

In verse 3, David said, *"For I know my transgressions and my sin is ever before me."* Notice that phrase, "my sin is ever before me." What David had done was so etched into his memory that it reverberated through his conscience all the time: day and night. Another test as to whether you're saved is not if you can sin, but if you can sin and then just ignore it and forget about it. If you're one of God's kids, the Holy Spirit will put his finger of conviction on that sore spot of sin and push on it until it's dealt with. You see, there are really only two wounds that can come to the human psyche: one is sorrow and the other is guilt. Sorrow is a clean wound. If you have a broken heart or are dealing with a major loss in your life, give it some time and your heart will begin to heal itself. Guilt, however, is a dirty wound. It's like a cancer that spreads, festers, and rots, never stopping until it is cleansed.

> " *Have mercy on me, O God, according to your steadfast love; according to your abundant mercy blot out my transgressions. [2] Wash me thoroughly from my iniquity, and cleanse me from my sin! [3] For I know my transgressions, and my sin is ever before me. [4] Against you, you only, have I sinned and done what is evil in your sight, so that you may be justified in your words and blameless in your judgment. [5] Behold, I was brought forth in iniquity, and in sin did my mother conceive me. [6] Behold, you delight in truth in the inward being, and you teach me wisdom in the secret heart. [7] Purge me with hyssop, and I shall be clean; wash me, and I shall be whiter than snow. [8] Let me hear joy and gladness; let the bones that you have broken rejoice. [9] Hide your face from my sins, and blot out all my iniquities. [10] Create in me a clean heart, O God, and renew a right spirit within me. [11] Cast me not away from your presence, and take not your Holy Spirit from me. [12] Restore to me the joy of your salvation, and uphold me with a willing spirit.* "*
> - Psalm 51

> "An unsaved person feels bad about what his sin does to him; a saved person feels bad about what his sin does to God."

Sin brings disgrace to the God we love.

In verse 4, David was speaking to God, *"Against you, you only, have I sinned and done what is evil in your sight."* Who exactly did David sin against? Some would say that since he committed adultery, he sinned against his own body and against Bathsheba and her husband. He certainly committed sin against his family and ultimately against the entire kingdom he was leading. But none of these is mentioned. He saw his sin for what it primarily was – an affront to a holy God! David truly loved God, and that's why his heart was broken. It dawned on David, "God, you were watching me. Your eyes saw what I did. I've sinned against You. Not only have I broken Your law, I've broken Your heart." Here's something we need to understand: **An unsaved person feels bad about what his sin does to him; a saved person feels bad about what his sin does to God.**

Sin causes our heart to be depressed.

As David continued to talk about the consequences of his sin, he said in verse 8, *"Make me hear joy and gladness, that the bones You have broken may rejoice."* He was despondent; there was no joy or gladness. Sin may be fun while you're doing it, but it always leaves a bitter aftertaste. Proverbs 20:17 says, *"Bread gained by deceit is sweet to a man, but afterward his mouth will be filled with gravel."* David had lost his joy. That's why he prayed to God in verse 12, *"Restore to me the joy of Your salvation."* Notice that David didn't ask for God to restore his salvation. He never lost it. He prayed that God would restore to him the *joy* of his salvation. It's been said that the most miserable person on the face of this earth is the saved person who is out of fellowship with God. You need to understand that there is only one thing that can take away your joy, and that's sin. There's a big difference between joy and happiness. Your happiness depends on what happens to you; the joy that comes from your relationship with Jesus remains constant despite what's going on around you. Happiness is based on outside circumstances; joy is based on inside conditions. When your heart is right with God, there is a joy on the inside of you and a peace that surpasses all understanding.

Sin causes our spirit to be defiled.

In verse 10, David said, *"Create in me a clean heart, O God, and renew a steadfast spirit within me."* David's sin caused him to have a sour and defiled spirit. It's amazing how when we get out of fellowship with God, it causes us to be pretty cantankerous and hard to get along with. We get a sour spirit, and nothing can please us. One of the marks of someone who has lost their close intimacy with God is the development of a critical spirit. In another passage of Scripture, we see what David was like before he came back to God. He still had not repented from either his adultery or the cover-up of Uriah's murder. The prophet Nathan knew it, and he came before David telling him a fictitious story about a rich man who had everything he could ever wish for – houses, land, large farm, and a big family. The man lived next door to a poor man, who has nothing but a pet lamb. This lamb was like one of his own children; it even ate from the same table. And the man who was very rich and had everything stole the poor man's lamb, killed it, and had a big barbecue party! Nathan asked David, "So what do you think ought to be done to this rich man?" David was livid! He immediately ordered that the rich man be punished and forced to repay the poor man four-fold! Nathan created this parable just to show how defiled David's spirit had become. The king was judging a man for stealing a lamb when he himself had stolen a woman. He was criticizing someone for killing an animal when he had killed a man. He was so quick to see the sin in someone else's life, but he was unable to acknowledge the sin in his own life. The person who is out of fellowship with God is always quick to find fault in everybody else. Hermann Hesse said, "If you hate a person, you hate something in him that is part of yourself. What isn't part of ourselves doesn't disturb us. We tend to react negatively to the dark shadows in others that also reside in ourselves."

Sin distracts us from our purpose.

This is one of the most damaging aspects about sin in the life of a Christian. David went on to pray, *"Restore to me the joy of Your salvation ... then I will teach transgressors Your ways, and sinners shall be converted to you"* (vs. 12-13). He is saying in effect, "Lord, put my feet on the right path, and I'm going to get back to serving you."

In Psalm 51:2-3, David prayed to God: *"Wash me thoroughly from my iniquity, and cleanse me from my sin. For I acknowledge my transgressions, and my sin is always before me."*

Notice what David called it. He emphasized that it was "my" iniquity, "my" sin, and "my" transgressions, not somebody else's. He was owning up to the failures and the mistakes he made. There is one thing that God will never accept for sin, and that is an excuse. When the Holy Spirit convicts us of a shortcoming in our life, we need to own up to it and confess it.

Why do you think we are sometimes hesitant to confess our sin, even when we know God will forgive and cleanse us?

_____

_____

_____

_____

_____

_____

_____

_____

Satanic accusation vs. Holy Spirit conviction

It's important for us to understand the difference between satanic accusation and Holy Spirit conviction. The Bible says that the devil is the "accuser of the brethren" (Revelation 12:10), and he does it in two primary ways:

1. The devil will accuse you of sin that has already been confessed. The devil will sometimes keep dredging up your past to you to make you feel guilty and unworthy. Satan loves to dig up your past mistakes and throw them back in your face. But when God buries your sin, it is gone. God will never bring you into double jeopardy. Acts 11:9 says, *"Do not call anything impure that God has made clean."*

2. The devil will try to make you feel guilty for no reason. That is, you just feel bad all over, but not over any specific. You feel like a loser and doubt that God could ever love you or use you. The devil loves to either dredge up sin that has been forgiven or make you have a general sense of angst without giving it a name. When that happens, take it for what it is – satanic accusation.

What is the Holy Spirit's conviction? Conviction is the Holy Spirit putting a firm pressure on a very specific sin you have committed and reminding you it was wrong. Like a good doctor, God will put His finger right on that specific sore spot and push. He will call it by name and want you to confess

> **" Happiness is based on outside circumstances; joy is based on inside conditions. "**

NOTES _____

_____

_____

_____

_____

_____

_____

_____

_____

_____

_____

_____

_____

_____

_____

_____

_____

_____

_____

143

> **"**Though your sins are like scarlet, they shall be as white as snow; though they are red like crimson, they shall be as wool.**"**
> - Isaiah 1:18

it and be cleansed. Satan will accuse you generally, but the Holy Spirit will convict you specifically.

So can a Christian still sin? Yes. Can a Christian sin and not suffer? Absolutely not. The two most expensive things in this world are salvation and sin. Salvation is so expensive because it cost God His Son. Sin is so expensive because, if it is not dealt with, it will cost you your soul. The way that you deal with your sin will determine the way that God will deal with you. Spend some time today asking the Holy Spirit to reveal to you any sin in your heart that is unconfessed or unrepented.

Sin makes you feel dirty, but God wants to give you a spiritual bath. In Isaiah 1:18 we read, *"Though your sins are like scarlet, they shall be as white as snow; though they are red like crimson, they shall be as wool."* That's the power of the cleansing grace of God. You don't have to carry your baggage around.

In your own words, how would you explain the difference between Holy Spirit conviction and Satanic accusation?

_____

_____

_____

_____

_____

_____

_____

Unloading your garbage

In 1986, in the city of Philadelphia, the sanitation workers went on strike during the Democratic National Convention. This meant that over 15,000 tons of trash was accumulating in the city, and they needed a place to put it. This trash was loaded onto a huge ship called the Pelicano. The Pelicano collected all the trash and sought out a place to offload its toxic cargo. But after more than two years of traveling and more than 11 countries, the Pelicano became the most unwanted ship in the world. No place would take it in and no place would relieve it of its burden. What is true of the Pelicano is true of many lives today. They're carrying around the burdens of life that have accumulated over the years. They are carrying around the difficulty and the disappointments, the pain and the circumstances that are weighing them down, and they have no place to offload them. The answer is simple. Jesus said, *"Come to me all of those who are carrying those heavy burdens and I will give you rest."* Jesus Christ offers you a harbor in which to dock and offload life's burdens. He is your rest.

NOTES _____

_____

_____

_____

_____

_____

_____

_____

_____

_____

_____

_____

_____

_____

_____

_____

_____

_____

_____

_____

_____

Day 2

What Is Spiritual Warfare?

vimeo.com/138215262

You need to realize that you are in a war that is unlike any other war ever fought in human history because it's a spiritual war. In Ephesians 6:12 we read, *"For we do not wrestle against flesh and blood, but against principalities, against powers, against the rulers of the darkness of this age, against spiritual forces of wickedness in heavenly places."*

What does that mean? The Bible teaches us that we actually live in two worlds. The physical world is the one we're all aware of, but then there is the world behind this world, the spiritual realm. Here's what you need to understand: Everything visible and physical is controlled by something invisible and spiritual. Therefore, if you want to change the realm that you know, you must draw from the invisible spiritual realm that you do not see. Behind every conflict, temptation, or issue we face is a spiritual root. And unless we first identify and deal with the root spiritual cause, our attempts to fix the physical problems will only provide temporary relief at best. In other words, everything that your five senses experience physically is first generated by something your five senses cannot detect.

The invisible world

The invisible (spiritual) world is just as real as the visible world, and both Old and New Testaments refer to it often. In 2 Kings 6:15-19, the evil king of Aran was determined to find and kill God's prophet Elisha. One morning, Elisha's servant woke up at sunrise and went outside. Surrounding the city of Dothan were hundreds, maybe thousands, of horses, chariots, and warriors. They had come to the city with one goal, and Elisha, who was sound asleep inside, was the target. The servant panicked and woke Elisha. When Elisha walked outside and assessed the situation, he offered one of the strangest statements in all of Scripture: *"Do not fear, for those who are with us are more than those who are with them"* (2 Kings 6:16). Elisha's servant was probably thinking that the old man had lost his mind. His prophecies were great, but his math was terrible. They were completely surrounded by this vast enemy army. But Elisha said, "Don't worry. We have the upper hand." Elisha then prayed and said, *"'Oh LORD, please open his eyes that he may see.' So the LORD opened the eyes of the young man, and he saw, and behold, the mountain was full of horses and chariots of fire all around Elisha."* When the servant's eyes saw what was going on in the unseen spiritual world, he was amazed. God's heavenly forces were ready to fight supernaturally for these servants of God. For just a brief moment, God allowed the invisible to become visible, and it was incredible.

NOTES _____

> **"Everything visible and physical is controlled by something invisible and spiritual."**

NOTES

Satan often tries to keep you from taking the spiritual realm seriously. He knows that if he can just divert your attention away from the spiritual realm, he can keep you away from the only place where true victory may be found. But we must remember that if all you see is what you see, you will never see all that there is to be seen. The physical world simply manifests what is already happening in the spiritual realm.

Paul reminds us *"our battle is not against flesh and blood."* Your battle is not against your neighbor, spouse, co-worker, child, or even our own weaknesses in the flesh. All of those things are simply the fruit and not the root behind our battle. People are simply conduits of the spiritual battle that is taking place in another realm – the *"heavenly places."* Whether you realize it or not, you're in a war. There is an unseen spiritual battle that is taking place all around you.

Because of the decisive move by God to save you and transform your life, Satan no longer has authority over you. His only means to overcome you is to deceive you. C.S. Lewis stated, "There is no neutral ground in the universe: every square inch, every split second is claimed by God, and counterclaimed by Satan."

Satan's four-fold attack on your life

1. Satan wants to *choke* out your prayer life.
Acts 16 tells us that as soon as Paul and Silas went to pray, the woman with a demonic spirit came to harass them, interrupting their prayers. Satan doesn't want you to pray! When you don't pray on a regular basis, it's like you're not breathing. He wants to choke out your prayer life. He wants you to worry about everything and pray about nothing.

2. Satan wants to *constrict* your faith.
Another interesting note about Acts 16 is that this demonic attack took place as Paul and Silas were stepping out on their missionary journey. This was the first time Paul had gone to this part of the world, and Satan decides to show up on the scene! I've seen it happen so many times when you're trying to break out, you're trying to expand your influence for the Lord, you're launching a new dream, or you're going into new territory. That is when Satan comes in and tries to limit you and constrict your faith. He wants to hold you back and keep you from moving forward, making you feel as if there's an invisible force around your business or your ministry. You feel like you're doing all you can, but you just can't go any further.

3. Satan wants to *conflict* your relationships.
The wrong words exchanged between two individuals can give power to the devil. Take marriage for example. Married life starts out as the *ideal*. A few months later, there's an *ordeal*. Before long you start thinking you've got a *raw deal*. Then you start looking for a *new deal*. Why? Because this constricting, conflicting spirit has come into your marriage. Scripture says, *"Death and life are in the power of the tongue."*

4. Satan wants to *cause* you to fall morally.
Jesus said that Satan has come to steal, kill, and destroy (John 10:10). The word "devil" comes from the Greek word *diabolos*. It's a compound word made up of the Greek words *dia* and *ballo*. This name is used 61 times in the New Testament. The first part of that word is the prefix *dia*, which means "through," and it has the idea of "penetrating something all the way through." The devil is looking for some sort of "entry point" to gain access into your life. The second part of the word is *bolos*, which means "to throw."

When you put those two words together to form the word *diabolas*, it paints a vivid picture of the devil as one who repeatedly throws accusations at the mind, striking again and again until he ultimately penetrates the mind with his slanderous lies and relationship-destroying insinuations.

So how do we combat this? Any military official would tell you that the most difficult enemy to fight is the one you cannot see. Fortunately, God's Word shows us how to combat it. Paul compares our weapons of defense to a suit of armor that a warrior would wear. Ephesians 6:11 says, *"Put on the whole armor of God, that you may be able to stand against the schemes of the devil."* Paul wrote these words when he was sitting in a jail cell, probably looking at a Roman soldier standing guard. Paul was making the point that everything this soldier needed to successfully combat his enemy was at his disposal. Likewise, we have the whole armor of God at our disposal. *Everything* that you and I need to live our life of victory is there, and *nothing* is lacking.

Read Ephesians 6:10-17. What are the six pieces of armor that Paul lists? Write down any other observations or questions that you may have.

_____

_____

_____

_____

_____

_____

_____

_____

Armor for the war

Let's look at each of those pieces of armor individually and analyze their symbolic meaning and what they mean to us today.

Belt of Truth

What was the purpose of a soldier's belt? It had both a *utility* function as well as a *mobility* function. Not only would it hold additional pieces of armor, but it would also help the soldier move faster. When he was ready to head into battle, he could reach down and pick up the part of his tunic that was down towards his feet and tuck it into his belt. The purpose of the belt was to stabilize things by keeping them in their proper order.

When we understand and live by God's truth, all other areas of our life are stabilized. Jesus said in John 8:32, *"You will know the truth and the truth will set you free."* It's the *knowledge* of that truth that sets you free. One of Satan's greatest strategies is to set up worldviews, speculations, or viewpoints that are contradictory to Scripture (2 Corinthians 10:3-5). Our worldview (our belief system; frame of reference; and basic assumptions about what is true, real, and good) determines a person's behavior. Your worldview is the lens by which you see everything in life. Satan will use what you see in magazines, movies, music, and the media to plant erroneous thoughts into your mind. We need to make sure that our lives are anchored to the truth of Scripture, not just what we think feels good or is the most pragmatic viewpoint for us.

> Finally, be strong in the Lord and in the strength of his might. [11] Put on the whole armor of God, that you may be able to stand against the schemes of the devil. [12] For we do not wrestle against flesh and blood, but against the rulers, against the authorities, against the cosmic powers over this present darkness, against the spiritual forces of evil in the heavenly places. [13] Therefore take up the whole armor of God, that you may be able to withstand in the evil day, and having done all, to stand firm. [14] Stand therefore, having fastened on the belt of truth, and having put on the breastplate of righteousness, [15] and, as shoes for your feet, having put on the readiness given by the gospel of peace. [16] In all circumstances take up the shield of faith, with which you can extinguish all the flaming darts of the evil one; [17] and take the helmet of salvation, and the sword of the Spirit, which is the word of God.

- Ephesians 6:10-17

> **"Faith is never tied to your feelings; faith is based on your feet – what you do in response to what you believe."**

Breastplate of Righteousness

A soldier wore a piece of armor that went from the bottom of his neck down to his waist. It could be made of solid metal or a woven chain. Its purpose was to protect all of the vital organs, especially the heart. When the Bible talks about your heart, it's talking about the center of your being – your intellect, emotions, and will. It's the real battleground where Satan wants to wage war in your life. Paul is saying that we need to put on righteousness – literally put on purity over our heart. There are two sides to righteousness: the *being* side and the *doing* side. The Bible tells us that Jesus has credited ("imputed") His righteousness onto our account when we choose to receive Him as Savior (2 Corinthians 5:21). When you got saved, God not only *removed* the stain of sin but He also *replaced* that stain with the righteous standard of Christ. So now when God looks at you, He sees you through the blood of Jesus. He doesn't just see someone who has been forgiven of their sins. He sees someone who has the full standard of the righteousness of Christ. Only when we fully understand our *position* of righteousness do we walk in the *practice* of righteousness.

Proverbs tells us, *"Above all else, guard your heart, for it is the wellspring of life."* Putting on the breastplate of righteousness is saying, "Lord, I am going to live a life of purity!"

Shoes of the Gospel of Peace

Back in the ancient world, shoes weren't a matter of fashion as much as they were a matter of function. A Roman soldier's shoes were called *caliga*, which were sandals studded heavily with hobnails in the soles of the shoe. Not only would those shoes provide durability and stability, but they would also allow for greater mobility. They were like the cleats that football or soccer players wear today. It would allow them to be more mobile and also make it more difficult for them to be knocked down.

Paul is saying that we have this "gripping power" when we have the shoes of the gospel of peace. The word "peace" means different things to different people, but in the language of the Bible, peace means "completeness, wholeness, and an inner resting of the soul that does not fluctuate based on outside circumstances." Colossians 3:15 says, *"Let the peace of Christ rule in your hearts."* The word for "rule" essentially means "to umpire." In other words, peace is to be our umpire. In the game of baseball, the main joy of an umpire is to ultimately declare the way things are. If the umpire calls a runner out, that runner is out! So the peace of Christ is to make the call in your life. What does Satan want to do? He wants to eradicate peace and make you live your life always looking over your shoulder, always worried, and always doubting the intentions of the people around you.

That is why we always need to have on the shoes of the gospel of peace. In 1 Peter 3:15, we read that if we are ever asked about our Christian hope, we need to be ready to explain it. We need to always be ready, at a moment's notice, to seize those opportunities to share the gospel and to tell others about Christ.

Shield of Faith

The word for "shield" used here is *thureos*, which would be a large shield measuring four feet long by three feet wide. It was used to block and shield the entire body from arrows or hard blows from the enemy. So what is faith that acts like a shield to us in our life? The simplest definition of faith I've ever heard is that faith is acting as if God is telling the truth. Another way of putting it is, "Faith is acting as if something is so even when it appears not to be so in order that it might be shown to be so because God said so." Faith simply means that you are believing God to do what He has said He will do. When you are under attack and you feel like all hell is breaking loose in your

NOTES

life, you need to lift up your shield of faith! When your finances are so low and you don't see how you're going to make it another week, take up your shield of faith. When you're breaking down emotionally and have lost your passion in life, block Satan's arrows of doubt with your shield of faith. Faith is never tied to your feelings; faith is based on your feet – what you do in response to what you believe. It is acting on the truth, whether you feel the truth or not.

Helmet of Salvation

A helmet serves an obvious purpose – to protect the head. But it also is a reminder of a spiritual principle: every attack Satan will send will come through your mind. He knows the value of getting a foothold in your thoughts and imagination because this will prepare the way for that thought to translate into action. Beliefs always determine behavior. That's why we have to be on guard against the thoughts we allow our minds to dwell on because it can and will give the enemy leverage. You can't control everything you're exposed to, but you can control a few things. You can control what you watch on TV. You can control what you read and listen to. You can control what websites you visit. Be careful what you allow into your mind. Keep the helmet of salvation on.

Sword of the Spirit

Paul wraps up the description of the armor of God with *"take the sword of the Spirit, which is the Word of God."* Your Bible is a sword. Notice that this is the only offensive weapon we have in our possession from which to combat spiritual warfare. All the other pieces of armor are defensive in nature. In Hebrews 4:12 we read that *"the Word of God is quick and powerful, sharper than any two-edged sword."* When the devil attacks you, your best offense is to have a specific Scripture that deals with that specific issue of attack. That's why I want to encourage you to take in the Word every day, and become a great swordsman of Scripture. When you became a Christian, God not only put salvation in your heart, but He also put a sword in your hand.

If you're experiencing a lot of spiritual battles lately, congratulations! That means you're alive, you're active, and the devil is concerned about you. Charles Spurgeon used to say, "Satan never kicks a dead horse." We need to keep in mind that Satan is watching, searching, and waiting to find a crack in your armor. He knows where there is sin in your life. Paul says, *"do not give a place to the devil"* (Eph. 4:27). He knows where your tendencies and weaknesses are, and he will attack you repeatedly in that very place. But God hasn't left you defenseless. Put on that spiritual armor today!

Take a moment to reflect on today's lesson. What are three observations you have made today about spiritual warfare?

NOTES

Day 3

How Do I Keep My Mind Pure?

vimeo.com/138215312

vimeo.com/138215312

NOTES _____

_____
_____
_____
_____
_____
_____
_____
_____
_____
_____
_____
_____
_____
_____
_____
_____
_____
_____
_____
_____
_____

Your life will always move in the direction of the dominant images you allow to reside in your mind. Those images become thoughts that will eventually become actions. You can't always control what appears before your eyes, but you can control how long you look. Your mind is the line of scrimmage in your life. Whoever or whatever controls your mind controls you.

Mind control

Read 2 Corinthians 10:3-5: *"For though we walk in the flesh, we are not waging war according to the flesh. For the weapons of our warfare are not of the flesh but have divine power to destroy strongholds. We destroy arguments and every lofty opinion raised against the knowledge of God, and take every thought captive to obey Christ ..."*

According to that scripture, what are the measures we should take toward any thought that attempts to exalt itself above the Word of God?

_____
_____
_____
_____
_____
_____
_____

As you read that passage, there are a few words that jump off the page: war, weapons, fight, and strongholds. There is a battle that started the moment you began to think for yourself. Paul says that your mind is like a fort or a castle that is constantly under attack. Why is the devil so interested in your mind? Because he knows that if he can control your mind, he can control you. Your mind is the control center of who you are. Everything you do begins with a thought.

Ralph Waldo Emerson said, "Life consists of what a man is thinking about all day." Your thoughts determine your behavior. Proverbs 23:7 says, *"For as a man thinks within himself, so is he."* John Locke said, "The actions of men are the best interpreters of their thoughts." Sow a thought, reap an action; sow an action, reap a habit; sow a habit, reap a character; sow a character, reap a destiny. Notice that the first link in the chain is the thought.

If you could build a computer that could do everything the human mind can do and be just as powerful, that computer would be larger than the Empire State Building, a city block wide and a city block deep. Dr. Elinore Kinarthy noted that more than 10,000 thoughts pass between your ears every day. The average person has more than 200 negative thoughts a day, including worries, jealousies, insecurities, cravings for sinful things, etc. Depressed people have an average of 600. You can't eliminate all the troublesome things that go through your mind, but you can certainly reduce the number of negative thoughts.

If you are going to succeed in the Christian life, you not only need to learn *with* your mind, you need to learn *about* your mind.

We need to first understand that Satan wants to capture our minds. God has a wonderful plan for your life (Jeremiah 29:11), but Satan has a sinister plan for your life. And whomever you get into agreement with, that's whose plan is going to come to pass. 2 Corinthians 10:3 says, *"For though we live in the world, we do not wage war as the world does."* Paul immediately says that this war is not one that we can see; it's a war that we cannot see. It's a mental and spiritual war. From the time Satan entered into the world, he has had only one strategy: control, capture, and corrupt your mind. Satan has aimed his heaviest artillery at your mind because he knows that if he captures your mind, he captures you. If you can get someone to think in the wrong way, they will start living the wrong way.

Satan's strategy

Satan's strategy against our minds is aimed at both the lost as well as the saved.

For the lost, Satan's goal is to darken their mind. In 2 Corinthians 4:4 we read, *"The god of this age has blinded the minds of unbelievers, so that they cannot see the light of the gospel of the glory of Christ, who is the image of God."* Many people who aren't convinced that God is real quite frankly don't *want* to be convinced. Their minds are blinded. The gospel is so simple, but why do they not see it? That question is answered by 1 Corinthians 2:14: *"The natural man does not receive the things of the Spirit of God, for they are foolishness to him; nor can he know them, because they are spiritually discerned."* Satan's goal for those who do not yet know Christ is to continue to keep them in spiritual darkness. That's why you need to pray for them to be exposed to the light of God's truth.

For the saved, Satan's goal is to defile their mind. Every temptation we will ever experience comes to us via our thoughts. In 2 Corinthians 11:3 we read, *"But I fear, lest somehow, as the serpent deceived Eve by his craftiness, so your minds may somehow be led astray from your sincere and pure devotion to Christ."* Every day we are bombarded with contaminating thoughts in movies, media, and music. We're attacked with self-defeating thoughts such as fear, anxiety, depression, and low self-esteem.

When it comes to how our minds work, there are two laws that contribute heavily to our mental state of being – the Law of Concentration and the Law of Substitution. The Law of Concentration states that whatever we dwell upon grows in our life experience. Whatever we think about on a continual basis becomes a part of us. We become what we think, and the more we dwell on something, the more we have of it in our lives.

The Law of Substitution states that our conscious mind can only hold one thought at a time. Dr. Joel Santos stated, "It makes no difference to our mind whether the thought is 'negative' or 'positive,' it can only hold one at a time. However, we can choose to substitute 'negative' thoughts with 'positive' thoughts, thus changing our mental state of being."

> " Satan has aimed his heaviest artillery at your mind because he knows that if he captures your mind, he captures you. "

NOTES

> **"**For the mind set on the flesh is death, but the mind controlled by the Spirit is life and peace.**"**
> - Romans 8:6

How to win the battle of your mind

1. Refocus Your Mind.

In Colossians 3:2 we read, *"Set your mind on the things above, not on the things that are on earth."* That is a very powerful truth. The Bible teaches that you can determine the direction your mind goes. One author said, "Too many minds are like plankton, a small sea plant that goes wherever the current takes it." We need to learn how to form new habits and how to concentrate. In Romans 8:6 we read, *"For the mind set on the flesh is death, but the mind controlled by the Spirit is life and peace."* What does it mean to be spiritually minded? It means that you have allowed the Holy Spirit of God to always be bringing holy, pure, and godly thoughts to the forefront of your mind. Just like a compass always points north, the spiritually minded person will always point towards God.

So what do you do when sinful, negative thoughts enter your mind?

You reject them. Stay on the offensive and be aggressive. Scripture says that our weapons to win the battle for our minds are not physical but rather *"have divine power to destroy strongholds"* (2 Corinthians 10:4). A stronghold can be defined as a wrongful thinking pattern. It's an area of "stinking thinking" that has gotten you into a rut and is not in agreement with God's Word. What is your greatest stronghold in your thinking? When those thoughts even remotely flash across your mind, you need to take that thought *"captive to the obedience of Christ"* (vs. 5).

You replace them. Find a verse of Scripture to replace that negative thought. When the enemy tells you that you're a loser and you'll never amount to anything, quote Scripture such as Psalm 84:11, *"No good thing does He withhold from those who walk uprightly."* When Satan reminds you that you have too many weaknesses, quote 2 Corinthians 12:9, *"And He said to me, 'My strength is made perfect in your weakness...'"* We reject those negative thoughts by keeping our minds filled with God's Word.

You respond with just the opposite of what Satan is telling you. John 8:44 tells us that the enemy cannot tell the truth. So when he brings his lies about you and your family, you need to turn it around and tell the devil just the opposite. When you are negative, you are in agreement with the enemy, but when you're positive, you're in agreement with God.

2. Refill Your Mind.

You substitute the wrong thoughts by filling your mind with the right thoughts. If you're battling with lust, bitterness, worry, or anger, how do you get rid of that? By refilling your mind. When you travel through an airport, you have to go through security checkpoints with TSA. Before you can pass through, you have to go through a metal detector and take off anything that might set off the alarm – your watch, belt buckle, shoes, cell phone, and so forth. You need to have a checkpoint like that at the gate of your mind. Paul gives us a list of those things that we should only let through. In Philippians 4:8, he says, *"Finally, brethren, whatever is true, whatever is honorable, whatever is right, whatever is pure, whatever is lovely, whatever is of good repute, if there is any excellence and if anything is worthy of praise, dwell on these things."* Paul gives us a grid to test our thoughts before we allow our mind to dwell on them.

- **The Reliance Test** – *"whatever is true ..."*
  Can you bank on it and rely on it? Is it true? We live in a generation today that doesn't ask, "Is it true?" but rather, "Does it work?"
  Don't let anything dwell in your mind or enter into your philosophy of life or worldview of thought if it doesn't agree with the supreme source of truth – the Bible.

- **The Respect Test** – *"whatever is honorable ..."*
Do you allow dishonorable things to get into your mind – things that are not worthy to occupy so much of your "think" time. Some things are not necessarily bad because they're vile but because they are just not worth spending time thinking about it.

- **The Rightness Test** – *"whatever is right ..."*
The word "right" means "straight" as opposed to crooked. Don't let any crooked thinking come into your mind.

- **The Reverence Test** – *"whatever is pure ..."*
The word "pure" means "free from contamination." It was a word that was used for an animal sacrifice to determine if it was good enough to be used in worship. In other words, could this thought be offered to God? Is this something that I would be ashamed to offer to God? Can I take this novel, this movie, this relationship and say, "Lord, I want to bring glory to you through this."

- **The Relationship Test** – *"whatever is lovely ..."*
The word "lovely" doesn't mean beautiful. It literally means "causing you to love." Does this thought that you're dwelling on cause you to love in a way that honors God and is kept pure? If there is something that comes into your mind that causes you to criticize unjustly or brings division between you and another person, then you need to refuse to dwell on it in your thoughts.

- **The Good Report Test** – *"whatever is of good repute ..."*
This means those things that are "high toned," meaning that it sounds good. People who are gossips and those who love to listen to gossip enjoy receiving things that are not of "good repute" about other people.

- **The Radiant Test** – *"if there is any excellence and if anything is worthy of praise, dwell on these things."*
This means that you focus and dwell on the positive side of life.

The reality is, we cannot always control the fleeting thoughts that flash upon the screen of our minds, but we can choose the thoughts that we dwell on. Billy Graham used to say, "You can't keep a bird from flying over your head, but you can keep it from making a nest in your hair." Keeping your mind pure involves avoiding "stinking thinking" and allowing those thoughts to make a nest in your head. A lot of people don't realize we can choose our thoughts. Just because a thought comes into our minds doesn't mean that we have to think on it. We can either dwell on that thought or ignore it. James Allen said, "Good thoughts bear good fruit. Bad thoughts bear bad fruit. And man is his own gardener."

You can't just make up your mind to stop thinking about something. If I were to tell you: Stop thinking about an elephant! Don't think about an elephant! What are you thinking about right now? An image of Dumbo just popped into your mind. Just trying to "stop" thinking the wrong thoughts doesn't work. The wrong thoughts must be replaced with something else. Keep your mind off the thoughts you don't want by keeping it on the thoughts you do want.

Why is it that when we have the freedom to think any thought we choose, we still select thoughts that bring us down?

> **"** Good thoughts bear good fruit. Bad thoughts bear bad fruit. And man is his own gardener. **"**

NOTES _____

_____

_____

_____

_____

_____

_____

_____

_____

_____

_____

_____

_____

_____

_____

_____

_____

_____

_____

_____

"If you want to change your life, you must *first* change your thinking."

3. Renew Your Mind.

In Romans 12:2 we read, *"And do not be conformed to this world, but be continuously transformed by the renewing of your mind."* We are transformed by the renewing of our minds. We're not totally transformed when we are born-again; our mind needs to be renewed day by day. You've probably heard that little axiom computer programmers use: "Garbage in, garbage out." Well, I have some great news for you: as soon as the Word of God goes in, the garbage goes out! For some people, they have allowed the devil to make a bed in their mind. (And he doesn't pay any rent or buy any groceries.) Every day, he torments you, contaminates you, dirties you, and leads you astray. He's got a stronghold in your mind. You need to pray, "God fill my mind with the knowledge of You!"

When God wants to communicate with you, all He has to work with is your mind. When God wants to change you, He does it by renewing your mind. When God wants to calm you, He does it by the renewing of your mind. But if we don't allow our minds to be renewed, we will limit ourselves in our relationship with God. If you want to change your life, you must *first* change your thinking.

I once heard a story about a Native American on a reservation who gave his heart to the Lord and was born again. He went to his pastor a few weeks later and said, "Pastor, I have a problem. Now that I'm saved, every day I feel like there is an internal fight going on in my mind. It's like there is a white dog and a black dog fighting each other to the death."

The old, wise pastor understood the new Native American Christian was referring to the invisible war that we all fight between our new nature that feeds on the Word of God and spiritual things on the one hand and the old nature that feeds on the lust of the flesh, the lust of the eyes, and the pride of life on the other. The pastor asked the man, "So Joe, which dog wins the fight?"

The man paused for a moment and said, "You know, I never thought about it before, but the dog I feed the most wins the fight."

The same is true for you and me. We have to understand that we are constantly feeding ourselves. Everything we watch and listen to, the people we choose to be around, the thoughts we dwell on – they all feed our inner man. When it comes to the battle for your thought life, if you feed your carnal nature on impure thoughts, then that dog will win the battle for your thought life. On the other hand, if you feed the new nature you have been given on the Word of God, uplifting messages, and wholesome thoughts, then your new nature will defeat the power of temptation to sin. Which dog are you feeding the most? That's the one that will win the fight.

Day 4

How Can I Come Clean With God?

The greatest single attribute of God is his Holiness. The adjective "holy" is used to describe God more than any other adjective in the Bible. Right now in Heaven, the angels around God's throne are saying, *"Holy, holy, holy is the LORD Almighty; the whole earth is full of his glory"* (Isaiah 6:3). The word "holy" is used three times, not because the angels have a stuttering problem, but because in Hebrew, repeating something three times was their way of emphasizing something or saying, "This is of the greatest importance."

Like Father, like son

Tony Evans says this about God: "Holiness is the centerpiece of God's attributes. Of all the things God is, at the center of His being, God is holy. Never in the Bible is God called, 'love, love, love,' or 'eternal, eternal, eternal,' or 'truth, truth, truth.' On this one aspect of His character, God has laid the most stress." This is important to emphasize because your view of God determines your relationship with God.

In 1 Peter 1:15-16 we read, *"Be holy yourselves also in all your behavior; because it is written, 'You shall be holy, for I am holy.'"* Because God is holy, we as His children are expected to be holy.

Have you ever heard that phrase, "Like father, like son"? You would expect to see the nature of the father reproduced in the child. There was a young man getting ready to go off to college, and his father said to him, "Son, I don't have much to give you, but one thing I have given you is my name. Please do not do anything with my name that I wouldn't do with it." That son knew that for him to sin without regard to the name that he carried would cause his father the deepest pain.

I am a Park. My father's name is W.T. Earl Park. Because he fathered me, I have become a partaker of his nature. You would expect to find his traits and characteristics in me because he is my dad. As Christians, we bear the name of Christ, yet every time we set a poor example or live in a sinful way, we not only cause a breach in our own fellowship with God, but we also cause others to misunderstand the holiness of the God we say we serve.

So what does "holiness" mean? It means to be separate and distinct. Jesus said that as His disciples we are to be *"in the world but not of the world"* (John 17:15). That doesn't mean that we need to be *isolated* from the world, but we do need to be *insulated* from it. It's like a ship out on the open sea. It's ok for a ship to be out on the water – that's what it was made for. But it's not ok for the water to be inside the ship! Too many people have shipwrecked their lives because they've allowed sin to sink them into the

vimeo.com/138215362

NOTES _____

155

> ## "If you don't understand grace, you'll never be relieved of guilt."

abyss of guilt and shame, and they can't see any way back.

The good news is that the holiness that God demands from you is the holiness that only He can give to you. God is not only *why* we are to be holy; God is the *way* to be holy.

When you have a heavy heart full of regret and remorse, and you decide to come back to God, He is willing to claim the baggage of your past guilt. But here's the reality: If you don't understand *grace*, you'll never be relieved of *guilt*.

What did Jesus mean when He said we are to be "in the world, but not of the world?" What does that look like for a disciple of Jesus today?

_____

_____

_____

_____

_____

_____

_____

Prodigal son

I believe that the greatest picture we have in the Bible that illustrates God's grace and how we can come clean with God is the story of the prodigal son. In Luke 15, the story Jesus told begins with a son who evidently had a good home and godly parents – everything you could want in life. But somehow, the root of ingratitude had grown into the fruit of rebellion. He went to his father and demanded his inheritance. He said, *"Father, give me my share of the estate."* Normally, the inheritance of an estate wouldn't be given until after the father dies, but this son wanted his inheritance *immediately*. Basically, this young man was saying to his father, "I wish you were dead already. I want what you have, but I don't want you."

People today treat God like the prodigal son treated his father. They want what God has to give – they want to enjoy God's world, but they don't want God.

This father did what he wasn't required to do. He gave his son what he asked for – his portion of the inheritance. And Jesus said, *"Not long after that, the younger son got together all he had, set off for a far country and there squandered his wealth in wild living"* (Luke 15:13). He let the good times roll. He slept by day and partied by night. Basically, if it felt good, he did it! But the prodigal soon found out that the pleasures of sin eventually turn into the poison of sorrow. I'm not going to lie to you and say there isn't any fun in sin. If that were the case, none of us would ever do it! Hebrews 11:25 speaks of the *"pleasures of sin,"* but that's not the end of that verse. The Bible says that the pleasures of sin are *"for a season."* You can get plenty of kicks out of sin, but sin always comes with its kickbacks.

After the prodigal had spent all of his money, and had all of his fun living high on the hog, he ended up living lower than the hogs. Scripture says that he eventually got to the point where he was so destitute he found himself in a field feeding pigs and wishing that he could eat what the pigs were eating. The most dishonorable job a Jew could ever have would be to work with swine because pigs were considered unclean. And yet here was a Jewish boy who once had everything in life he could have ever wanted slopping around with pigs. He had learned a lesson that every prodigal will learn sooner or later: Sin will take

you further than you want to go, keep you longer than you want to stay, and cost you more than you want to pay.

The father agreed to give the son his inheritance. What does this teach us about God, our Father?

_____

_____

_____

_____

_____

_____

_____

> ❝ Sin will take you further than you want to go, keep you longer than you want to stay, and cost you more than you want to pay. ❞

Fortunately, the story doesn't end there. In Luke 15:17 we read, *"When he came to his senses, he said, 'How many of my father's hired men have food to spare, and here I am starving to death!"* When he finally understood how wrong he had been, he knew what he needed to do. He planned to go back to his father's house and say, *"I am no longer worthy to be called your son; make me like one of your hired men."* Notice that phrase, *"make me."* Before he left home, the prodigal was saying, *"Give me,"* but now he's taken a much different tone. He's saying, *"Make me."* That is the key to unlocking the door to change in your life. When you come before God with a heart that says, "Make me. Fashion me. Mold me." You would be surprised what God can do with such a life.

When the prodigal son started his long journey home, Jesus said that as soon as his father saw him *"while he was still a long way off,"* he was filled with compassion towards the son who had been lost for so long. The father ran toward him, threw his arms around him, and kissed him. You see, although the son had forgotten about his father, the father had never forgotten about his son. You can read the Bible cover-to-cover, and you will never find God running away from man. God never runs from you; He always runs toward you. For every step you take toward God, He will take two steps toward you.

In verse 21 we read the son's confession to his dad: *"Father, I have sinned against heaven and against you. I am no longer worthy to be called your son."* The son didn't even have time to add that he would be willing to work as his dad's hired servant. The father was so busy with compassion he didn't have time for confession. Notice that the father never brought up the past. That illustrates the fact that when you come back to God, your sins are buried in the grave of His forgiveness and cast into the sea of His forgetfulness (Micah 7:19). When you come back to God, all you will find is forgiveness. *"But the father said to his servants, "Quick! Bring the best robe and put it on him. Put a ring on his finger and sandals on his feet. Bring the fattened calf and kill it. Let's have a feast and celebrate."* Notice the four things the father gave to his son and what they represent:

1. Forgiveness
The father gave his son the best robe, representing his forgiveness. Here was a young man who had come home in rags, but the father said, "I have forgiven his sins, let's cover up his rags. Let's cover up the evidence of his sin and failure." When you cover your sin, God uncovers it, but when you uncover your sin, God covers it. When you come before God in repentance, God exchanges your filthy rags with His robe of righteousness.

NOTES _____

_____

_____

_____

_____

_____

_____

_____

_____

_____

_____

_____

_____

_____

_____

_____

_____

_____

_____

_____

2. Family

The father gave his son a ring, representing family. More specifically, the ring represented his sonship. In those days, the ring had the family crest in it, which made families easily visibly identified in a community. This was the father saying, "I want everybody to know that he belongs to me."

3. Favor

The father gave him sandals, representing his favor. As he came home, his shoes had long since worn out. The father gave him new shoes, which were an emblem that he was no longer a slave.

4. Fellowship

The father killed thc fattened calf, representing his fellowship. In those days, when they killed the fatted calf for a sacrifice, the head of the house would take the blood of the animal and apply it to the threshold of the door. When the honored guest would step through the door, they would step over the blood, which was symbolic of a new covenant. When that son stepped back into his old home, he knew that that he was in a new relationship with his father. The reason we know we have a right to come into our Father's house is because an innocent victim, Jesus Christ, shed His blood for you. The way back to the Father's house is Jesus.

Jesus goes to great lengths to describe how the father responded to his prodigal son. What does this teach you about God, our Father?

_____

_____

_____

_____

_____

_____

_____

_____

The story of the prodigal son illustrates for us three wonderful truths that we shouldn't ever forget:

- No matter how far away you have gone, you can come back.
- No matter how far out you have gone, you can come in.
- No matter how far down you may have gone, you can come up.

So how can we come clean with God?

1. Confess your sin to God.

When you read the gospels, one thing you'll discover is that Jesus *never* condemned or turned away anyone who was a sinner and came to Him. Every time a sinner came to Jesus and said, "I'm guilty," He said, "I forgive you." Confession is the only knife that can lance the boil of guilt and get rid of the infection. The word "confess" means "to agree with." When you confess your sin, you're taking God's side against it. Spiritual freedom doesn't come in a plea of innocence but in an admission of guilt.

2. Repent of your sin.

"Repentance" is the word used in the Bible for sincere confession. *Re* means "to turn back." *Pent* means "that which is highest," like a penthouse. When someone repents, he turns back to God's highest way of living instead of the lower ways of sin. There's a big difference between *remorse* and *repentance*. Often times, when someone is caught red-handed, they feel remorse: "I wish I didn't get caught." Repentance is more than just sorrow for getting caught. It's a deep sorrow for choosing our own route instead of God's. It's ownership of how you have hurt His heart through your own selfishness.

3. Believe that you have received His forgiveness.

There is no sin too dark for His light. There is no sin too gross for His grace. There is no sin you have committed that God will not forgive when you confess to Him and turn from your sin (1 John 1:9).

Forgiveness

The word "forgiveness" in the Hebrew language means to lift a burden off of someone else and to carry it away where it could never be seen again. It is where the strong hands of a loving God carry the heavy stone of sin off your shoulders.

A man once came to his pastor and confessed, "There's something I've done in my past that is so bad, and I don't think God could ever forgive me. I must have asked God to forgive me at least a thousand times." That pastor looked at him and said, "Then you've asked God to forgive you 999 times too many. You should have asked for His forgiveness one time and then thanked Him 999 times for forgiving you."

That's exactly what God wants you to do. Satan says look at your sin; God says look at my Son. In Isaiah 1:18 we read, *"Though your sins are like scarlet, they shall be as white as snow; though they are red like crimson, they shall be as wool."*

The time has come for a fresh start and a clean slate. God does not see the marks of your past. Instead, He sees this: *"See, I have inscribed you on the palms of my hands"* (Isaiah 49:16). God has written your name where He can see it. In the end, that is the only tattoo that matters.

> " Satan says look at your sin; God says look at my Son. "

NOTES

159

Day 5

How Can I Overcome Temptation?

vimeo.com/138215424

NOTES _____

_____
_____
_____
_____
_____
_____
_____
_____
_____
_____
_____
_____
_____
_____
_____
_____
_____
_____
_____
_____
_____

What has mastered you? In 2 Peter 2:19 we read, *"For a man is a slave to whatever has mastered him."* What are you a slave to? What is it that is bigger than you? I'm not talking about a bad habit like biting your fingernails. I'm talking about something that's much stronger than a habit. For some men and women, this could be an addiction to pornography. For others, it's going too far physically in a relationship. Some turn to drugs and alcohol. For many, their struggle resides beneath the surface as their continual sin is the hurt, resentment, bitterness, and grudges from their past. We must take seriously the sin that is in our life because **what you fail to destroy will eventually destroy you.**

The sin struggle

Sometimes believers wonder, "Am I really a Christian? Because if I were really a follower of Christ, I wouldn't struggle with all of this." Paul wrote a passage in Romans 7 that gives us a lot of hope and a lot of help. Outside of Jesus, Paul was probably the godliest man who ever lived. Most scholars believe he had memorized major chunks of the Old Testament, and he wrote two thirds of the New Testament. He even had an encounter with Jesus face-to-face. If anyone was a Christian, it was the apostle Paul. Yet I wonder if you can identify with what Paul says in Romans 7:15: *"For I do not understand my actions. For I do not do what I want, but I do the very thing I hate."* Ever feel like that? I'm grateful that the godliest man who ever lived was transparent enough to say that he sometimes did things and couldn't figure out why he did them.

We read in verse 16, *"Now if I do what I do not want, I agree with the law, that it is good."* In other words, Paul is saying, "I'm glad there's a law. Thank God we have the Bible that can be our moral compass that is greater than our feelings." All of us have been in situations where we "felt" like something was ok, but then we looked back and realized how wrong we were.

"So now it is no longer I who do it, but sin that dwells in me" (vs. 17). In another passage, Paul said this about himself: *"I am the chief of sinners"* (1 Timothy 1:15). Our evil desires are constantly searching out temptations to satisfy their cravings. You have a sinful nature within you that is constantly at work to wear your self-resistance down and to keep you from doing the good things you desire to do.

"For I know that nothing good dwells in me, that is, in my flesh. For I have the desire to do what is right, but not the ability to carry it out. For I do not do the good I want, but the evil I do not want is what I keep on doing.

Now if I do what I do not want, it is no longer I who do it, but sin that dwells in me." (vv. 18-20). When I first read that, I thought, "Thank you, Paul, for being so real!" He was saying that everywhere he went, evil was right there with him. Some days we want to do good, but we just can't seem to pull it off.

Don't miss this: Paul was not looking for a reason to sin, he was looking to be rescued from it. Sometimes people ask, "Can I be a Christian and still struggle with the same sin?" The reason they ask is because they *want* to struggle with the same sin. They want to raise their hands in worship on Sunday, but not talk about *where* they put their hands or *who* they put their hands on Monday through Saturday. Paul was not asking, "Can I live like that?" Paul was saying, "I'm struggling with sin, and I want to be rescued. So where was his hope? It's in verse 25, *"Thanks be to God who delivers me through Jesus Christ our Lord!"* Paul knew that the power of sin was broken through the person of Jesus.

How is our struggle with sin actually an indication of our spiritual growth?

_____

_____

_____

_____

_____

_____

_____

The process

The Christian life is a decision followed by a process. And if you want to overcome the power of sin and temptation in your life, you need to follow a process:

1. Cry out to God

Perhaps God is going to convict you to the point where you decide that you are not going to live in darkness anymore. You're *not* going to go there. You're *not* going to let something else control your body. You're *not* going to be in bondage to something that is not the presence of Christ.

Watchman Nee told a story of his trip to China when he and some of his friends went for a swim in the river. On one occasion, one of the men got a cramp in his leg and began sinking fast. Because Nee didn't know how to swim, he motioned to one of the other men who was an excellent swimmer to go and help the drowning man. To his astonishment, however, the guy didn't move. He just stood there and watched the drowning man. Watchman Nee was agitated. He kept yelling at the only man who could rescue the drowning man, but the man stood on the shore calm and collected. As the drowning man went under the water for what looked like the last time, the swimmer was there in a moment, and he brought him safely to the shore. After the rescue, Watchman chewed this guy out and accused him of loving his life too much and being selfish. The response of the swimmer revealed, however, that he knew what he was doing. He told Watchman that if he had gone in too soon, the drowning man would have put a death grip on him and they would have both drowned in the river, and he was right. He told Mr. Nee that a drowning man cannot be saved until he is utterly exhausted and ceases to make the effort to save himself.

> " What you fail to destroy will eventually destroy you. "

NOTES _____

_____

_____

_____

_____

_____

_____

_____

_____

_____

_____

_____

_____

_____

_____

_____

_____

_____

_____

_____

_____

_____

_____

_____

_____

_____

> "You will never have a breakthrough until you first have a break down."

NOTES

The same is true for us spiritually. You will never have a breakthrough until you first have a break down. Paul got to the point that he said in verse 24, *"Wretched man that I am! Who will rescue me from this body of death?"* Because Paul had spent many years in prison, he had watched how Romans executed criminals with uncanny brutality. Many times, if a man had committed a murder, he was bound hand-to-hand, leg-to-leg, and face-to-face with the corpse of his victim and then thrown out into the heat of the Mediterranean sun. As the corpse decayed, it literally ate death into the living man and became to him, in the strictest literal sense, "A body of death." Paul saw his carnal, sinful human nature in the same way. But he said there is someone who can provide his deliverance. In the following verse, he said, *"Thanks be to God through Jesus Christ our Lord."* He transferred all dependence for doing the will of God from himself to Christ alone.

If you're ready for a breakthrough, get on your knees and cry out to God for help. Until you see your sin as serious, you will not be serious about getting it out of your life.

2. Confess it to God

As a kid, I never understood the point of confession. I was told by my Sunday school teachers, "God is watching you ... and He knows *everything* that you do!" So I thought, "Well, if God already knows everything, why do I need to tell Him that I sinned if He already knows what I did?" Maybe you've wondered the same thing. But here's the reality: confession has nothing to do with information; it has everything to do with transformation. Confession is not me telling God I did something wrong, because He already knows. A transformation is taking place in my mind and heart because I'm looking at something from God's point of view and acknowledging and admitting, "God, this is wrong. It's a sin and I hate it. I want you to cleanse this out of my life." When I begin to see as God sees, I'll begin to do what God says.

3. Communicate your struggle to another Christian

If you're anything like me, your initial gut reaction to this is "Umm ... I don't think so. I'm a very private person." And yet this is perhaps the number one reason why Christians continue to remain in bondage.

Let's be honest. Confessing to God is the easier part of the process of cleansing you from the toxic residues of sin. God already knows your sin, so you might as well talk to Him about it anyway. Other people, however, don't know unless you tell them or they discover it themselves. This aspect takes more courage, but it's worth the risk.

The purpose of confessing to people is much different from why we confess to God. We confess our sins to God for forgiveness, but we confess our sins to other Christians for healing. James stated this clearly: *"Therefore confess your sins to each other and pray for each other so that you may be healed"* (5:16).

Our secret sins continue to have power over us while they reside in darkness. But they begin to lose their power once they are exposed to the light. Whenever someone confesses to me, "I'm about to tell you something I've never told anyone!" I know that this person is about to experience a breakthrough. They may have confessed it to God countless times, but something begins to change once they bring it out and in the open towards a trusted friend.

You're probably tempted to think, "I can just confess my sin to God. That's all I need to do." If your goal is forgiveness only, then you are right. But if you would like strength and encouragement to overcome that sinful trap, you need to realize that our God loves to work through His people.

Proverbs 28:13 sums it up this way: *"Whoever conceals their sins does not prosper, but the one who confesses and renounces them finds mercy."*

As believers, how can we help each other fight the battle against the sin in our lives?

_____

_____

_____

_____

_____

_____

_____

" We confess our sins to God for forgiveness, but we confess our sins to other Christians for healing. "

4. Commit to your plan of action before temptation strikes.
When it comes to not fulfilling the desires of the flesh, John Piper provides a set of strategies in the war against wrong desires in the form of the acronym A.N.T.H.E.M.

A – Avoid as much as is possible and reasonable the sights and situations that arouse unfitting desire. I say "possible and reasonable" because some exposure to temptation is inevitable. And I say "unfitting desire" because not all desires for sex, food, and family are bad. We know when they are unfitting and unhelpful and on their way to becoming enslaving. We know our weaknesses and what triggers them. "Avoiding" is a Biblical strategy. *"Flee youthful passions and pursue righteousness"* (2 Timothy 2:22). *"Make no provision for the flesh, to gratify its desires"* (Romans 13:14).

N – Say No to every lustful thought within five seconds. And say it with the authority of Jesus Christ. "In the name of Jesus, NO!" You don't have much more than five seconds. Give it more unopposed time than that, and it will lodge itself with such force as to be almost immovable. Say it out loud if you dare. Be tough and warlike. As John Owen said, "Be killing sin or it will be killing you." Strike fast and strike hard. *"Resist the devil, and he will flee from you"* (James 4:7).

T – Turn the mind forcefully toward Christ as a superior satisfaction. Saying "no" will not suffice. You must move from defense to offense. Fight fire with fire. Attack the promises of sin with the promises of Christ. The Bible calls lusts *"deceitful desires"* (Ephesians 4:22). They lie. They promise more than they can deliver. The Bible calls them *"passions of your former ignorance"* (1 Peter 1:14). Only fools yield. *"All at once he follows her, as an ox goes to the slaughter"* (Proverbs 7:22). Deceit is defeated by truth. Ignorance is defeated by knowledge. It must be glorious truth and beautiful knowledge. We must stock our minds with the superior promises and pleasures of Jesus. Then we must turn to them immediately after saying, "NO!"

H – Hold the promise and the pleasure of Christ firmly in your mind until it pushes the other images out. *"Fix your eyes on Jesus"* (Hebrews 12:2). Here is where many fail. They give in too soon. They say, "I tried to push it out, and it didn't work." I ask, "How long did you try?" How hard did you exert your mind? The mind is a muscle. You can flex it with vehemence. Take the kingdom violently (Matthew 11:12). Be brutal. Hold the promise of Christ before your eyes. Hold it. Hold it! Don't let it go! Keep holding it! How long? As long as it takes. Fight! For Christ's sake, fight till you win! If an electric garage door were about to crush your child you would hold it up with all your might and holler for help, and hold it and hold it and hold it and hold it.

NOTES _____

_____

_____

_____

_____

_____

_____

_____

_____

_____

_____

_____

_____

_____

_____

_____

_____

_____

_____

> "We need to starve what we want to kill and feed what we want to build."

E – Enjoy a superior satisfaction. Cultivate the capacities for pleasure in Christ. One reason lust reigns in so many is that Christ has so little appeal. We default to deceit because we have little delight in Christ. Don't say, "That's just not me." What steps have you taken to waken affection for Jesus? Have you fought for joy? Don't be fatalistic. You were created to treasure Christ with all your heart – more than you treasure sex or sugar. If you have little taste for Jesus, competing pleasures will triumph. Plead with God for the satisfaction you don't have: *"Satisfy us in the morning with your steadfast love, that we may rejoice and be glad all our days"* (Psalm 90:14). Then look, look, look at the most magnificent Person in the universe until you see Him the way He is.

M – Move into a useful activity away from idleness and other vulnerable behaviors. Lust grows fast in the garden of leisure. Find a good work to do, and do it with all your might. *"Do not be slothful in zeal, be fervent in spirit, serve the Lord"* (Romans 12:11). *"Be steadfast, immovable, always abounding in the work of the Lord"* (1 Corinthians 15:58). Abound in work. Get up and do something. Sweep a room. Hammer a nail. Write a letter. Fix a faucet. And do it for Jesus's sake. You were made to manage and create. Christ died to make you *"zealous for good works"* (Titus 2:14). Displace deceitful lusts with a passion for good deeds.

5. Continue to walk in the Spirit

I've got some bad news for you. If you're trying to beat sin on your own, it may never happen. You cannot change you. If you could, then you would already be changed. You've probably tried for years and have so far been unsuccessful. Only Jesus can change you. And the best news of all is that Jesus already did change you! That's why we can't say, "Well, this is just the way I am. This is how I was born. This is the person I've become because of my environment." No! In Jesus, the power of sin has been broken in our lives, and we can live in freedom in response to what has held us in bondage for years. The key to living the Christian life is not found in trying; it's found in trusting.

In Galatians 5:16 we read, *"Walk by the Spirit, and you will not gratify the desires of the flesh."* If you live your life as the Holy Spirit directs you, then you will never follow through on what your corrupt nature wants. We need to starve what we want to kill and feed what we want to build.

When temptation comes you will yield every time, either to the Lord or to your sin. Stop fighting temptation! Why fight a battle already lost when you can enjoy a victory already won. Don't fight temptation – yield to Jesus! And when temptation comes, say, "Hey, that old self is dead! I don't have to obey him ... I'm no longer Satan's slave. I died. I was buried. I was raised. Christ's power lives in me ... Lord Jesus, I yield to you!" Incredible power will come into your life the moment you yield to Jesus Christ.

Satan wants to make your past your future. Don't ever allow sin to define who you are. You are not a drunk. You are not a worrywart. You are not a homosexual. You are not a mental adulterer. You are a blood bought saint of God who may have some temptations residing in your flesh, but God has given you victory over them.

The late great preacher Billy Sunday said, "I'm against sin. I'll kick it as long as I've got a foot, and I'll fight it as long as I've got a fist. I'll butt it as long as I've got a head. I'll bite it as long as I've got a tooth. And when I'm old and fistless and footless and toothless, I'll gum it till I go home to Glory and it goes home to perdition!" May we have that same attitude about overcoming sin as well!

Reflect on what you've learned today. In your own words, describe how you would help someone else overcome a temptation they are struggling with:

_____

_____

_____

_____

_____

_____

_____

NOTES _____

_____

_____

_____

_____

_____

_____

_____

_____

_____

_____

_____

_____

_____

_____

_____

_____

_____

_____

_____

_____

_____

_____

_____

_____

_____

_____

_____

Day 1

What Is My Role as a Church Member?

vimeo.com/138215475

NOTES _____

_____

_____

_____

_____

_____

_____

_____

_____

_____

_____

_____

_____

_____

_____

_____

_____

_____

A Christian without a church home is like an orphan without a family. Being actively involved in the body of Christ is vital to our spiritual growth. In his book *Stop Dating the Church*, Joshua Harris gives a quick profile of someone he refers to as a "church dater." Do you see any of these characteristics in yourself?

- A church dater's attitude toward church is "Me-Centered." We go for what we can get. The driving question is, "What can this church do for me?"

- A church dater is very independent. They go to church because that's what Christians are supposed to do, but they're just not willing to get too involved. They may go to church, but they don't want to invest themselves in a small group.

- A church dater tends to be critical. Since they fall short on allegiance, they're quick to find fault in the church. Many people treat church with a consumer mentality, looking for the best product for the price of their Sunday morning. As a result, Harris says, "We're fickle and not invested for the long-term, like a lover with a wandering eye, always on the hunt for something better."

As our society grows increasingly secular, more and more people are leaving the church. For every one person who comes into the church, there are three that are going out. In the United States alone, 60 to 70 churches close per week. People today think, "Who needs the church? Why should I belong to it? I can worship God on the golf course!" But R.G. Lee said, "Your absence from church is a vote to close its doors."

Whereas it's discouraging to see the state of the church in America, it's awe-inspiring to see how the church is exploding in growth in countries where their faith is persecuted. In China, the church's growth is out of control. It's estimated that 20,000 come to faith every day! The same is true in sub-Saharan Africa. In Latin America, the conversion rate is 10,000 people a day! The church flourishes in those parts of the world where we are persecuted most. I truly believe that the greatest days for the church of Jesus Christ are not behind us but before us!

A true disciple of Christ is someone who loves Jesus. If you love Jesus, you will love what He loves. We read in Ephesians 5:25, *"Christ loved the church so much that He gave Himself for it"*. If Jesus loved the church enough to give His life for it, we should love the church enough to give our lives to it.

Why do we need the church?

We need God's people.
Every human being has some need to belong to a family or a group. We all yearn for community. Sociologically, people gravitate toward the group that reflects their hobby, value system, or culture. People gather in groups, whether it is the Boy Scouts, the Elks Lodge, or the Ruritan Club. This is one place where the church should excel. Psalm 68:6 says, *"God sets the solitary in families."* In other words, God's cure for isolation is to put people with His people. When I'm struggling, I've never really felt like going down to City Hall or the Elks Lodge and pouring out my heart, but I will pour out my heart to my church family. 1 Corinthians 12:26 says, *"If one member suffers, all the members suffer with it. If one member is honored, all the members rejoice with it."*

This is one of the reasons I believe the best days of the church are still ahead of us. We live in such a busy and complex world where we are more connected than ever, but people are starting to sense the lack of human touch. People are crying out for more than just an email, text message, or a Facebook status update. There's a longing now more than ever for face-to-face real community.

We need God's principles.
Hebrews 10:23 says, *"Let us hold fast the confession of our hope without wavering."* In other words, we are to stand up for what we believe. We need steady doses of truth, which is why we need to expose ourselves to the teachings of the Word of God. In a world cluttered with so many voices, opinions, and values of how we should live our lives, we need to hear that clarion call that cuts through it all that says, "Thus saith the Lord."

Interestingly, the me-centered church dater can benefit and grow with that voice. The reality is, **you cannot grow like you should if you do not go like you ought.** All living organisms are comprised of cells, and the cells in your body basically need two things to survive. First, they need other cells with which to live and interact. Second, they need food. When cells have these two things, they are considered healthy, and healthy cells will naturally reproduce. The same is true in the Body of Christ. We need God's people, and we need God's principles.

We need God's purpose.
Every human being yearns to know the meaning of life: "Who am I? Where did I come from? Where am I going?" We would love to know that we are a part of some big cause that is greater than ourselves. The great news is that if you're an active member of a church, you are a part of the greatest cause in the entire world. Our cause is greater than any charitable, political, or societal cause. In Philippians 1:3, Paul said, *"I always thank God for your partnership in the gospel from the first day until now."* Think of your church as a family partnership. Even when Jesus was a child, He had to remind His mother, Mary, *"Don't you know that I must be about My Father's business?"* (Luke 2:49). It was this cause that motivated Jesus. That's our purpose and meaning as well – the cause of the gospel! **The church is the vehicle that Jesus chose to take the message of the gospel to every generation and people.** The message that the church has is the world's only hope. It's through the local church that we are attached to God's work around the world.

We need God's Presence.
God's presence is available to you at all times, but there's a special promise to those who gather together, worship together, and meet together as the Body of Christ. Jesus said in Matthew 18:20, *"Wherever two or three are*

> **"If Jesus loved the church enough to give His life for it, we should love the church enough to give our lives to it."**

NOTES _____

169

> "The church is the vehicle that Jesus chose to take the message of the gospel to every generation and people."

NOTES

gathered together in my name, I am there in their midst." The church is far more than just a social gathering; it's a place we go to encounter the presence of God. The more genuine our worship, the more His presence shows up! The more you fellowship with God, the more you will want to fellowship with God's people. And the more you fellowship with God's people, the more you will want to fellowship with God.

Acts 2:42-47 is a snapshot of what the first church looked like: *"And they devoted themselves to the apostles' teaching and the fellowship, to the breaking of bread and the prayers. And awe came upon every soul, and many wonders and signs were being done through the apostles. And all who believed were together and had all things in common. And they were selling their possessions and belongings and distributing the proceeds to all, as any had need. And day by day, attending the temple together and breaking bread in their homes, they received their food with glad and generous hearts, praising God and having favor with all the people. And the Lord added to their number day by day those who were being saved."*

What are some of the characteristics of the New Testament church? What stands out to you the most about this passage?

_____

_____

_____

_____

_____

_____

_____

Thom Rainer says, "The main reason people leave a church is because they have an entitlement mentality rather than a servant mentality." Look at some of the direct quotes from exit interviews of people who left local congregations:

- "The worship leader refused to listen to me about the songs or music I wanted."
- "The pastor did not feed me."
- "No one from my church visited me."
- "I was out two weeks and no one called me."
- "I told my pastor to go visit my cousin and he never did."
- "They moved the times of the worship services and it messed up my schedule."

We have somehow turned Biblical church membership into country club membership where people think that you can pay your dues and be entitled to certain benefits. That's completely opposite of the Bible's definition. In 1 Corinthians 12:12-31, Paul describes church members not by what they should *receive* in a local church, but by the ministry they should *give*.

What is your role as a member of the church?

Be faithful in your attendance.
You are either worshiping or you are wavering. Faithful church attendance isn't always an accurate measurement of the state of a person's heart, but

it is a good place to start. If a person calls himself a "Christian" but never bothers to darken the door of any church, it's obvious that their spiritual sentiment doesn't run very deep. Think about it: if Jesus is the head and the church is the body (Ephesians 5:23), you cannot walk away from the body of Christ without walking away from Christ. In order to abide in Christ, you must abide in His church. Don't get me wrong, there's considerably more to Christianity than just being faithful in going to church, but we must never fool ourselves into thinking that you can be faithful to Jesus and give up being a part of the church.

In the early church, people were expelled for not attending church, assuming they were not saved in the first place. The writer of Hebrews admonishes us to *"not neglect our meeting together, as some people do, but encourage one another, especially now that the day of his return is drawing near"* (Hebrews 10:25).

There is a village in Southern Europe that has a church named "The House of Many Lamps." When it was built in the 16th century, the architect provided no light except for a receptacle in each pew where every person would place their own lantern. When someone didn't show up to church that Sunday, his spot in the church would be left dark, and if many stayed away, the darkness became greater than the whole. It was the regular presence of each person that lit up the church. The same is true for your faithful attendance.

Be careful to protect the unity.

The Bible talks more about the unity in the church than it does about the subjects of heaven or hell. As a member of God's church, it's your job to protect the unity of the body. In John 17, Jesus prayed that His followers *"will be one."* I believe that our community will be *won* when the church is *one*. When people find a church where its members really love each other unconditionally and Biblically, you will have to lock the doors to keep people out. The church is a fellowship, and when someone destroys the unity, they work to destroy the church. Any attitude that causes disunity is sin. This doesn't mean that there cannot ever be a disagreement. When there is a conflict, it needs to be handled Biblically according to Matthew 18:15-17. Notice that passage does not include gossip, sharing a problem or a criticism with someone who is neither a part of the problem nor the solution.

Growing churches love, and loving churches grow. When a church develops the *unity* of the book of Acts, it will discover the *power* of the church of Acts. Get everybody to love Jesus, and you've got a wonderful church. They don't have to agree on anything else. When God wants to put a bunch of new baby Christians into a church, He looks around for the warmest incubator He can find. Why would God send those who are new to their faith to a place where they might be caught in the crossfire of a church conflict? People make mistakes. Church members will disappoint you. Sometimes we needle each other, but we still need each other. Understand this: outside influences have never killed a church. Jesus said, *"Upon this rock I will build my church and the gates of hell shall not prevail against it"* (Matthew 16:18). The devil is no match for a church that is unified. Satan cannot defeat a unified body because there is no place for him to plan an attack. There is only one way that a church can be killed, and that is from within. People, even believers, can be used as tools of Satan in the Body of Christ. How? By causing division (Titus 3:10-11). Negativity can kill a church. Gossip can kill a church. Dissension and criticism can kill a church. Be careful to protect the unity of the body.

Be prayerful for your pastor and leaders.

The Bible teaches that pastors are held accountable by God for how they lead, manage, and direct the church (1 Peter 5:1-3; 1 Timothy 3:1-7). With

> " ... if Jesus is the head and the church is the body, you cannot walk away from the body of Christ without walking away from Christ. "

NOTES

that accountability comes authority. God has given your pastor the authority to make decisions and set the course of direction for the church. Hebrews 13:17 says, *"Obey your leaders and submit to them, for they are keeping watch over your souls, as those who will have to give an account. Let them do this with joy and not with groaning, for that would be of no advantage to you."*

Peter Drucker, the father of modern management, said that the four hardest jobs in America (and not necessarily in any order) are the President of the United States, a university president, a CEO of a hospital, and a pastor. America is now suffering from a shortage of pastors. According to Jimmy Draper of LifeWay Christian Resources, for every 20 pastors who go into the ministry from seminary, only one of them will retire as a pastor. I don't know of any other profession where there is a 95% drop out rate. Your pastor desperately needs your prayers. If a church wants a better pastor, they only need to pray for the one they've got!

Be bountiful in your financial support.
God's method of financially supporting the church is called the tithe. The word "tithe" literally means "tenth." We are to bring at least 10% of our income and give it back to the Lord as an act of worship. If every member obeyed God in this area of their life, the church would not have any financial problems and our missions budgets would be fully funded. Ron Blue, a Christian financial counselor, noted that the average active church member only gives 2.5% of his income to the church. He said that if everyone in the average church were reduced to a welfare income, and the people tithed off of that amount, the church would double the receipts! God says, *"Bring the full tithe into the storehouse, that there may be food in my house. And thereby put me to the test, says the LORD of hosts, if I will not open the windows of heaven for you and pour down for you a blessing until there is no more need"* (Malachi 3:10).

Be mindful about your own preferences.
Opinions are like noses – everybody has one. Far too many church members are guilty of making a principle out of a preference. We must be on guard against this. I don't even agree 100% with the pastor of my church – and *I'm* the pastor! We all have a preferred style of how the church ought to look and function. But we must be careful not to allow our opinion to cause division in the body. We must be careful not to major on the minors. There's a big difference between the message (the principles of the Bible) and our methods (how we go about engaging our culture with the message). My seminary professor, Dr. Elmer Towns, used to say, "Methods are many; principles are few. Methods may change, but principles never do." Before you open your mouth to criticize something, first ask, "Is this about my preference, or is this about a principle? Is this an essential core element to our faith, or is this my opinion on a disputable matter?" Churches very seldom ever divide over doctrinal issues; they split over issues pertaining to philosophy of how to do ministry. And that is a shame.

Be thoughtful in encouraging others.
Hebrews 10:24 says, *"Let us consider one another in order to stir up love and good works."* That's an interesting thought. We are to go to church out of consideration for one another. There is something that every Christian needs to give as well as receive, and that is encouragement. The following verse says, *"Let us exhort one another ..."* To exhort literally means "to come alongside to help." Begin to ask God to show you who you can bless and encourage next Sunday. Look for that individual that might be alone, and sit with them. Treat everyone you see in the hallway as if they have a sign on their forehead that reads: "I really need a word of encouragement today."

Be purposeful in fulfilling the mission.

The main reason you need to be an active member is not because of what you can get out of the church but what you can give to the church. The more you give, the more you get. **What you receive from the church is in direct proportion to what you are willing to give to the church.** It's high time we stop asking the question, "What can my church do for me?" and start asking, "What can I do for my church?"

A church in Kansas was finally forced to close its doors. There were no longer any funds available to keep the church going and attendance had been in decline for decades. The pastor finally made the sad announcement that the church would be closing the doors. He invited everyone whose names were still on the church membership roll to come that Sunday for the funeral service of that church because it was everyone's duty to give it a decent burial. When the church members showed up that Sunday, they noticed a closed coffin covered in flowers in front of the pulpit. After the eulogy, the pastor invited every person to come forward and peek inside the coffin so they could see the reason this church had died. One by one, the church members came forward, and as each one peered inside the coffin, they saw a large mirror showing their own reflection.

Here's a question for you to consider: What kind of church would my church be if every member were just like me? What would happen if every member prayed for your church the way you pray for it? What would happen if every member were as involved in service as you are? If every member gave the same proportion that you give financially, would the church still be able to keep its doors open? It's time that we stop asking what our church can do for us, but what we can do for our church.

Based on these eight different roles of a church member, which one(s) do you feel you excel in? Which one(s) would you like to improve upon this year?

> " What kind of church would my church be if every member were just like me? "

NOTES

Day 2

Why Should I Be in a Small Group?

vimeo.com/138215547

NOTES _____

_____
_____
_____
_____
_____
_____
_____
_____
_____
_____
_____
_____
_____
_____
_____
_____
_____
_____
_____

Small groups are meant to be a microcosm of the church where you worship. There's a big difference between just attending church and being in community with that church. One of the things you discover when you get involved in a really good church is that the church isn't a building you go to, it's a family you belong to. And for each person, the center of that family life is usually a small group that meets together regularly so that people can study spiritual truth together, and in the process, come to a place where they can know and be known, love and be loved, serve and be served, celebrate and be celebrated.

Secrets of the early church

I've often wondered how the early church grew exponentially – so fast and so strong. But when you do a survey through the Book of Acts, the reason becomes obvious. The power of God was moving mightily in the early church and the people were on fire for the Lord. But there was something about their structure, what the New Testament church *did*, that contributed to their growth. Let's take a survey walk through the Book of Acts together to see what that secret was.

Acts 1:15 says, *"... Peter stood up among the believers (a group number about a hundred and twenty)."* So we know that this is the number the church had in the very beginning. In the Upper Room, prior to Pentecost, we know that they started with around 120.

Acts 2:41 says that on the day of Pentecost, the greatest revival the world has ever seen with the Holy Spirit came down, *"... about three thousand were added to their number that day."* On the very first day of the church, they instantly became a mega church! 3,000 people were saved and worshipping Jesus as the Messiah!

Acts 2:47 says, *"... the Lord added to their number daily those who were being saved."* Now if you're adding at least one person a day, how many is that in a year? A minimum of 365. Yet I think that there were many more than that being added to the church because of what we see in the next verse.

Acts 4:4 says, *"... the number of men grew to about five thousand."* Whenever you have 5,000 men, how many women and children do you have? I think a conservative estimate would be at least 10,000 or more! So by this time, you have a church with a minimum of at least 15,000 individuals.

Acts 5:14 says, *"Nevertheless, a multitude of men and women believed in the Lord and were added to their number."* How do you know when you have a multitude? You can't even count them!

Then you get to Acts 5:28, and the critics are saying, *"... you have filled Jerusalem with your teaching."* Well, no wonder! Scholars think that within the first 20 years, the early church was approximately 100,000 people in Jerusalem. The population in Jerusalem at that time was 200,000 (maybe 250,000 at the most). So when you consider that half of Jerusalem has been won to Christ during this time, that's what you call "filling a city with your teaching and doctrine!"

Acts 6:1 says, *"Now in these days, when the number of the disciples was multiplying."* Notice that we have now moved from addition to multiplication! We now have the number of disciples rapidly multiplying.

Acts 6:7 says, *"So the Word of God spread. The number of disciples in Jerusalem increased rapidly, and a number of priests became obedient to the faith."*

Acts 20:21 says, *"... tens of thousands of the Jewish people have become followers!"* That's the kind of rapid, exponential growth that God wants to see in the church today!

So how do you get New Testament growth? You must use New Testament methodology. We need to ask the question: If the church was growing this rapidly, how did they pull that off? Where did they meet? They couldn't possibly build a multi-million dollar worship center to house all those people. The answer for how the early church operated is in Acts 5:42, *"They met day after day, in the temple courts and house to house."*

This dual strategy of both large church worship and small group fellowship is the key Biblical strategy and structure for God's church, not just back then, but also for today. When we do things like the New Testament followers did, in the power of the Holy Spirit, we're going to have the kind of results that we saw in the Book of Acts. The early church met in the temple courts for their large church worship gathering, but then they spent most of their time going "house to house" for their small group gathering. Why did they do this? Because they needed to be connected to one another in their fragmented and persecuted world, and we desperately need to be connected too.

Small groups are a big deal because God doesn't want just *fans* of a church; He wants *family*. He doesn't just want *attendance*; He wants *attachment*. He doesn't just want people to *go*; He wants people to *grow*.

Made for community

In every church service, people sit in rows. It's the "sit still while I instill" approach, and I'm not knocking it. It's one way that we learn and grow. But that approach also needs to be coupled with a small group environment where you can flesh out what you're learning, discuss, ask questions, and deepen relationships. We need a bridge between information and application. Reading the Bible on my own has been vital to my spiritual growth. But some of the greatest catalysts for my spiritual development have occurred on the horizontal level as I've gleaned insights, advice, and encouragement from others in my small group community.

What we do is heavily influenced by whom we are doing life with. All of us have those "at-the-wrong-place-at-the-wrong-time-with-the-wrong-people" stories. When we hear about people making good changes in their lives, there is always a "right-people-at-the-right time" element.

The reality is we must be intentional about going deeper in our relationships. Why? Because it's our natural human tendency to drift away from it. The gravitational pull of our lives is to drift towards isolation, independence, and autonomy, none of which are healthy. We've been taught to admire the "Lone Ranger" individualists in today's culture. We're afraid of community because we fear rejection and awkwardness. Our introverted nature makes us want to withdraw inside of our safe little bubbles. But we can't use that as an excuse not to engage in a small group.

Satan knows that there is power in numbers. That's why he strives so hard to make sure that we stay lonely and alone. Remember, that's how sin entered the world. Satan watched until Eve was by herself – separated from

> " ... the church isn't a building you go to, it's a family you belong to. "

NOTES

> **"You need community, and somebody in community needs you."**

NOTES _____

Adam – before he tried to tempt her to eat the forbidden fruit.

There's a connection between stumbling and being involved in a group. You can stumble away from your faith. You can stumble away from God. You can stumble away from church. But it is very difficult to stumble out of genuine community because real community won't let you go that easily – they are your family! Not *if* but *when* you stumble, you will need most what you desire the least. You need those individuals in your life who will not let you go that easily. When we stumble, we need people who will insist that we get up, whether we want to get up or not.

Solomon, the wisest man who ever lived, said, *"Two are better than one, because they have a good return for their labor: If they fall down, they can help each other up. But pity those who fall and have no one to help them up."*

Autonomy is a myth, a trap, an unworthy goal. You were created for community. You need community, and somebody in community needs you. Donald Joy is a relationship guru, and he believes that every one of us needs support from four different people groups: 1.) close family (parents, spouse, and children), 2.) Relatives (uncles, grandparents, cousins), 3.) lifelong friends (a collection of people you can stay close to and share life with), and 4.) associates (people you enjoy working with, going to the gym with, going to church, etc.). These four groups of people represent a support system, which can be thought of as a trampoline. Donald Joy goes on to say, "How many people can you count that are holding that trampoline? Research shows that a healthy system has at least 12 or more individuals that are holding you up." He also mentions that a neurotic system has fewer than 10 people, and a psychotic system has fewer than five. You might think, "Well, I don't need anybody. I have my spouse and my kids and that's all I need." You are so wrong. You need others to provide that support.

From spectator to participator

There are many reasons why you need to move from being a spectator in church worship to a participator in small group community. Here some of them:

You will understand the Bible better through group discussion, and you will be able to apply it to your own personal situations. There's something about discussing and hearing from others how the Bible is being applied in their life that helps to accelerate spiritual growth in our own. Colossians 3:16 says, *"Let the word of Christ dwell in you richly as you teach and admonish one another with all wisdom."* The call to teach what God has taught us is for every Christian. God did not create us to be reservoirs; He made us to be conduits. We're not just to soak up spiritual truth for our own benefit; we are to share so other people can grow from how God has grown us.

You will develop close relationships with other believers who will walk beside you in your journey as a follower of Jesus. The Bible tells us that when God made Adam, He put him in a perfect environment in the Garden of Eden. There were no problems, no pressures, no pain. Yet God looked down on Adam in that perfect environment and said, "It's still not good enough." In Genesis 2:18 He says, *"It is not good for man to be alone."* It's not God's will for you to be lonely. You were made for relationships.

You will find answers to the needs in your life through group prayer. It's incredible to know that you have a group of people who are interceding in prayer for you during the week. In my small group, we have someone who sends an email of all of our prayer requests so that we can continue to pray for one another on a daily basis.

You will get support in times of crisis or major changes from

people who really care for you. The church where I pastor is too large for me to be able to visit with all of the members who are sick and in the hospital. But technically, that's not the pastor's job anyway. He is there to *"equip the saints for the work of the ministry"* (Ephesians 4:12), and the individuals in our small groups are the ones who are to minister to one another.

You will be able to demonstrate to your lost friends the love of Jesus in a non-church setting. There are many people who may never darken the door of a church service, but they will come to your small group if you invite them. What I have discovered is that when they get around other believers and grow in that community, they start coming to church, and eventually make the decision to become followers of Christ as well. Our greatest outreach to the community is our small group ministry.

You will be able to contribute to the body of Christ. We can accomplish so much more when we are all working towards a common goal. The Bible says that one will put a thousand to flight, but two will put to flight ten thousand (Deuteronomy 32:30). It's one thing to show up for a small group; anyone can do that, but a good group bonds and gels when the members of the group make a conscious effort to be contributors to the group. What does that look like? Somebody makes dessert for the group. And somebody calls those who are absent or late. And during the group meeting, everyone pays attention and adds a comment or two so that a really good discussion happens. The bottom line is that you learn to do life together, speak the truth in love to one another, and make each other's lives better as a result of it.

Small groups are the perfect place to welcome your friends into the church and introduce them to Christ. People don't just need principles to live by, they need people to live with. If a new church member or new Christian doesn't make seven meaningful relationships at a church, statistics show that they will be gone after the first year. A worship service or dynamic speaking abilities of a pastor might get people to come, but it's small groups that get people to stay.

Small groups are the perfect place to practice our call to be discipled and make disciples. Disciple-making relationships are built primarily through small groups. It's an entry point for us to invest in someone's life and help them grow towards spiritual maturity.

What role has community played in your faith journey?

The need for relationships
Maybe you're reading this thinking, "Yeah, that's great, but it's not for me." Perhaps you're like me, and you're struggling with having a full plate in life – or maybe an overflowing dish. It's when you're feeling overloaded and

NOTES

NOTES

overwhelmed that you need to be in a small group the most. When you get busy, the very first thing in your life to get short-changed is your relationships. The first relationship to get hurt is your relationship with God. You think, "I don't have time to talk to God or to read my Bible." The second area where you start cutting back is in your relationship with your family. The third area you start cutting back on is your relationship with other Christians. When we get too busy what happens? Our priorities get all out of whack. The very thing we need the most is given the least attention. Whenever you start skimping out on those three categories of relationships, it always comes back to haunt you.

Jesus said that we are to love each other in the same way that He loves us (John 15:12). The phrase "one another" is used over 50 times in the New Testament to describe our relationship to other believers. Many of these are commands that we cannot fulfill unless we are active and engaging with our church in community and not just sitting as idle spectators on the sidelines.

Rick Warren says, "If you are a member of a small group or class, I urge you to make a group covenant that includes the nine characteristics of biblical fellowship: We will share our true feelings (authenticity), forgive each other (mercy), speak the truth in love (honesty), admit our weaknesses (humility), respect our differences (courtesy), not gossip (confidentiality), and make group a priority (frequency)."

If you're already a part of a small group, I want to encourage you to pursue those relationships more fully. Also, it's always important to remember that building meaningful relationships thrives on participation. Are you one of those who could share a little more so people know what's going on or talk a little less giving others a chance to speak?

If you've taken some time off from being in a small group, I want to encourage you to re-engage. If you're already in a group, make a call or send a text and invite someone to join you at your small group this week.

Do you feel that you are engaged in the small group community of your church and growing in those relationships? If not, what changes do you think you need to make?

_____

_____

_____

_____

_____

_____

Could you ever see yourself leading a small group in the future? Why or why not?

_____

_____

_____

_____

_____

_____

_____

Day 3
Why Are Relationships Vital to My Growth?

Let's take a pop quiz:
- Can you name the five wealthiest people in the world?
- Can you name eight people who have won the Nobel or Pulitzer Prize?
- How about the last 10 Academy Award winners for best picture?

Here's another quiz:
- Think of three people you most enjoy spending time with.
- Name five friends who have helped you through a difficult time.
- List four people who have taught you something worthwhile.

The second quiz was a whole lot easier, wasn't it? The lesson? The people who make the most difference in our lives are not the ones with the most credentials, but the ones with the most concern.

Most people are not living at the peak of their spiritual experience. They know how to fire it up, but they don't know how to keep it going. Living the Christian life is not a solo gig. It requires teamwork. God has given you an incredible resource in your brothers and sisters in Christ, and by investing in those relationships, you can begin to tap into that resource.

Someone once said that God gives us our relatives, but thank God we can choose our own friends! Having true blue friends is vitally important. Howard Hughes, who at one time was worth $4 billion dollars, once said, "I would be willing to give it all for one good, loyal friend." You must understand that those closest to you will determine your level of success or failure in this life. If you bring godly people around you, they will *bless* you. If you bring the wrong people around you, they will *curse* you. There is no neutrality when it comes to friends; they will either bring you up or they will bring you down. The relationships you choose will greatly determine the quality and direction of your life.

Proverbs 13:20 says, *"He who walks with the wise will be wise, but the companion of fools will be destroyed."*

Think about the closest friends you have in your life right now. Would you say they are helping further you in your relationship with God or are their attitudes and actions hindering your walk with Him?

vimeo.com/138215585

NOTES _____

179

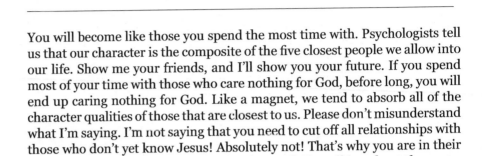

"Show me your friends, and I'll show you your future."

You will become like those you spend the most time with. Psychologists tell us that our character is the composite of the five closest people we allow into our life. Show me your friends, and I'll show you your future. If you spend most of your time with those who care nothing for God, before long, you will end up caring nothing for God. Like a magnet, we tend to absorb all of the character qualities of those that are closest to us. Please don't misunderstand what I'm saying. I'm not saying that you need to cut off all relationships with those who don't yet know Jesus! Absolutely not! That's why you are in their life – to help influence them towards the Lord. I'm talking about those you intentionally allow into your inner circle. This isn't about who you are trying to influence, it's about who is influencing you?

David and Jonathan

A Biblical friend holds you up when you stumble and holds you down when you stray. When it comes to friendship, quality is more important than quantity. One such friendship you find in Scripture is that of David and Jonathan. After David defeated the giant Goliath, he became the most popular figure in ancient Israel. You could say that he was the next *Israeli Idol*. As a result, Saul, the king of Israel, was eaten up with jealousy. People still *respected* Saul, but they *loved* David. Even though David tried to build many bridges to King Saul, Saul burned down every single one of them. It even got to the point that Saul was attempting to hunt David down and take his life! David was facing the biggest trial of his life, and he was in desperate need of a friend to come alongside him. That's where Jonathan comes in.

If there was ever a friendship with the cards stacked against it, it would be this one. Jonathan was King Saul's son. He was the rightful heir to the throne. David was anointed by Samuel to be the next King of Israel. That's a little awkward. Jonathan could have easily been jealous. Yet through his own attitude and actions, he basically said, "David, even though I know you are going to take my place as King, I am going to be your friend for life." Jonathan was David's best friend; therefore, he gave him his personal loyalty. He was okay with being number two as long as David was number one. You would never expect these two to become friends, but they did. Out of their adversity, we have a great picture of Biblical friendship and what it means to be a genuine friend to others in the body of Christ.

1 Samuel 18:1-4 says, *"As soon as he had finished speaking to Saul, the soul of Jonathan was knit to the soul of David, and Jonathan loved him as his own soul. And Saul took him that day and would not let him return to his father's house. Then Jonathan made a covenant with David, because he loved him as his own soul. And Jonathan stripped himself of the robe that was on him and gave it to David, and his armor, and even his sword and his bow and his belt."*

Jonathan had the highest love that one could have for another because we read, *"Jonathan loved him as himself."* What Jonathan gave David that day symbolized his personal loyalty:

- He gave David his robe, which was a symbol of both his status as prince and future role as king.
- He gave David his armor, a symbol of his role as commander-in-chief over Israel's army.
- He gave David his belt. Worn only by the wealthy and royalty, it

represented all that he could have had as king but was willing to give up for David.

In 1 Samuel 23:16, we read that Jonathan encouraged David in the Lord. The Bible says that he *"strengthened his hand in God."* We need friends who will take us to God, and we need to be that kind of friend to those who are struggling. When David was running for his life away from his best friend's father, I can hear Jonathan saying, "David, I can't solve this, but I know who can! We need to take this to the Lord."

If you are going to be a Jonathan in someone else's life, what kind of characteristics do you need to have based on your reading of that Scripture?

_____

_____

_____

_____

_____

_____

_____

Choosing wisely

Aristotle once said, "Friendship is a single soul dwelling in two bodies." Your relationships in this life are vital. If you show me who you listen to, I'll show you who you are becoming. If you show me who you are being influenced by, I'll show you the type of person you will be.

Proverbs 12:26 says, *"The righteous should choose his friends carefully, for the way of the wicked leads them astray."* The word for "choose" is the Hebrew word tur, which is the idea of searching out land you are interested in investing in. This verse has the idea of a person who explores and evaluates prospective friendships carefully. Henry Ford said, "My best friend is the one who brings out the best in me."

You may be just one relationship away from changing the course of your destiny. In the Bible, Saul became the Apostle Paul. After a dramatic encounter with Jesus on the road to Damascus (Acts 9), Saul was converted. He went from being a persecutor and killer of Christians to becoming the man responsible for the most exponential growth of Christianity. But outside of Jesus, there was one man who changed Paul's destiny – Barnabas. When everyone in the early church was afraid of him and nobody trusted Paul, Barnabas was the encouraging friend who strengthened him, discipled him, and vouched for the sincerity of his faith. He said to the early believers, "It's safe. He's changed! You can trust him!" That one relationship changed Paul's destiny.

I'm so grateful for the godly Christian relationships I have in my life. I would not be where I am today if it were not for them. One of the great benefits of having friendships where both individuals are mutually vulnerable is that they can sharpen you and keep you accountable in your walk with the Lord. Proverbs 27:17 says *"As iron sharpens iron, one man sharpens another."* I had a moment of truth when I discovered the words of an 18th Century French writer who observed: "We discover in ourselves what others hide from us; and we recognize in others what we hide from ourselves." When I read those words, I vowed to retire my masks and get real.

> " A Biblical friend holds you up when you stumble and holds you down when you stray. "

NOTES _____

_____

_____

_____

_____

_____

_____

_____

_____

_____

_____

_____

_____

_____

_____

_____

_____

_____

_____

_____

_____

_____

> **"** *As iron sharpens iron, one man sharpens another.* **"**
> - Proverbs 27:17

NOTES

Accountability

In *Character that Counts: Who's Counting Yours?*, Ron Handley gives a number of great questions that you can have your accountability partner ask you on a weekly basis. These are the same questions that my friend asks me each week. Take a look at this list of 10 questions and ask yourself, "Where do I need to be kept accountable? Who is it that can help me grow in these areas of my life?"

1. Have you spent daily time in God's Word and in prayer this week?
The bottom line is that all areas of your life will be more achievable when this one discipline is carried out. I've noticed that when I'm spending daily time with God, all the other areas of my life seem to fall into place.

2. Have you had any flirtatious or lustful attitudes, tempting thoughts, or exposed yourself to any explicit materials, which would not glorify God?
I've seen so many men and women fall in this area. Perhaps they could have been protected if they had a trusted friend to hold them accountable in that area. Jerry Kirk says, "Choosing to let Jesus be in control of your sex life will shape every other area of your life because sexuality is at the center of our being ... Practicing sexual purity, even though it's hard, is also one of the most accurate reflections of the depth of our relationship with Christ." I could not agree more. Approximately 70% of Christian men admit to viewing pornography at least monthly. One of the major reasons I'm able to walk in victory and avoid this temptation is because I know that at least once a week, I have a trusted friend who is going to ask me this question.

3. Have you been completely above reproach in your financial dealings?
The Bible has a lot to say about our personal wealth and how we manage it – 2,000 verses to be exact. Many Christians think their responsibility to God is giving their 10% but the reality is that all of our money belongs to God, and we are simply caretakers of it. Do you have anyone to keep you accountable when it comes to tithing, going into debt, managing your finances, and your general attitude towards money? I personally have a tendency to be a little too materialistic in my attitude towards money, and I benefit greatly by having someone keep my greed in check. It's been said, "You can't store up treasures in heaven if you're holding on to the treasures of earth."

4. Have you spent quality relationship time with family and friends?
Developing and maintaining quality relationships is vitally important. Are you making any effort in investing in those that are closest to you? If you're married, how is the relationship with your spouse? If you have kids, how intentional are you being in parenting them? If you're single, how are you investing in your friends and family members?

5. Have you done your 100% best in your job, school, etc.?
God expects our best effort in all of our endeavors (Colossians 3:23-24). Whether it be on the job, at home, or in the classroom, we're not to just merely drift through life. We're to do our best for God's glory. Do you try to keep learning or have you stagnated? Do you give a minimal effort or do you strive for excellence? Do you work diligently, or are you hanging out too much at the coffee pot? Does Jesus shine through you on your job?

6. Have you told any half-truths or outright lies, putting yourself in a better light to those around you?
Often half-truths are spoken out of convenience rather than taking the

needed time to be absolutely correct. If we kept track, I think we'd be shocked at how many times we tend to be dishonest even if they are innocent "white lies." Someone once said, "Tell the truth, and you can forget about it. Tell a lie, and you will have to remember it forever." Every lie we tell leads directly and indirectly to more lies. I believe most of us do not deliberately want to lie, yet it can be very easy to stretch the truth, but that is lying.

7. Have you shared the gospel with an unbeliever this week?
Regardless of how bold you may or may not be, we are called to live as the "salt of the earth" and the "light of the world" (Matthew 5:13-16). Have you been intentional about trying to live "on mission" for Jesus Christ?

8. Have you taken care of your body through daily physical exercise, proper eating, and sleeping habits?
Rod Handley says, "Amazingly, when these disciplines are in good working order, I feel fresh, confident and balanced – ready to take on any challenge. When ignored, I feel lethargic and frustrated." Knowing that our body is the temple of God, it's wise to have someone keep us accountable when it comes to the upkeep and maintenance of that temple.

9. Have you allowed any person or circumstance to rob you of your joy?
How you react to those difficult situations can have tremendous impact not only on your own spirit but also on the spirit and attitude of those around you. Paul Sailhammer says, "Joy is that deep settled confidence that God is in control of every area of my life." A person can only steal that joy away from us if we allow them to.

10. Have you lied on any of your answers today?
This is a pretty deliberate question! Sometimes as we look back over our responses, we may realize that we need to come clean on a previous answer.

What should I do now?
Is being accountable to another person in the Body of Christ easy? Of course not! But I have been amazed and astounded at how much I have grown just by being answerable to people in my personal life. Andy Stanley once said, "Giftedness ensures a good start; accountability ensures a good finish."

Maybe you're thinking to yourself, "I sure wish I had someone like this in my life, but I don't right now." If that's the case with you, let me offer a few suggestions:

Start now in investing in relationships around you.
Proverbs 18:24 says, *"A man who has friends must himself be friendly."* I read a poem that said, "I went out to find a friend and could not find one there. I went out to be a friend, and friends were everywhere." Be active in expanding your connections with other believers and watch the sovereign hand of God lead you to the right individual(s).

Pray that God will send a Jonathan into your life.
During a lonely and difficult season, I prayed that prayer for about six months, and I can tell you that God directly answered that prayer.

Realize that no one will be vulnerable with you unless you are first vulnerable with them.
Full disclosure to another godly Christian friend (of the same sex) can be your way out of a dangerous fog. The value you receive from accountability

> **"** I went out to find a friend and could not find one there. I went out to be a friend, and friends were everywhere. **"**

NOTES

NOTES

is only as great as the extent to which you are willing to be open and honest with that person. Deep friendships grow out of the vulnerability of allowing another person to see who you really are beneath the polite exterior. If you are not transparent with others – if you put a wall up to people so they cannot hurt you – that will certainly work. By stiff-arming them, they will not get close enough to hurt you, but the downside is that they won't get close enough to help you.

My wife is from Northern Maine, near the Canadian border. I'll never forget one winter when I went ice fishing with my father-in-law. Having been raised in south Florida, the idea of walking on ice and drilling holes in it to fish just defied common logic to me. What if I fell through the ice?! When we arrived at the lake, I could see through the cloudy snow an ice shack that was about 500 yards out. I thought to myself, "Ok ... I'm going to walk out there on the ice ... today might be the day I go home to Jesus!" Very delicately I tried to displace the weight of my body as I took wide, gentle strides on top of the ice. All I could think about was how quickly hypothermia would set in if I fell through, and I was hoping it would be a quick and painless death. All of the sudden, I heard this rumble, and I felt the ice vibrating underneath my feet. I thought, "Oh Lord! This is it! I'm going down!" But then as I looked up, I saw my wife's cousin coming through the cloudy snow to greet us – *driving his Ford F-350 pickup truck on top of the ice!* Needless to say, after seeing that, I was ready to go fishing!

What happened? I learned that if that ice could hold up a Ford F-350 thundering across it, it could certainly hold me up! Hang around people who are riding with God in a pickup truck so that you'll know He can carry you with whatever you're facing. If you want more confidence and more faith in God, you've got to spend more time around other believers who are pursing the same thing.

Do you have anyone in your life that you feel you could be mutually vulnerable with and can hold you accountable? Why or why not? How might having this kind of friend help you grow spiritually?

Day 4

What Are My Spiritual Gifts?

Spiritual gifts are not for my benefit; they are for the benefit of others. According to 1 Peter 4:10, *"As each has received a gift, use it to serve one another, as good stewards of God's varied grace."* The gift that God gives you is to bless other people and His church. In 1 Corinthians 12:7 we read, *"A spiritual gift is given to each of us so we can help each other."*

Paul tells us in 1 Corinthians 12:1, *"Now concerning spiritual gifts, brethren, I do not want you to be <u>ignorant</u>."* According to one study, 87% of all Christians don't know anything about their spiritual gifts. God doesn't want us to be ignorant about how He has blessed us. So how can you know what spiritual gift you have?

Imagine that you are at your family's house for a large dinner or a family reunion. Someone has prepared a tray of delicious desserts full of pies, cakes, and cobblers of all varieties. Unfortunately, as they are bringing the tray of desserts from the kitchen to the dining room, she happens to trip over a toy in the hallway, and now all of the desserts have come crashing down to the floor. What would be your response?

If you have the gift of prophecy, you'd probably say something like, "I told you something like this was going to happen! Whose kid left their toy in the hallway? I saw this coming and warned you all about it!"

If you have the gift of teaching you might say, "I've done some research on this, and there's actually a better way to get the tray of desserts to the dinner table. Step one, you do this ..."

Some of you would immediately get up and say, "I'm on my way to help! I'll get the mop!" They have the gift of service.

Those with the gift of exhortation would say, "You know, that happened to me one time. It's ok. We can learn from this and we can be better people as a result of it!"

For some, their gut reaction would be to say, "Ok everybody, I'm going to run to the store, and I'll buy everyone a dessert! Be right back!" They have the gift of giving.

Then there are those individuals who just take charge. "We can get this place cleaned up in no time! Billy, you grab the mop. Janet, please get some paper towels. Bob, bring the trash can over ... I've got a vision to make this better!" They have the gift of leadership or administration.

Then there are those comforting individuals who just come over to where the hostess is and put their arm around them, saying, "My heart hurts for you. When I saw that tray falling, I was hurting for you and with you. I'm just so devastated you're going through this right now." They have the gift of mercy.

In today's lesson, we're going to examine some of the main spiritual gifts taught in the Bible. There are others, but these are some of the more

vimeo.com/138215638

NOTES _____

185

> *"Having gifts that differ according to the grace given to us, let us use them: if prophecy, in proportion to our faith; ⁷ if service, in our serving; the one who teaches, in his teaching; ⁸ the one who exhorts, in his exhortation; the one who contributes, in generosity; the one who leads, with zeal; the one who does acts of mercy, with cheerfulness."*
> — Romans 12:6-8

predominant ones. With each gift, we'll provide a definition, the purpose for the gift, characteristics of it, as well as some potential misunderstandings, problems, and precautions for those who have this particular gift.

Prophecy

This is the distinctive ability to boldly declare the truth of God, regardless of the consequences, calling people to righteous living. The church needs those individuals who will deliver the truth of God with divine insight and authority in order that people might repent of their sins and live for God. They're motivated to see people live holy lives and they get their greatest joy when someone comes back to the Lord.

Characteristics

They feel compelled to express their thoughts, feelings, and attitude *verbally* in regards to right and wrong, and they are very persuasive when it comes to defining what is right or wrong.

They have a bold sense of confidence when it comes to speaking God's truth. They speak with a sense of urgency that comes from a deep reliance upon the Word of God to validate their convictions. They make it clear to others where they stand.

They are very discerning. The have an uncanny ability to identify character and motives of other people. While they speak firmly about an issue, they will be that person's number one supporter when they do repent of their sin. They are open and honest about their own sin.

They have a tremendous hatred for sin and especially despise any form of lying. Hypocrisy, insincerity, and manipulation grieve the heart of this person. They know that when a person is lying, they are nowhere close to repenting as they're seeking to cover their sin.

Precautions

They can tend to be impulsive, making quick judgments without getting all the facts. As a result, they have a tendency to be impatient with others and have poor listening skills.

They can focus more on law than grace. Sometimes the one with the gift of prophecy has difficulty relating to people as individuals. They're not as concerned about a person's feelings as much as they are communicating truth.

If they are not led by the Spirit, the prophets may have a tendency to speak their minds as opposed to speaking for God.

Service

This is the ability to identify unmet needs involved in a task related to God's work and to make use of available resources to meet those needs. It can also be the provision of physical labor to accomplish tasks within the body of Christ, which enables the church to move forward. They love to meet the practical needs of fellow Christians and God's church.

Characteristics

They have a keen insight to needs. Their mental radar goes off when they see a task in the body of Christ that needs to be done. They are hard workers, self-starters, and get stuff done. They have a tremendous sense of fulfillment when they see that their efforts met a real tangible need.

NOTES

186

They don't need to be asked, and they don't care about being in the limelight of recognition. While they don't want public attention, they do have a need for appreciation as that confirms to them that the service they're providing is necessary and has been done in a satisfactory manner.

They will help others regardless of how much it costs them or inconveniences them.

They prefer doing rather than talking or planning. Sometimes if they are promoted to positions of leadership, they can be weak in delegation. Their gift tells them they should do it, not someone else.

Precautions
They can be misunderstood sometimes because they may appear to be pushy.

They have a difficult time saying "no," and as a result can easily become involved in a lot of activities. They can get so involved in serving that they fail to get their own things done.

They may become resentful and bitter if they feel taken advantage of and not shown some appreciation.

Because they make things happen and get things done, they are many times asked to lead a project, which they're not gifted for and it quickly fails. This brings about frustration and causes them to feel bad about themselves.

Teaching
A person with this gift loves to mine the gold nuggets of truth out of God's Word. The teacher communicates information relevant to the health and ministry of the body of Christ in such a way that others will learn. They make the truth of God's Word clear with accuracy and simplicity so that others can learn and understand these truths.

Characteristics
Chuck Swindoll says that the teacher will have four loves:
1. *They love the body of Christ.* They have a burning desire for every person to be equipped with truth. The teachers are great when we face the "hard questions" about faith or the Bible. Many look to them as the "defenders" of the faith.
2. *They love studying the Bible.* It's a joy to them to dive into the meaning of Biblical words. They enjoy outlines and finding hidden treasures. They have an alertness to factual details and are quick to detect error.
3. *They love delivering the truth.* It's not enough just to find the truth; they also are looking for an avenue to share the truth. It's a passion for them.
4. *They love simplicity.* They're gifted in taking the complicated and making it simple. It's easy for them to connect the dots so that a passage of Scripture can be understood. Their notes are often systematized and easy to follow.

Precautions
They may get so "lost" in the details of study that they get sidetracked from the ultimate purpose of that passage of Scripture. They may share too much information without enough application. As a result, they can be boring as a speaker if they seek only to communicate facts and may come across as cold or indifferent.

They can become overly critical of other teachers, especially when they spot

> " *Now there are varieties of gifts, but the same Spirit; [5] and there are varieties of service, but the same Lord; [6] and there are varieties of activities, but it is the same God who empowers them all in everyone. [7] To each is given the manifestation of the Spirit for the common good.* "
> - 1 Corinthians 12:4-7

NOTES

> "When God's Spirit came to live in your heart, He didn't come empty-handed. He brought a spiritual gift to give to you."

a factual error in their message. 99% of their theology may be accurate, but they'll dismiss them over the 1% they disagree on.

They can get so caught up in research that they don't rely enough on the Holy Spirit for enlightenment. They may find that they're seldom taking the time to pray, "Lord, what are you saying to me? How does this apply to my life?" They're reading the Bible to find their next lesson, rather than to find God's Word specifically to them.

Exhortation

This spiritual gift is given to those who minister with their words in offering comfort, consolation, encouragement, and counsel in such a way that people feel helped and healed. They motivate others to pursue a course of action. They are the "how to" teachers of the Word who coach others in reaching their maximum potential. The teacher gives us the what, the exhorter tells us the how. The teacher is motivated that we know the truth; the exhorter is motivated that we apply the truth.

Characteristics

A person with this gift is interested in where you are with Christ. They will want to know what steps you are taking to grow as they sense a responsibility to help you grow spiritually. They are great for giving you practical steps towards growth. They stress the importance of discipleship, and nothing excites them more than to see someone implement their advice and begin to grow.

When hearing a sermon, they're listening for the application. They're looking for the message to be practical. They want Scripture to be taught in ways that apply directly to daily living.

They have the ability to see potential in you and can visualize spiritual achievement for you down the road. They are great to have around when you're thinking about taking a step of faith.

They have strong people skills and usually have a very healthy self-image and are very confident when it comes to God, life, and people.

Precautions

The exhorter can be misunderstood sometimes because they make something that is difficult in your life seem so small and simple. "Just do steps 1, 2, and 3, and your life will be all better!" The exhorter must be careful not to over-simplify a very complex problem. As a result, they may appear over-confident because, for them, the answers seem simple.

Many get overloaded with people's demands. Everyone's problem becomes their problem.

They can come across as uninterested in a person's feelings. If they're not walking in the spirit, they can be judgmental. They can also become apathetic because they get tired of people having the same problem.

Giving

If you have the passion and ability to contribute yourself, your money, your time, and/or your material resources to the work of the Lord, you may have the gift of giving. These are individuals who want to make a real difference by giving far beyond a tithe to discover and provide for the physical needs of the Body of Christ. They do so in such a way so that God gets the glory, not the giver. However, it should be noted that this gift is not just limited to people who have lots of money.

Characteristics

One of the most important things to know about givers is that they don't want people to know that they are givers. They watch for opportunities and then quietly meet the needs. They are not motivated by praise or applause. They are not seeking public approval.

They have a keen ability to make wise purchases and investments in order to have money to give away. Most people want to save money in order to have more money. The giver desires to save so that he will have more to give.

They are people of faith and are motivated to support projects that step out in faith. They also have a desire to use their giving to motivate others to give.

Givers want to do more than just give. They want to feel a part of the work that they have given to. Many times, if they have given to a missionary project, they enjoy being invited to see the completion!

Precautions

Givers may tend to judge other people by their giving or lack thereof.

If they are not walking in the spirit, they may try to control programs and projects with their gifts, or they may give with the wrong motives. If not in check, pride has a way of creeping into a person's life who has the gift of giving.

Because they focus on money, many times they are misunderstood by people who think they are more focused on the temporal as opposed to the eternal.

Administration

The gift of administration or leadership is defined as a person with the motivation to coordinate the activities of others for the achievement of common goals. They preside over, lead, and distinguish major objectives and help those around him to visualize them. They have the ability to organize a larger group of Christians so that each one is released to perform his or her ministry without the hindrance of disorganization. These organizational leaders have an understanding of God's goals for the church and are able to create a structure that produces the values God intended the church to have.

Characteristics

This individual organizes people and projects according to the "big picture." They are gifted at breaking down the major goals into smaller achievable tasks. The size of a project doesn't discourage them. What makes them so valuable is that they can see the big picture in small pieces.

They enjoy planning and goal setting. They are self-starters who feel a great sense of fulfillment in seeing the parts come together. They are motivated to organize those areas in which they are responsible.

They are good at decision-making. It comes natural to them and others seek them out for direction.

They have the ability to delegate and they know what can and cannot be delegated. They know how to remove themselves from distracting details in

> " Spiritual gifts are not for my benefit, but for the benefit of others. "

NOTES

189

NOTES _____

_____
_____
_____
_____
_____
_____
_____
_____
_____
_____
_____
_____
_____
_____
_____
_____
_____
_____
_____
_____
_____
_____
_____
_____
_____
_____
_____
_____
_____
_____
_____

order to stay focused on the big picture.

Precautions
Their ability to delegate may come across to some as laziness and a tendency to avoid work. Many times they fail to explain why a task needs to be done, and people feel used.

They may appear to be more interested in the project than they are people.

Because they endure the criticism and complaints of people they are at times viewed to be callous and insensitive.

Because they want to finish the project, they may become insensitive to the weariness and priorities of others. While they strive to stay orderly, they can cause others to get out of order.

Mercy
Those with this gift feel genuine empathy and compassion for individuals (both Christian and non-Christian) who are suffering, and they translate that compassion into cheerfully done deeds that reflect Christ's love and alleviate the suffering. They are the best at comforting those who are in distress and they help to restore them to a place of peace and productivity.

Characteristics
They have the great ability to feel and empathize with the joy or distress of another person or group. They have a heightened sense of discernment when it comes to emotions. They don't have to ask, "How are you doing?" They just intuitively know.

They can vicariously experience what others are going through. They have a great hope and desire to be able to help others by their presence and friendship.

They are very sensitive to statements or actions that may hurt others. Those with this gift are reluctant to speak against any person, regardless of what they have done.

Precautions
They can get so absorbed with another person's personal problems, which can be detrimental to their own health.

If they're not careful, their on-going sympathy may enable that person to continue to live in that state and not make the necessary changes in their life.

Because they err on the side of grace, they may not speak up in times when they do need to confront the sin in someone's life. Mercy must also be balanced with justice.

Reflect on what you learned today? What did God teach you about spiritual gifts?

_____

Out of this list, which one do you think is your primary spiritual gift and why?

What do you feel may be your secondary spiritual gift? Why?

Day 5
How Has God Shaped Me to Serve?

vimeo.com/138215680

God has given you talents and abilities that you are designed to express, but you have two options: you can live your life by design or you can live your life by default. You can either live your life intentionally, or you can live your life accidentally. You can either make the most out of what God has given you, or you can waste it.

When it comes to knowing your purpose and calling in life, it can all be summed up in one word: service. God wants you to serve Him by serving others.

Ephesians 2:10 says, *"For we are his workmanship, created in Christ Jesus for good works, which God prepared beforehand, that we should walk in them."*

God didn't put you here on this earth for you to be some selfish little clod where you live totally for yourself and everyone else exists to meet your needs, to give you pleasure, or to peel grapes for you. No, Jesus taught us that the real mark of greatness is not how many people are serving you, but how many people you serve. The highest calling of any Christian is to be a servant. Jesus said in Matthew 20:28, *"Your attitude must be like my own, for I did not come to be served, but to serve."* The greatest title anyone could ever give you is not "leader" but rather "servant of God." The greatest people are those that serve the most.

It's been said that humility isn't thinking less of yourself. It's thinking of yourself *less*. The opposite of humility isn't pride; it's self-absorption. You cannot lead, inspire others, or serve others when you are absorbed with yourself.

We need to understand what it means to truly have a servant's heart. You never hear a servant complaining about "my rights" because he doesn't have any rights. He belongs to His master. You never hear a servant complaining about "my programs" because he doesn't have any programs. They belong to Jesus Christ. If you're not careful, church can be a place where it's really easy for egos to get bruised. Someone once said, *"How can you know if you have a servant's heart? Answer this question: 'How do I feel when people treat me like one?'"* How do you respond when someone treats you like a servant? Maturity is when you take off the bib and put on the apron. You stop expecting people to feed you and you start feeding other people.

Saddleback Church has developed a great assessment tool for finding and fulfilling your unique purpose for life. They use the acronym SHAPE to help you discover how God has uniquely crafted you. Think of your unique shape as a puzzle piece that is meant to fit into and fulfill the total picture of the spiritual body, which is the church. The SHAPE acronym stands for Spiritual Gifts, Heart, Abilities, Personality, and Experiences. Since we covered spiritual gifts yesterday, we'll take a deeper look at the other four components of your shape.

Heart – *What are you most passionate about?*

The dictionary defines your heart as "your emotional constitution of your disposition. It's the vital or driving impulse." The Bible uses the heart to represent the center of your motivations, desires, and inclinations.

My heart determines three things:

1. It determines why I say the things I do. Luke 6:45 says, *"For the mouth speaks what the heart is full of."*

2. It determines why I think the way I do. Hebrews 4:12 says, *"For the word of God is...able to judge the thoughts and intentions of the heart."*

3. It determines why I act the way I do. Proverbs 4:23 says, *"Above all else, guard your heart, for everything you do flows from it."*

In *The Purpose Driven Life*, Rick Warren explains it well:

Physically, each of us has a unique heartbeat, just as we each have unique thumbprints, eye prints, and voice prints...It's amazing that, out of all the billions of people who have ever lived, no one has had a heartbeat exactly like yours.

In the same way, God has given each of us a unique emotional "heartbeat" that races when we think about the subjects, activities, or circumstances that interest us. We instinctively care about some things and not about others. These reveal the nature of your heart...[and] are clues to where you should be serving.

Your passion is a pointer to the problem you were created to solve. Psalm 33:14-15 says, *"From the place of His dwelling [God] looks on all the inhabitants of the earth; He fashions their hearts individually; He considers all their works."* What you love is a clue to something you contain. What is it that makes your heart come alive? Your attractions, desires, commitments, and prayers are an indication of what you were created to do. What is the one thing you would love to pursue if you had nothing holding you back?

Determining what you have a heart and a passion for is a great indication of where you need to serve your church. If you have little love for what you're doing, you'll never have a great sense of personal fulfillment. God has given you a unique emotional heartbeat that races when you encounter activities, subjects, or circumstances that interest you. We instinctively feel deeply about some things and not about others. That's there by intentional design. This God-given motivation serves as an internal guidance system for our lives.

What are you most passionate about? Is there an issue, activity, cause, or people group that makes your heart race? If time and money weren't an issue, to what cause would you donate yourself?

_____

_____

_____

_____

_____

_____

_____

SHAPE:
Spiritual Gifts
Heart
Abilities
Personality
Experiences

NOTES _____

193

> **" *... I have given him skill, ability, and knowledge in all kinds of crafts.* "**
> **- Exodus 31:3**

NOTES _____

_____
_____
_____
_____
_____
_____
_____
_____
_____
_____
_____
_____
_____
_____
_____
_____
_____
_____
_____
_____
_____
_____
_____

Abilities – *What are you naturally good at?*

God is the one who gave you those abilities. God says in Exodus 31:3, *"I ... have given him skill, ability, and knowledge in all kinds of crafts."* You may have the same spiritual gift as others, but coupled with your own unique abilities, how you express that spiritual gift can look differently. In 1 Corinthians 12:6 Paul notes, *"There are different abilities to perform the same service."* God wants us to use both our spiritual gifts as well as our natural abilities for His service. The difference is that one was given to you at your physical birth or throughout our life (skills and abilities), while the other was given at our spiritual birth (spiritual gifts).

One of the most common excuses that people give for not getting involved in ministry is their belief in the lie that they just don't have any abilities to offer. Nothing could be further from the truth. National studies have proven that the average person possesses somewhere between 500 and 700 different skills! You are probably unaware of most of them. A good percentage of the skills that you have seem to be inborn and develop very early in infancy. When people say things such as, "She just seems to have a natural talent for that," it's probably true.

One of the things that allowed me to go to the next level of my life and ministry was when I was able to identify and develop the abilities that God had given me, and to stop doing those things I had no ability to do.

Think about it. Do you have any skills or abilities in administration (accounting, office, secretarial, software)? Building or maintenance (painting, landscaping, roofing, etc.)? Recreation (skiing, sports, hiking, coaching, personal training)? Music and the arts (choral, crafts, drama, instruments, painting, etc.)?

Arthur F. Miller, Jr. writes: "Understand that you are God's idea. You will be held accountable for what he gave you to work with."

What are some of the abilities you have? Where do you seem to naturally excel?

_____
_____
_____
_____
_____
_____
_____
_____

Personality – *What's your take on your temperament?*

We each have a different personality that influences everything about us. Our personalities help define who we are. Have you ever tried writing your name with your opposite hand? When you try doing something that isn't natural to you, you feel uncomfortable doing it; it takes extra time and effort, and you still do a pretty lousy job at it! The same things are true when we try to minister in areas that are not suited to our own personality. Take a look at the descriptions of the four main personality types below and think about which type seems to describe you the most. Keep in mind that there isn't a "right" or a "wrong" temperament.

Lion (Choleric)
- naturally outgoing
- assertive
- businesslike
- at ease with large groups
- confident
- direct
- decisive
- success-oriented
- optimistic
- dislikes slow decision-making
- dislikes incompetence
- strong-willed
- not overly dependent on others
- wants to be the best
- natural leader
- deals well with pressure and stress
- presses hard to reach goals
- bold during times of adversity and hardship
- risk-taker
- influential

Otter (Sanguine)
- bubbly and enthusiastic
- fashionable
- at ease with groups
- expressive
- spontaneous
- deep desire to be popular or liked
- excitable
- persuasive and motivational
- dislikes monotonous routines and rigid rules
- upbeat and positive
- initiates fun
- tells great stories
- makes decisions and asks questions later
- humorous
- charming
- wants others' happiness above all else
- independent
- good at improvising and "shooting from the hip"

Golden Retriever (Phlegmatic)
- loyal and gentle
- likes to be comfortable and practical
- low key
- good listener
- sensitive to others' needs
- tolerant of others' mistakes
- easygoing
- relationships are a high priority
- peaceful attitude
- good peacekeeper between those at odds
- dislikes abruptness, insensitivity, and confrontation
- doesn't overestimate himself
- has a servant's attitude
- consistent

NOTES

NOTES

- team player
- strives for group agreement
- cooperative
- tough negotiator and good at bargaining

Beaver (Melancholy)
- reserved
- thorough and thoughtful
- often prefers privacy over large groups
- systematic
- perfection is a priority
- dislikes surprises and unexpected situations
- fears embarrassment
- thinker
- meticulous
- thorough
- devoted
- philosophical and well-researched
- sticks with what works and has worked
- efficient and often organized
- cautious in unfamiliar territory
- not overly affected by criticism or popularity issues

Evaluate your personality based on the descriptions above. Number the personality types with the one that you identify with the most.

_____

_____

_____

_____

_____

_____

_____

_____

Experiences – *How has God used your past to shape your present?*

God has given each of us experiences in life: the good, the bad, and the ugly. Every experience you've had can be used for God's glory whether it is to allow Him to maximize your past blessings or redeem your past mistakes. Paul knew this full well. He said, *"Now I want you to know, brothers, that what has happened to me has really served to advance the gospel"* (Philippians 1:12). Since our greatest life messages come out of our weaknesses, not our strengths, we should pay close attention to what we've learned in the "school of hard knocks."

In 2 Corinthians 1:3-4 we read, *"Blessed be the God and Father of our Lord Jesus Christ, the Father of mercies and God of all comfort, who comforts us in all our affliction, so that we may be able to comfort those who are in any affliction, with the comfort with which we ourselves are comforted by God."* Paul knew that God never wastes a hurt. The best person to counsel someone who has lost a child is another person who has lost a child. He wants you to be open to ministering to people who are going through what you have already been through.

What are the life experiences you have had that have taught you the most valuable lessons?

_____

_____

_____

_____

_____

_____

_____

_____

It's important to give some prayerful thought to what your unique, God-given SHAPE really is. Without that knowledge, your life will lack direction. Everything that God created is a solution to some problem. You needed to see, so God gave you eyes. You needed to hear, so God gave you ears. Dentists solve teeth problems. Lawyers solve legal problems. Your assignment here on earth is to solve a problem somewhere.

Remember, God loves you because of who you are, but He blesses you because of what you do. How do you think God feels when He invests into us gifts and abilities straight from His hand and yet we fail to use them for His glory? Since God has invested His life into me, I want to make sure that He gets the best return on His investment. Your talent is God's gift to you; what you do with it is your gift back to God.

66 Your talent is God's gift to you; what you do with it is your gift back to God. 99

NOTES _____

_____

_____

_____

_____

_____

_____

_____

_____

_____

_____

_____

_____

_____

_____

_____

_____

_____

_____

_____

_____

_____

_____

DISCOVERING GOD'S PLAN FOR YOU

week 8

Day 1

What Do I Do When I Feel Like God Can't Use Me?

vimeo.com/138215738

I think all of us struggle with feelings of inferiority sometimes. I heard about a guy who was getting ready to go out to eat with his wife. He had just gotten out of the shower when he looked in the mirror in disbelief and said, "Where did that great athletic body go? Who is this old man staring back at me? These arms look like pencils, and I've got the stomach of three men! Hon, this is awful, please tell me something positive!" With a big smile she said, "Well, at least there's nothing wrong with your eyesight."

Psychologists tell us that it takes seven positive words of affirmation and encouragement to compensate for the negative affect of one negative criticism we receive. No wonder so many of us feel so insecure! However, I believe that God turned your ears forward for a reason – so you would listen to His promises for your future and not what people are saying behind your back.

We all know what it's like to feel inadequate. Maybe you've thought that God just couldn't use you. But I want to challenge you in that thought and cause you to realize that He does want to do something significant through you!

Feelings of inadequacy

Can I just be honest with you? I've been insecure in just about every area of my life. I pastor a mega church, but I sometimes feel completely inadequate to be a pastor. I've felt unqualified to be both an author and communicator of God's Word. I've felt inadequate in being a husband and a dad. I can certainly say that I'm well acquainted with feelings of inferiority and trying to overcome the sense that everyone else around me is better, stronger, bigger, and smarter.

Inferiority complexes are killers. They are destroyers of hope and joy and vision, striking victims with a paralysis that prevents them from taking any kind of action.

When I talk to most Christians, it doesn't take long before I begin to hear the "inferiority complex" come through in their conversation: "Oh, I could never lead a small group." "Oh, I'm not spiritual enough to serve in that capacity." "Me? No... I'm not qualified to do anything like that for God."

In what areas of your life do you feel most insecure or inadequate?

_____

_____

_____

_____

_____

_____

_____

_____

_____

If there's one thing the Bible teaches us about this subject, it's this: God doesn't call the qualified, He qualifies the called.

Read 1 Corinthians 1:26-29: *"For consider your calling, brethren, that there were not many wise according to the flesh, not many mighty, not many noble; but God has chosen the foolish things of the world to shame the wise, and God has chosen the weak things of the world to shame the things which are strong, and the base things of the world and the despised, God has chosen, the things that are not, that He might nullify the things that are, that no man should boast before God."*

From the previous passage, point out the five types of people God is looking to use:

_____

_____

_____

_____

_____

_____

God's Most Wanted List

We find in this passage a description of the kind of person who's on "God's Most Wanted List":

1. God uses those who don't feel *smart* enough.

Notice it says that God chose the *"foolish"* things of the world. This word for foolish in the original language of the Bible is where we get our English word "moron." In this context, it literally means the non-intellectual or those individuals without any kind of formal education. Maybe you have an IQ that's less than average. Congratulations! The Bible says that God chooses the non-intellectuals to confound the wise. Now obviously, this isn't an excuse for not growing or maturing as an individual. But what it does mean is that if you don't feel as if you're the brightest crayon in the box, God will not exempt you from being used by His Spirit.

2. God uses those who don't feel *strong* enough.

The Bible says, *"God has chosen the weak things of the world to shame the things which are strong..."* Weak means those who are physically weak, sickly, or emaciated. If you feel like you're not healthy enough to serve God, He takes that excuse out of the equation as well!

You may not make the cover of *Vogue* or *GQ* magazines. You may be dealing with some health issues. It doesn't matter. Regardless of what kind

> **"** God doesn't call the qualified, He qualifies the called. **"**

NOTES _____

_____

_____

_____

_____

_____

_____

_____

_____

_____

_____

_____

_____

_____

_____

_____

_____

_____

_____

_____

_____

_____

_____

> "Our God loves to take the insignificant things of this world and use them for His glory."

of condition your body may be in, every nerve, every fiber, every corpuscle must be given to Jesus Christ. It's been said that it doesn't take much of a man to be a Christian, just all that there is of him. Anything less than all is not enough for the Lord Jesus Christ.

One of my favorite stories in the Bible is the miracle of Jesus feeding the 5,000. Next to Jesus, the little boy who brings his bag lunch is the hero of this story. That kid barely had enough food to feed himself. The Bible says he brought five loaves and two fish. When we think of a loaf of bread, we think of what we can buy at the grocery store down the street. But these were more like wafers that were flat, hard, and brittle. It was about the size of a small pancake, because barley was the bread for poor people.

What about the fish? Well, the word for fish is actually a word that refers to little pickled fish, which would be about the size of a sardine. Don't get the idea that this was some big salmon or great sea bass. It was really about the size of a minnow. So I guess you could call this story "The miracle of the saltines and the sardines!"

But the important thing to see in this is that this little boy was willing to give to Jesus everything that he had. And when you give your all to Christ, you'll be amazed what He can do with it! Remember this awesome principle: anything that you transfer to Jesus can be transformed by Jesus. What that little boy had was valuable because it was available. We should never insult God by thinking that He could not use us. It's not our ability He's looking for; it's our availability. On that particular day, it wasn't Simon Peter, Philip, or any of the disciples that God used. It was a little boy who dared to give his all to Christ. I've seen people who were too big for God to use, but I've never seen anyone too small for God to use. Our God loves to take the insignificant things of this world and use them for His glory.

Jesus took the bread and broke it, and about 5,000 were fed that day. Jesus will take the bread of your life and ask simply, "May I break this with you?" If you nod and say, "Yes," you will be multiplied in ways you would have never dreamed or imagined.

3. God uses those who don't feel *sophisticated* enough.
The phrase *"base things"* refers to those of no degree or pedigree. If you feel like you were "born on the wrong side of the tracks," it makes no difference to God. The Bible says, *"not many noble are called."* God can surely use celebrities and Ph.D.s who love Jesus, but sometimes He has more difficulty in using them because of their pride.

In the Book of Judges, we find a story about a man named Gideon (Judges 7:1-8). He found himself in some dire circumstances as an evil army was plotting to destroy his people, the Israelites. An angel of the Lord came to Gideon and told him that God had chosen him to deliver his people from the hands of their enemies. But what was Gideon's response? He didn't feel like he was good enough for that God-assignment. Just in case God forgot, Gideon wanted to remind Him of his lack of social standing. Basically, he told God that he came from the poorest family in Manassah and out of all the kids in the family, he was the runt of the litter! He was saying, "Lord, you've gotten to the bottom of the barrel, and you can't use me!" But God responded, "Gideon, I think you've gotten to the point where you are *low enough* that I *can* use you!" God reduced Gideon's army from 32,000 to a mere 300 to make sure that He alone would get the glory, not man. The Bible says that *"The Spirit of the Lord clothed Himself with Gideon"* (Judges 6:34). It wasn't Gideon, it was God's Spirit in Gideon. God took an ordinary man and did extraordinary things through him.

4. God uses those who don't feel *special* enough.
The word *"despised"* refers to what the world laughs and mocks at. The root

form of this word means "to be considered as nothing" – this would be the "nobodies" in society. The life of David teaches us that you are a candidate for God to use when others think you're not. In 1 Samuel 16, God told Samuel to find and anoint the next King of Israel. So Samuel visited the household of Jesse, a home with several potential candidates for King. The first was Eliab. He looked like a contestant on *The Bachelor*. He had the looks, the physique, and the brains. But God said, *"Do not consider his appearance or his height, for I have rejected him"* (1 Samuel 16:7). When Samuel asked if there were other sons, Jesse's reply was, *"There is still the youngest ... but he is tending the sheep."* God told Samuel, *"The Lord does not look at the things man looks at. Man looks at the outward appearance, but the LORD looks at the heart."*

Why did God choose David – the one voted most unlikely to succeed, the youngest shepherd boy – to be king over Israel? Because God specializes in accomplishing His plans through unlikely people. You need to understand that God has put more in you than those around you can see. And He looks past what the world looks for. Others look on the outside, but God sees His perfect work on the inside.

5. God uses those who don't feel *significant* enough.

The last type of person that is on the list that God is looking to use would be the *"are not"* ones. What does that mean? This is a person who not only didn't make the list of "Who's Who," but they didn't even make the list of "Who's Not!" This would have been one of the most offensive word phrases in the Greek language. Having a sense of "being" was everything to the Greeks, so to be called a "nothing" was the worst of insults. This phrase refers to people who feel invisible, as if nobody even knows or notices that they are here.

Have there been times when you've felt that way? Then understand this: Your limitations are not a prohibition to God using you, but rather a platform upon which God's grace can flow through your life. In 2 Corinthians 12:9, it says, *"And He said to me, 'My grace is sufficient for you for my strength is made perfect in your weakness.' Most gladly, therefore, I would rather boast about my weaknesses that the power of Christ might dwell in me."* To focus on my inability is not just false humility; it is rebellion against the God who works His greatest work through my weaknesses.

Out of those five descriptions of the type of person God is looking to use (foolish, weak, base things, despised, etc.), which one do you feel like you can identify with the most and why?

_____

_____

_____

_____

_____

_____

Perfect fit for the job

Here's one thing I've learned as a follower of Christ: God will use you in spite of your insecurities and He will often use you in areas where you're *most* insecure! When I was younger, I was absolutely scared to death of public

> " God specializes in accomplishing His plans through unlikely people. "

NOTES _____

> **"His strength is made perfect in your weakness."**

speaking. At one time, it was my number one fear. Now it's what I do almost on a daily basis, and I love it! So what life skill do you feel is your weakest? Leading? Praying? Sharing your faith? Teaching? Parenting? God's grace is all that you need. His strength is made perfect in your weakness.

To the extent that you depend on yourself and what you can do, that is how much you defuse the power of God in your life. Whether in your job performance or your ministry for the Lord, if you're depending half on your own intellect and ability to make it happen, that's 50% of God's power you *won't have.* John the Baptist said, *"He must increase, and I must decrease"* (John 3:30). Why? Because less of me means that there can be more of Him. The more dependent you are on God, the more He is able to move in and through your life.

So what do you do with those feelings of inadequacy? You simply turn them over to the Lord Jesus Christ. Remember: anything that you *transfer* to Jesus can be *transformed* by Jesus.

When I was a kid, my dad would have me work with him and help him out in the garage. Sometimes if Dad was working underneath the car, he would ask me to reach up and grab a tool for him on the shelf. If I didn't know what that particular tool was, Dad's verbal instructions would go something like this: "Brandon, it's over there … just a little bit higher … a little more to the left … never mind, I did the job with this screwdriver." Then Dad would say to me, "Brandon, that tool would have been better to use. It was made for this job, but I used this screwdriver because it was close to me."

What kind of person does God use? It's not always the one who is the most qualified and seems to have all the "bells and whistles" and be the perfect fit for the job. The person who God uses is the person who stays close to God and is available to be used. I may be a simple screwdriver, but I want to be close to God's hand so He can use me.

Read 2 Corinthians 12:9 once again. Put in your own words what God is saying to you in this verse:

_____

_____

_____

_____

_____

_____

Day 2

What Is God's Will for Me?

God wants us to know His will more than we are willing to know it. He doesn't play "Marco Polo" with you. He has a plan for you to discover His plan; He has a way for you to discover His will. In fact, it is not really your responsibility to find the will of God; it is your responsibility to do the will of God. If God wants you to know His will, it is His responsibility to reveal it; it is simply your responsibility to obey it.

vimeo.com/138215809

The definition
When we talk about the "will of God," let's make sure we clarify the terms. When you think about God's will, think of it in three categories:

1. God's Providential Will
This refers to those things God is going to do, regardless. When you think of God's creation, redemption, and second coming, these are all a part of God's providence. There are certain things about history that are destined to happen because God has providentially willed them to happen.

2. God's Principled Will
This refers to the moral will of God. The 10 Commandments, the moral law, the "do's" and "don'ts" of the Bible are the things He has commanded. We don't have to question God's will in this area. It's clearly defined; we just obey it.

3. God's Personal Will
This is the area where we have so many questions. This would be God's individualized will for your personal decisions and plans in your lives. God has a specific plan for your life. Whether you're a plumber or a pastor, God has a plan for your life. God never deals with people en mass, He deals with them as individuals, and God has as many methods as He has men.

Here's the key: the more familiar you are with the *providential* will of God and the more surrendered you are to the *principled* moral will of God, the easier it will be to discover the *personal* will of God for your life.

Since God has a will for us, He must want us to know it. If so, we could expect Him to communicate it in the most obvious way – through His Word! So everything you need to know about God's will is clearly revealed in Scripture.

NOTES

> "Success is progressing in the will of God."

George Truett said, "To know the will of God is the greatest knowledge; to do the will of God is the greatest achievement." I believe everyone wants to be successful to some degree. We want to know that our lives are significant and will count for something. But the best definition of success I have ever heard is this: Success is progressing in the will of God.

So what is God's will for your life? One of the best books I ever read on this subject is John MacArthur's book *Found: God's Will*. He helps us to understand that in order to know God's will for our lives, we must first answer the following questions:

Are you Spirit-filled?

Ephesians 5:17 says, *"Do not be unwise, but understand what the will of the Lord is."* That verse tells us that if we don't know God's will, we're not just uninformed, we're unwise! Notice that it's a command from God for us to know His will, and God's commandments are always His enablement. Anything God asks us to do, He will always make sure that we have resources or the capacity to do it. The way to know God's will is revealed in verse 18, *"Be not drunk with wine wherein is excess but be filled with the Spirit."*

Many times people are facing a crisis of decision: "Should I marry this person?" "Should I enter into this business deal?" "Should I purchase that new home?" They ask, 'Why doesn't God do something for me and show me His will?' Yet at the same time, they're not surrendered or filled with God's Spirit. Why should God show a person what to do if he's not already obeying what God's clearly told him to do?

Are you letting the Holy Spirit of God, who lives inside of you, guide you to know God's will. The Bible says in Romans 8:14, *"As many as are led by the Spirit of God, they are the sons of God."* The Spirit of God is there to lead us. In John 16:14, Jesus (speaking of the Holy Spirit) said that He was going to give us another "Comforter." The word in the Greek for "Comforter" is *parakletos*, which literally means "a guide who walks by your side."

Jesus said, *"My sheep hear my voice ..."* It may sound mystical, but the Holy Spirit wants to guide you in your daily decision making. The Bible says that the Holy Spirit prompted Phillip to go and share the gospel with an Ethiopian eunuch who was riding in a chariot. Because Phillip was obedient in sharing the gospel, it opened up all of North Africa to the Gospel! I'm so glad that Phillip listened to the voice of God's Spirit.

In Nehemiah 7:5, Nehemiah says that God put it in his heart to gather together the nobles and the rulers and the people. Have you ever had God put anything on your heart? Have you ever had the Holy Spirit just speak to you?

You need to understand that you don't need more of God's Spirit. When you were re-born spiritually, you received as much of the Holy Spirit as you're ever going to get! God's Holy Spirit just needs more of you! Spirit-filled people do not stumble and mumble around trying to figure out what God wants. They just go! We need the Spirit of God to be released in our lives.

Are you saturated in God's Word?

If you are saved and Spirit-filled, you will want to be saturated in God's Word. The Bible is the primary means through which God desires to lead us and direct us.

Psalm 119:105 says, *"Thy word is a lamp unto my feet and a light unto my path."* When you get into the Word of God, you're going to find out that God will begin to direct your life right out of the Bible. Nothing that God leads you to do will ever disagree with Scripture. You cannot know the will of God without first knowing the Word of God. Most Christians today are floundering in finding God's plan for their lives because they don't know God's Word. The Bible says this book is a lamp unto our feet and a light unto our path.

When facing a crucial decision, we must get in the Word! Without God's Word, we are guided only by our fears and our desires. A man was struggling in a certain area of his life, and his pastor recommended that he read the book of 1 Peter. He read the entire book every day for several weeks, and each day he would underline portions of Scripture, make notes in the margins, and highlight some verses. After several weeks, he said to his wife, "Honey, look how dirty the pages of my Bible are in 1 Peter!" She said, "Yes, but look at how clean your life is now!" The one issue he struggled with was overcome through the power of God's Word.

It is surrender to the known will of God that paves the way to discovering the unknown will of God. And as you begin to let God's Word flow through you, you will begin to think God's thoughts after Him.

Are you being sanctified?

Paul, in 1 Thessalonians 4:3, says, *"For this is the will of God, even your sanctification."* God desires for every believer to be sanctified. The word "sanctified" means that you are looking more and more like Jesus. Your life is becoming pure. In the next few verses, Paul gives four suggestions for living a pure and sanctified life:

    1. Vs. 3 – "Abstain from fornication"
    2. Vs. 4 – "Control your body"
    3. Vs. 5 "Subdue your passions"
    4. Vs. 6 – "Treat others fairly"

In verse 7, Paul sums it all up, *"For God has not called us for impurity, but in holiness."* If you want to be used of God, you must be holy, pure, and sanctified. It is not great talent that God uses; it is not great ideas that God uses; it is great likeness to Jesus Christ. So how can you be sanctified? It's simple. Ask the Holy Spirit to reveal to you anything in your heart that's not glorifying to Him. Confess any known sin, ask for God's forgiveness, and repent of it. Make sure there's nothing standing in the way between your soul and your Savior!

In the process of trying to know His will, we get to know Him. God is more interested in your discovery of Him than He is of your discovery of His will. The Bible says in Proverbs 4:18, *"But the path of the righteous is like the light of dawn, that shines brighter and brighter until the full day."* I love that visual picture. In the early hours of the morning before the sun rises, it's pitch black! You can't see a thing! Then the sun begins to peek over the horizon, and you can begin to make out the silhouette of the trees. Then it gets brighter and brighter until high noon (*"the full day"*) when the light illuminates everything and there are no shadows.

That is how God reveals His will to the person that is walking down a righteous path. It may seem dark at first, but as you walk down the path of righteousness and obedience to God, our Lord has a way of illuminating the details as you journey together with Him.

Are you submissive?

Paul wrote in I Peter 2:3-15, *"Submit yourselves to every ordinance of man for the Lord's sake: whether it be to the king as supreme, or unto governors, as unto them that are sent by him for the punishment of evildoers, and for the praise of them that do well. For so is the will of God."*

> " Without God's Word, we are guided only by our fears and our desires. "

NOTES

> ## "God's will for you is not a road map; it is a relationship!"

What is it that God wills that you do? Submit to those over you. You can't have any God-given authority in this life if you are not submissive to those authorities that are placed over you. It is God's will that you be submissive, not just to His Spirit but to others whom God has placed over you.

Are you a submissive Christian? One of the things I've noticed in being a pastor is that broken people have a very easy time discerning God's will. They have emptied themselves of pride and selfishness to the point that they are in tune with the Holy Spirit. Thomas Merton said, "We receive enlightenment only in proportion as we give ourselves more and more completely to God by humble submission and love."

Are you fully surrendered?

Romans 12:1-2 says, that we are to present ourselves as a *"living sacrifice"* to God so that we may *"prove what is that good, and acceptable, and perfect, will of God."*

Do you want to know the will of God? Then don't surrender to a Plan, surrender to a Person! Sometimes I hear people say, "I surrendered to the ministry!" I think to myself, "What a shame! You should have surrendered to Jesus!"

Remember: God's will for you is not a road map; it is a relationship! You do not find the will of God; the will of God will find you as you obey Him and surrender to Him. You cannot say to God: "Tell me what You want me to do, and then I will decide if I want to do it." You just sign a blank check and say to God, "Lord, anywhere, any time, at any cost – I will do it!" Have you ever done that? Before God will reveal His will to you, you must surrender your life to Him. Paul says, *"present yourself as living sacrifices."* You must literally "make a present" of your life to God.

Proverbs 3:5-6 says, *"Trust in the Lord with all your heart, and do not lean on your own understanding. In all your ways acknowledge him, and he will make your paths straight."* As you go about acknowledging the Lord with you life surrendered, He will direct your path. The phrase, *"make your paths straight"* has the idea of something bulldozing or clearing the way. As you commit your life to the Lord, He will clear a path for you and open up doors of opportunity.

Now you might be thinking, "Ok, this is really great stuff, but it doesn't help me with this specific decision I need to make. What does God want me to do *specifically* in this particular area?" If you are saved, Spirit-filled, sanctified, saturated in His Word, submissive, and surrendered, here's what the will of God is for you: *do whatever you want!* If these five elements or qualifications are true and operating in your life, then who is the one running your wants and desires? God is!

A.W. Tozer said "The man or woman who is wholly and joyously surrendered to Christ can't make a wrong choice; any choice will be the right one."

In a real sense, when these qualities are operating in your life, you don't find God's will, God's will finds you. Psalm 37:4 says, *"Delight yourself in the Lord, and He will give you the desires of your heart."* God does not say that he will give all the desires that are there. But if you are living a godly life and delighting yourself in Him, you will have the right desires! God will give you the desires of your heart when He is what your heart desires most.

You see, the will of God is not primarily a place. The will of God is not primarily for you to go there or work here or buy this or do that. The will of God is primarily concerned with who you are as a person. If you are the right you that God wants you to be, then you can follow the God-given desires He has placed in your heart, and in so doing, fulfill His personal will for your life! When you put God in His rightful place, He will put you in the right place.

Light to guide you

There's a harbor in Italy that had a problem with boats shipwrecking at night if they took the wrong approach into the harbor. Because there were too many rocks, shoals, and reefs in the surrounding area, there was only one safe angle that the ships could enter. So the engineers came up with a brilliant idea. They built four large poles and put four lights on top of each of the poles. As you would come down the channel, you would see each of those four lights, but it was only when they saw the four lights merge into one single light that they knew that they now had a straight line to approach the harbor safely.

God has given us many points of light to determine His will in our decision-making. When all of these converge into one direction, we can rest in the confidence of knowing that we're making the right choice. So what are those points of light?

Knowing Biblical principles

God's direction will never contradict God's instruction. I've been told this, and I believe it's true: 95% of what we ought to do with our life, God has already clearly told us in His Word. If you are saturated in His Word, it will tell you what you ought to do with the other 5%. Ask yourself: "Does God's Word *prohibit* or *promote* what I'm thinking about doing?'

Receiving spiritual prompting

One of the reasons God has given us the Holy Spirit is to guide us through the promptings and inner workings of His Spirit with us (1 Corinthians 2:12). I believe that on the road of life, we have two guardrails: one is *Scripture* the other is the *Spirit*. As we go through life trying to make difficult decisions, God has given us both of those guardrails to keep us from falling off the side of a cliff. I've found that when you're walking in the Spirit and really thinking through the Scriptures, when you're really open to doing what God wants you to do and going wherever God wants to take you, it's almost as if the Spirit of God takes the Word of God and, like a magnet, pulls you along in the right direction.

Listening to godly counsel

Proverbs 11:14 says, *"Where there is no guidance the people fall, but in the abundance of counselors there is victory."* Seek counsel from godly individuals who have been proven trustworthy in the past. They should know all the facts about the decision you're facing and can still be completely objective. As they pray with you in making those decisions, God can use them many times to confirm His will to you.

Experiencing inner peace

Is there a settled peace in your heart about this decision (Colossians 3:15)? One Scripture that really assures me is Isaiah 30:21 where God says, *"Whether you turn to the right or to the left, you will hear a voice behind you saying, 'This is the way, walk in it.'"* The will of God will never lead you where the peace of God cannot keep you.

On the move

Here's one final thought. We need to remember that God likes to use people who are already moving. Think of a trailer truck for example. With its payload, one of these vehicles may weigh up to 36,000 pounds! Just imagine how difficult it would be to try to steer or change the direction of one of these trucks when it's parked. It's impossible. But get it moving down the interstate, and you can steer it with your pinky finger. One of the things I've

> **"** When you put God in His rightful place, He will put you in the right place. **"**

NOTES

209

> ❝You just get rolling and moving in the Lord's direction, and He takes over the wheel!❞

learned in being a disciple of Jesus is that the people whom God uses the most and guides the most are those that get moving! God saves His richest ministries for His busiest saints. You just get rolling and moving in the Lord's direction, and He takes over the wheel!

In Acts 16, Paul was on the move. He didn't always know where he should go or what he should do, but he kept moving! He kept looking for a place to preach, or to serve God, or to start a new church, and the Bible says that he encountered a lot of closed doors. Paul wanted to go to a place called Bithynia, but "the Spirit of Jesus did not allow them" (Acts 16:7). Paul bounced off a lot of closed doors, but that was God's way of leading him to the open door. God led him to Macedonia, which is where Paul really needed to be. Because Paul was already rolling, God could easily steer him.

Too many times we allow indecision to paralyze us from taking any action. So we just sit around and say, "I just don't know what God wants me to do!" You need to get moving so God can lead you. Psalm 37:23 says, *"The steps of a good man are ordered by the LORD: and he delights in his way."* You just get into the mainstream of what God is doing and let Him lead you to that perfect will. You may reach a lot of closed doors, but soon God will open a door so wide, you won't be able to see around it, only through it!

Suppose your friend is facing an important decision. What advice would you give him or her as to how to find God's will?

_____

_____

_____

_____

_____

_____

_____

_____

_____

In what area of your life are you currently seeking God's will? How does what you studied today give you insight on your next step?

_____

_____

_____

_____

_____

_____

_____

_____

_____

Day 3

Does God Have a Plan for My Problems?

The fact of the matter is that you are going to have some problems in life, and God is even going to orchestrate your circumstances so that you do have some problems. Trouble is a part of who we are. It is a part of our fallen human nature. No one ever gets beyond the reach of problems. There is no wall high enough, there is no door strong enough, and there is no man wise enough to escape all the problems this world has to offer. But there is one thing we need to keep in mind: the struggle that you're in today is developing the strength you need for tomorrow.

What would you say is the biggest problem or struggle you are facing today?

_____

_____

_____

_____

_____

_____

_____

_____

I think it's interesting to learn that the Chinese symbol for the word "crisis" is really two words combined into one: Crisis = problem + opportunity. How true that is! Your problems are God's opportunities for Him to reveal Himself working directly in your life. Let me give you five ways that God uses problems in our lives:

God uses problems to *direct* me.

The problem that irritates you the most is the problem that God will assign to you to solve. God uses problems to direct us. He will sometimes allow our pain to be the launching pad of our greatest calling. Sometimes it is those problematic irritations in life that reveal what we are passionate about changing.

God may sometimes place an obstacle in your path so that you do not miss the opportunities that He has to direct you. I think of the prophet Elijah after he had defeated the 450 prophets of Baal (1 Kings 19). After that incident, Elijah ran into conflict, became depressed, and started to run away. He even got to the point where he asked God to kill him. He wanted

vimeo.com/138215855

NOTES _____

_____

_____

_____

_____

_____

_____

_____

_____

_____

_____

_____

_____

_____

_____

_____

_____

_____

_____

_____

_____

_____

> " ... the struggle that you're in today is developing the strength you need for tomorrow. "

his life to end. But God led Elijah by a brook for rest and refreshment. God supernaturally provided for Elijah by directing him to the brook, but then He did something else. He supernaturally caused the brook to dry up! That proved to be yet another problem for Elijah. What was God doing in all of this? Why did God allow the brook to dry up? It was because He wanted to move Elijah and redirect him towards His next plan for this prophet's life.

Another similar story is that of Jonah and the whale. God instructed Jonah to go to Ninevah and pronounce His judgment upon those people. Ninevah was east, but Jonah decided to go west as far as he could, and he ended up in the belly of a whale. That's a problem! But God allowed that problem to redirect Jonah to where He intended him to go all along.

God may have allowed the problem that is in your life to redirect you. Perhaps you have been through a relational breakup. It hurts, but God says, "I'm directing you. I'm drying up something in order to move you towards My choice for your life." It kind of reminds me of the song by the country group Rascal Flatts that speaks of how the breakups in the past lead us to the "one" we are to be with. The song says, "God blessed the broken road that led me straight to you."

Sometimes, we ask for a small blessing and get no answer, but find out later that God denied us because He wanted to give us something bigger. You have to leave what you have before God can bring you to His best.

God uses problems to *inspect* me.

How you respond to your problems speaks a lot about who you are as a person. God wants to see what's down in the well of our hearts because when the problems of life arise, it will come up in the bucket! You don't know how you will respond to a problem until you have the problem.

You see, your life is like a tea bag: when you go through a little bit of hot water, your true nature will come out. God told the Israelites when they were wandering around the wilderness for 40 years that His purpose in keeping them in the problem was to uncover their real nature. Deuteronomy 8:2 says, *"Remember that the Lord your God led you on the entire journey these 40 years in the wilderness, so that He might humble you and test you to know what was in your heart, whether or not you would keep His commands."* God said to the Israelites, "I brought you into the wilderness because I wanted to test you."

Any time there is a problem in your life, you can be sure that two things are going on: your faith is being tested by God and contested by Satan. Satan wants to discourage you, but God is testing your faith because He knows that faith is a muscle. Problems develop the muscle of faith. Problems let the world know what is really inside of you. When you're in a problem, forget what you want, and ask God what He wants you to have. God sends you into a problem so you can find out who you really are. God doesn't give us what we can handle; God helps us handle what we've been given.

God uses problems to correct me.

Ken Whitten said, "Life is a school and problems are the curriculum." We learn more through suffering than we do from succeeding. God knows you will learn more through pain and problems than you do from prosperity. Sometimes those problems will reveal wrongful attitudes or motives in our heart. When we are faced with rules, there is something inside every one of us that says, "I'm not doing that." If we see a sign that says, "Wet Paint," what's the first thing you want to do? You want to touch the wet paint!

Mark Twain said, "A cat who sits on a hot stove will never sit on a hot stove again ... and he will never sit on a cold stove either." Sometimes we have to get burnt in order to really learn the lesson God is trying to teach.

Ask yourself, "What is this problem teaching me? Is it showing a weakness? A blind spot? A character defect? Remember, how you conduct yourself in the problem determines how long you stay in that problem.

Growing up, I loved to go outside and play with my cocker spaniel, Galaxy. They say that dogs are man's best friend, and I can certainly say that is true. I always had a blast playing outside with my dog. But Galaxy wasn't always the kind of dog that listened very well. When it was time to come home for supper, I would yell, "Galaxy, come!" But he more or less ignored me and continued to play in the puddles and chase after squirrels. I would continuously yell for him to come and follow me home to no avail. Finally, I decided I was going to have to do something clever to get his attention. So I picked up a large branch and threw it in his direction. Galaxy thought I wanted to play "fetch," so he ran after the branch as fast as he could, picked it up in his mouth, brought it to me, and laid it at his master's feet. He had finally come home.

I wonder if the burden that you have today has been given to you by God to cause you to come to His feet. Maybe He's tried to call you in other ways, but you wouldn't come. What you are facing today may very well be the burden that God is using to bring you to His feet. God sends the storm to show us that He is the only shelter.

God uses problems to *protect* me.

In 1 Peter 3:17 we learn, *"For it is better to suffer for doing good, if that should be God's will, than for doing evil."* Sometimes suffering is a blessing in disguise. Sometimes it is better to do what is right, but it is easier to do what is wrong.

The problems in your life may be God's ways of protecting you. If you don't believe that, go back to your 15-year class reunion and look at all those people you could have married! That will make you grateful for all those hard breakups!

Rick Warren told a story about how a businessman in his church came to him and said, "I have been asked in business to do something that is very unethical. If I do it, I will sin against God, but if I don't do it, I will lose my job." Rick told the man that if he wanted to do the right thing, he really had no other option Biblically. He needed to take a stand for what was right.

The man didn't do what his company was asking of him, and he was immediately fired. Two weeks later, he came to church carrying that morning's newspaper to show Rick Warren. The newspaper showed all of the top management of that company on the front page. They were all indicted for fraud and sent to prison. That man said, "Rick, if I had not done the right thing, that is where my picture would have been!"

God can use problems in life in order to protect us. The truth is we don't know about our tomorrows, but God does. That is why there is no substitute for a consistent daily walk with God. Only when we get to heaven will we discover all the problems in life we avoided because we walked with Christ. We will never know on this side of eternity how God has protected us.

God uses problems to perfect me.

Here's another good problem principle: The success that you have in life will be determined by the problems you solve or create.

It was said of General Douglas MacArthur that the one thing that made him a great general was that he could see 50 problems and 50 solutions all at the same time.

What is God's ultimate goal for your life? It is to make you more like

> " ... how you conduct yourself in the problem determines how long you stay in that problem. "

NOTES

213

> ❝ Jesus Christ did not come to get us out of trouble; He came to get into trouble with us! ❞

NOTES

Christ (Romans 8:28-29). God uses problems to knock off everything in your life that doesn't look like Christ. He keeps molding you and transforming you into the likeness of His Son, Jesus.

Pain and problems are a type of preparation like no other, allowing the unimportant to fall away and the critical to rise to the top.

Your greatest times of praise will never be when you're on the mountain top experiences of life, but when you're walking through the valleys. The deepest level of worship is praising God in spite of the pain, thanking God during the trials, trusting Him when you're tempted to lose hope, and loving Him when He seems so distant and far away. At my lowest, God is my hope. At my darkest, God is my light. At my weakest, God is my strength. At my saddest, God is my comforter.

Based on what you read today, how do you think God could be using your greatest problem for His glory and ultimately for your good?

_____

_____

_____

_____

_____

_____

_____

_____

God does not save us from the valley of the shadow of death. He does something far better. He walks with us through the valley of the shadow of death. Jesus Christ did not come to get us out of trouble; He came to get into trouble with us!

Fixed on Him

Many years ago Dr. Charles Stanley, a famous Christian author and televangelist, said that he was struggling with some opposition in his ministry. During that time, an elderly woman from his church invited him to come to her retirement community for lunch. Although he was very busy and under serious pressure, he went and ate lunch with her. Afterwards, she took him up to her apartment and showed him a picture hanging on her living room wall. It was a picture of Daniel in the lion's den. She said, "Young man, look at this picture and tell me what you see."

Dr. Stanley looked at the picture and then began to describe what he saw. All of the lions had their mouths closed, some were even lying down, and Daniel was standing with his hands behind him. Stanley told the lady everything he knew to tell her as he observed that portrait. Then she asked, "Anything else?" He knew there must be, but he couldn't see anything else. She put her arm on his shoulder and said, "What I want you to see is that Daniel doesn't have his eyes on the lions. He has his eyes on the Lord." Like Daniel, our eyes should be steadfastly and confidently fixed upon Him during the good times and the bad.

214

Day 4

How Can I Make My Work My Ministry?

How do we as Christians take our faith into the marketplace so that God would use us in the marketplace to lead people in His direction? For many, it is difficult to make the mental shift because they've been raised to think that church is where you talk about God, and work is where you talk about work. We like to compartmentalize everything. Yet that approach is found nowhere in the Bible. Remember, being a disciple is a relationship with Christ that transforms every aspect of your life. As stated earlier in the study, you cannot compartmentalize the sacred from the secular. That would be like a husband saying to his wife, "You know, Honey, when I'm at home, we're married and I'm your husband. But when I go to work on Monday, I'm not your husband anymore, and I don't have to act married because home is home and work is work. So I can't put your picture on my desk, and I also need you to know that I'm going to need to take my wedding ring off and leave it in the car." That wife would probably tell her husband, "If you're leaving your ring in the car, how about you live in that car!" Every married person understands that they don't leave their relationship at home. Here's what I want you to understand: You can't leave Christianity at home or at church. We take our relationship with Jesus with us wherever we go.

So much of the teaching of Scripture applies directly to the workplace. And in today's lesson, we'll look at a few key Biblical truths that we need to keep in mind.

God loves it when we work.

I used to think of work as something that was the result of sin. But when you read Genesis 2:15, you find that before sin ever entered into the world, God gave Adam the gift of productivity and the fulfillment that comes from work.

The Apostle Paul wrote a letter to the Christians of the church at Colossae, and he spoke about how believers are to respond in a work environment. The first group of people he addressed is not those with jobs and careers like a lot of us have; he addressed those who were slaves. What was Paul's advice to them? He basically told them that if they were a slave, then be the very best slave their master has ever had. Don't just do what you're asked to do; go beyond it!

Work with all your heart

Read Colossians 3:23-34: *"Whatever you do, work heartily, as for the Lord and not for men, knowing that from the Lord you will receive the inheritance as your reward. You are serving the Lord Christ."*

vimeo.com/138215921

NOTES

"You can't leave Christianity at home or at church."

NOTES

The first thing Paul says in Colossians 3:23 is, *"Whatever you do, work at it with all your heart ..."* That phrase literally means "out of your soul." It describes an athlete pouring every ounce of his energy into an event. Our service to God in our workplaces ought to be characterized by energy and enthusiasm, diligence and dedication, confidence and commitment.

Notice what Paul says next: *"... as working for the Lord, not for men ..."* In other words, when you go to work on Monday morning, you are to go in as if your employer were Jesus Christ Himself! We are to work as if we're working for the Lord, not for men. What does it look like when we're "working for men?" For most, it means they do as little as possible to get by unless their boss is watching. For others it means to appear to be busy, even though you're not. The attitude of "working for men" also shows up in territorial attitudes, jockeying for position, or taking credit for ideas.

What would it look like if someone approached their job with the mindset that they are working for God, not for men? What difference should it make in the work ethic of the average Christian?

In verse 24, Paul gives us some added motivation: *"... since you know that you will receive an inheritance from the Lord as a reward."* We will someday give account for every single part of our lives to the Lord. God isn't just looking at how you live your life in worship on Sunday; He is looking at your whole life. And someday in eternity, when God gives us a "new heaven and a new earth" to dwell in, we are still going to work! We're going to still have positions of responsibility, and we'll still be productive in eternity. The implication of this verse, and others, is that God is watching your diligence now in order to determine what you can be trusted with later. Jesus taught us that he who is faithful with little worldly responsibility will be given much greater responsibility in the life to come (Matthew 25:23). Bruce Wilkinson put it this way: "Our eternal destination is the consequence of what we believe on earth. Our eternal compensation is the consequence of how we behave on earth."

Ultimately, *what* you do is not as important as *how* you do it. The significance of your work is not found in the details of your job, but rather in your ability to put your heart into whatever it is that God has called you to do at this time. I believe with all my heart that it is a sin for you *not* to do your best on the job. Elbert Hubbard said, "Do your work with your whole heart and you will succeed – there's so little competition." Most people on the job will not put in the extra effort to excel – that's what should make you stand out as a Christ-follower.

And just in case we didn't get it the first time, Paul reminds us once again to remember, *"It is the Lord Christ you are serving."* Ephesians 6:5 echoes this same teaching when it says, *"Slaves, obey your earthly masters with respect and fear, and with sincerity of heart, just as you would obey Christ."* Even if your boss is a two-legged devil, you still need to work for him as if you were working for the Lord Jesus Christ (because ultimately God owns the company that he thinks he owns). Daniel is a great example of this. He was a diplomat who served the wicked king of Babylon. Eventually, because of the fact that Daniel was not willing to compromise his Biblical convictions, he was thrown into the lion's den, yet the hand of God protected him from harm. When the king realized that Daniel lived through this experience through the protection of His God, a great fear came over him, and he said, *"Daniel, servant of the living, God, has your God, whom you serve continually, been able to rescue you from the lions?"* (Daniel 6:20). The king had to acknowledge that even though this man was his employee, Daniel ultimately was a *"servant of the living God."* Even if you're a stay-at-home parent, your job is a sacred job when you understand the One for whom you're primarily working. When you work, you are reflecting the image of God where you are. I once saw a sign at an office cubicle that read: "Work is more than an occupation; work is more than an obligation; work is an opportunity to reveal the excellency of God."

You ought to go into your job tomorrow with the understanding that God loves to watch you work! And one day you'll be rewarded for your diligence and commitment to excellence.

There's another Scripture that has a direct application to how we live our lives in the workplace.

Light of the world

Read Matthew 5:14-16: *"You are the light of the world. A city set on a hill cannot be hidden. Nor do people light a lamp and put it under a basket, but on a stand, and it gives light to all in the house. In the same way, let your light shine before others, so that they may see your good works and give glory to your Father who is in heaven."*

Jesus tells His people, *"You are the light of the world ..."* The world is in darkness. People are trying to figure out if God is real, and if so, how they can know Him. They are faced with all sorts of unanswered questions. And God intended for *you* to be the type of person whom the world could look at to know about God.

Jesus then said, *"A city on a hill cannot be hidden."* In ancient Israel, you never wanted to be out traveling at night. It just wasn't safe, as robbers would come out at night to prey on any traveler still on the road. So when you planned your travels, you would go from village to village during the day because it wasn't safe to spend the night out on the side of the road. So if a family was on the road and the sun was going down, they were hoping they could make it to the next city. And as the sun went down, they would look for the lights of the cities that would be built on top of the hills and make a beeline straight there in order to take refuge. Just as a city on a hill served as a beacon of hope for the weary traveler who is fearful for his own life, so also Jesus intends for you and me to be that beacon of hope among those we live and work with.

Jesus goes on in Matthew. *"Neither do people light a lamp and put it under a bowl. Instead they put it on a stand, and it gives light to everyone in the house."* In other words, when the environment you're in is dark and you light a lantern, you don't put it under anything that would shield its light. Instead, you put it in the highest place so that it gives light to everyone who's in darkness.

Verse 16 says, *"In the same way, let your light shine before men that they may see your good deeds and praise your Father in heaven."* We are to live life in such a way that it gets noticed, in such a way that there's something that stands out about you that is different than the people around

> " ... your job is a sacred job when you understand the One for whom you're primarily working. "

NOTES

217

> **"**Don't shine so that others can see you; shine so that through you, others can see Him.**"**

NOTES

you. And somehow, you would help them make the connection between how you live your life and the fact that you have a relationship with your Father in heaven. They may first look at you, but eventually, you want to turn their focus to God in heaven. In other words, God wants you to live in such a way that those who know you, but don't know God, will come to know God because they know you.

Sometimes, I hear people say, "Man, I've got to get out of my job. This is such a godless environment. There aren't any other people here who are followers of Christ." Think about it: what kind of environments need the most light? Those that are the most shrouded in darkness.

Where is the darkest environment of your life?

_____

_____

_____

_____

_____

_____

_____

_____

The truth of the matter is, the place the most light is needed is definitely not your church, and it's probably not your home. The environment where it is the darkest is probably in your workplace. That's why God has you there – to be a light! Don't dampen that light by complaining about your job or letting others down with your job performance. You stay full of joy by staying full of Jesus and the light of Jesus that is within you will radiate on the outside of you.

Notice *how* our light is to shine. The Bible says to *"let your light shine"* – not *try* to make it shine. People need to see the light, not the candle. Don't shine so that others can see you; shine so that through you, others can see Him. God intends for us to glow, not to glare. This means that we can't have a "holier-than-thou" attitude that preaches down to others through our words or actions. When people ask us the reason for why we're different, don't respond with, "Well, I'm a Christian and obviously you're not!" What we want to communicate is *not* "I believe something." What we want to communicate is "I'm in a relationship with somebody." If there is no noticeable difference between you and your co-workers in how you speak, how you think, where you go, and what you do, then you are in effect covering over your lamp and not allowing the light of Jesus to shine through you to minister to others. Francis Chan said, "Something is wrong when our lives make sense to unbelievers."

Make your workplace your mission field.

What are some practical ways you can make your workplace your mission field? Here are some ideas and suggestions:

Be a resource person for others at work

When you know that someone in your office is going through a difficult time, experiencing a conflict, or going through a divorce, you can be the one to pick up a book, CD, or some other Christian resource and give it to them. Don't say, "Here! You need to read this!" Say, "Hey, I know you're going through a hard time right now and I want to give you something that has really helped me in this area." There are plenty of tools, books, CDs, pamphlets, and other resources that can provide some practical help as well as inch them closer to the gospel as well.

Invitations
In your church, you have worship services every week you could invite your co-workers to. You can invite them to have lunch with you and take some time during lunch to open the conversation towards spiritual things. Look for those God-ordained opportunities.

On-Site Gatherings
This is a trend that excites me! There is a growing number of Christian employees that are holding "on-site gatherings" in their workplace, such as morning or lunchtime Bible Studies. They ask their boss if they can use a room at the office during off hours (breakfast or lunch), and they hold a small discussion group where they watch a video clip that shows them how to manage stress, set goals, increase productivity, or deal with other problems, with all of those videos having the gospel interwoven in them. It's a powerfully effective way to be on mission in the workplace, and people may eventually look to you to be the "chaplain" of your employment!

Always remember, if you are a disciple of Jesus, you are a light! You may have had your faith hiding under a bucket up until this week, but from this point forward you need to function according to how God has called and equipped you. Let people see your good deeds and glorify your Father who is in Heaven!

Not of this world
When I was growing up, my favorite superhero was Superman. He was faster than a speeding bullet, more powerful than a locomotive, and able to leap tall buildings in a single bound. But what fascinated me about him was the fact that as Clark Kent, he seemed like a pretty average guy. He always wore black suits to work along with those nerdy glasses. He would get into trouble with his boss at *The Daily Planet* as well as have constant conflict with his co-worker Lois Lane. But should this average, ordinary guy happen to pass by an empty telephone booth, he would walk in as Clark Kent, but then emerge wearing that red cape and a massive letter "S" written across his chest to stand for that heroic title – Superman.

What was it that made Superman so powerful? If you read the comics or watched the movies, you'd remember that Superman was not from this world. He was from a planet called Krypton. And he drew upon his power from up there and lived it out down here. The strength and abilities he possessed in this world were the result of him being from another world.

How does that apply to you? As a disciple of Jesus, the Bible says that you are not of this world (John 15:19). Through Christ, you've been made a new creation and you have a new nature within you – the Holy Spirit! When you step out of your home and into your workplace tomorrow, to the world, it ought to be as if you have a massive letter "S" written across your chest. It may not stand for Superman or Superwoman, but it will stand for Saved, Sanctified, Spirit-filled, Sold-out for Jesus Christ Saint, who is ready to make an impact in their workplace for the glory of Jesus Christ.

NOTES

Day 5

How Can I Follow the Promptings of God's Spirit?

vimeo.com/138215990

One of the most exciting things I get to do as a follower of Jesus Christ is to partner with the Holy Spirit to accomplish God's work here on this earth. It's an incredible thing to think about – God in the person of the Holy Spirit who lives and dwells within me wants to use me (my body, my words, my brain) to help and to encourage others we come into contact with.

The Bible tells us in many places that the Holy Spirit will prompt us, lead us, and guide us to do certain things in this life. That's why it's important to learn how to follow His lead and to obey His promptings. Romans 8:14 says, *"For all who are led by the Spirit of God are sons of God."* So how does the Spirit of God do that? At times it may seem like a little voice speaking in your heart. Some people describe it as an impression, a nudge, or a "knowing." I like to describe a "prompting" as a tap on your heart by the Holy Spirit. It's like having God's GPS in our heart. He's just trying to get your attention to help guide you in the right direction. Have you ever felt something alerting you to pay attention or pulling you in a particular direction? Perhaps you were listening to a sermon and you sensed God telling you to follow Him in obedience. Or maybe you walked into a building and were filled with dread, as if you should leave quickly. If you are a follower of Jesus, then most likely these feelings were the prompting of the Holy Spirit.

Have you ever sensed God prompting you to do something? What was that like?

_____

_____

_____

_____

_____

_____

_____

God Nudges

Promptings of the Holy Spirit or "God nudges" typically come in one of three forms:

NOTES _____

1. A nudge to avoid a compromising situation or to take a course of action

When you walk by the Spirit, you will not fulfill the desires of the flesh (Galatians 5:16). Beth Moore says, "Any day not surrendered to the Spirit of God will likely be lived in the flesh." Galatians 5:25 says, *"If we live by the Spirit let us also walk by the spirit."* Perhaps you're wondering what the phrase "walk by the Spirit" means in your life. How can you live each moment in dependence on the Holy Spirit, sensitive to His voice and obedient to Him?

To walk in the Spirit means obeying His initial promptings. You do it by going through each day aware of the Holy Spirit's presence with you. You submit to Him as you feel Him pulling you in a certain direction or tugging at your heart to take a particular course of action, even if you don't quite understand why. In Acts 20, Paul sensed the very strong prompting of the Holy Spirit to go to Jerusalem, even though he didn't fully know what was in store for him there. The Holy Spirit also nudged him with an uneasy feeling that trouble was ahead, but he was also given the confidence to bear up under it because of the God He served. (See Acts 20:22-27.)

For example, you may be convicted to drop a conversation, turn away quickly from what's on TV or in a movie, or leave a place that is questionable. Whatever it is, do so immediately. The Spirit is warning you about a temptation to sin that you may be unable to resist unless you obey Him instantly.

2. A nudge to share the love and message of Jesus with someone

Maybe there's someone that comes to your mind during the day. You may or may not know that he or she has been going through a difficult time and needs some words of support and encouragement. Immediately obey that prompting and call or write that person. Trust that the Holy Spirit will give you the right words to encourage him or her. God wants to minister to that person, and He wants to use you to do it. As a result of following His prompting, we receive the blessing of being a part of the process. When God puts love and compassion in your heart toward someone, He is offering you an opportunity to make a difference in that person's life. You must learn to follow that prompting of the Holy Spirit. Don't ignore it. Act on it. Somebody needs what you have.

Sometimes this kind of nudge grows heavier as the day wears on. It is a sense of intense spiritual heaviness that God is underlining this person for you. In Acts 8:26-31, we read how Phillip was wandering on a desert road and felt that the Spirit had given him a nudge to approach a stranger on the roadway. As a result of obeying that prompting, God was able to use Phillip to lead an Ethiopian eunuch to place his faith in Jesus Christ.

3. A nudge to be God's blessing to an individual

In *The God Pocket*, Bruce Wilkinson describes how you can partner with God to provide a small miracle in someone else's life. Let's say you are going through a hard time and you are in desperate straits. You've cried out to God for help. Let's assume God wants to answer your prayer, but how is He going to do it? God might respond in one of three ways:

- God might give it to you directly. He's God. He could make money drop out of the sky and onto your kitchen table if He wanted to. But it's not likely.
- God might send an angel. He could provide an angel to give you the exact provision you need. But again, God doesn't seem to work that way as a norm. That just leaves one more option.
- God can partner with another person in delivering His miracle. This is how God most often works in meeting needs. As Wilkinson states: "God chooses to rely primarily on human partners to get funds to people in need."

> " As a result of following His prompting, we receive the blessing of being a part of the process. "

NOTES

221

NOTES

It's also the same way He has chosen for the gospel to be spread as well. God could have written John 3:16 in big giant letters in the sky, but instead He depends upon us as His people to deliver the greatest news in all the world.

What happens though, is that more often than not, God's people are too busy and distracted to be able to sense those "God promptings" of our heart, and, therefore, we choose not to get involved. If that should happen in your case, even though God said yes to your desperate prayer for help, today you could end up staring into empty hands because the person chosen to help you with that need ignored the prompting. "Every day and all over the world, God sends out a symphony of invitations for people to partner with Heaven … God is asset rich – He owns it all. But He is cash poor – all His funds are in our hands," Wilkinson says.

As you think about obeying those God nudges and inner promptings in your spirit, think of yourself as being one of God's delivery agents. In 1 Timothy 6:18, Paul gives young Timothy a picture of how Christians can invite God into their giving in a big way. Scripture says, *Let them do good, that they be rich in good works, ready to give, willing to share.*

What do you suppose keeps us from not being able to recognize the Holy Spirit's promptings in our life?

Be prepared to be nudged

Here's how this works: Ask God to lead you in deciding how much you should set aside to meet a need or be a blessing to someone else. It could be $10, $20, $100, or more. No amount, when devoted to God, is too big or too small. Then you just devote that money to God. Pray something like, "God, I wholeheartedly devote this money to you. None of it belongs to me. All of it belongs to you. I promise that I will deliver it whenever and wherever and to whomever you choose." Then you just depend upon God to lead you to the exact person He has in mind. Sometimes I've found myself giving this money away the same day. Other times, I might find myself carrying those funds in a special compartment in my wallet for weeks at a time.

Recently, I was talking to a young man who started attending our church with his wife. He was a believer. She was not yet a believer, but they both attended church faithfully. One day, I was talking to the husband, and he had mentioned to me that he had been looking for work for quite some time and was waiting to hear back on a couple of interviews. Even though he never once asked for money or indicated that they were in financial stress, I felt the "God nudge," and the Holy Spirit prompted me to give him the $100 I had set aside for God to use to meet a need. I immediately gave it to him and said, "I want you to understand that this money belongs to God, not me. I've been carrying this around until He tells me who to give it to. So don't thank me. I'm just the delivery person! I really sense that God wants me to give this to you. May it be a reminder of just how much He really does love and care about you."

I also had a grocery store gift card I left him in addition to the $100 cash. Tears welled up in his eyes, and he gave me a big hug and went on his way. About a week later, I received this email from him:

> Brandon, I want to share with you the amazing things that God has done not just in my life but in my wife's life as well. After leaving your office, I found out that my cell phone had been cut off. As you know, I have been avidly looking for work, and without a working phone, an employer would not be able to offer me an interview or a possible position. We had not budgeted for the bill and wouldn't have the money for service to be restored for at least 10 days. God provided.
>
> Once I got my phone re-activated with the cash you'd given me, I had several messages from prospective employers, and every one of them offered me an interview. God provided.
>
> I was nervous because my professional attire and wardrobe has been lacking as of late, and it's impossible to make a great first impression if your appearance is not deemed acceptable. So I went to the thrift store, hoping that I could find something appropriate for my interviews. Within minutes I had a brand new pair of slacks, two very expensive shirts, and a jacket worth several hundred dollars, for a whopping total of $18.97 – the remainder of the money God provided!
>
> That night, I went grocery shopping with the gift card you provided us. I filled up our refrigerator and pantry with so many things that I actually had to reorganize the fridge. God provided.
>
> After making dinner for my lovely wife and before eating our bountiful meal, we did something we had never done together ... we prayed. We prayed and thanked God for all of the wonderful things that He had done for us and how truly grateful we are for everything He has done in our lives. God provided.
>
> The next day I was ready for my interviews. No detail overlooked. I was offered two different jobs. I started work the following day. God provided.
>
> That following Sunday, my wife prayed and gave her life to Jesus Christ! She will be baptized next week. Thank you again for your brotherly love, care, and concern. God provided you in my life.

When I read that email, I wiped the tears away from my eyes and prayed, "God thank you for using me to provide your funds in meeting a small miracle in someone else's life." I pray that I never miss an opportunity to be a conduit in the hands of God.

A couple weeks ago, I was leading a small pastor's conference, and at the end we prayed over a bi-vocational pastor who was really struggling to balance his work schedule with pastoring a small country church. We gathered around him and prayed over him, and as we were praying, I felt the Holy Spirit give me a "nudge" to take all the cash I had in my pocket and give it to him. That day I had nearly $200 in my wallet! I don't normally carry that much money around with me, but on this particular day I did. I felt God say to me, "Give what is in your wallet to this pastor. He needs it more than you do." I immediately obeyed. While we were praying, I took out my wallet

> " **Following the promptings of the Holy Spirit is one of the most enjoyable aspects of walking with God.** "

NOTES

> **66** *I will instruct you and teach you in the way you should go; I will counsel you with my eye upon you.* **99**
> - Psalm 32:8

and very delicately placed a roll of $200 cash into this man's pocket. I wish I could have been there later to see the look on his face when he reached in and pulled out that wad of cash. That night when I got home, I checked the mailbox and discovered that I had received a check in the amount of $1,000 that I wasn't even expecting to receive for a speaking engagement! It was as if God was saying to me, "You put My agenda ahead of yours, and I will always make sure your needs are supplied." Proverbs 11:25 says, *"A generous man will prosper; he who refreshes others will himself be refreshed."* Sometimes when you give to God, He refreshes your resources by giving back to you in return. Other times, God gives back to you in other ways. You may get back an experience that you wouldn't trade for 10 times the money!

Following the promptings of the Holy Spirit is one of the most enjoyable aspects of walking with God. I've given away something as small as a tie I was wearing to a gentleman who said he liked it and as large as a car to a single mother who needed transportation. You don't always have to give money. Follow the prompting of God if He asks you to deliver fresh-baked cookies to a neighbor or a co-worker, bring flowers to someone, offer to babysit for free, pay for someone's Starbucks coffee, pay for someone's fast food meal behind you in the drive thru, or send a note of encouragement to someone.

One of my favorite sayings of Jesus was, *"He who has ears to hear, let him hear."* That phrase is repeated throughout the gospels and even in the book of Revelation. God wants us to learn how to "tune in" to Him. Psalm 32:8 says, *"I will instruct you and teach you in the way you should go; I will guide you with my eye."* As you walk with God, expect His guidance. Never postpone a prompting. Be quick when the Spirit speaks.

As you obey those initial promptings of the Holy Spirit, the voice of God becomes stronger and more prevalent in your life. Eventually, you begin to see spiritual realities that only a person who is in constant communion with the Father can perceive (Psalm 25:14).

Pray this simple prayer, "God, I'm available to be used by You today. Make me sensitive to Your promptings and to what is happening around me in the lives of those I meet. Use me today for Your purposes. I surrender fully to You."

Jesus said "He who has ears to hear, let him hear." What do you need to do to hear His voice today?

_____

_____

_____

_____

_____

_____

_____

_____

_____

SHARING YOUR STORY
week 9

Day 1

What Are Some Ways I Can Share My Faith?

vimeo.com/138216054

NOTES _____

_____
_____
_____
_____
_____
_____
_____
_____
_____
_____
_____
_____
_____
_____
_____
_____
_____
_____
_____
_____

God wants you to have not just a ministry in the church, but also a mission in the world. Ministry is serving believers; mission is sharing with unbelievers. Jesus came as a missionary from Heaven that He might make us missionaries for Heaven.

C.S. Lewis said, "The Church exists for nothing else but to draw men into Christ ... if they are not doing that, all the cathedrals, clergy, missions, sermons, even the Bible itself, are simply a waste of time. God became man for no other purpose."

Some Christians try to excuse themselves from the Great Commission by saying, "Well, evangelism just isn't my spiritual gift." No. Evangelism is to be the work of every Christian.

Philemon 1:6 says, *"I pray that you may be active in sharing your faith, so that you will have a full understanding of every good thing we have in Christ."* You may have heard the saying that you don't really understand something fully until you're able to teach or communicate it to others. The same is certainly true about the gospel. There's something special that happens on the inside of me while I'm sharing my faith. I'm reminded of what Christ did for me, the ultimate sacrifice He made on the cross, the fact that He took my deepest, darkest sins I've ever committed upon Himself when He died, and that He has exchanged my awful sinful nature for His grace and righteousness. I've experienced Philemon 1:6 for myself. Sharing the gospel gives me a deeper understanding of what Jesus did for me.

When Jesus approached those that would become His first disciples, He said, *"Follow me and I will make you fishers of men"* (Matthew 4:19). What He was basically saying to them was, "What you are now doing for a living, I want you to do with your life." When Jesus said, *"I will make you fishers of men,"* He was saying, "I will take you – your personality, your background, your influence – and I will use you to catch men and women and bring them into my family."

F.I.S.H.

Learning to share your faith is as easy as learning to F.I.S.H. for men. Here are four easy steps for how you can reach your friends and family members for Christ:

F - Find whom God wants you to reach.

This vitally important step involves prayer, asking God to show you who He wants you to reach out to. Look at those in your own sphere of influence. How many people do you know who are not yet active followers of Christ?

I - Invest yourself in their lives.
It may be trite, but it's true: people don't care how much you know until they know how much you care. You must invest your time in them first.

S - Share your story and God's story.
At the appropriate time, God will give you an opportunity to communicate the gospel to them.

H - Help them grow and reproduce.
Once they have accepted Christ, the job has just begun. Remember, God wants us to make not just disciples, but disciple-makers.

Write down the names of three people that you know who at this moment in their life are "fish" and not "followers." As you write down their names, commit to pray that their heart will be open to coming to know Christ, but also that God will give you opportunities to move them closer to that decision.

_____

_____

_____

_____

_____

_____

_____

_____

> " ... How beautiful are the feet of those who bring good news! "
> - Romans 10:15

NOTES

The church exists primarily for those who are not here yet. Or to put it another way, the church exists for the fish that have not yet been caught! Unfortunately, most of our churches are filled with individuals who are quite content to be keepers of the aquarium rather than fishers of men. Growing up in South Florida, I did a lot of fishing as a teenager, and there's one thing I learned: fish do not naturally come to the fishermen. Fishermen have to go to the fish. Only people can reach people.

Romans 10:14-15 says, _"How then, can they call on the one they have not believed in? And how can they believe in the one of whom they have not heard? And how can they hear without someone preaching to them? And how can anyone preach unless they are sent? As it is written: 'How beautiful are the feet of those who bring good news!'"_

Statistics tell us that the majority of people who know Christ today have entered that relationship because someone cared enough to share with them the gospel story. Relationships have always been, and still are, God's primary path for bringing people into His kingdom. God has one plan for bringing the story of His salvation to the world, and it's you and me.

Six examples of how to share your faith

What do you think of when you hear the word "evangelism?" For some people it may conjure up images of standing on a street corner with a sign and a megaphone. The word "evangelism" simply means the announcement of good news, and there are actually numerous ways you can share your faith in a way that fits your personality and style.

> " ... the majority of people who know Christ today have entered that relationship because someone cared enough to share with them the gospel story. "

NOTES _____

1. Peter's Intentional Approach

Peter was a pretty confrontational guy! In Acts 2, he proclaimed the gospel of Jesus to an audience of Jews by saying, *"This Jesus whom you crucified, died on the cross for your sins."* That's bold and direct! As a result, 3,000 people came to faith that day.

The intentional or confrontational approach is what most people think about when it comes to evangelism. If you have the type of personality where you can walk up to anyone and talk about anything, this style might be for you. This type of person doesn't beat around the bush. They cut straight to the facts. However, if it is not done with a humble and caring heart, you can come across as harsh or pushy in your approach.

2. Paul's Intellectual Approach

In Acts 17, Paul finds himself in Athens where all of the philosophers and intellectuals would hang out. He looks around and sees all of these idols, and the Bible says he was deeply troubled in his spirit. Paul, who himself was one of the best intellects of his day, said to these men, *"I noticed that you have this idol made to an Unknown God ... I know that one's name."* Paul used that as springboard to reason with these philosophers about the one true God, and His Son Jesus, and the plan of salvation.

This approach is for those who enjoy giving logical and reasonable presentations of their faith. They lay out a sound explanation, work with ideas and concepts, present their case, and allow the other person to ask questions. They are the folks who enjoy reading books on apologetics and how to defend the faith. You may not consider yourself an intellectual, but you can read a lot of great books that smart people have written. This approach is for the person who loves to break down the barriers that people have when it comes to their false assumptions about God and Christianity. However, if you're not careful, you can over-intellectualize the faith or try to argue someone into the kingdom of God.

3. The Blind Man's Testimony Approach

In John 9, the blind beggar who was healed by Jesus was questioned by the Pharisees about the identity and methods of Jesus. I love his response. He didn't try to engage them in their theological discussions. He simply stated the truth that was lived out of his own experience. He said, *"I once was blind, but now I see."* His personal experience was irrefutable.

As a Christian, you have a spiritual autobiography. There is so much power when it comes to sharing your own personal story of how God has saved you. In fact, this week, we're going to devote a whole day's lesson to learning how to articulate and communicate your own personal story of salvation effectively. The great strengths of this approach are that it can be shared briefly and it's very non-threatening. You're not "preaching down" to anybody when you share your testimony. And we share stories about ourselves all the time, so why not use your testimony as a story to communicate the greatest Story of all time?

4. Matthew's Relational Approach

Before Matthew became a disciple, he was a notorious sinner. He was a tax collector, which meant that he earned a lucrative living by ripping people off on their taxes. But Matthew was radically saved! He wasn't a strong preacher like Peter or Paul, but he did have a large home, so he decided to invite all of his friends over and introduce them to Jesus.

The relational approach of evangelism is for those who like to build deep, long-term friendships with non-believers. They are people-centered individuals who enjoy deep levels of friendship and communication. Over the course of time and building their relationship, the gospel is shared after they have had a chance to observe your life and gotten to know you. The benefit to this approach is that it communicates true care and sensitivity for the other person, but if you're not careful, you can put too much emphasis on building the relationship that you ultimately neglect to share the gospel. There needs to come a point in time where you say, "This is what the Lord means in my life, and I want to share Him with you because I care about you."

5. Dorcas' Servant Approach
Scripture tells us that Dorcas was a woman who was *"full of good works and acts of charity"* (Acts 9:36). This approach is for those who express their faith in service projects to others. They share their faith first through some tangible form of action, such as feeding the homeless, working in a soup kitchen, or volunteering in neighborhood projects. Jesus is credited as the motivation for why they serve, and they use their act of service as a segue to not only share the love of Christ but also to provide the platform to share the message of Christ.

There are few things in life that show God's love more than real charitable action. The only weakness though is that we must be careful not to misuse this approach as a cop-out by thinking, "Well, I'm loving people so loudly with my actions that I don't really need to say anything." No. We must serve people radically, but then we must verbally tell them about Jesus.

6. The Samaritan Woman's Invitation Approach
One day Jesus was in Samaria when he told a woman at a well about how He Himself can be the "living water" that she needs to experience the cleansing and forgiveness from her past sins. This woman then went back to town and told everyone that they needed to come and see the Messiah – Jesus! Because of her simple invitation, people began to flock to Him by the hoards, and they too got saved. In John 4:42 they said to the woman, *"We no longer believe just because of what you said; now we have heard for ourselves, and we know that this man really is the Savior of the world."*

The greatest strength of this approach is that you don't have to know anything. It's as simple as saying, "Hey, would you like to come to church with me this weekend?" It doesn't take a lot of knowledge, but you're simply pointing people to Christ. The only weakness is that this is a good place to start, but not a good place to stay. Of course, we should be inviting people to our church, but you also need to learn to be equipped to share your faith so that you too can lead a person to Christ and help them grow and reproduce.

Look back over the list of six examples of how you can share your faith. What are the top two or three methods that seem to fit your personality? Why do you identify with those methods?

_____

_____

_____

_____

_____

_____

_____

In 2 Corinthians 5:20 Paul says, *"We are therefore Christ's ambassadors, as though God were making his appeal through us."* No matter what your career

NOTES

> **"We are never responsible to save, only to share. Our goal is to bring revelation, not to broker a response."**

is, you are now an ambassador of Jesus Christ. We are never responsible to save, only to share. Our goal is to bring revelation, not to broker a response. The end result is up to God; we only have to be obedient to share. By His power, He will give us both the opportunities to share as well as the words.

One day, I felt convicted that I wasn't doing enough to share my faith with others. That morning I prayed that God would open up my eyes to the opportunities that were around me. That afternoon, a pickup truck ran out of gas right in front of me. I pulled over to see if I could help and ended up giving him a ride to the gas station and back. I knew that while this man was in my car, God had given me a "captive audience" of someone who needed to have the love and message of Jesus shared with them. I want to encourage you to pray, "God, open up my eyes to the people around me who need to hear the gospel, and open up doors of opportunity for me to share Your wonderful message with them." That is a prayer that God loves to answer.

What questions do you have about sharing your faith with others?

_____

_____

_____

_____

_____

_____

_____

NOTES _____

_____

_____

_____

_____

_____

_____

_____

_____

_____

_____

_____

_____

_____

_____

_____

_____

_____

_____

_____

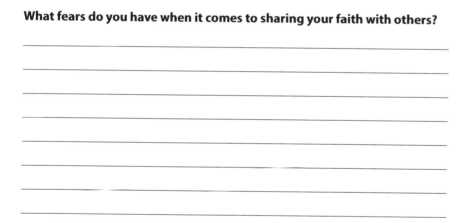

Day 2

How Can I Start the Conversation?

Like many Christians, sharing my faith hasn't always been easy. I didn't know what to say, when to say it, or how to say it. My primary concerns were: "How do I bring the subject up?" and "what if they ask me something I'm not prepared to answer?"

As it turns out, I'm not alone. In talking to a lot of other believers, I've discovered that their fears of inadequacy are a big barrier when it comes to sharing their faith. Rebecca Manley Pippert offers this insight: "Having taught evangelism around the world I have discovered that the fears are remarkably the same. *What if I offend? What if I'm rejected? What if they ask me a question that I can't answer?* However, over time I realized that the deeper, unspoken fear was the assumption that evangelism is all about us and our skills."

vimeo.com/138216099

NOTES _____

What fears do you have when it comes to sharing your faith with others?

_____

_____

_____

_____

_____

_____

_____

Critical Openings

The majority of people are most open to the gospel during three critical times in their life: When they are under tension, during transition, or in trouble. Let's unpack those three:

Under Tension

Maybe they are facing increasing pressure at work or worried about the rumor of layoffs. Perhaps they are concerned about a parent whose health is failing. Sometimes the stress and tension of life reminds them that their strength really isn't sufficient to face the demands that are placed on them, so they are more willing to turn to God during those seasons of life.

During Transition

Perhaps they are facing a move to a new area or expecting their firstborn child. Maybe they've just lost their job and are seeking new employment. When people are going through transitions; they have left the comfort zone that has been their sole source of security for so long. Now they realize that the ground which they used to stand securely on has shifted, and that can open up their awareness to a God who never changes.

In Trouble

Maybe they're facing a divorce or their marriage is in jeopardy. Perhaps they're worried that they may have cancer or some other health crisis. Falling into legal trouble can also be an eye-opening experience that reminds them of the God-shaped vacuum that they have within their heart.

Each of these seasons of life has one thing in common: they are life-shifting events that shake up our status quo and make us reconsider our purpose and our need for God in our life. Watch when those around you are going through these three seasons. This is when they are most likely in the "red zone" of their spiritual journey and may be most ready to cross the line of saving faith.

The Red Zone

In *Red Zone Evangelism,* Kent Tucker teaches us to think about sharing our faith in terms of bringing that person closer and closer to the goal line of saving faith. Sometimes just a simple chat or sharing a key insight is what they need in order to move them one step closer to making that decision.

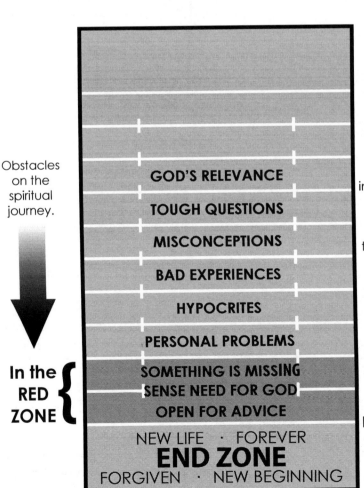

Obstacles on the spiritual journey.

The Spirit of God and the positive influence of Christians draw the seeker toward the goal.

GOD'S RELEVANCE

TOUGH QUESTIONS

MISCONCEPTIONS

BAD EXPERIENCES

HYPOCRITES

PERSONAL PROBLEMS

SOMETHING IS MISSING

SENSE NEED FOR GOD

OPEN FOR ADVICE

In the RED ZONE {

Line of Faith

NEW LIFE · FOREVER
END ZONE
FORGIVEN · NEW BEGINNING

Drawn to God

Jesus said in John 6:44, *"No one can come to Me, unless the Father who sent Me draw him …"* I used to think God drew people to Himself in some mystical way, by picking and choosing who He was going to draw to a knowledge of Him. The good news is that God does not desire anyone to be lost. So how does God draw them? The answer is in the following verse: *"It is written in the Prophets, 'And they will all be taught by God.' Everyone who has heard and learned from the Father comes to me."* One of the primary ways God draws people to Himself is by hearing, learning, and being taught the message of the gospel. How does that exposure take place? It happens through everyday conversations with ordinary believers like you and me. God can draw people unto Himself when you and I just take the time to talk about Jesus with those who have yet to meet Him. It was as the Apostle Paul was engaging Lydia in a conversation about the gospel that *"the Lord opened her heart to respond to Paul's message"* (Acts 16:14).

In his book, *The Unexpected Adventure*, Lee Strobel said, "Evangelism is never a solo activity. God is always working behind the scenes to draw people to Himself. And one of the greatest thrills in sharing our faith is to catch occasional glimpses of his covert activity. It's almost as if he's winking at us and saying 'You ain't seen nothin' yet. Stick with me and I'll show you some "divine coincidences" that will rock your world and exponentially expand your faith.'"

We need to remind ourselves that it's not our job to get a person saved. We need to differentiate God's part, the unsaved person's part, and our part. Our job is to simply have the conversations so that the Holy Spirit can do His work in their hearts. Our role is not to get a person to cross the red zone and make a salvation "touchdown." Instead, we should be inching them closer and closer to the goal line of saving faith by having conversations, answering their questions, and doing our best to remove the intellectual barriers that are keeping them from hearing and believing the gospel. God's power transforms the hearts of individuals, but He releases that influence through His people. Don't allow your fear of not knowing what to say next or how to respond to their questions hold you back from bringing the subject up. There's an encouraging promise that Jesus made that should give us confidence. In Matthew 10:19-20, Jesus said, *"at that time you will be given what to say, for it will not be you speaking, but the Spirit of your Father speaking through you."* There have been times when I would be sharing the gospel with someone and all of a sudden, just the right words would flow out of my mouth. Afterwards, as I reflected back on our conversation, I had no idea where that thought or those words came from. It was simply the Holy Spirit using me as His mouthpiece to speak to that person's heart. Christians who are engaging non-believers in spiritual conversations don't have to be afraid of what to say. Instead, they should be confident that God will empower them with the right words at just the right time.

The right questions

If we want to influence others, we must learn how to be good conversationalists. Conversation is an art to be studied and practiced until it becomes an effective instrument in your life. In a way, our conversation can be thought of as a bridge because it connects your mind to the mind of others. This bridge is built out of words and good questions, and the better you learn to use words and questions that show genuine interest, the stronger the bridge and the greater your impact for Christ.

William Wilberforce (1759-1833) was one who was intentional about the questions he would ask to people he would meet.

Everywhere he went, and with everyone he met, he tried, as best he could, to bring the conversation around to the question of eternity. Wilberforce prepared lists of his friends and next to their names he

> ❝ God's power transforms the hearts of individuals, but He releases that influence through His people. ❞

NOTES

233

> **"Questions are great conversation starters. It seems everyone has a story or an opinion to share."**

made notes on how he might best encourage them in their faith, if they were believers, and to know Christ if they were not. He listed subjects to bring up with each individual that might launch a conversation about spiritual issues. He described these subjects and questions as 'launchers' and was always looking for opportunities to introduce them. (Amazing Grace: William Wilberforce and the Heroic Campaign to End Slavery in the British Empire by Eric Metaxas).

Questions are great conversation starters. It seems everyone has a story or an opinion to share. And to get it, you need only ask. Good questions invite people to open up about themselves and divulge their thoughts and feelings on a wide variety of topics. Gary Poole added, "Don't you appreciate it when someone asks *you* sincere questions? It conveys an interest in your opinions and insights. It demonstrates a desire to know who you are and what you really think. And that means a lot. There is something powerful about questions that force you to think, look within yourself, examine your heart, and search for answers. And it's in the process of responding to those questions that you often make discoveries about yourself – things you never even realized before."

Some of the biggest shifts that have ever taken place in my life happened through someone asking me a pivotal question that got below the surface and made me question my motives, my purpose, or my goals. When you preach down at people, they instinctively put up their intellectual barriers. But when you engage them in conversations about the gospel, they cannot answer those questions without first tearing those self-protective barriers down. Why? Because our brains love questions. They have the power to engage us and shift our mindsets. They drive knowledge and growth and fuel both creativity and critical thinking.

Often, people won't be willing to listen to the message of the Gospel until you've first engaged them in spiritual conversations that prepare their hearts and minds to hear it. We share the gospel best not when we tell people what they should or should not believe, but when we tactfully ask probing questions in ways that allow them to surface the truth for themselves and evaluate the strengths of their beliefs. For example, when someone says, "I'm a pretty good person so I know I'm going to heaven," you can ask, "What do you mean by 'good'?" Sometimes asking the right questions can expose cracks in the foundation of their worldview.

Getting started

When I talk to other believers, I find that a lot of them really do have an interest in wanting to talk about their faith; they just don't know how to get the conversation started. How do you go from talking about the weather, your career, and what was on TV last night to talking about how you know you'll go to Heaven when you die? For most, just getting started is the most difficult task of all.

I'm going to give you a list of 20 questions that I've compiled over the years that can help you get the conversation of the gospel going in the right direction. As you go through this list, make a mental note of the questions you could see yourself using in your everyday conversations:

1. How can I pray for you? I love to do this at restaurants. Many times I'll say to the waiter or waitress, "We're going to pray over our food in just a few minutes, but first I wanted to ask how we can pray for you." You'd be surprised how this simple question can open up such a huge door of opportunity to share the gospel.

2. How can I best serve / help you? People don't care how much you know until they know how much you care.

NOTES

3. What has been the high point and low point of your week? This is a great "getting acquainted" or "catch up" question to get the conversation going. But the great thing about this question is that it often goes below the surface and gets to the root of the struggles they're dealing with in life.

4. Do you think much about spiritual things? People today are willing to talk a lot about spirituality. This open-ended question gives you an opportunity to talk about their spiritual beliefs.

5. What is your church background? Notice that this is a lot less threatening than asking, "Are you a Christian?" or "Do you go to church regularly?" Instead, it's asking about their background, their parents' religious influence. If the person is a believer and actively involved in church, they will let you know.

6. We've never had the chance to talk about your religious background. Where would you say you are on your spiritual journey?

7. How has this experience affected the way you look at God? Ask this after someone has gone through a personal difficulty.

8. What is your concept of God? Do you view Him positively or negatively?

9. Do you find that your faith and spiritual values play a role in your work / day / marriage / perspective on life?

10. If you could ask God one question, and you knew He would answer right away, what would it be?

11. Most people in America say they believe in God. What does believing in God mean to you?

12. Did you hear about that horrible tragedy that was in the news last night? In talking to people, I've discovered that not many of them have the assurance that they'll go to Heaven when they die. Have you thought about Heaven recently?

13. If you could be sure there is a God, would you want to know Him? Or if you could know God personally, would you want to?

14. How do you think someone becomes a Christian?

15. Can I share with you how I discovered a personal relationship with God?

16. Have you ever come to a point in your life where you trusted Jesus as your personal Savior and Lord, or do you think that is something you're still moving toward? May I share with you how I came to that point?

17. We've been friends for quite some time now, and I've never really talked to you about the most important thing in my life. May I take a few moments and do so?

NOTES

NOTES

18. Before I came to know Christ personally, God was a vague concept that I could not relate to or grasp. How would you describe your view of God? Jesus? Is He a reality to you or more of a vague concept?

19. Are you 100% certain that you will go to Heaven when you die?

20. If you were to meet God face-to-face and He were to ask you, "Why should I let you into Heaven?" What do you think you would say?

Out of this list of questions, which ones are your "fave five" that you could see yourself using?

When you're talking with people, let everything revolve around them at first and around Christ at the last.

There was a pastor who kept a painting of a shipwreck in his office. The painting depicted sailors in lifeboats reaching out their hands to people floating on debris from the ship. The pastor's son looked inquisitively at that painting for a while and then asked his dad, "Are those in the lifeboats trying to save those people or are they just shaking hands?"

I sometimes wonder about us. It's great to be growing in our relationships with others, but are you doing more than just socializing? Wouldn't it be a shame if all you did was shake the hands of those around you when you could be helping them into the lifeboat of salvation.

W. E. Baxter said, "The two most embarrassing questions you can ever ask a Christian is this: 'When was the last time you personally led someone to faith in Jesus Christ? When was the last time you tried?'"

What impact would it make on your life if you could say with confidence you know how to help others come to faith in Christ?

Day 3

How Do I Share My Personal Story?

O ur lives are compilations of stories: the stories of where we came from, where we are, where we're going, what we think, and what we believe all work together to make us who we are. At our core, we are walking anthologies made up of the stories we experience.

When you accepted Christ as your Savior, your story changed. When we share the story of what Jesus Christ has done in our lives, the Bible calls that a "testimony," and it is the most effective way you can share the gospel message with an unbeliever.

vimeo.com/138216152

One thing I know
Read John 9:1-34. Jot down any interesting insights or questions you have from this passage in the margin.

This Scripture presents one of the great miracle healings by Jesus in the Bible. There was a man who was blind since birth. Jesus and His disciples were walking by him one day at the Pool of Siloam, and Jesus was moved to heal him of his blindness. The Bible says that Jesus spat on the ground and made mud with his saliva and then put it over this man's eyes. Why would Jesus use spit to heal somebody? As it turns out, people of that day had a high view of saliva's healing properties, so Jesus used their common understanding to communicate to this blind man His intention to heal him. Jesus never healed anybody the same way twice. He used a variety of methods in order to eliminate confidence in any one technique. Healing isn't the product of a special formula or a process. It ultimately comes from the power of God. We know from the story that after the blind man washed his eyes out in the Pool of Siloam, he was immediately given his sight!

But the story doesn't stop there. Some critics of Jesus, the Pharisees, were looking for ways to incriminate Christ, so they began asking this man all sorts of questions. Finally, the blind man basically tells them that he wasn't able or qualified to answer all of their theological questions. His response to them was simplistically perfect, *"One thing I know: that though I was blind, now I see"* (John 9:25).

What I love about this story is that here was a man who had lived his life as a beggar on the street. He was uneducated and had a low social stature, yet he was able to stand before the intellectual religious leaders of that day with confidence in telling what Jesus had done for him.

People love stories
Sharing your story is a natural way for you to tell others how God has changed your life. The emphasis is on telling the story of how you personally came to

NOTES

> **"Your story is living proof that there really is a God who stands behind His promises and has changed your life."**

faith in Jesus and the new changes that are happening within you. But why are stories so effective?

People are interested in stories

Sometimes I wish I could put a camera up on stage to show you what an audience looks like when I'm speaking at an event. I could be talking about any subject and a good percentage of the people are either taking notes or they're looking down at their shoes, or their neighbors shoes, but as soon as I start to tell a personal story, every eye in the room looks up and fixates on me as the speaker. Why? Because psychologically, God has wired us to be interested in stories! We tell stories all the time, stories about where we grew up, how we met our spouse, or what we did over the weekend. Why not start telling the greatest story of all time? The story of how you yourself were once blind in your sin, but now you see!

People can relate to your story

When someone is sharing their story, we subconsciously put ourselves in their shoes for a moment and vicariously live through them. It's what happens to us when we watch a heart-wrenching movie like *Unbroken*. We can almost feel and sense the pain and anguish that the main character is going through. When you are telling someone what your life was like before you came to know Christ, how you experienced a turning point in your faith by believing and receiving Him as your Savior, and then what your life has been like since becoming a Christian, people can identify and relate to that. For just a brief moment in history, they are putting themselves in your shoes. And many times, whether they are conscious of it or not, they begin to ponder in their own heart, "If God could do this in their life, just maybe God could bring about the same change in my heart too." Your stories, regardless of how dramatic they may be, are relatable.

By sharing your testimony, you're demonstrating that your faith has substance – there is a reality behind it. It's not just your opinion or an attitude that has helped you. Your story is living proof that there really is a God who stands behind His promises and has changed your life. And when people listen, they may feel that if God did that for you, maybe He could change the course of their lives too.

No one feels threatened by your story

Evangelism has gotten a bad rap in today's world because a lot of people feel like they are using the gospel in the same way a used car salesman tries to get you to buy a car. But sharing your story takes away all of that negative stigma. You're not asking someone to do something. You're not preaching a "turn or burn" gospel message to them. You're just sharing what God has done for you, and not too many people will ever feel threatened by that.

No one can argue with your story

Why do we need to be able to share our experience of discovering faith in Christ? Because the man with an experience is not at the mercy of a man with an argument. A skeptic may disagree with what we say, but he cannot truly deny what we've experienced.

A few years ago, I was invited to speak at a Philosophy of Religion class at the University of Miami. The professor asked if I would be interested in coming and talking to the class about what Evangelical Christians believe. I thought to myself, "You mean you're asking me to come and talk about Jesus and the gospel for a whole hour in a university? You betcha! I'm in!"

On the day that I was delivering my lecture, I happened to notice two men sitting near the back who were obviously mocking and making fun of just about everything I was saying. Then towards the end of the class time,

I spent a few moments sharing my personal story of what I used to be like and how I came to faith in Jesus. The amazing thing is you could have heard a pin drop in that room! Even those guys who were mocking me for my faith couldn't say another word. Why? Because no one can argue with your story.

Our personal experience is irrefutable. When someone says, "I used to be a runaway drug addict, but now I'm addicted to Him," no one is able to argue with that! When God does a work in a human heart, there is a life change. You cannot have a genuine experience with God and *not* be changed by that encounter.

Your three-part story

If you have never developed your personal testimony, here is an outline that will help you do so now. Write a few sentences that fall under each part of this outline.

Before: *My story before I committed my life to following Jesus*
What was life like for you before you became a Christian? Tell what was missing in your life. What was it that made you aware of your need for Christ? Most people have a way of rationalizing why they don't need Jesus. What did you use to justify yourself?

_____

_____

_____

_____

_____

_____

_____

_____

_____

_____

During: *My story of how I made a commitment to following Jesus*
Tell how you made that commitment and what you did. What influenced that decision? Were there any specific realizations that led to that decision? Who was involved in leading you to Christ? What did they say that made a difference?

_____

_____

_____

_____

_____

_____

_____

> **" You cannot have a genuine experience with God and *not* be changed by that encounter. "**

NOTES _____

NOTES

After: *My story after I made a commitment to following Jesus*
Tell about the difference that following Jesus has made in your life and eternity. What has changed? Why has it changed? What is the single biggest difference you see between the old you and the new you?

Paul gives his testimony three times in the book of Acts, and each time, he includes those three essential elements – a "before" picture, how he came to believe, and an "after" picture.

What *not* to do
As you think about how you share your testimony, allow me to give you a few words of caution:

The goal of this practice is not to craft a memorized speech.
The idea is to develop a few talking points that you can naturally move through in articulating what your faith means to you. In each of the three times Paul shared his testimony in Acts, how he shared it was different each time. When he was speaking to Jewish people (Acts 22), he emphasized his own education as a Pharisee and zeal for Judaism. When he was speaking to Roman authorities (Acts 26), he portrayed himself as an obedient citizen of Rome. To the philosophers of Athens (Acts 17), his approach was to show how his teaching agreed with the thoughts of the philosophers of that day. Paul adapted the details of his story to fit his audience. He said, *"I have become all things to all men, that I might by all means save some"* (1 Corinthians 9:22).

Don't be long-winded.
People are interested in stories, but if you drone on and on, they will either run or tune you out. The goal is to be able to articulate your testimony in less than 90 seconds, dividing each category up into about 30 seconds. By not sharing too much detail, hopefully this will result in leaving them wanting more and asking probing questions to continue to conversation.

Be careful not to emphasize the past too much.
Sometimes a person who has a dramatic life-changing experience will talk about how they used to be a drug addict, prostitute, bank robber, or murderer, "but then I came to know Jesus and everything got better!" The goal isn't necessarily to highlight all of the ugly and bizarre things that used to be part of your past; those details should only serve as an illustration in order to highlight the work that Jesus Christ has done in your life.

Don't worry if you feel like you don't have a "dramatic" testimony.

You may not have had a Damascus Road experience (Acts 9) like the Apostle Paul, but you have experienced the same risen Lord Paul experienced. You were once on the road of sin. You saw the light, and the Lord opened your blinded eyes. The emphasis again is on Jesus and what He has done, not on you. Sometimes the most powerful testimonies come from ordinary people who found God in ordinary ways, but share their story with passion because they know where they would be without Jesus.

Life-changing story

Amanda, a young woman from Miami, Florida, used to describe herself as a devout atheist. She honestly felt that a person had to be simple-minded and uninformed in order to believe in Jesus. Today, she is a committed follower of Christ! If you were to ask her, "What was it that led you to find your way to God?" Her answer would be simple. She wouldn't tell you that it was some sort of intellectual or philosophical argument that convinced her. What she would tell you is how a close friend of hers told her the story of how Jesus had radically changed her life. Months went by and Amanda could see the obvious change in her friend's life. She said she just didn't know what to do with that. Amanda said that late at night the story of life change that her friend experienced would just tug at her, and it lived in her heart and mind for years. And when Amanda finally wrestled with the idea of a God who loved her personally, it was her friend's story of what God had done in her life that made all the difference.

Don't worry about whether or not you know enough about the Bible. Just share your story. When people hear how you "once were blind but now you see," God can plant a seed in their heart that could someday lead them to faith in Jesus Christ as well.

> **" Don't worry if you feel like you don't have a "dramatic" testimony. "**

NOTES

241

Day 4

How Can I Share the Gospel? (Part 1)

vimeo.com/138216202

NOTES _____

The way that people build bridges today is pretty ingenious! You build a foundation on one side, build a foundation on the other side, and then connect a bridge deck somewhere in the middle. We cross bridges all the time. We even have all these little idioms we say, like, "Don't burn your bridges" or "I'll cross that bridge when I come to it."

When you think about it, the gospel can best be illustrated as a *Bridge to Life*. We can do nothing to build a bridge to God; He is the one who chose to build a bridge to us by sending His Son, Jesus.

Why the Bridge?

Sharing the gospel by using the bridge diagram is extremely powerful for several reasons:

- People think in pictures. We are the multi-media generation. We consume most of our information visually through pictures. TV and the Internet have had that effect on us. That's why telling the gospel in picture form can be so much more effective.
- You don't have to memorize a bunch of information. It's easier to remember a picture than it is to remember a script. All you have to do to share the gospel with someone is to re-draw this picture and tell the story of the gospel while you're doing it.
- I personally feel that it's less intimidating. I remember when I first became a Christian and I would try to share the gospel with my friends. I did my best to recite word-for-word the "script" and the "Romans Road," hoping that I wouldn't mess it up. Sketching out a picture on a scrap sheet of paper and talking about it is so much less intimidating than trying to preach a mini-sermon to them. It's also much more openly received by the person you're talking to.
- Once you've shared the gospel with them on a scrap sheet of paper, you can give it to the person to take with them. If they didn't accept Christ, you've given them something to think about. If they do accept Christ, they now have something of value that they can keep to reflect back on and hopefully share with others.

Dr. Kent Tucker and *Share Your Faith Ministries* have written an incredible resource to help you share your faith using the *Bridge to Life* diagram. It's called *Red Zone Evangelism*. I highly recommend you pick it up if you really want to sharpen yourself in this area!

The Bridge step by step

Let's walk through step-by-step how to communicate the gospel using the Bridge diagram from today's video. Remember, there are eight key words to help trigger your memory:

Relationship

God loves us and wants to have a *relationship* with us. He created us for that purpose. God desires for you to know Him and for you to allow Him to guide you in this life. Jeremiah 31:3 says, *"I have loved you with an everlasting love; I have drawn you with unfailing kindness."*

Separation

Maybe you've wondered, "If God is real and wants to have a relationship with me, why is it that I feel so isolated from Him? We have chosen to go our own independent way, and our sins (mistakes we've made, times we've lied, lust, greed, anger, and so forth) have caused a *separation* between us and God.

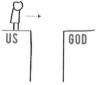

Good Works

Most of us can sense this separation, so we try *good works* to earn our way back to God. This could include trying to live a good life, going to church, volunteering in the community, and giving to worthy causes.

Fall Short

But no one is perfect. We all sin, and all of our attempts to cover over the bad things we've done *fall short* of God's standard.

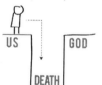

Death

The Bible says that the penalty for our sins is *death*. This is not just physical death but a spiritual separation from God in a place called hell.

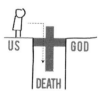

Bridge

But God did for us what we could not do for ourselves. He provided a *bridge* to make a way for us to make our way back to God.

Paid

When Jesus died on the cross, He *paid* the penalty for our sins and rose again to be our Savior. He took all of the sins you've ever committed – past, present, and future – into Himself so that you will not have to suffer the consequences for your sins.

Receive

But it's not enough just to know this. To cross over the bridge, we need to believe in who Jesus is and *receive* Christ by asking Him to forgive us and come into our lives.

> **❝** He provided a bridge to make a way for us to make our way back to God. **❞**

NOTES

> **"**Salvation isn't found in some magical incantation or formula ... It's not about what a person says; it's about what's going on in their heart that matters most.**"**

NOTES _____

_____

_____

_____

_____

_____

_____

_____

_____

_____

_____

_____

Their response

That's it! You've shared the gospel! But there are still a few more questions to get their response and their feedback. To remember these questions, use the following phrases to help jog your memory:

Make sense?

Ask them, "Does this diagram make sense to you? Is there anything I said that seems confusing to you?" This gives them an opportunity to provide feedback and to ask you any questions. Don't be afraid of the questions they'll ask. The Holy Spirit may give you the answer right then and there. Other times, you can just say, "You know, that's a great question. Let me look into that and get back with you."

Where are you?

This allows the person you're talking with to do a little "self-diagnosis." Many times I'll give them the pen and say, "Put an 'X' where you can see yourself in this chart." Many times I'll ask them, "Is there any reason why you would not want to place your faith in Jesus Christ and receive His gift of salvation?" Sometimes they do bring up objections. That's ok. It lets me know what they're struggling with coming to Christ, and I can help them find the answers they're looking for.

Cross Over?

If the person seems receptive, simply ask, "Would you like me to lead you in a prayer right now to believe and receive God's gift and to make Jesus your Lord and Savior?

If the answer is yes, simply lead them in a prayer. Let them know that it's not the words they say that save them. Salvation isn't found in some magical incantation or formula. It's simply a decision of their mind, their emotions, and their will to give their whole lives to Jesus Christ, placing faith in Him for their forgiveness of sins. Again, don't focus on getting the words of the prayer just right. It's not about what a person says; it's about what's going on in their heart that matters most.

I usually offer to lead them in a prayer phrase-by-phrase by asking them to repeat after me:

> *"Dear Lord Jesus,*
> *Thank you for dying on the cross for me.*
> *I believe in who You are,*
> *And I place my faith in You.*
> *Please forgive me for all my sins.*
> *I turn away from how I've been living,*
> *And I know turn my life over to You.*
> *I receive Your gift of salvation today.*
> *Thank you for saving me*
> *and for giving me eternal life.*
> *In Jesus name, Amen."*

E.S.P.N.

Now once they've accepted Christ into their heart and life, you've got a perfect opportunity to help them on the very first step of discipleship. I love the easy-to-remember analogy of E.S.P.N. we covered in today's video and in week 1 to help you remember the four things that happen to us when we choose to believe and receive. Share with them that if they prayed that prayer sincerely, here is what Christ has done for them:

E - Eternal Life — When you close your eyes in this life, you will open your eyes in the presence of God in Heaven! God has written your name in the Lamb's Book of Life. You can be just assured of your future home in Heaven as if you were already there (John 6:47)!

S - Sins Forgiven — God has given you a fresh start. All of your sins – past, present, and future – are covered by the blood of Jesus. He has cleansed you from everything you've ever done wrong (Acts 10:43)!

P - Personal Relationship — Today you began a personal friendship with Jesus Christ that can grow from this point forward for the rest of your life! You can now grow as a follower of Christ (Matthew 11:28-30). I can help disciple you on your journey of faith by becoming your LifeCoach.

N - Never Leave You — Once you have chosen to accept Christ, the Holy Spirit of God came to live within you. Scripture tells us that God has made this promise: *"Never will I leave you; never will I forsake you"* (Hebrews 13:5).

Your turn

Now, let's have you practice. You've seen me demonstrate it on video, and you've read it in this lesson. Don't skip this part! This may be the most important practice you do because it has the potential to forever change someone's eternal destiny.

Draw the bridge diagram and write what you would say to the person you're sharing your faith with in your own words.

NOTES

Day 5

How Can I Share the Gospel? (Part 2)

vimeo.com/138216250

A person can understand something much better if he can *see* what you are talking about as well as *hear* what you're trying to say. You've heard it said that a picture is worth a thousand words. That's why visually illustrating the gospel helps the person you're talking to have a better comprehension of what you're trying to say. Another benefit is that when the person you're talking to is looking at something, you have a better chance of explaining it without being interrupted or chasing rabbit trails.

Communicating the life-changing message of the gospel is the greatest privilege we have as disciples of Christ. In reality, I'm just a nobody telling everybody about a Somebody who can save anybody! It's not your words that God blesses; it's your obedience to tell others about Him. In today's lesson, we're going to review what you just learned in the video by walking you through, step-by-step, the process of using those visual illustrations as a clear and understandable way of communicating the greatest story ever told!

Hand-to-Hand Evangelism

Thumb – Good News
God loves you and has a purpose for your life
God created you to be in a relationship with Him. He wants you to experience His love, forgiveness, and purpose for your life. He wants to give your life meaning.

"For God so loved the world that He gave his one and only Son, that whoever believes in Him, shall not perish, but have eternal life." - John 3:16

"I have come that they may have life and that they may have it more abundantly." - John 10:10

But if God loves you and desires a relationship, why do you feel isolated from Him?

Pointer Finger– One problem of sin
Sin separates you from God
Nobody is perfect. Every day you and I both will sin and make mistakes. The Bible says, *"For all have sinned and fall short of the glory of God"* (Romans 3:23).

Week 9

Day 5: **How Can I Share the Gospel? (Part 2)**

Sin is the cause for physical and spiritual death. Romans 6:23 says, *"For the wages of sin is death ..."*

Next, I'll illustrate the barrier that sin causes between us and God by using my cell phone, a wallet, etc. I'll say something like, "This hand represents me, and this wallet represents sin. As we've stated, we've all sinned and come short of the glory of God. We're not good enough to go to heaven, and we are separated from Him. We may try to do many things (go to church, do good works, be religious) to try to cover over our sin, but it doesn't remove the problem of sin. We have to be sinless to go to heaven. No bridge reaches God except one. So how can we get past this isolation and get in good with God?

Middle Finger – Jesus Christ
God sent His Son Jesus to pay for our sins

Let's allow your middle finger, which is the tallest, to represent Jesus Christ. The only way our relationship can be restored with God is that our sins must be forgiven. Jesus Christ died on the cross for this very purpose. Jesus said in John 14:6, *"I am the way, and the truth, and the life. No one comes to the Father except through Me."* So, Jesus is the only way to God.

Going back to our wallet illustration, let's say my other (empty) hand represents Jesus Christ. The Bible says in 2 Corinthians 5:21, *"He made Him who knew no sin to become sin on our behalf, so that we might become the righteousness of God in Him."* While saying this verse, I transfer the wallet from one hand to the other.

You see, Jesus never sinned at all. Because He was both fully God and fully man, He was able to take our sin debt, and He carried that with Him on the cross. He died, He was buried, and He rose again. And because of His blood that was shed, He could wipe away every sin from our heart. I then clasp my hands together and say that because I've accepted His gift of salvation, God now looks upon me the same way He looks upon Christ. He now sees in me the same righteousness as in Jesus. Sometimes people think, "Well, I'm too big of a sinner." But there is not a sin that Christ did not die for.

Now, I hold up my first three fingers and explain that the Bible says that when Jesus died on the cross 2,000 years ago, He didn't die alone. There was also a thief on both sides of Him. One thief chose to receive Jesus as His Lord and Savior, but the other thief chose to reject Him. That is the same decision that every person has to make – either to *receive* or *reject* His offer of eternal life. To not make any decision is to reject Him. His death made it possible to be forgiven, but you have to ask for it!

Ring Finger – Our reponse
Making a decision to accept Christ as Savior and Lord

For those who are married, the ring they wear on their ring finger reminds them of the decision they made and the vows they spoke  when they married their spouse. When a couple gets married, they surrender their lives to one another. When a person becomes a Christian, they make an even greater life-altering decision to become a life-long follower of Christ.

> **" I'm just a nobody telling everybody about a Somebody who can save anybody! "**

NOTES _____

_____
_____
_____
_____
_____
_____
_____
_____
_____
_____
_____
_____
_____
_____
_____
_____
_____
_____
_____

Our response is as easy as ABC:

A – Admit that you have sin in your life and that you are willing to turn 180 degrees from your sin. Acts 3:19 says, *"Repent, then, and turn to God so that your sins may be wiped out."*

B – Believe in what Jesus did for you – that he died for your sins and rose again from the dead.

C – Confess verbally and publicly your belief in Jesus Christ. Romans 10:9 says, *"That if you confess with your mouth, 'Jesus is Lord,' and believe in your heart that God raised him from the dead, you will be saved."*

Pinky Finger – Our faith
We are too weak to save ourselves so we must receive God's gift
Your pinky finger is the weakest finger on your hand. That reminds us that we are too weak to save ourselves. A lot of people think that doing good works, going to church, or being religious will get them to Heaven. But think about it this way: If you could be a good person and still get to Heaven, why would Jesus have to die? The Bible says in Ephesians 2:8-9, *"For it is by grace you have been saved, through faith – and this is not from yourselves, it is the gift of God – not by works, so that no one can boast."*

Palm of Hand – Eternal life
When you are saved, you are secure in the hand of God
After you make that decision to accept Jesus, you can be certain that you have a relationship with Him and a home in Heaven. Jesus said in John 10:28, *"I give them eternal life, and they shall never perish; no one will snatch them out of my hand."*

Stop for a moment and review how to share your faith by using the fingers on your hand to jog your memory. Try going through it without looking at your notes. How much did you remember?

The Morality Ladder

The second illustration you saw in today's video is what Bill Hybels calls "The Morality Ladder." This is an excellent way to communicate to a person who seems to believe that their own goodness and morality is sufficient enough to get them into Heaven. They think they are decent, moral individuals and, therefore, sense no need for God or His forgiveness.

Just like the *Bridge to Life* diagram, all you need is something to write on and a pen. Start by writing "God" at the top of the page and explain that God is holy, just, and pure, so he would be at the top of this ladder of morality. Then draw a straight line to the bottom of the page, and at the bottom make a box to symbolize all the purest forms of evil that are in the world – the serial killers, child abductors, and the Adolf Hitlers of society.

Then you ask, "Where you would place yourself on this ladder? Would you say that you're right up here next to God and you're perfect and holy, or would you put yourself down here with those with the lowest forms of morality?"

I might say, "Before you answer that, who do you think is the most moral person who has lived in recent history?" A lot of times people say someone like Mother Theresa or Billy Graham. I usually put them on the upper half of the ladder and explain to the person I'm sharing with that both of these individuals have confessed their need for the forgiveness of Jesus Christ for their sins. They both have admitted that they've done things they shouldn't have done and have thought things they shouldn't have thought. So by their own admission, they acknowledge they're not perfect, and they need Jesus to fill their gap."

Next, I talk about myself and where I would put myself on this morality ladder. I might say something like, "Now, you don't know me too well, but I don't bat in the same league as Billy Graham, so I would put myself way below him."

Now I give the pen to the individual and ask, "Where would you place yourself on this diagram?" They usually put a mark somewhere near mine. I then explain that by their own admission, they have a gap between where they are and where God is. What is their plan for dealing with that gap? The Bible says that you can't bridge it on your own. It requires that you come to the cross of Jesus Christ and you believe upon Him, receive His gift of salvation, so that what He did on the cross might be applied to your gap, in order to bring you to Himself.

Try it yourself! Use the space below to practice drawing "The Morality Ladder."

NOTES

Week 9

Day 5: **How Can I Share the Gospel? (Part 2)**

NOTES

This week, you've learned three simple and easy-to-remember approaches to share the story of the gospel. Just start the conversation, share your own personal story when you get the chance, and don't forget to communicate the gospel message as clearly as you can.

It's not enough just to live a godly Christian life before our unbelieving friends. We've got to *talk* about our faith putting spiritual concepts into plain everyday words. Paul was adamant about this in Romans 10, where he warned that people wouldn't figure out the message on their own. Someone has to articulate the gospel to them by explaining who God is, what kind of damage our sin has caused, and how each of us can receive forgiveness and experience the new life Jesus Christ has in store for us!

Over the last two lessons, you've learned three ways to share your faith: Bridge to Life, Hand-to-Hand, and the Morality Ladder. Which one is your favorite and why?

BECOMING A DISCIPLE-MAKER

Week 10

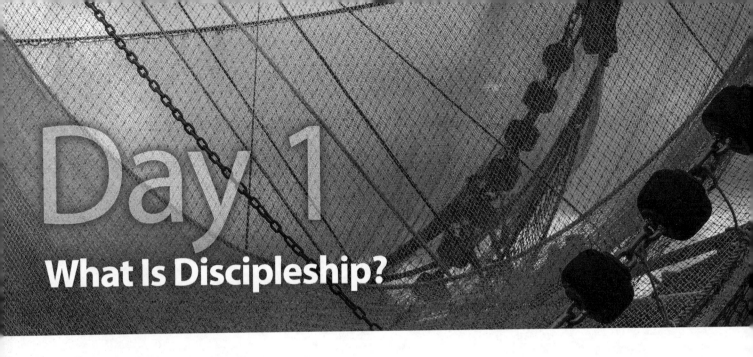

Day 1
What Is Discipleship?

vimeo.com/138216312

vimeo.com/138216312

NOTES _____

_____
_____
_____
_____
_____
_____
_____
_____
_____
_____
_____
_____
_____
_____
_____
_____
_____
_____
_____

"*Follow me and I will make you fishers of men.*" Those were the first recorded words that Jesus spoke to a handful of men who would become His first devoted followers, and it's a promise. Jesus would take His disciples and turn them into disciple-makers. What began as a simple call of obedience, ended up being a decision that would transform not just their lives, but the entire world. Jesus did not come to make us Christians. It was the world that gave us that name (Acts 11:26). Jesus isn't looking for decisions; He's looking for disciples. That's why He came to earth. Francis Chan said, "The church should be known for this. If we are going to call ourselves followers of Christ, we should be making disciples."

Sometimes I sit back and wonder, "How have we missed this as a church?" Why is it that we see so little disciple-making taking place in the church today? How is it that we have so many "come and see" seeker churches but so very few investor churches that are committed to helping each individual have a healthy balance of both evangelism and discipleship? We have created a church culture where the pastor ministers as the rest of the church sits back at a comfortable distance, enjoys "doing church," and leaves feeling inspired or "fed." This was never what God intended. We've moved so far away from Jesus' command to go and make disciples that believers today have no frame of reference for what making disciples looks like. If you were to ask the average Christian today what "discipleship" is, you would get some ambiguous answers or maybe even some blank stares. We have ceased to make the main thing the main thing. Maybe this is why statistics show that traditional church is losing ground to population growth.

So what is discipleship? When I was a student at Liberty University, we had to memorize the following definition of discipleship and be ready to spout it off at the drop of a hat. It's a quotation by Allen Hadidian that has been engrained into my memory after all these years:

> "*Discipling others is the process by which a Christian with a life worth emulating commits himself for an extended period of time to a few individuals who have been won to Christ. The purpose being to aide and guide their spiritual growth to maturity and to equip them to reproduce themselves into a third spiritual generation.*"

Jesus' definition of discipleship

As Jim Putnam says in *Real Life Discipleship*, "The invitation is the definition." When Jesus said, "*Follow me and I will make you fishers of men*" (Matthew 4:19), he defined for us what true discipleship entails.

252

"Follow Me" – A disciple knows and follows Jesus using their *head*. A disciple follows the teachings of Jesus (John 8:31-32).

"... and I will make you ..." – A disciple is being changed by Jesus in their *heart*. A disciple puts Jesus first in all things (Mark 8:34-38). As we spend time following Jesus, He begins to change us from the inside out. Jesus said we would know a tree by its fruit (Matthew 7:17-20). That doesn't mean we'll have perfect fruit, but we should have growing fruit.

"fishers of men" – A disciple is committed to making disciples for Jesus with his *hands*. A disciple is someone deeply committed to Christ's mission: to make disciples of others (Matthew 28:18-20). When we spend time with Jesus and we walk in the fullness of His Holy Spirit, we cannot help but to care about what He cares about. God's mission is now our mission.

Based on Matthew 4:19, how would you define a disciple of Jesus?

> **Follow me and I will make you fishers of men**
> - Mark 4:19

NOTES

Definition of a disciple

A disciple is someone who 1.) knows and is **following** Jesus, 2.) is being changed by Jesus and **becoming** more like Him, and 3.) is committed to **making** disciples for Jesus. Based on what you just read about how Jesus defined discipleship, if we are not making disciples, can we say that we are really disciples ourselves?

When you ask people for their definition of discipleship, those who have grown up in church might give an answer that involves growing as a Christian and becoming more like Jesus. Whereas that's true, it's also incomplete. You cannot separate the command to mature as disciples from the call to multiply disciples.

Discipleship means intentionally partnering with another Christian in order to help that person obey Jesus and grow in relationship with Him so that he or she can then help others do the same. A disciple is one who embraces and obeys all the teachings of Christ and endeavors by words and actions to make more disciples.

The word "disciple" is *mathetes* in the Greek, and it simply means "an apprentice." That's not uncommon for us to think about in today's modern world. Before a med student begins operating on patients, they first must complete a residency under the tutelage of an experienced physician. Disciples in Jesus' day would follow their rabbi (teacher) wherever he went, learning from his teaching, and being trained to do whatever the rabbi did. Jesus said, *"A disciple is not above his teacher, but everyone when he is fully trained will be like his teacher"* (Luke 6:40).

A disciple is first of all a learner, but a disciple is also one who teaches what he or she has learned to someone else. It's the principle of *learn and*

> **"If we are not making disciples, can we say that we are really disciples ourselves?"**

return. Colossians 3:16 says, *"Let the word of Christ dwell in your richly as you teach and admonish one another with all wisdom ..."* In other words, the natural by-product of dwelling in the Word is that you are teaching and admonishing one another in the Word as well. It's like everything else you learn – if you don't use it, you lose it! Every time you learn something from Scripture, find someone to share it with.

The Word of God has some strong words for those who have been saved for years but are still unable to teach another person the basic beliefs of our faith: *"Concerning him we have much to say, and it is hard to explain, since you have become dull of hearing* [literally means "mule-headed"]. *For though by this time you ought to be teachers, you have need again for someone to teach you the elementary principles of the oracles of God, and you have come to need milk and not solid food"* (Hebrews 5:11-12). In other words, the writer of Hebrews is saying that some of us need to "grow up." These believers had been saved for so long, they should have been teaching and discipling others. But instead, they were still over in "spiritual kindergarten" playing with little ABC blocks.

WHAT A DISCIPLE LOOKS LIKE

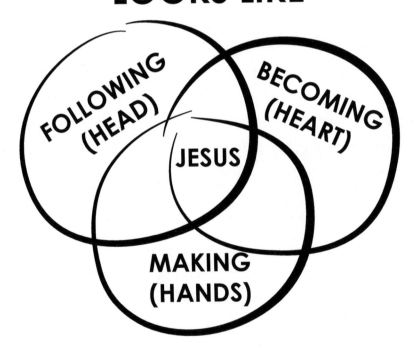

Discipleship is not ...

Discipleship is not teaching.
Although we can grow tremendously from great teaching on the Bible, discipleship is far more than that. It's not some "sit still while I instill" approach to learning.

Discipleship is not preaching.
As a mega church pastor, I used to think that discipleship could happen by solid Biblical preaching. Want better disciples? Preach better sermons! My friend, Robby Gallaty used to think the same thing. He tells a story about how he emailed Avery Willis, creator of *Masterlife*, and asked about the role of preaching in making disciples. Avery's response was classic. He said, "I really don't

believe much discipling is done through preaching, Robby. Yes, you can impart information and emotion in preaching, but discipleship is more relational, more one on one ... preaching to make disciples is like going to the nursery and spraying the crying babies with milk and saying that you just fed the kids." He went on to say, "I'm not against preaching; I do it all the time. But Jesus chose twelve and lived with them, explained to them, gave them assignments, debriefed them ... to shape and mold them to be like Him. His sermons no doubt helped convey the truth, but He had to follow up most of it with what I call *discipling*."

Discipleship is not mentoring.
Mentoring has to do with what the mentor can offer to someone else through his or her own wisdom and experience; discipleship has to do with what Jesus can offer to someone else through His wisdom and experience.

Discipleship is not a program.
My hesitation in writing *LifeCoach: Discipleship* was that I did not want this to become just another church program where once a person completes it, they check that off their list and consider themselves "discipled." Been there, done that, bought the t-shirt! But making disciples is far beyond some program. It must become the mission and practice of our lives.

Discipleship is not "just me and Jesus."
In their book *The Invested Life*, Joel Rosenberg and T.E. Koshy suggest that a discipleship relationship is "more personal, more practical, and more powerful. A teacher shares information, while a discipler shares life; a teacher aims for the head, while a discipler aims for the heart; a teacher measures knowledge, while a discipler measures faith; a teacher is an authority, while a discipler is a servant; and a teacher says, 'Listen to me,' while a discipler says, 'Follow me.'"

You don't need a slew of qualifications to be a disciple-maker. You just have to be following and obeying Jesus. Remember that the Bible says that the first disciples were just *"unschooled, ordinary men,"* but the people didn't care. They took note that these men *"had been with Jesus"* (Acts 4:13).

How would you define what Biblical discipleship is to someone who is unfamiliar with the concept?

_____

_____

_____

_____

_____

_____

_____

Who are you investing in?
Bill Hull was once teaching his class at Biola University in Southern California. On the first day of class, Bill outlined the plan for the next 15 weeks to the students. "After every class," instructed Bill, "you will find one person to teach everything you learn from me each week. This will continue for the entire semester. At the end of the semester, that person will come to class and take the final exam for you. Your grade depends upon how well you

> **" You don't need a slew of qualifications to be a disciple-maker. You just have to be following and obeying Jesus. "**

NOTES _____

_____

_____

_____

_____

_____

_____

_____

_____

_____

_____

_____

_____

_____

_____

_____

_____

_____

> **"**This isn't just the job of pastors or church leaders; it's for anyone who calls themselves a follower of Christ.**"**

NOTES _____

invest what you learn in another person." How do you think you would do if you were Bill's student?

God calls the process of investing in others "making disciples." The two questions that every disciple of Christ needs to answer are: 1.) Who is investing in you? and 2.) In whom are you investing?

Robby Gallaty says, "How many people have you personally discipled who are not repeating the process in others? When the church becomes an end in itself, it ends. When Sunday School, as great as it is, becomes an end in itself, it ends. When small groups ministry becomes an end in itself, it ends. What we need is for discipleship to become the goal, and then the process never ends. The process is fluid. It is moving. It is active. It is a living thing. It must continue to go on. Every disciple must make disciples.

Paul, Barnabas, and Timothy

We need to have three different types of relationships in our lives:

Paul – A Paul type of relationship involves someone who is like a mentor to you. They are pouring their life into you by transmitting the wisdom and knowledge and life experience that God has given to them. You need someone who is at a place in life that you want to go. God uses people like this to pour a tremendous amount of emotional and spiritual capital into you.

Barnabas – A Barnabas type of relationship is someone who is more like a peer equal. They sharpen you and make you stronger. They encourage you. When you think of the best friends you have in your life, these are the Barnabas relationships that you have. He and Paul traveled together and did ministry together.

Timothy – A Timothy type relationship is someone in whom you are investing. They are the person you're discipling just like Paul discipled young Timothy who was called to pastor a church.

Do you have these three types of relationships in your life? Who is your Paul, who is your Barnabas, who is your Timothy?

_____

_____

_____

_____

_____

_____

_____

_____

Making disciples makes me

There is a surprising side effect when it comes to making disciples: I will not reach my maturity in Jesus apart from the task of making disciples. It's not about teaching a curriculum or memorizing Bible verses. Faith is relational. Jesus spent three years taking 12 people and forming them into His disciples. The things he taught were important, but faith is relational not propositional.

The two greatest needs of every follower of Christ are to be a disciple and to make disciples. Dallas Willard says, "We talk about the Great Commission, but it's really the Great Omission because we think that it's always someone else's job to make disciples." This isn't just the job of pastors or church leaders; it's for anyone who calls themselves a follower of Christ.

We grow best when we help others grow. There is some part of my maturity that will never be accomplished apart from making disciples. Jesus taught us that we will not be mature until we raise others up. That's true in both the physical realm as well as the spiritual.

Russian Christians vs. Chinese Christians
The way our world is going and the fulfillment of Bible prophecy we see today, I believe we may be approaching the end times. Time is running out. We know that things aren't going to get easier for Christians. In fact, they'll get increasingly more difficult as the persecution of our faith grows more mainstream in our society. There may even come a day when we are not able to gather in public worship. Already, around the world, more Christians are being put to death for their faith than any other time in history. As scary as that may sound, don't let that intimidate you. I believe the greatest days for the church are still ahead of us. It's been said that the blood of the martyrs is the seed of the church. Christianity actually grows faster in places where our faith is more marginalized and persecuted, rather than in the center of society. But the difference-maker is whether or not disciples are being trained to become disciple-makers.

In the last century, we've had two major communist revolutions both in Russia and in China. In both revolutions, the objective of the communist party has been to try to kill and destroy the church.

In Russia, Christianity was centered on its churches, cathedrals, and priests. Every believer was dependent upon them for their spiritual growth. The moment the communist-driven Russian government arrested these teachers and took away their buildings, Christianity in Russia crumbled almost overnight. They didn't know where to turn. They didn't know how to grow. They didn't know how to disciple. The result? The Church in Russia basically died.

In China, the same communist revolution happened in that country under Mao Zedong's dictatorship. They did the same thing. Immediately, they went to work to arrest the pastors and to destroy the churches in an effort to root out the presence of Christianity from their country. But there was something different about the Chinese Christians. Many of their pastors had already empowered their people to become disciple-makers. The ordinary church-attender knew how to lead a person to Christ and help them grow in their faith. So when they took away the leaders and the church buildings, the Church continued moving forward! As a matter of fact, under Mao Zedong, the Church grew from 2 million believers to a staggering 80 million disciples meeting together in underground gatherings. Why? Because they knew how to minister to other people and disciple one another.

I want you to look at your own life. Which camp would you fall into? Would you be more like the Russian believers – dependent upon Christian leaders and the church for spiritual growth – or would you be like the Chinese Christians – able to make disciples on your own and grow the kingdom of God?

The next reformation
The first Protestant reformation took place in 1517 with Martin Luther. The result was that it put the *Word of God* back into the hands of the people. I believe another reformation in the church is yet to happen. It will only come when we put the *work of God* back into the hands of the people. God has called you to make disciples. Join me in being a revolutionary reformer!

NOTES

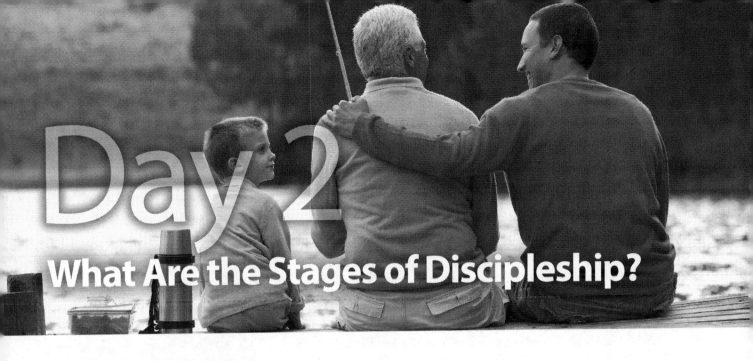

Day 2
What Are the Stages of Discipleship?

vimeo.com/138216374

Warren Wiersbe said, "After forty years of ministry, I'm convinced that spiritual immaturity is the number one problem in our churches." Sadly, there are millions of Christians who grow older, but they never grow up. They never mature in the Lord, when growth should be the goal of every disciple.

I heard a story of a little boy who fell out of bed in the middle of the night. When his mother rushed into his room to see if he was ok, she asked, "What happened?" He said, "I don't know. I guess I stayed too close to where I got in." So many Christians do that with their faith. They stay too close to where they got in, and they haven't gone on to the next stage of spiritual growth.

Five stages of discipleship

In *Real Life Discipleship*, Jim Putman outlines the five stages of the discipleship journey, which you can see throughout Scripture. Putman lists the characteristics of each stage as well as the next steps that person needs to take in order to move on to the next stage. One of the things that I found most helpful is the way that he summarizes the statements that people make that reveal what stage they may be in. Our words reveal the condition of our hearts (Matthew 12:34). People reveal where they are spiritually by what they say and by what they do. When you understand these five stages, you're able to ascertain where a person is on their spiritual journey so that you can help them get to the next stage of maturity.

When you think about the following individuals, what are some of the characteristics that come to your mind?
1. **Dead** – cold, lifeless, indifferent, unresponsive
2. **Infant** (1-2 years)– dependent, need to be served, innocent
3. **Child** (3-12 years) – self-absorbed, learning, immature, demanding
4. **Young Adult** (13-25) – energy, independent, searching, hungry
5. **Parent** (26+) – creating life, sense of responsibility, selfless, giving

Let's unpack each of these five stages more in depth and look at the spiritual parallels behind each one.

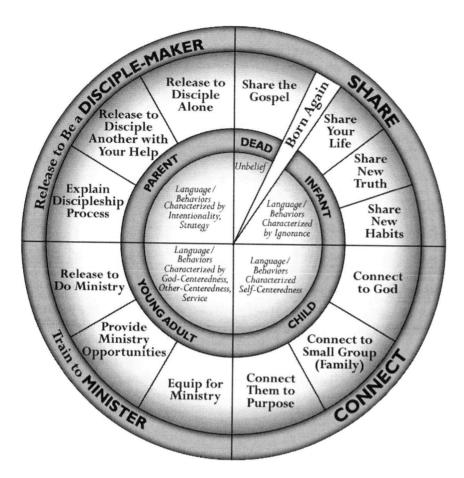

Stage #1: Dead

When someone is dead, they are cold, lifeless, and unresponsive. Scripture says that every person born into this world may be alive physically, but they are dead spiritually. Ephesians 2:1-2 says, *"And you were dead in your trespasses and sins in which you once walked, following the course of this world ..."*

The person who is spiritually dead can be characterized by their *unbelief*. This can manifest itself in a rebellious attitude towards God or an attitude of indifference. They may have a total disbelief in the supernatural, or they may embrace many forms of the supernatural (karma, reincarnation, astrology, etc.) They may have a belief in God, but that belief is different than the God revealed in Scripture. They may even believe that there are many different ways that a person can get to God. They are characterized by spiritual blindness (1 Corinthians 2:14). The spiritually dead person is relying on their own good works to get them to heaven, or they think they are just as good as anyone else, so they don't need a Savior. Here are some of the common phrases you hear a person say who is spiritually dead:

- "I don't believe there is a God."
- "The Bible is just a bunch of myths."
- "Evolution explains away a need for God."
- "There are many ways to get to God."
- "I'm a Christian because I go to church and I'm a good person."
- "I'm a good person, so I'll be ok."
- "It doesn't matter what you believe as long as you are sincere."
- "I don't know for sure where I'm going when I die."
- "I believe in heaven, but there is no such thing as hell."

So what does a person who is spiritually dead need? They need another

> **"All good disciple-makers don't start out ready; we become ready as we start out."**

disciple of Christ to come alongside them and show them through their own life what it means to have a real and genuine relationship with Jesus. They need someone to help them find the answers to life's hard questions and perhaps even to help show them the evidences for Christianity. It's ok if you don't have all the answers to the questions they're asking. We need to be humble enough to say, "I don't know for sure how to answer that, but I will find out. Let's meet next week to talk about it." All good disciple-makers don't start out ready; we become ready as we start out. Most importantly, they need that individual to articulate the gospel for them and to give them an invitation to receive Christ.

When someone is dead, they have no hope in their own strength and power. There is absolutely nothing they can do to make themselves come back to life again. Once a person "believes and receives" Christ, the Holy Spirit moves in and they become a spiritual "babe in Christ." That's a great picture of salvation and what it means to be "born-again."

Stage #2: Infant

In verse 12, John writes, *"I am writing to you, little children* [think infants]*, because your sins are forgiven for His name's sake ..."* The Bible compares someone who has just become a new Christian to a "babe in Christ." I used to think that a great church was a church that had all mature believers. That's not a great church, that's a *failing* church. The church should be, in one sense, like a maternity ward: always bringing in new souls who have been born again. The problem, however, is that some Christians stay in that maternity ward way too long. *"Like newborn infants, long for the pure spiritual milk, that by it you may grow up to salvation."* There's nothing wrong with being an infant, but there is something wrong with staying an infant. If a person has been saved for years, but they're spiritually still drinking their bottle and sucking their thumb, they're looking to be served and not to serve, then they are living in disobedience and are neglecting their spiritual growth.

Babies love to put anything in their mouths! When my kids were infants in the crawling stage, they were like human vacuum cleaners. Anything on the ground was fair game! They would go after cigarette butts, roaches, and hairballs – literally anything and everything! For those who remain in the spiritual phase of infancy, you'd be amazed what they allow inside of them. The apostle Paul was frustrated with the Corinthian church for this reason. Many of them should have long gone on to the next phase of discipleship, but they still remained as infants. He says to them, *"Brothers and sisters, I could not address you as people who live by the Spirit but as people who are still worldly – mere infants in Christ."*

A good percentage of Christians are stuck in this stage because they were converted and then allowed to stay in the nursery. According to Jim Putman, "When spiritual infants stick around long enough to become a part of the church culture, they can pick up the Christian lingo and eventually mimic the behaviors of more mature believers at least while they are in public. When this is the case, there is little substance or depth behind their words and actions." They are ignorant about what they need spiritually and what the Bible says about life and the purpose of a Christian. They still have a worldly perspective about life along with some spiritual truth mixed in. Some of the statements you might hear them say are:

- "I believe in Jesus, but I sometimes make the lake or the golf course my church."
- "I don't have to go to church to be a Christian."
- "I gave my life to Jesus and I go to church, but I don't need to get close to other people."
- "People have hurt me, so it's just me and God."

- "My spouse is my accountability partner. I don't need anyone else."
- "I pray and read my Bible. That's good enough for me."
- "My work is my ministry. I provide for my family. I don't have time for church."
- "I didn't know the Bible said that."

So how do we go about meeting the needs of the spiritual infant to get them to the next stage? Just like a newborn needs protection and care, the new believer also needs some individual attention from another follower of Christ. The Word of God needs to be explained to them, and the habits of a believer need to be modeled. Spiritual infants need spiritual teaching because by themselves, they won't get much right in their spiritual lives.

Stage #3: Child

John moves from speaking to infants to speaking to *"little children,"* those who have just been born-again. In verse 13, John writes: *"I write to you, children, because you know the Father."* Your physical age has nothing to do with your spiritual maturity. The Greek word for "children" here in verse 13 refers to someone who is born-again, but is immature in their faith. They're no longer an infant, but they still have a lot of growing up to do.

These Christians still remember who they were as unbelievers, and they are grateful and appreciative of how God has changed them. They are growing in their faith and getting more connected with the body of Christ. So much of their Christian life at this point seems rooted in their feelings, so they have a lot of highs and lows. Sometimes they are easily led to believe things about life and faith that are Biblically inaccurate. They are increasingly doing the right things, but often for the wrong reasons. They know more about what Christians say than what the Word of God says. Their service to God and His church is often conditional: they will serve in ministry as long as the benefits to them outweigh the costs.

You might recognize some of the thoughts and attitudes of the spiritual child:
- "I love my small group; just don't split us up or add any more people to it."
- "Who are all these people coming to my church? Maybe they should go somewhere else."
- "I'm not sure I like this church anymore. It's becoming too big and has too many people."
- "My small group is not taking care of my needs."
- "I don't have anyone at church who notices me or is spending enough time with me."
- "I really didn't like the music today ... if only they did it like ..."
- "I'm not being fed in my church, so I'm going to a church that meets my needs better."

How can we help this type of Christian move from where they are to where God wants them to be? What this person needs more than anything is deeper connections, both to God as well as to other mature believers. They need to learn how to become a "self-feeder" of the Word and not allow the church to be the only source of their spiritual growth. They need to also be connected to a small group where they can grow in their knowledge and understanding of Biblical truth as well as have someone come alongside them and help them discover their purpose and spiritual gifts.

Unfortunately, it's quite common for Christians who have been saved for decades to get stuck at this phase. The writer of Hebrews expressed frustration with believers who had been saved for a long time because by this

NOTES

"Growing up is more than just showing up."

NOTES

time they should have become "spiritual parents." He says, *"For though by this time you ought to be teachers, you have need again for someone to teach you the elementary principles of the oracles of God, and you have come to need milk and not solid food."* In other words, they had been walking with God for so long, they should have been able to invest in others, but they were still in spiritual kindergarten playing with ABC blocks. Growing up is more than just showing up. Sometimes we think that if a person comes to church on Sunday morning, attends Bible study, or holds a position in the church, they must be a mature Christian. Unfortunately, some of the most immature Christians I've met have held these types of positions and have never missed a service. God wants us to thirst and hunger for more and not get satisfied with mediocrity. *"Therefore let us leave the elementary teachings about Christ and go on to maturity"* (Hebrews 6:1).

Stage #4: Young Adult

There are two major characteristics of those that fall in this category in the discipleship journey: they are *workers* and they are *warriors*. John says, *"I have written to you, young men, because you are strong and the Word of God abides in you."* The word "abides" means "to live with." This is a person who lives *with* the Word, because they are *in* the Word. Are you a worker and a warrior? Are you no longer being served but are being a servant?

John goes on to say in verse 14, *"the word of God abides in you and you have overcome the evil one."* A growing disciple will become a warrior for Christ and be able to overcome the enemy. Sometimes people say, "I'm not afraid of the devil." That's not the problem. The real question is, "Is the devil afraid of you?" Are you any threat to Satan's kingdom? Just as no thief is afraid of a gun still in its holster, the devil is not afraid of a Bible that is not being opened on a daily basis. Are you a victor or a victim? Are you an overcomer or are you consistently overcome?

The "young adult" is characterized by service. They are God-centered, and they put the needs of others ahead of themselves. They are action-oriented, zealous to serve, and mission-minded. This type of Christian is really sold out for Jesus, *but* they often don't think in terms of reproducing disciples. They have a desire to serve, but they're not strategic in how to train others. It's also worth noting that because they are growing strongly in their faith, they may encounter increasing spiritual warfare from the enemy who would much prefer that they go backwards toward mediocrity.

The thoughts and attitudes of a Christian who is a spiritual young adult may include:

- "I love my church / small group, but there are others who need a church like this!"
- "I think I could lead a small group if I had some help. I have three friends I've been sharing my faith with, and this group would be too big for them."
- "Look at how many are at church today! This is awesome! I had to walk two blocks from the closest parking spot!"
- "Randy and Rachel missed group and I called to see if they were ok. Their kids have the flu, so maybe our group can make meals for them. I'll start."
- "I was reading my devotions this morning and I came across something I have a question about."
- "I noticed that we don't have an old folks' visitation team. Do you think I could be involved?"

This type of growing Christian needs help finding a ministry to serve in the church as well as ongoing relationships with other believers for encouragement and accountability. They need help in discerning how to navigate complex ministry situations as well as how to set healthy boundaries for themselves and their family. They need to be taught how to defend their faith (apologetics) as well as how to work under the leadership of the church.

Stage #5: Parent

The ultimate goal of any disciple of Christ is to reach this fifth and final stage of discipleship: being a parent. John repeats himself twice in this passage. In 1 John 2:13-14 he says, *"Fathers have known Him who is from the beginning."* The ultimate mark of maturity is when you know God. You not only know the will of God, the work of God, or the Word of God, you know the ways of God. The more you know the Father, the more you're going to become like a father.

Again, when John is talking about being a spiritual father, this has nothing to do with your chronological age. You can still be a teenager and be a spiritual parent to someone else. A spiritual parent is characterized by two things: *reproduction* and *demonstration*. A parent is someone who has reproduced themselves into another generation. Do you have any spiritual children?

One of the most rewarding things for me in my life has been to see myself become a spiritual grandparent. The only thing more thrilling than discipling someone is to see that individual win someone to Christ and begin to disciple them. If you choose to follow Jesus on the discipleship journey, someday you too will be able to bring those individuals you've won to the faith and be able to bring them before God and say, "Father, this is my spiritual family, because I have become like You, a father."

A spiritual parent is also capable of demonstration. They illustrate how a believer is supposed to live. Now I want you to download this truth deep into your heart: Spiritual maturity is demonstrated more by how you behave than by what you believe. *"Who among you is wise and understanding? Let him show it by his good behavior"* (James 3:13). Sometimes we get the idea that if a person knows a lot about the Bible, they must be spiritually mature. No. Maturity is not how much you know about Jesus in your *head*; it's how well you know Jesus in your *heart* and how much you show Jesus in you *life*.

You typically hear a spiritual parent say things like:
- "This guy at work asked me to explain the Bible to him. Pray for me that I'll be able to win him to the Lord."
- "We get to baptize someone from my small group tonight!"
- "I realized that discipleship happens at home too. Will you hold me accountable to spend some time discipling my kids?"
- "I have a person in my small group who is passionate about children. Can you have the children's ministry people call me?"
- "I just led Randy to faith in Jesus Christ, and I'll be meeting with him every Tuesday for lunch to disciple him."

The longer I walk with God, the more I see discipleship as the ultimate priority in life because our spiritual growth, or lack of it, controls every other area of our lives. When we are growing as disciples of Jesus, every other area of our lives is growing as well.

Don't read this and get discouraged by how far you still have to go and how much you still have to grow! Sometimes I too get discouraged when I look at my life. I feel that I should be further along than where I currently am. It's in those times that I hear the Holy Spirit speaking to my heart, saying, "You're a far cry from perfect, but you're much better than where you were,

> **"** Spiritual maturity is demonstrated more by how you behave than by what you believe. **"**

NOTES

263

and I'm not finished with you yet!" Just keep plodding along, taking those next steps, and you will find that you will grow!

I read about a man who took his young daughter to a carnival. She ran over to one of the booths and asked for some cotton candy. When the attendant handed her a gigantic ball of cotton candy, her dad said, "Sweetheart, are you sure you can eat all of that?" The little girl said, "Don't worry, Dad, I'm a whole lot bigger on the inside than I am on the outside!" That's what our Heavenly Father wants from us – that every day we will grow bigger on the inside than we are on the outside.

Based on your understanding of the characteristics of the five stages of discipleship, where do you think you are today? What led you to that conclusion?

_____

_____

_____

_____

_____

_____

_____

_____

What do you think should be your plan to go from where you are to the next phase of discipleship?

_____

_____

_____

_____

_____

_____

_____

Day 3

What Is the Power of Multiplication?

The other day, I asked my son, "Would you rather have $1,000 a day for 30 days or a penny that is doubled each day for 30 days? Of course, he went for what seems like the obvious choice. A thousand bucks given each day over a month would equal $30,000. But a penny today that is doubled each day for a month amounts to $5,368,709! That is the power of multiplication over addition.

Think about it another way. Suppose you start with a checkerboard of 64 squares. On the first square you place one tiny grain of wheat. On the second square you double it with two grains, and on the third square you place four grains. How much wheat would you have to place on the last square if you continue doubling each succeeding square? It would take enough wheat to cover the entire country of India to a depth of 50 feet! The multiplication process is explosive!

Long-range discipleship

Multiplication is one of the foundational laws of the universe. Everything that is alive and growing today operates on the principle of multiplication. All the way back in the book of Genesis, God said *"be fruitful and multiply"* (Genesis 1:28). God's design for disciple-making ministry is built on exponential growth – the principle of spiritual multiplication. The goal of the church isn't just to add new believers but to multiply disciple-makers. Paul demonstrates this for us in 2 Timothy 2:2, *"And the things you have heard me say in the presence of many witnesses entrust to reliable men who will also be qualified to teach others."* The emphasis of this verse is on multiplication. This is a long-range view to discipleship versus a terminal one. It's this vision of exponential multiplication that God wants to set as a fiery passion inside your heart. You can be a part of something so huge that it not only affects the people you see today but also the legacy of spiritual generations to come that will outlive you.

Billy Graham said this about 2 Timothy 2:2: "This is like a mathematical formula for spreading the gospel and enlarging the church. Paul taught Timothy; Timothy shared what he knew with faithful men; these faithful men would then teach others also. And so the process goes on and on. If every believer followed this pattern, the church could reach the entire world in one generation! Mass crusades, in which I believe and to which I have committed my life, will never finish the Great Commission; but a one-to-one ministry will."

If the world can be won to Christ within one generation, then why hasn't it already happened? Because personal evangelism will never result in spiritual multiplication if it is isolated from effective disciple-making. In the church I pastor, I discovered we were awesome at reaching the lost. Unfortunately, we were equally as good at losing the found.

vimeo.com/138216418

NOTES

265

> ❝The goal of the church isn't just to add new believers but to multiply disciple-makers.❞

Paul, Timothy, and faithful men

In *The Seven Habits of Highly Effective People*, Steven Covey popularized the notion that effectiveness is linked to viewing a worthy goal before one begins working on a task. I want to encourage you to have a vision to multiply out to four generations just as Paul did! Paul reproduced discipleship into Timothy, Timothy into faithful men, and those faithful men into others also. Remember, the Great Commission (Matthew 28:19-20) commands us to go

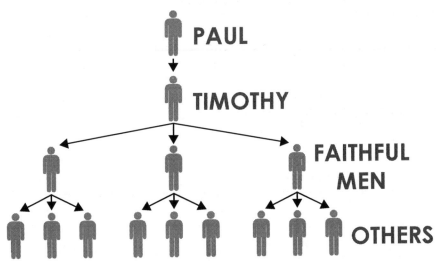

and make disciples, not simply converts. Think about it: If you led 1,000 people to faith in Christ every single year for 36 years, how many people would you have reached with the gospel? The answer: 36,000. However, if you led three people to Christ, discipled them over the course of the year, trained them how to reach and disciple other people as you have just learned in *LifeCoach: Discipleship*, and then they reached three other people each year, how many disciples would you have after 36 years? The answer: 1,048,576! That's over a million people you would meet someday in heaven who could all trace their spiritual heritage back to you!

Don't misunderstand. Evangelism is critical to our mission! True multiplying discipleship requires getting into proximity with those who don't know Jesus and building those relationships. It requires knowing how to lead another person to Jesus and helping them to do the same with others. If you can't lead someone to Jesus (addition), then you can't make disciples who make disciples (multiplication). Unless the evangelized are becoming the evangelists, our evangelism isn't going full circle.

Philippians 4:9 best demonstrates this foundational principle: *"Whatever you have learned or received or heard from me, or seen in me, put it into practice ..."* What we hear equates to teaching, and what we see equates to training. Paul focused on multiplication through modeling. He said, *"Follow my example, as I follow the example of Christ"* (1 Corinthians 11:1). You can only reproduce what you are. If you try to be a disciple-maker without being a disciple, you will frustrate yourself and those you're trying to lead.

Jesus' model for discipleship

In his book, *Mentoring 101*, John Maxwell reminds us that we only remember 10 percent of what we hear, but we'll remember 90 percent of what we hear, see, say, and do. This is why Jesus' model for discipleship multiplication was so effective. Think about what Jesus did. He took 12 ordinary, uneducated men, and He poured His life into them and equipped them to do the same. The result? Within two years they *"filled Jerusalem"* (Acts 5:28). In just over four years they were multiplying churches (Acts 9:31). Within 19 years, they *"turned the world upside down"* (Acts 17:6 NKJV). Within 30 years, Colossians tells us, *"all over the world this gospel is bearing fruit and growing"* (Colossians 1:6).

In Jesus' model, we see that He first spent considerable face-to-face time with His disciples. He lived with them and did life with them. They shared life together nearly 24 hours a day for three years. Not only were the disciples able to watch Jesus model His character before them, but He was also able to give them input as they reacted to the situations that were happening around them.

Secondly, the disciples had the benefit of hearing Jesus preach and teach to the crowds. Afterwards, He would spend additional time giving them private explanations of some of His more challenging teachings. This allowed for more questions and discussion on a more intimate level, and He was able to emphasize what they needed to hear as individuals and as a group.

Thirdly, Jesus modeled ministry before them. He would teach, preach, heal the sick, cast out demons, and teach them to do the same. He would then give them detailed instructions and send them on their way to put it into practice. He did it first with his inner circle, Peter, James, and John (Matthew 10), and then with 70 of His followers (Luke 10). Afterwards, Jesus would debrief them when they came back and offered further instruction and direction.

Finally, Jesus commissioned His disciples to go out and start their own ministry (Matthew 28, Acts 1), but He promised He would never abandon them and would still be available to help them.

John Maxwell summarized this leadership practice in this way:
- Modeling – The learner watches the teacher.
- Mentoring – The teacher explains the task and the learner assists.
- Monitoring – The learner performs the task, but the teacher assists and corrects.
- Motivating – The learner performs on his own, with encouragement and help as needed.
- Multiplying – The learner now becomes a teacher, training others to complete the task.

This is how a multiplying discipleship practice works. We invest in others, teach them how to invest in others, and support them along the way. Jesus did not personally disciple hundreds of people. Instead, he picked out a handful of ordinary men who joined Him in building the disciple-making movement. Our discipleship is only successful to the degree that those we have trained are in turn multiplying and reproducing.

A lot of times people think you've got to be trained a certain way, earn a seminary degree, or be saved for decades in order to be a disciple-maker. Nothing could be further from the truth! As a matter of fact, new believers often make the best disciple-makers because they still have natural relationship bridges with non-Christians. When we show them how to grow, how to share their faith, and how to disciple their friends, their own rate of spiritual multiplication takes place more naturally than someone who has been saved, yet stagnant, for decades.

Greater things
Jesus made a promise to those who would be His devoted followers that to this day I still have a difficult time fully understanding. In John 14:12, He promises that we will do even greater things than He did! How is that possible? Well, to begin with, we have more time. While Jesus had only three years to make disciples before He would be crucified, we, by God's grace, could have decades to make disciples! Take the Apostle Paul for instance. After 16 years of ministry, Paul had planted multiple churches in multiple countries and equipped more than 40 leaders to follow in His footsteps.

> " Our discipleship is only successful to the degree that those we have trained are in turn multiplying and reproducing. "

NOTES

NOTES

Jesus' promise that His followers "will do even greater things than these" was fulfilled in Paul's life as he sought to be a devoted disciple of Christ.

Read John 14:10-15. According to Jesus, how did He accomplish the things He accomplished?

How might your priorities change if you focused on multiplication?

Discipleship Essentials

Keith Phillips's chart compares the numeric difference between one person a day coming to Christ and two people a year being discipled to become a disciple-maker.

Year	Evangelist	Discipler
1	365	2
2	730	4
3	1095	8
4	1460	16
5	1825	32
6	2190	64
7	2555	128
8	2920	256
9	3285	512
10	3650	1,024
11	4015	2,048
12	4380	4,096
13	4745	8,192
14	5110	16,384
15	5475	32,768
16	5840	65,536

Day 4

How Do I Know Who I Should Disciple?

Perhaps you're starting to catch God's vision to be a disciple who makes disciples, but you have one lingering question: "Where in the world do I start? How do I know who I should be intentionally investing in?" It shouldn't be a surprise to us to discover that the same God who gave us the mission also gave us the method. So what is His template for disciple-making?

Person of Peace strategy

Before Jesus sent His disciples out to go and make disciples, He gave them some pretty specific details. Perhaps this was in order to ease their angst of not knowing where or how to get started. We basically have a composite view from two of the Gospels on what Jesus taught them, and there are some rich insights that we can apply to our lives as well. Let's take a look at these Scriptures, and then we'll make some more in-depth application.

vimeo.com/138216474

Matthew 10
- Jesus says, *"As you go, preach this message: 'The kingdom of heaven is near.'"* (vs. 7)
- *"Heal the sick, raise the dead, cleanse those who have leprosy, drive out demons."* (vs. 8)
- *"Freely you have received, freely give."* (vs. 8)
- *"Do not take along any gold or silver or copper in your belts; take no bag for the journey, or extra tunic, or sandals or a staff; for the worker is worth his keep."* (vv. 9-10)
- *"Whatever town or village you enter, search for some worthy person there and stay at his house until you leave."* (vs. 11)
- *"If anyone will not welcome you or listen to your words, shake the dust off your feet when you leave that home or town."* (vs. 14)
- *"I am sending you out like sheep among wolves. Therefore be as shrewd as snakes and as innocent as doves."* (vs. 16)

Luke 9 (additional comments not contained in Matthew 10)
- *"Whatever house you enter, stay there until you leave that town."* (vs. 4)

Luke 10 (additional commands not contained in Matthew 10 or Luke 9)
- *"Go out by two ahead of Me to every town and place I am about to go."* (adapted from vs. 1)
- *"Ask the Lord of the harvest ... to send out workers into this harvest field."* (vs. 2)

NOTES _____

NOTES

- *"Go! I am sending you out like lambs among wolves."* (vs. 3)
- *"Do not greet anyone on the road."* (vs. 3)
- *"When you enter a house, first say, 'Peace to this house.' If a man of peace is there, your peace will rest on him; if not, it will return to you. Stay in that house, eating and drinking whatever they give you, for the worker deserves his wages. Do not move from house to house."* (vs. 5-7)
- *"Heal the sick who are there and tell them, 'The kingdom of God is near you.'"* (vs. 9)

The Person of Peace is the one individual God has prepared to receive the gospel for the first time in a community. Instead of going after the meanest, toughest, and hardest to reach, the disciples simply impacted those whom they found it easiest to naturally befriend. That takes a lot of the worry out of disciple-making, doesn't it? When it comes to making disciples, it's far easier to work with those whom God is already at work in rather than to try to force-feed the Gospel onto someone who is not yet ready. Alex Absalom summarized this approach by saying: "They like you and you like them."

How do I know who I should invest in?

When it comes to finding that "Person of Peace," let me give you a few practical steps to help you determine what individual(s) to invest in a disciple-making relationship.

1. Begin with prayer.

I don't want this to sound simple or trite, but there is no better way to begin the endeavor of disciple-making than by starting with prayer. Jesus set the example. Before He selected His disciples, He made it a point to pray ... *all night long!* Luke 6:12-13 says, *"In these days he went out to the mountain to pray, and all night he continued in prayer to God. And when day came, he called his disciples ..."* This is a decision that shouldn't be entered into lightly; it's a decision that needs to be saturated in prayer. Ask God to lead you to the right person. Ask him to show you who to choose and who to initiate this conversation with. God is already at the center of this disciple-making movement. He only invites us to be equipped and ready to listen to His voice, discern His opportunities, and join Him in His work.

It was in the context of speaking about finding this "Person of Peace" that Jesus said, *"Ask the Lord of the harvest ... to send out workers into this harvest field"* (Luke 10:2). When you are ready and willing to say, "God, I'm ready. I want to disciple someone for You. Show me who I need to intentionally reach out to!" That is the kind of prayer that God loves to answer. The Person of Peace is found through prayer and active ministry.

2. Begin to "out" yourself as a disciple of Jesus.

Jesus made it clear that the disciples were to go out on this mission to make disciples, and that you were to basically "out" yourself as a follower of Christ and see how people responded. He didn't send them out as undercover agents. They were openly proclaiming that God's Kingdom had come near in the person of Christ.

As much as possible, let as many people as possible know that you are a follower of Christ. The approach that you use may look different for everybody. For me, it can be as simple as asking the waitress at the restaurant, "We're about to pray over our food. Is there anything I can pray for you about?" Or when someone asks me, "How are you doing?" I simply respond with, "I'm blessed!" It's simple and subtle, but it might be the very thing to initiate a conversation about the gospel.

We need to live a life that is naturally supernatural. Treat your non-Christian friends the same way you would treat your Christian friends. When one of your Christian friends is sick or is going through a hard time, you probably offer to pray for them. When one of your non-Christian friends is struggling, treat them the same way. Pray for them on the spot. Don't live a dualistic life where you act one way around your church friends and another way around your work friends.

3. Don't just look for "good people;" look for good soil.
Neil Cole says, "Don't invest in potential. Everybody has potential. Invest in obedience. When you see simple faith and obedience, invest there." He goes on to say that when God wants to start a movement, He doesn't begin with the best people, He begins with the broken. Sometimes it's the people with the darkest past that make the best soil because there's plenty of fertilizer in their life. Any gardener will tell you that if you want to see something grow, plant where there is a lot of dark fertilized soil. It stinks. It's messy. But it's going to bear forth fruit 30 fold, 60 fold, and 100 fold.

Jesus said, *"I have not come to call the righteous, but sinners to repentance"* (Luke 5:32). You don't call a doctor when you're well, but when you're sick. So don't ever be afraid to invest in someone who is currently "sick" because of their past lifestyle of sin. Those are some of the folks whom God can use the most because they're broken.

4. Don't worry about being rejected. In fact, you should expect it.
No one likes rejection. We all like to be loved and accepted. But Jesus taught us that if someone rejects us, they're not really snubbing us; they are rejecting the One we represent. Before Jesus sent His disciples out, He made it clear that they would experience both welcome and rejection. Jesus told His disciples that when they were rejected by a town, they were to simply shake the dust off of their feet (Luke 10:10). In other words, don't waste your time trying to reach someone who is insistent on remaining unreachable. The enemy would love nothing more than to suck up all of our time engaging people who aren't ready or who have already made up their minds that they are not accepting Jesus. If we don't move on, we may not find the Person of Peace that is waiting in the next person God wants us to invest in.

There will be people you are discipling that will fail you. You may get halfway through a discipling relationship, and they may no longer respond to you. When that happens, we just need to move on. You may be tempted to think, "This was a waste of my time. I invested all this energy, and it didn't go anywhere." Not if, but *when* that happens to you, you've joined the club. Jesus discipled Judas, and we all know that didn't turn out too well. Paul discipled Demas, and he ended up forsaking him (2 Timothy 4:10). Some people you try to disciple will eventually disappoint you and break your heart. But we must not allow the inevitable disappointments or rejections to keep us from endeavoring to fulfill the Great Commission.

How do I identify a "Person of Peace"?
Jo Saxton says that there are six marks of a Person of Peace from Luke 10:

1. They welcome you.
Our role as disciple-makers is to recognize where the Holy Spirit has gone ahead of us. God is already at work behind the scenes stirring people's hearts and prompting people to hunger for something more than what this life can fulfill. God is already at work in people's hearts even before we walk into their lives.

2. They receive you.
Jesus is already at work in their life, so they are open to those who carry the

> " God is already at work in people's hearts even before we walk into their lives. "

NOTES

presence of Jesus with them. Jesus said, *"When you enter a house, first say, 'Peace to this house'"* (Luke 10:5). This word for "peace" is *shalom*, which is still an everyday greeting in Israel. It would be the equivalent of our saying, "How are you?" Based on how a person responds to you when you try to approach them lets you know how receptive they are.

3. They are open to you.
As we live out our faith publicly and let others know Who we belong to, we need to watch and see who responds to that. You can't be rejected for Jesus until you've been connected to Jesus. Let as many people as possible know you're connected as His disciple. In Luke 10:6, Jesus goes on to say, *"If someone who promotes peace is there, your peace will rest on them; if not, it will return to you."*

4. They will be open to what you have to say about Jesus.
When you're around them, you can sense that they are open to discuss the things of God. The person who is most responsive to our message ought to become the focus of our attention. Jesus said, *"He who receives you receives Me"* (Matthew 10:40).

5. They are open to the life you live because of Jesus.
When you are present in a situation, you naturally draw persons of peace to you because of your Jesus-inspired difference. Finding the "Person of Peace" is really more about us than it is about them. If we are really the kind of disciple that God wants us to be, and if we are engaging those around us by implementing these practices, then those who want to discover Christ will begin to be drawn to us.

6. They serve you.
Not only do we recognize a Person of Peace as someone who welcomes us and likes to be with us, but they also attempt to serve us in some way. So often when we're seeking to minister, we want to do everything for somebody else, but the Person of Peace will want to make a contribution back to the relationship in some way. There's something about mutual serving that puts both parties on equal footing.

David Watson and Paul Watson say that you can identify a Person of Peace as having three primary characteristics:
- They are *open* to a relationship with you.
- They *hunger* for spiritual answers for their deepest questions.
- They will *share* whatever they learn with others.

You can use the acronym O.H.S. to remember those three key characteristics: Open, Hunger, Share.

How do I recruit a potential disciple?

Put down some roots relationally
It's important for us to learn to put down some roots in our relationship with that individual. Once we find that Person of Peace, Jesus admonishes us to *"Stay there, eating and drinking whatever they give you ... do not move around from house to house"* (Luke 10:7). In other words, Jesus was telling them not to go around like a door-to-door salesman. Once they found someone who was open and responsive to them, they were to stay a while and invest in building that relationship deeply, until Jesus tells you that it's time to move on.

Find a place to get together regularly
In Luke 10:8, Jesus says, *"When you enter a town and are welcomed, eat what*

is offered to you." In other words, we need to be willing to shift ourselves to their culture and their preferences. Eating together was a central part of doing life back then, and it's certainly a central part of doing life together today. I love the principle taught here. Nearly all of the discipling relationships I have with others today take place at either a restaurant as we gather for breakfast or lunch, or at a coffee shop. One of the best words of wisdom my seminary professor gave me was, "Never eat alone." You're always going to eat – at least three times a day. So why not share in that activity with someone else?

Begin to invest in them spiritually

Jesus says that our message to them needs to be *"The Kingdom of God has come near to you"* (Luke 10:9). Your friends might think that they are far from God, but He is really near to them and ready to come right in. You need to show them the truths of the Kingdom – what Jesus has done for them and how He can go about changing their life.

Alex Absalom says that we can begin this relationship by asking four questions:
1. How can I pray for you?
2. How can I serve you?
3. Can I share my story?
4. Can I share God's story?

Teach them how to disciple others

The next step is to equip this person to be the disciple-maker for his own community or sphere of influence. A Person of Peace is also someone who opens up their network of relationships to you.

In Greek and Roman society, this network of relationships was called *oikos.* Your *oikos* would have been your family, friends, neighbors, colleagues – those you do life with on a regular basis. What's interesting is that when Jesus told his disciples to greet the "house" there, the word is *oikos.* The implication there is that when we find and invest in our relationship with our Person of Peace, we are really investing in their entire *oikos.* We inevitably open the door to disciple their network of relationships.

This is a reproducible strategy. We see this over and over again in the New Testament. We see it in Luke 9 when Jesus sends out the 12 disciples. We see it in the Book of Acts with Peter and Cornelius, Paul with Lydia, Phillip and the Ethiopian eunuch. It's how the early church grew from a small group of disciples to 20 percent of the adult population of the Roman Empire! I want to encourage you to spend some time seeking God today and ask Him to direct you to your Person of Peace!

Describe the type of person (or community) that you think your heart is best shaped to reach for Jesus? Who are you called to love intentionally?

NOTES

NOTES _____

_____

_____

_____

_____

_____

_____

_____

_____

_____

_____

_____

_____

_____

_____

_____

_____

_____

_____

_____

_____

_____

_____

_____

_____

_____

_____

_____

_____

_____

Who do you most want to see saved or who would you most love to see become a disciple of Jesus?

_____

_____

_____

_____

_____

_____

_____

_____

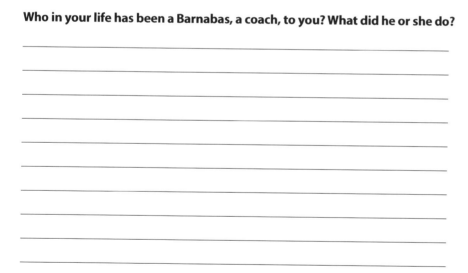

Day 5

How Can I Coach for Life?

Barnabas was perhaps one of the greatest coaches in the Bible. His original name was Joseph, but he was so effective at coaching that his name was eventually changed to Barnabas, which means "son of encouragement." He was one of Paul's closest friends and traveled with him on many missionary journeys. In Acts 11:23-24, we read this regarding Barnabas: *"When he arrived [in Antioch] and saw the evidence of the grace of God, he was glad and encouraged them all to remain true to the Lord with all their hearts. He was a good man, full of the Holy Spirit and faith, and a great number of people were brought to the Lord."* That's a pretty good example of a coach. It's someone who is called to encourage, prepare, help, and equip others to succeed in the plan God has for them. And as a result of his investment in people's lives, *"a great number of people were brought to the Lord."*

Who in your life has been a Barnabas, a coach, to you? What did he or she do?

_____

_____

_____

_____

_____

_____

_____

_____

_____

The doctrine of the priesthood of believers is incredibly important to disciple-making. It affirms the work of the Holy Spirit in the lives of all believers in how He has empowered them to function in accomplishing the mission of God. Through Jesus, we all have equal and direct access to God. What has bottlenecked the mission of the church is this idea or insistence that only the "professional clergy" (i.e. seminary-trained pastors) can teach others, answer questions, or coach others to be fully devoted disciples.

vimeo.com/138216531

NOTES _____

_____

_____

_____

_____

_____

_____

_____

_____

_____

_____

_____

_____

_____

_____

_____

_____

_____

_____

_____

_____

> **"When you truly listen to a person, you form a bond with them that becomes the platform upon which you influence and expand their life."**

NOTES

Five habits of an effective LifeCoach

How can you begin a coaching relationship with another person to fulfill God's calling on your life and to help them in their disciple journey? Let me give you five habits you should incorporate when you meet together using the acronym C.O.A.C.H.

C - Connect with them Relationally

It's been said that people don't care how much you know until they know how much you care. A coaching relationship is one that is totally focused on the other person. Coaches have no other agenda other than your personal growth and spiritual success. So when you enter into a discipling relationship, don't skip the small talk and get right down to business. You need to remember that at its core, coaching is all about relationship. It's about qualities such as trust, connection, support, and understanding. I like to think of this disciple-making-coach relationship as a friendship with a purpose. The relationship is what gives power to coaching. I want you to think about the people in your life who have made the most impact on you. It's probably not the conference speaker who delivered a great keynote address. It's probably the person who took the time to care enough about investing in you.

How does a person feel truly cared for? It's simple really. You just listen to them. Of all the qualities of a great coach, this one attribute is perhaps the most important. Can you ever think of a time when a friend really listened to you and helped you figure out on your own what plan of action you needed to take? That was coaching. Too often we confuse listening with doing nothing, but listening is anything but passive. It is an active and powerful tool that God has given us to help people grow. We practice active listening by summarizing and mirroring back to the person what we heard them say as well as by inviting them to share more of what they're thinking about a certain topic. When we communicate, most of us edit down what we're trying to say because we've become used to the short attention spans of the people we're talking to. A person really feels cared for and valued when we invite them to unpack their thoughts about a topic of interest to them and genuinely listen to what they're trying to say. When you truly listen to a person, you form a bond with them that becomes the platform upon which you influence and expand their life.

Some simple, yet great connecting questions are:
- How are you doing?
- What's happening in your life this week?
- How can I pray for you?
- What's been the high point and low point this week?
- What good things are happening in your life right now? What are you excited about?

O - Outline key issues to explore

Coaching is simply coming alongside a person so they can find out what God wants them to do and then helping them do it! People learn best not from listening to the advice of others, but by talking and verbally processing their thoughts out loud. So many times people come to me seeking advice. Most of the time, I don't tell them to do anything. I just sit there and ask questions. After 30 minutes of this, they'll sometimes shake my hand and say, "Brandon, thank you so much for your advice and input. I know exactly what I need to do." The truth of the matter is, I didn't give them any advice or counsel! I didn't tell them anything. I just asked good questions and let the Holy Spirit do the rest. Some people are able to hear God's voice as they process with others.

Here's a great question to ask the person you're coaching: "Is there an area of your life in which you sense God calling you to grow?" We need to learn to scratch where they itch. Let them set the agenda. Look for where they're struggling or what they're thinking about and dig a little deeper. When a coach says, "Here's what you need to work on," the coach ceases to become a coach and becomes the "expert consultant." A great coach is like a GPS system – they are always looking to see where you are and where you need to go next. Their questions, coupled with the guidance of the Holy Spirit, help determine the right turns you should make, and as a result, they'll help you arrive at your destination.

Here are some great questions to outline the issues that need to be discussed:
- What's one area where you sense God wants you to grow?
- What's one thing you'd like to change about yourself?
- What's really important to you? What do you value most?
- What has the Holy Spirit been tapping you on the shoulder about?
- What obstacles are you facing? What frustrates you?

A - Ask thought provoking questions
The best LifeCoach will truly *listen* to you rather than just hear you. They're picking up everything you're communicating, beyond what you're communicating. When you *direct* somebody, you reinforce the idea that they need to always go outside of themselves for all of their answers. This limits a person from really depending upon the Holy Spirit and the Word of God to be their primary source of truth. Jesus said, *"When the Spirit of truth comes, He will guide you into all the truth ..."* (John 16:13). The Holy Spirit can reveal truth to anyone through His Word. Our job is to help the individual remove the obstacles so they can hear His voice. The more non-directive you are, the more powerful your influence will be. Asking a certain kind of question is the key to unlocking the door of untapped potential. It's like holding up a mirror to the person and showing them what's there beneath the surface. One of my favorite Scriptures when it comes to coaching is Proverbs 20:5, *"The purposes of a man's heart are deep waters, but a man of understanding draws them out."*

Here are some of my favorite questions to ask:
- What are your deepest passions? What really satisfies and fulfills you?
- What energizes you? What drains your energy?
- What legacy do you want to leave? What do you want to be remembered for?
- What are your strengths? Where are you gifted?

C - Challenge them with next steps
A LifeCoach accepts you just the way that you are, but they care too much to allow you to stay that way. They are not some "expert" who just gives advice. Remember, the power is in the process, not in the coach. The answer is not in the "guru." The coach just facilitates the environment for growth. Remember, Coaching is not about you being an expert. Coaches don't need to have all the right answers; they just need to know how to help people find them. This isn't about you giving advice to people as to how they are to live their lives. It's not about listening to the coach; it's about helping the individual learn to listen to God for themselves.

Good coaching doesn't create dependency upon you as coach, but dependency upon the Holy Spirit working in them and through them. For most people this is a big relief. There's a misconception out there that if you want to make disciples, you have to be the "Bible Answer Man" and have completely mastered all aspects of the Christian life. Absolutely not! All that is required is that you yourself are growing. God isn't looking for experts; He's looking for examples – people who can say, *"follow me as I follow Christ"* (1 Corinthians 11:1). If you need to offer solutions instead of asking questions, then speak out of your own experience. Rather than preaching down to them

> " A LifeCoach accepts you just the way that you are, but they care too much to allow you to stay that way. "

NOTES

277

> **"God uses men, not just methods; God uses people, not just principles."**

and saying, "This is what you should do," it's more effective to say, "This is what I did that helped me in that area" or "This is what God is teaching me."

In Coaching 101, Bob Logan says, "One of the cardinal rules of writing is, 'Show, don't tell.' Likewise, one of the cardinal rules of coaching is, 'Ask, don't tell.' Never tell people something they can discover on their own ... A good coach doesn't need to know all the answers, only some good questions ... Good coaches resist being the answer person; they recognize that their primary role is to be the question person."

When someone shares a challenge or problem they have in their life, my driving impulse is to fix it! I want to give them three easy steps towards finding their solution. But we need to remember that courses of action that people determine for themselves are followed with much more conviction and enthusiasm than those they are told to follow.

Here are some good questions to help the person you're coaching progress towards an action step:
- What do you need to do next?
- What are the possible ways to get there?
- What resources do you need?
- What are you willing to endure to see your vision become a reality?
- What do you sense God wants you to do between now and the next time we get together?

H - Help them to grow and coach other disciples
The goal of life coaching for discipleship is for the disciple to become a disciple-maker. This is what makes the Gospel go viral. We catch the "virus" and then pass it on to others. The core of our faith ought to be highly "sneezable!"

The best coaches keep us accountable. They watch our progress and debrief with us as to how we are doing. They understand that discipleship takes time. Don't worry about the methodology of coaching. It's 99% just being who you are and 1% technique. If you want to be used by God, all you must do is simply make yourself available to be used. Don't worry if you feel like you don't have all this figured out. I don't either! But there's one truth that can't be denied: God uses men, not just methods; God uses people, not just principles.

I can't stress enough the importance of the relationship of meeting together on a regular basis with the person you're coaching. The most effective coaching relationships have regularly scheduled meetings. Once a week is ideal, but you could probably get by with every other week if your schedules don't allow for weekly meetings. The "call me when you need me" approach hardly ever works. People don't always know when they need you, and if you don't meet regularly, the relationship slowly fades away and many times the person you're discipling may revert back to a life of mediocrity and a lack of spiritual growth. Even after you complete this season of coaching, it's still beneficial to touch base from time to time.

Some good questions to get feedback are:
- What's working for you? What's not working for you?
- Is there anything that needs to change?
- What are you learning?
- Who can you invest in?

What does C.O.A.C.H. acronym stand for? Recap what you just learned:

_____
_____
_____
_____
_____
_____

Too often, we believe the lie from Satan that we don't really know enough or haven't been a Christian long enough to make a difference. Nothing could be further from the truth. Spiritual growth doesn't just magically show up in a gift box some day. It's more like walking into a lake – the longer you walk with God, the deeper He takes you and the more He overwhelms you with His person and presence. Regardless of where you may think you are in your spiritual maturity, you can lead a person to go through this *LifeCoach: Discipleship* journey in which you've invested 10 weeks of your life. Now that you've gone through it, you can turn around and guide someone else through it and fulfill your calling to be a disciple-maker. But don't worry. I won't leave you hanging. Through the LifeCoach app, I will continue to give you training on how to be a LifeCoach for others, and I'll give you step-by-step resources on how you can guide your disciple(s) through each session. Once you complete this last session, your app will promote from participant mode to coach mode where you can access the additional training, get cue cards of questions for your discipleship meetings, and manage and keep in touch with those you're discipling.

The benefit of making disciples

Could it be that in the act of making disciples, we actually become more of who Christ designed us to be? I know personally that I grow most and learn most when I am helping others to learn and grow. It gives me a place to apply what I'm learning and to take the focus off of myself and place it on Christ and others, where it belongs. We don't mature in order to minister; we minister in order to mature. God designed ministry to be the pathway towards spiritual maturity, not the other way around.

God gives the work to us not because He needs our help but because we need to be developed. Neil Cole made a statement that convicted me to my core. He said, "Ultimately each church will be evaluated by only one thing, its disciples. Your church is only as good as its disciples. It does not matter how good your praise, preaching, programs, or property are. If your disciples are passive, needy, consumerist, and not moving in the direction of radical obedience, your church is not good." What a challenging word. If the church is to make disciples of Jesus, and we're not doing that, what does that say about us?

Living an empowered life

People often view discipleship through the lens of becoming a better Christian. They think it's about helping Jim become a better father, Jane a better wife, or Bob a better employee. It's about helping Sarah overcome her sin issues or encouraging Sam to become more disciplined in his devotional life. Yes, discipleship does encompass all of those things, and it is about helping others bring every aspect of their lives under the controlling influence of the Holy Spirit.

But the question is, "How?" Over the last few years, I've spent some time thinking about my calling as a disciple-maker. One of the things I've realized

> **"** ... the longer you walk with God, the deeper He takes you and the more He overwhelms you with His person and presence. **"**

NOTES _____

_____
_____
_____
_____
_____
_____
_____
_____
_____
_____
_____
_____
_____
_____
_____
_____
_____
_____
_____
_____

> **"**... the only way to help someone become a disciple of Christ is to help them become a disciple-maker.**"**

NOTES

is that the only way to help someone become a disciple of Christ is to help them become a disciple-maker. Or to state it another way, the only way to help people become sanctified is by helping them become agents of sanctification in the lives of others. We will never help Jane, Bob, Sarah, and Sam realize the fullness of the Spirit-filled life until we've helped them become channels through which the Spirit of God flows into the lives of others.

Whenever you see the expression "filled with the Spirit" occur in the Bible, it is always in connection with disciple-making activity. We don't read, "And Paul, filled with the Spirit, overcame his anger problem." Or "Peter, filled with the Spirit, became a better husband." Instead, we read things like, *"And they were all filled with the Holy Spirit and continued to speak the word of God with boldness"* (Acts 4:31).

In other words, the gift of the Holy Spirit is meant to flow into us and then through us. Like an electric current, the Holy Spirit can't flow into a person unless he's flowing through a person into the lives of others. In order to truly know Christ, you must be about making Him known.

Maybe this is why a lot of people struggle with living the Spirit-filled life. We're trying to tap into the Spirit's sanctifying power without simultaneously engaging in disciple-making activity. Sure, we want to have our lives cleaned up (It's no fun being a sin addict.), but we don't want to re-orient our lives toward the priority of the Great Commission.

If you want to realize everything that God has for you, then you need to grab hold of this vision for discipleship that goes far beyond the American dream. The Holy Spirit will flow into you as much as you are willing to let Him flow out of you into the lives of others. Only when you get to Heaven will you realize the full results of your obedience to Christ. May God richly bless you as you fulfill His calling to become a disciple-maker!

Give us your feedback. Do you have any questions or topics for discussion before your last coaching meeting?

Made in the USA
Lexington, KY
07 March 2016